Principles of economics: Micro

THE IRWIN SERIES IN ECONOMICS

Consulting Editor   Lloyd G. Reynolds   *Yale University*

Principles of economics
MICRO

WILLIS L. PETERSON
University of Minnesota

Fourth edition   1980

RICHARD D. IRWIN, INC.   Homewood, Illinois   60430
Irwin-Dorsey Limited   Georgetown, Ontario   L7G 4B3

ISBN 0-256-02337-9
Library of Congress Catalog Card No. 79–89953

Printed in the United States of America

1 2 3 4 5 6 7 8 9 0 ML 7 6 5 4 3 2 1 0

LEARNING SYSTEMS COMPANY—
a division of Richard D. Irwin, Inc.—has developed a
PROGRAMMED LEARNING AID
to accompany texts in this subject area.
Copies can be purchased through your bookstore
or by writing PLAIDS.
1818 Ridge Road, Homewood, Illinois 60430.

Preface

This book is designed to be used as a core text in a one-quarter or one-semester course in microeconomics. It is intended for students who have either taken the macro principles course, or who have had no previous training in economics. Although the text takes the reader somewhat further along than has been customary in principles courses, the general reaction from the several hundred students I have taught using the first three editions of the text is that the material is challenging but not more difficult than that found in many of their other courses. Thus it seems that students are able to benefit from a slightly larger dose of economics than they traditionally have received in their principles courses. Because concepts and analysis of problems are emphasized as opposed to pure description, the text tends to be relatively compact. Therefore it is easy to underestimate the amount of material presented.

Probably the largest change in this Fourth Edition over the Third is the addition of an introductory section on demand and supply in Chapter I. This section is designed primarily for schools that offer the principles courses in a micro-macro sequence. It is intended to provide an overview of the more in-depth demand and supply material presented in Chapters II through VI.

The other changes consist mainly of a rewriting of sections I felt could be improved or supplemented. These changes will be most evident in Chapter III on the income and substitution effects, in Chapter IV on total physical product, in Chapter V on the rates of return to equity capital by industries, in Chapter VI on pollution control, in Chapter VIII on government regulation of industries and advertising, in Chapter IX on the labor-leisure choice, and in Chapter X on the price/earnings ratios of stocks. In addition many of the end-of-chapter questions have been changed with the intent of making them more stimulating and thought provoking.

Comments and suggestions from the reviewers of the third edition—Kurt Rethwisch, Duquesne University, and Dale W. Adams, Ohio State University—other adopters, and my students have been most beneficial. My thanks to all.

December 1979   Willis L. Peterson

Contents

minimize monopoly? Monopoly power. Monopoly power and inflation. Advertising. Pollution by imperfect competition. Marginal cost and supply. Demand facing the firm: A summary. The imperfectly competitive buyer.

1

Introduction to microeconomics

"Micro" versus "macro" economics

As economics developed into a discipline, two major areas of study emerged: micro and macro. Microeconomics is concerned mainly with the economic activities of individual consumers and producers or groups of consumers and producers known as *markets*. Macroeconomics, on the other hand, is concerned with economic aggregates or the economy as a whole. The two major problem areas of macroeconomics are unemployment and inflation. To be sure, these are of great concern to individuals, but they are also problems over which the individual has relatively little control. Both the cause and the solutions to these problems tend to lie in the realm of government action, which affects the entire economy.

It would be a mistake, however, to conclude that the micro and macro areas are distinct or unrelated fields of study. There is a certain amount of overlap between the two. For example, we will see in later chapters that much of what the government does in terms of enacting laws or levying taxes directly affects individuals and markets, and these effects can be analyzed with the tools of microeconomics. On the other hand, the actions of large groups of individuals, such as the increased desire to save on the part of many people, are analyzed with macroeconomic tools.

Because it is impossible to completely separate the micro from the macro, some economists argue that a more appropriate division would be price theory versus monetary and income and employment theory. In more advanced courses, particularly at the graduate level, microeconomic principles are generally referred to as *price theory,* mainly because the material deals with the determination of prices and their effect on the output and input mix in the economy.

The problem of scarcity

In studying economics, as in any other activity, we like to have some reason for exerting effort. We attend the theater or go to a ball game because it is enjoyable. We attend school to learn or to make it possible to have a job and earn a living. But why study economics?

There may be a few people who would be willing to study economics purely for the enjoyment it brings. For most, however, learning economics is not 100 percent entertainment. To be sure, mastering a subject provides a certain amount of intellectual satisfaction, but it is hard to justify economics on only this basis. Crossword puzzles or chess might do just as well (or better) on this score. The social science of economics must rest on a different foundation. I have posed this question to my students and so far all have been too kind (or too smart) to say that we study economics because it is a required subject. But that would beg the question: Why is it required?

The answer we are looking for can be simplified to a single word —*scarcity*. Human wants are greater than the resources available to satisfy them. In fact, economists traditionally have argued that human wants are unlimited or insatiable. At first you may find this hard to believe. Surely, you might argue, there is some level of income or standard of living where one would be completely satiated. But if you spend a few hours, or even a few minutes, making a list of the goods and services that you wouldn't mind having, chances are their purchase would put a millionaire in a financial bind. Of course, you need not limit your list to the familiar "private" goods and services, such as housing, cars, or vacation trips. You might want to include cleaner air and water, or a comfortable and convenient public transportation system.

Suppose by some stroke of magic all the items on your list were supplied. Would you then be completely satisfied or satiated? Probably not, especially if everyone else also were granted their fondest wishes. Human nature being what it is, we always seem to be just a little dissatisfied with what we have. A new compact car may satisfy for a time, but eventually we would be giving admiring glances to a Mercedes or a Cadillac. In addition, we must remember that entirely new goods and services, many of which do not even exist in our imagination, will be developed and come on the market in the future, as they have in the past. A "dream list" prepared by your great-grandparents certainly would not have contained many of the items on your own list, simply because they were not even imagined at the time.

It is less difficult to envision the scarcity of resources at our disposal. In recent years attention has been drawn to the day when our nonrenewable natural resources, especially fossil fuels, will be exhausted. Although less newsworthy, it is important to realize that most resources, including land area, labor, and man-made capital such as buildings and machines, are in limited supply. Being finite, these resources can produce only a finite amount of goods and services. Since human wants appear to be much greater than the resources to satisfy these wants, people must decide what they will produce and what they will have to forgo. In other words, we are forced to make economic decisions.

Economic decisions

We must make these decisions (or, if you wish, economize) from the time we are aware of the world around us. This harsh reality becomes apparent the first time a child stands in front of a candy counter clutching a dime or a quarter. The coin might buy a candy bar, a package of gum, or a roll of Lifesavers, but not all three. An economic decision must be made.

It would be misleading, though, to conclude that economic decisions all involve money. They do not. Probably the best example of a nonmonetary economic decision is how we allocate our time

—a scarce resource that seems to become scarcer as we become older. The student must decide if he or she will spend the evening studying, say, mathematics or history, or, perhaps even more fundamentally, whether to devote time to study or to leisure. Allocating time to its best use is one of the most important economic decisions we have to make. It could well be one of the most important things learned in school.

More traditional types of economic decisions involve the operations of households and firms. For the household, a continuing array of economic decisions must be made on how to allocate the weekly or semimonthly paycheck. How much goes to housing, how much to food, clothing, transportation, entertainment, and so forth? Managing just a modest income for a family requires thousands of economic decisions each year.

Considering the complexity of a household's economic decisions, we can appreciate the decisions that must be made in managing a business firm. What kind of things should the firm produce? Should it specialize or diversify? Should it produce a large volume and sell at a low price or produce less and charge more? How do the decisions of rival firms affect each firm? Should the firm employ more labor and save on machines, or should it substitute machines for labor? These are some examples of economic decisions each manager must make. How well these decisions are made largely determines the success or failure of the firm.

The need to make economic decisions, of course, does not stop at the level of the household or firm. Economic decisions must be made at all government levels, ranging from local governments, such as townships and municipalities, to the states and federal government. Perhaps the most basic of these economic decisions concerns how much of the total production of society is provided through the public sector and how much through the private sector. In a democracy, government decisions tend to reflect the broad wishes of society, but, of course, they cannot please everyone. People of a more conservative philosophy tend to desire a greater share of production in the private sector, while those of a more liberal bent stress the need for more public goods and services.

Once society settles on a mix between public and private goods, it must decide what kinds of public goods and services should be produced. For example, what is the appropriate mix between military and nonmilitary public goods? Should we have fewer weapons and greater public expenditures for slum clearance, public parks, pollution control, and so forth? Economic decisions involving governments or nations have this in common with those made by the child at the candy counter: Both require making a choice among alternatives, although one involves a dime or quarter, whereas the other may run into billions of dollars.

The usefulness of theory

Economic theory has suffered from a bad press for many years, and not entirely without justification. Students tend to be turned off by theory because they visualize dry, abstract material that has little relevance to their world. But theory does not have to be dry or irrelevant. In fact, little is to be gained by theory if it cannot be of help in making day-to-day economic decisions or resolving economic problems.

The main value of theory is that it provides a framework for thinking. We need such a framework because the world is too complex to take into account every bit of information that affects a decision or problem, and we have to sort out the important from the unimportant. But information does not come in neat categories labeled "important" and "unimportant," nor is it always obvious which is which. For example, some goods or services increase in price during their peak seasons, such as Christmas cards and hotel rooms on Miami Beach. Other products decrease in price during the time of the year they are most actively bought and sold, such as fresh fruits and vegetables in the northern states. For some commodities price rises when the quantity exchanged increases; for others, it declines when the quantity increases. To the person untrained in economics, there may appear to be very little order in markets. But after gaining an understanding of the theories of demand and supply (by the end of Chapter 6, I hope), you should be able to explain such phenomena and even predict future changes in price and the quantity of goods and services. In the latter sense, theory serves as a sort of "crystal ball."

Theory has come to be known by a number of names. One synonym is *principle,* as in the title of this book. A theory is also sometimes referred to as a *model,* probably because theory represents and predicts reality without necessarily duplicating it exactly or in detail.

Production possibilities

We have established that economics exists because we cannot have everything we would like and thus we are forced to make economic decisions. These decisions take the form of choosing among alternative goods or services those that will best satisfy our wants. Thus society must decide what to produce out of an almost infinite range of possibilities. Economists have traditionally represented this range of choices by what they call a *production possibilities schedule* (Table 1–1). This schedule can also be represented by a diagram (Figure 1–1) and called a *production possibilities curve.* Figure 1–1 is a representation or picture of the relationship expressed by the numbers in Table 1–1. Economics uses diagrams a great deal because a diagram is a relatively efficient and concise way of presenting an idea or concept.

TABLE 1–1
Production possibilities schedule

Wheat (million bushels)	Corn (million bushels)
0	80
10	75
20	65
30	50
40	30
50	0

The production possibilities schedule or curve is a way of illustrating the idea that a nation or individual faces limits on what can be produced and must make choices among many possible combinations of goods or services. In the simple example used here, if this nation devoted all its resources to the production of corn it could produce 80 million bushels of corn and nothing else.

FIGURE 1–1
Production possibilities curve

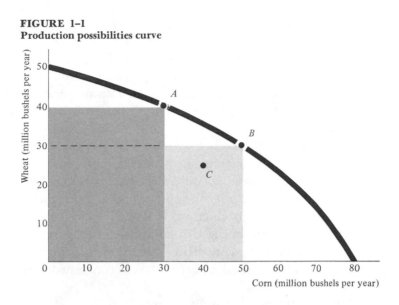

Or if all resources were devoted to wheat, 50 million bushels could be produced but no corn. The nation might like to have 50 million bushels of wheat *and* 80 million bushels of corn, but this combination is not possible because it does not have the resources to produce both. It would be more realistic, of course, for the country to choose some combination between the two extremes, say 40 million wheat and 30 million corn or 20 million wheat and 65 million corn. We will postpone for now just how a country goes about making this choice. The important point here is that such a choice must be made.

Efficiency and full employment

The best economic condition that can be achieved is to be on the surface of the production possibilities curve. Any point outside the curve is by definition impossible. Essentially the curve bounds or defines what it is possible to achieve, but it would be a mistake to believe that a nation or an economy always achieves the possible. To be on the surface of the curve, say at point *A* or *B*, requires two conditions: (1) all production is carried on in the most efficient manner possible, and (2) all resources are fully employed.

You might ask what we mean by efficiency. Essentially there are two types, and both are necessary to be on the surface of the production possibilities curve. One, engineering efficiency, requires that maximum output is obtained from a given amount of resources; that is, resource waste is kept to a minimum. Economics generally is not concerned with engineering efficiency, leaving this to engineers and physicists. The other kind, economic efficiency, also is required to reach the surface of the curve. By economic efficiency we mean producing products that consumers most desire at the lowest possible cost. In the production of most products there is some opportunity to substitute one input for another. For example, in wheat production, if labor is priced high relative to machines, as is true in the United States, wheat production should be highly mechanized, utilizing machines to substitute for high-priced labor. A large part of this book is concerned with achieving economic efficiency.

The second major condition required to reach the surface of the production possibilities curve is full employment of resources. The resource that we are most concerned with is the human resource. If there are people who are unemployed but would like to be working, the economy is not getting the goods or services these people could produce. Thus unemployment is wasteful for society, and, of course, for the individual who is unemployed the loss of income is a critical problem. Much of the material in macroeconomics deals with achieving full employment.

Only an extremely unusual economy would be able to achieve both maximum efficiency and full employment. Most economics probably operate somewhat below the surface of the production possibilities curve. This does not prevent them, however, from striving to reach the maximum production possible, subject to environmental constraints and conservation needs. Much of the work in economics is concerned with helping society move toward its maximum possible output.

Opportunity cost

Assume that a simple economy is achieving maximum production so that it is now on the surface of the curve, say at point *A* in

Figure 1–1. At this point it is producing 40 million bushels of wheat and 30 million bushels of corn per year. Suppose it wished to increase its production of corn, say up to 50 million bushels per year. To do this the nation would have to reduce its production of wheat from 40 to 30 million bushels. In other words, it would have to give up 10 million bushels of wheat to obtain the extra 20 million bushels of corn. Thus we can define *opportunity cost* as the amount of a good or service that must be given up to obtain more of another good or service.

Numerous combinations of goods or services might be used to illustrate opportunity cost. The only restriction is that two goods or groups of goods can be considered at a time because of the two-dimensional nature of the diagram. This does not in any way make the idea less relevant or useful, however.

An important decision facing the United States at the present concerns the choice between military and nonmilitary goods and services. A decision to maintain a large military establishment means that the nation must forgo a certain amount of nonmilitary goods and services, such as housing, transportation, a cleaner environment, and so forth. These goods and services represent the opportunity cost of military goods. (You might want to illustrate this choice with a production possibilities curve. What happens to a nation's position on the curve when it goes to war, assuming it is on or near the surface of the curve?)

Every economy must make a decision on the choice between consumption goods (items consumed to satisfy present wants) and investment goods (items such as machines and structures that increase future output). A nation that decides to devote a large share of its output to investment goods must give up some consumption goods. The Soviet Union, which has emphasized the production of investment goods, is a good example of this case. Another choice that must be made is between agricultural and nonagricultural products. Nations that must devote a large share of their resources to produce food because of relatively unproductive agriculture by necessity must give up the production of other things such as housing, transportation, and medical care. The less developed nations of the world illustrate this case.

So far the examples of opportunity cost have focused on the national level, but the opportunity cost concept applies as well to the individual firm, household, and person. The firm that uses its plant to produce shoes cannot produce belts or basketballs. The family that spends its vacation at the seashore must forgo the opportunity to spend this time in the mountains. When you are reading this book you cannot be doing something else, such as reading a novel, studying mathematics, or sleeping. Thus the opportunity cost of studying economics is the novel you did not enjoy, the mathematics you did not learn, or the sleep you lost. Everything you do has a cost; nothing is absolutely free.

The idea of opportunity cost applies particularly to the choice between labor and leisure. For a person paid by the hour, the opportunity cost of going fishing or to a baseball game on a weekday afternoon is the wages forgone from a job. There is little chance that a person who values income highly or what it will buy will take off to go fishing, because the opportunity cost would be too high. Another individual might place a high value on leisure; the person who not only values freedom and leisure highly, but because of a lack of skills, can earn only a low wage will probably choose more leisure. Of course, wage earners who support a family generally take their welfare into account when deciding whether the value of their leisure is greater than the income forgone.

We should stress again the importance of being on or near the surface of the production possibilities curve. If a nation is experiencing substantial unemployment, it may be able to increase its output of all goods and services simultaneously. This can be illustrated by Figure 1–1. If the nation is at point *C,* the movement to point *B* results in more of both corn and wheat. The same applies to an individual. Given the "gray matter" at your disposal, are you learning as much as possible during the hours you spend in class and studying on your own?

Increasing opportunity cost

Increasing opportunity cost refers to a situation in which *increasing* amounts of one good or service must be given up to obtain additional increments of another good or service. This idea is illustrated by the example in Table 1–1, but to illustrate it a bit more clearly, we have computed the cost of additional increments of

TABLE 1–2
Cost of wheat in terms of corn*

Increment of wheat (bushels)	Corn given up (bushels)	
	Total	Per bushel of wheat
First 10 million	5 million	½
Second 10 million	10 million	1
Third 10 million	15 million	1½
Fourth 10 million	20 million	2
Fifth 10 million	30 million	3

* Computed from Table 1–1.

wheat in terms of corn given up. These costs are presented in Table 1–2.

Notice that in order to obtain the first 10 million bushels of wheat, this country had to give up 5 million bushels of corn (80 down to 75). Or, for each extra bushel of wheat obtained, one-half bushel of corn was given up. Suppose we go one step further and see what happens when this economy increases its wheat production from 10 to 20 million. Now corn production is reduced from 75 down to 65 million. In this step, for each extra bushel of wheat obtained, one bushel of corn is given up. At the range where we approach the maximum wheat, three bushels of corn are given up for each bushel of wheat obtained. Thus we see that the opportunity cost of a bushel of wheat increases from one-half bushel of corn to three bushels of corn.

The same thing would be true if we start at the bottom and move up. At first only one third of a bushel of wheat is given up per bushel of corn. At the top two bushels of wheat must be sacrificed to obtain an extra bushel of corn.

This idea of increasing cost is illustrated by the concave nature of the production possibilities curve shown in Figure 1–2. Note that when the curve is concave to the origin, the lower right-hand segment is relatively steep. This means that the first 10-million-bushel increment to wheat output takes us back along the corn axis a relatively short distance. But as we approach the maximum possible wheat output, corn output is reduced by a large amount, and the curve becomes flat. The increasing amounts of corn given

FIGURE 1–2
Production possibilities curve illustrating increasing opportunity cost

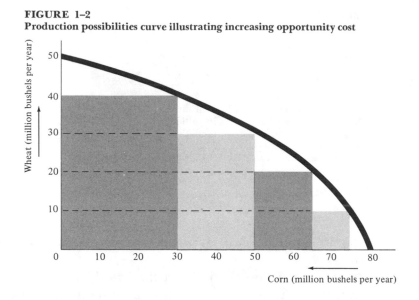

Corn (million bushels per year)

up in order to obtain the successive 10-million-bushel increments
of wheat are illustrated by the larger and larger distances on the
horizontal axis, moving from right to left.

The same result would occur if we started with all wheat and
no corn and moved down the vertical axis and out along the horizontal axis. With additional 10-million-bushel increments to corn
output, wheat output would decline by progressively larger
amounts. (It will be helpful to prove this to yourself with a diagram
of your own.)

The slope of this curve tells us, therefore, how easy or difficult
it is to transform one good into another. For this reason the production possibilities curve is sometimes called the *transformation
curve*. In this example, when we move down the curve we transform wheat into corn, or moving up we transform corn into wheat.
As we move along the curve, the rate of transformation changes
because of increasing costs. With little or no corn, it is easy to
transform wheat into corn; with almost all corn, it becomes more
difficult to make this transformation.

Does it make sense to believe that the idea of increasing costs fits
reality? Economists have argued that it does because they believe
that resources are more productive in some uses than in others. In
our example, it is reasonable to believe that some land is better

suited for wheat than for corn. In the United States the arid Great Plains area is an example. If all of this land were planted in corn, it would not yield very much. Taking the land out of corn and replacing it with wheat would not reduce corn production very much because of the low corn yield in this area, but it would increase wheat production considerably because wheat grows relatively well there.

In the production of other products, the idea of increasing costs is less clear. For example, if all our resources were devoted to the production of either automobiles or airplanes, would you expect increasing costs? Both use steel, aluminum, plastic, rubber, and semiskilled and skilled labor. In this case the rate of transformation probably would not change very much as you move down along the transformation curve, and we would come closer to a case of constant costs. In the case of constant costs, the opportunity cost of one good in terms of the other does not change at the various combinations of output. In this example, the opportunity cost of an additional airplane (in terms of automobiles given up) would not be expected to change very much over the range of production.

But, you might argue, if the point of all airplanes and no automobiles is reached, surely there will be a shortage of specialized people such as test pilots or aeronautical engineers, which will lead to increasing costs because less qualified people will have to do these tasks. True; and this brings up an important point. If resources are *rapidly* shifted from automobiles to airplanes, we would likely run into increasing costs of airplanes. On the other hand, if the move was very gradual and people anticipated the shift so that more would receive training in the needed skills, there would be less evidence of increasing costs.

This example brings out the importance of time for adjustment. Allowing little or no time for adjustment, a large-scale and rapid change to a different combination of products means that many resources will have to be used for other than their intended purpose. Automotive factories must be turned into airplane factories, mechanical engineers into aeronautical engineers, and so forth. Allowing a longer time to adjust will permit resources to become better adapted to new uses. New factories that are built will be designed for airplane production, and more people will train as aeronautical engineers. Thus the transformation curve would not exhibit as much curvature when a longer time is allowed for re-

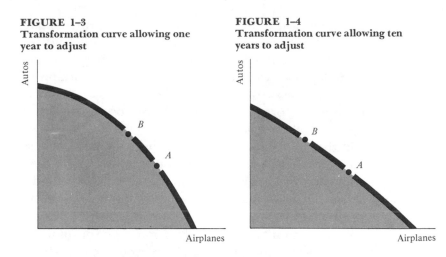

FIGURE 1-3
**Transformation curve allowing one
year to adjust**

FIGURE 1-4
**Transformation curve allowing ten
years to adjust**

sources to adjust as when a more rapid adjustment is forced. Figures 1–3 and 1–4 illustrate this difference.

A related and important point is the need to realize that no economy ever moves the entire distance along the transformation curve from one axis to another. Most changes are relatively small, say from *A* to *B* or *B* to *A* in Figures 1–3 and 1–4. And note that even though the transformation curve has a pronounced curvature, especially in Figure 1–3, the segment of the line between points *A* and *B* is close to a straight line. (You might check this by running a straightedge through points *A* and *B*.) A perfectly straight line represents constant costs throughout.

Thus it is reasonable to believe that in the range where you would expect changes to take place, there would not be as much evidence of increasing costs as over the entire range of the transformation curve. And the more time allowed for adjustment, the closer this segment would come to a straight line, as illustrated by the segment of the line between *A* and *B* in Figure 1–4.

Economic growth

So far we have been concerned mainly with moving along the surface of a given production possibilities curve. As long as all resources are fully employed, an increase in the production of one category of goods must be accompanied by a decrease in the output of the other category. Yet we observe in developed nations such as the United States, Canada, Japan, and the Western European countries an increase over time in the production of most broad categories of goods and services. For example, during the current year the United States has produced more of both private and public goods and services than it did during 1930.

An increase in the total output of goods and services over time is referred to as *economic growth*. Economic growth can be attained by an increase in the total quantity of resources, such as population or capital goods, or by an increase in resource productivity. Strictly speaking, the latter also amounts to an increase in the quantity of resources, since a more productive resource represents more resources than a less productive one. For example, a worker-day of skilled labor provides more labor than a worker-day of unskilled labor. The idea of productivity differences between resources is discussed more thoroughly in Chapter 12 on economic growth and development in the companion volume to this text, *Principles of Economics: Macro*. The main objective here is to recognize that nations need not be constrained to a given level of output for all time.

The phenomenon of economic growth can be illustrated by a shifting to the right of the production possibilities or transformation curve, as shown in Figure 1–5. At any time, such as 1930 or

FIGURE 1–5
Production possibilities curve illustrating economic growth

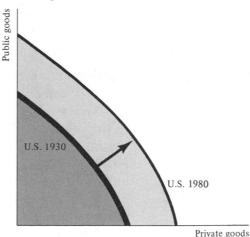

1980, more of one kind of good entails less of the other. Over time, however, more of both kinds of goods can be attained by economic growth.

We should point out that the production possibilities curve we have been discussing refers to total output rather than output per person. If population growth equals the growth in output, the individual really is no better off, even though the total output of the economy is growing. This is characteristic of many less developed countries. In the developed nations, output has grown more rapidly than population, giving each individual increasing amounts of goods and services.

The allocation of resources

Although the production possibilities curve is useful for illustrating the various possible combinations of goods and services an economy can produce with limited resources, it does not provide the answers to three important economic questions that face every society. These are (1) what and how much of each good should be produced, (2) how should each good be produced, and (3) for whom? A major share of the remainder of this book will deal with these three economic questions. In this section we will introduce in very general terms how these three questions are answered in three different economic settings: (1) the private sector of a market economy, (2) the public sector of a market economy, and (3) a communist society.

THE PRIVATE SECTOR OF A MARKET ECONOMY

Let us look first at the question of what and how much of each good are produced in the private sector of a market economy. At any time there are thousands of goods and services available to consumers in various quantities. With the passage of time some of these goods and services disappear or are no longer produced, while other new goods and services take their place. Who decides what is to be produced and in what quantities? In the private sector there are two groups of decision makers: producers and consumers. This is not to say that people are either one or the other. Certainly everyone has to be a consumer to stay alive. Also just about everyone is a producer, that is, one who contributes to the production of goods and services. (In Chapter 4 we will see that production takes place in both homes and places of business.) The producers we are mainly concerned with in this section include those who make decisions regarding what and how much to produce. In large part they are the entrepreneurs and managers of business firms.

In making decisions on what to produce, producers are constrained by the resources and technology at their disposal. For example, before the discovery of petroleum and the development of the internal combustion engine, producers of transportation vehicles were limited to those drawn by animals or powered by steam. Of course most resources are themselves the result of some production process as opposed to being a free gift of nature. The same is true of technology. As we will see in Chapter 11 and 12, knowledge and technology also are the result of production activities, i.e., education and research. For our purposes here, we will consider resources and the state of the art as given to the individual producer, recognizing that these do change over time.

Given the resources and technology available, probably the most important factor that producers must take into account is whether or not they will be able to sell the product and make a reasonable profit. In making a decision on whether to introduce a new product, producers must try to anticipate the reaction of consumers. In making such a decision, producers must rely on their own judgment regarding consumer behavior as well as information obtained from consumer surveys and test marketings.

Although producers must take the initiative in developing and introducing new products, consumers have the last word in determining whether a product stays on the market. If consumers receive a relatively large amount of satisfaction from a product in relation to its price, it will tend to stay on the market, providing, of course, that producers can make a profit at the price consumers are willing to pay. On the other hand, those products that do not provide a good measure of satisfaction to consumers in relation to what they cost will not be purchased and in turn will eventually go off the market.

For products that remain on the market, the question remains: How much of each should be produced? Products that enjoy a large demand because they yield a good measure of satisfaction will tend to bring a relatively attractive price (to producers) in the market. A favorable price serves as an incentive for producers to increase the output of the good or service. As the output increases, the price eventually will decline. As the price declines, producers know that the market is becoming saturated and that they should stop increasing the output of the good in question.

In addition, productive efficiency and resource prices influence what and how much is produced. Goods that can be produced efficiently and sold cheaply will enjoy a relatively large share of the total output of the economy. Of course, changes in resource prices will change production costs and also change the level of consumption. For example, if a resource becomes more expensive, the cost of producing products that utilize this resource also is likely to increase. As a result producers must ask a higher price for these products in order to cover their increased production costs. Some consumers will likely decide that these particular products no longer are a good buy and as a result quit buying or at least reduce their rate of purchase of the items in question. In response to this action, producers will have to reduce their output or face a buildup of inventories of goods they cannot sell at a price that will cover production costs.

Resource prices also influence *how* most goods and services are produced. For example, if labor becomes more expensive relative to capital (machines, buildings, tools, etc.), producers attempt to substitute relatively less expensive capital inputs for labor in producing goods and services. By changing the method of production, producers are able to minimize the increase in costs that stems from an increase in the price of a resource. This phenomenon is quite evident when comparing production techniques in the United States and other developed nations where labor is relatively expensive with those of the less developed countries (LDCs) where labor is relatively cheap. In countries where labor is expensive, producers have an incentive to substitute capital for labor and therefore utilize what is known as *capital-intensive* methods of production. Production techniques in the LDCs where labor is relatively inexpensive tend to utilize much labor compared with capital. Here producers utilize what is called *labor-intensive* methods of production. Thus we see that the second economic question, namely how each good and service is produced, is in large part determined by resource prices. Of course, the technical aspects of the production also influence the technique. Some production, such as the assembly of tiny components in computers or electronic equipment, is more labor-intensive than, say, the extraction of petroleum from the ground.

The third economic question, the "for whom?," is answered in very broad terms by saying that all production is carried out to satisfy the desires of consumers. Unless each good and service contributes in some way to the satisfaction of consumers, there is no demand for the item and therefore no reason to produce it. A somewhat more difficult question is "which consumers?" Obviously consumer tastes have some bearing on who buys what. The production of chicken livers, for example, is not carried out for people who dislike this product.

Given the tastes of individuals, the "for whom?" question depends largely on the incomes and wealth of people. Those who enjoy high incomes are able to claim a larger share of the total output of the private sector than their low-income counterparts. Incomes differ because of differences in wages and salaries and because of differences in the amount of capital owned. People who possess scarce and highly valued skills and are willing to work hard are renumerated by relatively high incomes. Similarly, people who own a large amount of capital are renumerated for their contribution to production. Hence the more resources a person is able to provide, the more output he or she will be able to enjoy. This means, of course, that people who lack skills, ambition, or the ownership of capital will not be able to lay claim on as many goods and services produced in the private sector as their higher-income counterparts.

Most societies including the United States have attempted to increase the amount of goods and services going to low-income people. This can be done in two ways: (1) by increasing the capacity of low-income people to produce, primarily through more and better education, and (2) by taking away income and wealth from high-income people through taxes and transferring them to low-income people through welfare payments and goods and services provided by the government.

To summarize this section briefly, we see that producers generally take the initiative in developing new products, but consumers ultimately determine which products stay on the market. The amount of each good and service that is produced depends in part on the demand of consumers for the item. Goods that are highly demanded will tend to bring a relatively high price in the market, which provides an incentive for producers to step up the production of such items. Productive efficiency and resource prices influence production costs, which in turn influences the prices that must be obtained to at least cover these costs. Resource prices also influence the method of production. The amount of goods and services that each person can claim from the private sector is determined in large part by the resources that the person contributes to the overall production process. In the main this contribution is reflected by the person's income and wealth.

Consumer decisions regarding what and how much of each good to purchase as well as who will purchase it are reflected by the demand for goods and services. Producer decisions regarding what and how much to produce and by what method are reflected by the supply of goods and services. Much of the discussion throughout the remaining chapters centers on consumer and producer decisions, how these decisions affect demand and supply, and how demand and supply influence prices and quantities exchanged.

THE PUBLIC SECTOR OF A MARKET ECONOMY

In the United States about one third of the total output is purchased and distributed by various agencies of the federal, state, and local governments. Thus it is important to consider each of our three economic questions from the standpoint of the so-called public sector. The goods and services purchased and distributed by the public sector tend to be those that do not lend themselves to individual purchase and use. They are frequently known as *public goods*. The major public goods include the military, police and fire protection, streets and highways, waste and water treatment, the postal service, and public parks. The government also provides regulatory services such as law enforcement, labeling, keeping harmful products off the market, and reducing pollution, with the aim of improving the working of the market economy. In addition, the government plays an important role in subsidizing the purchase of certain goods and services such as education, and in transferring income to certain people through the various welfare programs and Social Security.

In a democracy the short-run decisions of what and how much of each public good is to be produced are made by elected office holders and their appointed officials. Of course, over the long run the general public has the final say because elected office holders serve at the discretion of the electorate. Different people have different ideas regarding the "proper" kinds and amounts of public goods. As mentioned, people with a more conservative political philosophy tried to prefer fewer public goods (with the possible exeception of the military) and less government influence over private decisions than their more liberal counterparts. Thus the actual kinds and amounts of public goods produced tend to be a compromise between different wants.

The preference for public goods also is likely to be influenced by the incidence of benefits and costs. Those people who perceive the benefits of public goods to be small relative to the taxes they pay will likely favor a reduction in the production of such goods, or at least a slowing down of their growth. On the other hand, people who benefit from government spending more than in proportion to the taxes they pay are likely to favor increased government spending, or at least not a reduction in such spending.

It should be pointed out, too, that in the United States and most other market economies the actual production of most public goods is carried out by privtae firms under contract to the government. For example, aircraft companies produce the nation's military aircraft and construction companies build the highways and dams. However in the case of services, most of the people providing these services such as military personnel, teachers, postal workers, and regulatory personnel are employed by a government agency.

There is a class of goods and services that falls somewhere between the public and private goods categories. These are called *public utilities;* examples include local power and light or telephone companies. Goods and services provided by these companies generally are purchased by individuals in the marketplace, so in this sense they resemble private goods. But for reasons that will become clear in a moment, society has decided that the normal production of these goods by many firms in each area would not be desirable. Thus the government regulates their production, and in this sense public utilities resemble public goods.

The main reason for having public utilities is to avoid a costly duplication of facilities and services. Suppose, for example, there were ten telephone companies serving your area instead of one. Each of these companies would require its own lines, telephones, and so forth. Assuming comparable efficiency, the cost under this system would be high compared with that for one set of lines and one telephone per subscriber. It is also easy to imagine how difficult it would be to make calls; for example, you might buy telephone service from a different company than the person you wish to call. Thus in order to avoid duplication and unnecessary confusion, the government gives exclusive right to just one company to operate in each city or area.

By giving a firm exclusive right to operate, however, the government makes a public utility a virtual monopoly, free from the competitive forces in the market. In order to guard against excessive prices or inferior service to the public, the government also regulates these firms by setting the prices they charge and establishing standards of performance.

THE COMMUNIST SYSTEM

Communist countries such as the Soviet Union, mainland China, and their satellites are frequently described as centrally planned economies because the basic economic decisions regarding what and how much to produce, how each good shall be produced, and for whom are made by political leaders in the central government. Under a communist system the nation's resources are owned and controlled by the government, and it is up to the government to decide where and how the nation's available resources are to be used. For the most part these allocative decisions reflect what the authorities have decided is "best" for the country, at least at the macro level. For example, the Soviet planners have traditionally devoted a larger share of their resources to investment goods than has been the case in the U.S. economy. Although Soviet consumers have at times voiced a desire for more consumer goods, the authorities have in large part followed their long-run plans. At the micro level, however, the wishes of consumers appear to carry a bit more weight. For example, if the people desire less bread and more meat, there will be a tendency for some bread to go unsold and the meat shelves to empty quickly. As a result, the authorities may attempt to increase meat production while cutting back on bread production.

In recent years, the Soviet Union has begun to utilize prices a bit more in attempts to modify consumer behavior. If the authorities think the people should continue to eat a large amount of bread and very little meat, they will tend to lower the price of bread and raise the price of meat. Even though prices are set by the government, people in these countries respond to price changes just as people do everywhere, buying less of the item that is increased in price and more of the item that is less expensive.

The ability to set price is a powerful force in the hands of these governments. By manipulating price the authorities can often get people to do things voluntarily that they might otherwise not do, even under direct orders. For example, in order to reduce the consumption of cocoa, the Soviet authorities increased the price of chocolate candy bars. Similarly, the price of vodka was increased a few years ago in order to reduce the consumption of that beverage.

Bear in mind, though, that price manipulation does not solve all problems. If the price that is set for an item does not correspond to the price people wish to pay for the quantity produced, there will tend to be either a shortage or a surplus of the item. If price is set lower than would exist in a free market for this quantity, there will be a shortage; long lines of prospective buyers will form and "black-market" activities or bribing will tend to emerge, usually unobserved. If price is higher than what people would be willing to pay to buy all that is produced, unsold stocks will begin to pile up.

Those who favor such an economic system argue that it results in a more equal distribution of income than results from a "capitalist" or free market system. Because individuals cannot own capital, such as machines, buildings, and land, the income from property does not give rise to differences in personal income. Also the government sets all wages and salaries and as a result there is not so large a difference between the lowest and highest salaries as exists in a free market setting. In addition the government subsidizes (or provides "free") some of the basic necessities of life, mainly housing, medical care, and education. This is also intended to reduce the disparity between the "haves" and the "have nots." To pay for these goods and services as well as the military and other public goods, the government uses the income from capital and sets the wages of workers lower than their contribution to output. The latter method of obtaining income bears some resemblance to that used in the United States and other free market economies. In other words, the take-home pay of U.S. workers after deducting federal and state income taxes and Social Security taxes tends to be substantially less than their gross wages.

The disadvantages of a communist system have been well documented, at least in noncommunist countries. The loss of virtually all personal freedoms and the chance to own property stand out as being perhaps most significant. In order to establish and maintain a communist state, the government is forced to deal harshly with people who resist losing their liberty or their property. The millions of people who were shot or sent off to concentration camps in the Soviet Union is a case in point.[1]

Centrally planned economies also tend to be inefficient. Because of the millions of economic decisions that are required each day, it is impossible for a small group of central planners to have enough information to allocate resources to their most valuable uses. As a result the total value of output of the country is smaller than it could be if the decisions were made by people with more intimate knowledge of production and cost conditions. Central planners also are able to deal with a relatively small number of goods and services. This limitation is evidenced by the drab uniformity that one observes in communist countries. Incentives also tend to be a major problem. Because people have little to gain and much to lose by exhibiting too much ambition or being too innovative, it is to the advantage of each individual to do just enough to stay out of trouble. The incentive system in communist states resembles that if everyone taking a college course were limited to a "C" grade, regardless of the grades received by each individual on his or her exams. Needless to say there would be consid-

---

[1] See Aleksandr Solzhenitsyn, *The Gulag Archipelago, 1918–1956,* trans. Thomas P. Whitney (New York: Harper & Row, Publishers, 1974).

erably less studying and knowledge "produced" than if grades were assigned on the basis of what each person actually earned or learned.

It also can be argued that the equality of incomes and class claimed by communist governments is more an illusion than a fact. One can argue that there is in fact a greater concentration of economic power in communist countries than in market economies. It appears that high-level political leaders have power over workers and relative access to goods and services far in excess of their corporate counterparts in the United States. These differences may not show up in the money income statistics (if they were available), but one must look also at income in kind, including goods and services provided "free" by the government, opportunities for travel, and power over people for those who value this "good."

Introduction to demand and supply

Most of the material in the next five chapters will deal with demand and supply. Before undertaking this task, it will be useful to obtain a general idea or overview of what demand and supply are all about. Just as a builder must see a picture or blueprint of what will be built before work begins, it will help to first sketch a picture of demand and supply to see what we will end up with in Chapter 6.

DEMAND DEFINED

Let us begin with demand. We can define *demand* as a relationship between price and quantity. For most goods and services we can observe an inverse relationship between price and quantity. That is, when price is relatively high, the quantity of an item that people buy per week, per month, or per year will tend to be relatively low. Conversely if price is relatively low, the amount that people buy tends to be somewhat greater.

The idea that people buy less of an item when its price is high and more when its price is low has a certain intuitive appeal. There are two reasons for this behavior. First a relatively high price prompts people to look for lower-priced substitutes. For example, when the price of beef is high, people tend to cut back on beef

consumption and eat more pork, chicken, fish, cheese, or other protein source. On the other hand, when the price of beef is low, it
becomes a substitute for other relatively more expensive protein
sources. A second reason people buy less of an item when its price
increases is because their income does not go as far. In a sense a
higher price forces people to make do with a little less of the item.
Conversely if an item's price declines, people may use some of their
increased purchasing power to buy more of the item.

Economists often illustrate this relationship with a diagram.
Price is placed on the vertical axis and quantity on the horizontal
axis. By choosing various possible prices and observing the amounts
people will buy at these prices, we can trace out a downward slop-

FIGURE 1–6
A demand curve

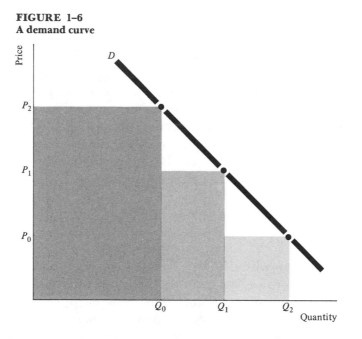

ing line, as illustrated by Figure 1–6. For example, if price is
high, say at P_2, quantity will be low at Q_0. As price declines to P_1
and P_0, quantity increases to Q_1 and Q_2, respectively. If we assume
that the same relationship holds between these points as on the
points, we can connect them and obtain a downward sloping line.

Economists call this a *demand curve,* even though it is often drawn as a straight, downward sloping line.

SUPPLY DEFINED

Let us turn next to the concept of supply. We also can define *supply* as a relationship between price and quantity. For most goods and services we can observe a positive relationship between price and quantity. That is, when price is relatively high, the quantity of an item that producers or sellers will place on the market will tend to be relatively large. Conversely, when price is relatively low, the quantity supplied also will be low.

The idea that producers will place more on the market when price is high and less when price is low also is intuitively appealing. In this case, a high price provides an incentive for producers to increase output because their profits will be greater than when price is low, other things being equal. The prospect of relatively high profits tends to result in producers cutting back on less profitable activities and increasing the output of the high-priced item. For example, if shoes are high priced, shoe manufacturers may build more manufacturing capacity for shoes and cut back on the production of other items. Also there will be a tendency for producers of other less profitable items to switch over to shoes in an effort to "get a piece of the action." The opposite occurs if shoe prices are low relative to those of other goods and services. Some shoe manufacturers may get out of the shoe manufacturing business entirely, while others cut back shoe production in an attempt to expand output of other more profitable things. After all, producers are consumers too. We would expect them to also try to get the most for their effort and money.

As in the case of demand, economists often illustrate the supply relationship with a diagram, again placing price on the vertical axis and quantity on the horizontal axis. With a positive relationship between price and quantity, the observed points will trace out an upward sloping line, as illustrated by Figure 1–7. For example, if price is relatively high, say at P_2, quantity supplied also will be high, as indicated by Q_2. As price declines to P_1 and P_0, quantity supplied also declines to Q_1 and Q_0, respectively. Economists call

FIGURE 1–7
A supply curve

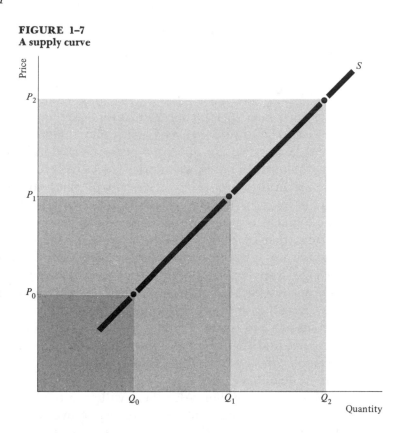

the line that is traced out by this price-quantity relationship a
supply curve, even though it is often drawn as a straight, upward
sloping line.

EQUILIBRIUM PRICE AND QUANTITY

It is important to recognize at this point that demand or supply
alone cannot tell us which price and quantity will actually exist.
They tell us only the various possible prices and quantities that
might prevail. But when we combine the two concepts, the exact
market price and quantity can be determined readily. The demand and supply curves are something like two blades of a scissors;
both are necessary to do the job.

The process of price and quantity determination can be understood best by superimposing the demand and supply curves on the

FIGURE 1–8
Determination of equilibrium price and quantity

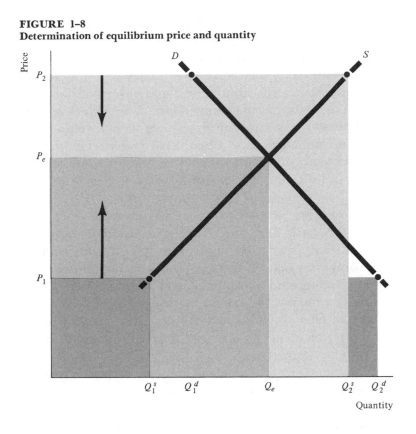

same diagram, as shown by Figure 1–8. This is possible because both have price on the vertical axis and quantity on the horizontal axis.

Perhaps the easiest way to see which price will prevail is to begin with a price that would not be likely to prevail, at least for long, say the high price P_2. At this price, consumers buy a relatively small amount, Q_1^d, but producers supply a relatively large amount, Q_2^s. As you can see, the outcome of this situation would be a buildup of unsold goods or services. As a result, there would be a downward pressure on price. Some buyers, seeing the glut in the market, may press sellers to lower the price. And some sellers, seeing the buildup of inventories, may initiate some price reductions in an effort to entice buyers to take a larger amount of their output.

Alternatively, let's see what happens if price is relatively low, say at P_1. In this case quantity demanded, as shown by Q_2^d, is larger than quantity supplied, Q_1^s. Now there will be a shortage of the item as demanders indicate a willingness to buy more than suppliers wish to sell. At this low price some buyers are not able to obtain all they would like to buy, while some sellers are experiencing empty shelves or are drawing down their inventories. As a consequence some buyers will be likely to offer sellers a higher price in order to obtain some of the scarce good. Also we can be quite sure that at least some sellers will ask for a higher price as long as they can be sure of selling their entire stock.

So far, we have seen that neither the high price P_2 nor the low price P_1 could long prevail in the market. Forces would be present to drive P_2 down or P_1 up. By now it is probably evident that there is only one price, P_e, that can prevail without the presence of downward or upward pressure. For at price P_e buyers are willing to take off the market exactly the same quantity that sellers are willing to offer. In other words, the market is in equilibrium. For this reason P_e and Q_e often are referred to as *equilibrium price* and *quantity,* respectively.

In summary, the demand for and supply of a good or service determine the price and quantity of that good or service. In the context of the production possibilities curve, demand and supply determine where on the curve a nation will be. If the demand for and the supply of the good on the vertical axis are large relative to those of the good on the horizontal axis, the economy will be at some point on the upper portion of the curve.

One might conclude at this point that once a market gets into equilibrium, price and quantity should remain unchanged for all time to come. Right? Wrong! What happens in virtually all markets is that the demand and supply curves themselves are continually shifting or changing positions. Once they are in a new position, equilibrium price, quantity, or both are likely to be different. Once this occurs, the equilibrating process must start over again.

SHIFTS IN DEMAND

The two possible shifts in demand are illustrated in Figure 1–9. The shift to the right from D_1 to D_2 represents an *increase* in de-

FIGURE 1–9
Shifts in demand

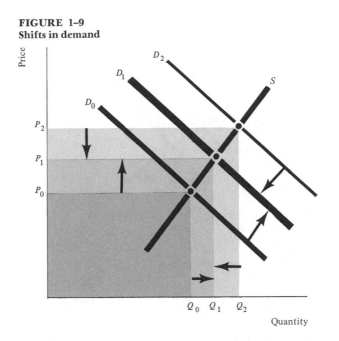

Quantity

mand. This means that buyers become willing to take a larger quantity off the market at any given price. On the other hand, a shift to the left from D_1 to D_0 is a *decrease* in demand. In this situation buyers decrease the quantity they will take off the market at any given price. The reasons demand may increase or decrease are discussed briefly in the section on demand shifters.

Notice the effects of shifts in demand on the equilibrium price and quantity. When demand increases, both price and quantity increase. Intuitively this makes sense; when people want to buy more of something they will generally bid up the price of the item, and producers are likely to respond by increasing its production as it becomes more profitable. Conversely when demand decreases, the equilibrium price and quantity both decrease. In this case the decrease in the desire of buyers to purchase the product causes a decrease in its price, and producers respond by decreasing the output of this item because it now has become less profitable.

SHIFTS IN SUPPLY

Figure 1–10 is intended to illustrate the two possible shifts in supply. The shift to the right from S_1 to S_2 represents an *increase*

FIGURE 1–10
Shifts in supply

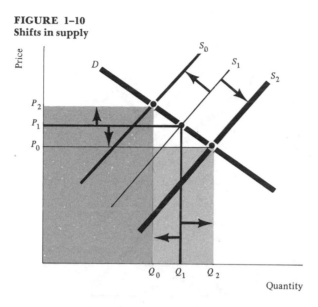

in supply. This means that sellers become willing to place a larger quantity on the market at any given price. On the other hand, a shift to the left from S_1 to S_0 is a *decrease* in supply. In this situation sellers decrease the quantity they will place on the market at any given price. The reasons supply may increase or decrease are discussed briefly in the section on supply shifters.

Notice the effects of the shifts in supply on the equilibrium price and quantity. When supply increases, quantity increases but price declines. As sellers place a greater quantity of the item on the market, it becomes more plentiful and its price declines. As the price declines, buyers find the item a better buy and as a result they become willing to take more off the market. Conversely a decrease in supply causes an increase in price because the good in question becomes less plentiful. The higher price discourages people from buying it, so the quantity decreases.

Before turning to the factors that cause demand and supply to shift, a distinction should be drawn between a change (shift) in demand or supply and a change in the quantity demanded or supplied. For example, an *increase in demand* refers to a shift to the right by the demand curve, whereas an *increase in quantity demanded* refers to a movement downward along a given demand curve. The latter would be caused by an increase in supply. The same distinctions should be made between a *decrease in demand* and a *decrease in quantity demanded*. The latter would be caused by a decrease in supply.

The same terminology should be applied to the supply side. For example, an *increase in supply* refers to a shift to the right by the supply curve, whereas an *increase in quantity supplied* refers to a movement upward along the supply curve. This movement would be caused by an increase in demand. The same is true for a *decrease in supply* and a *decrease in quantity supplied*.

Keep in mind that a change in price does not cause a change (shift) in demand or supply. Because price is shown on the vertical axis of the demand–supply diagram, a change in price causes a movement only up or down along the same demand and supply curves. Let us now briefly consider the main factors that cause shifts in the demand and supply curves. There are five demand shifters and five supply shifters that apply to most goods and services.

DEMAND SHIFTERS

1. Changes in prices of related goods or services. The demand for a good, say pork, will increase if the price of a substitute good, such as beef, increases. Consumers, in an attempt to avoid buying as much of the higher-priced beef, increase their purchases of pork, thereby increasing the demand for pork, that is, shifting the demand for pork to the right. The opposite would of course hold true if the price of a substitute good declines.

2. Changes in money incomes of consumers. The demand for most goods and services tends to increase or shift to the right as the money income of consumers increases.[2] Again this is reasonable; when we have more money to spend we are able to increase our purchases of certain items. By the same token, a decrease in consumer incomes, say because of an increase in unemployment, tends to decrease the demand for many items, or shift it to the left.

3. Changes in expectations of consumers regarding future prices and incomes. If consumers expect the price of an item to in-

---

[2] Some exceptions include cold-water flats, old fashioned washboards, and starchy foods.

crease in the future, they are likely to attempt to increase their rate of purchase of the item in order to stock up before the price rise. Similarly if people expect their future incomes to be larger than their present incomes, we can expect them to buy more at the present than if they expected "hard times" ahead. The opposite would be true, of course, for expected lower prices or incomes in the future.

4. Changes in tastes and preferences. Sometimes people step up their purchases of an item if they suddenly take a liking to it. For example, the demand for motorcycles and blue jeans has increased in recent years. On the other hand, yo-yos and bobby sox no longer are "in."

5. Changes in number of consumers. The total market demand for an item will be greater as the number of consumers in the market increases. Nationwide, the demand for most goods and services has been shifting to the right because of population growth. Of course, in places where the population has declined, such as in rural areas and small towns during the 1950s and 1960s, the demand for many goods and services has declined.

These five demand shifters include those that apply to most goods and services. There may be other demand shifters that occur because of special circumstances. For example, the passage of a law prohibiting the purchase or consumption of a good or service likely will decrease the demand for the item because most people prefer not to break the law. By the same token, making it legal to purchase a good, such as occurred at the repeal of prohibition, will tend to result in an increase in demand for that good. The markets for illegal goods and services are discussed in greater detail in Chapter 6.

SUPPLY SHIFTERS

1. Changes in the prices of resources. A decrease in the price of resources (hence a decrease in production costs) has the effect of increasing the supply of the item produced, that is, shifting its supply to the right. As costs decline, producers can sell an item for a lower price and still retain their previous profit margins. (Bear in mind that an increase in supply also means that producers are willing to supply a given quantity for a lower price.) Of course, an increase in resource prices has the opposite affect, namely, to decrease supply or shift it to the left.

2. *Changes in prices of alternative items that may be produced.* If there is a decrease in the prices of other goods or services that require about the same kinds of resources to produce, then we can expect the supply of the item in question to increase. For example, a firm that is producing both footballs and basketballs will be likely to increase its supply of footballs if the market price of basketballs declines. On the other hand, an increase in the price of an item can be expected to decrease the supply of alternative goods or services.

3. *Changes in expectations of producers regarding future prices.* If producers expect the price of their products to decrease in the future, they may sell off part of their inventories, thereby increasing present supply in order to take advantage of favorable prices at the present. Accordingly, if producers expect higher prices in the future, they may decrease their present supply in order to have more to sell when the price is expected to be higher.

4. *Changes in technology.* A change in technology always has the effect of increasing the supply of the item being produced because it has the effect of lowering production costs. Unless the new technology lowered production costs, producers would have no incentive to adopt it.

5. *Changes in number of producers.* The total market supply of an item will increase if the number of producers increases, assuming the average size of the producers remains constant. Finally, the supply of a good or service will decline or shift to the left with a decrease in the number of producers, again assuming no change in the average size of producers.

These five supply shifters include those that apply to most goods and services. There may be other supply shifters that occur because of special circumstances. For example, in the production of agricultural products, changes in weather or growing conditions are an important supply shifter. Unusually good weather should bring forth an increase in the supply of these products, whereas unfavorable conditions such as drought likely will decrease supply, or shift the supply curve to the left.

Main points of Chapter 1

1. Economics has evolved into two major fields of study: macro-economics and microeconomics, although there is considerable overlap between the two.
2. Economics exists because of the basic problem of scarcity. Human wants are greater than the resources available to satisfy these wants.
3. Because resources are scarce, individuals, households, firms, and governments must choose among alternative goods or services. Everyone from small children to the largest governments must make economic decisions. Not all economic decisions involve money; allocating time is an important non-monetary economic decision.
4. Economic theory is useful because it provides a framework for thinking, enabling us to separate important from unimportant information in making economic decisions or solving problems.
5. The production possibilities curve represents the idea that the total output of goods and services is limited by the resources available, and choices must be made among possible alternatives.
6. The surface of the production possibilities curve is reached only with maximum engineering and economic efficiency and full employment of resources.
7. With maximum efficiency and full employment of resources, more of one good or service can be obtained only by giving up a certain amount of another good or service. This is called *opportunity cost*.
8. Increasing opportunity cost exists when more and more of one good must be given up to obtain additional units of another good.
9. Increasing opportunity cost will occur if existing resources are not equally productive in all uses.
10. The allowance of a long period of time for resources to adjust to the production of different goods can be expected to reduce the incidence of increasing opportunity cost.

11. Economic growth is illustrated by an outward shift of the production possibilities curve and results from an increase in the quantity and/or productivity of resources.

12. The three economic questions faced by both the private and public sectors of a market economy and by a communist economy are *(a)* what and how much of each good to produce, *(b)* how to produce each good, and *(c)* who will enjoy the fruits of the production.

13. In the private sector of a market economy the decisions regarding what and how much of each good or service are made jointly by consumers and producers. Consumer decisions are reflected by demand and producer decisions by supply.

14. A relatively high market price resulting from a high demand for a product provides an incentive for producers to supply more of it.

15. A relatively high market price resulting from high production costs provide an incentive for consumers to use less of the product.

16. Resource prices also influence how each good is produced. Relatively high labor prices (wages) provide the incentive for producers to substitute capital for labor, utilizing a capital-intensive method of production.

17. The claim of each person on the output of the private sector is determined largely by his or her income.

18. Incomes differ because of differences in wages and salaries and differences in ownership of wealth or property. Most societies have attempted to increase the income or purchasing power of low-income people.

19. In the public sector of a market economy, decisions regarding what and how much of each public good to be produced are determined by the political process.

20. Public goods are those that do not lend themselves to purchase or use by individuals. They include the military, police and fire departments, streets and highways, and waste and water treatment.

21. People with a more conservative political philosophy tend to prefer somewhat fewer public goods and less government intervention into private economic decisions than their more liberal counterparts.

22. Public utilities were created to achieve greater efficiency by avoiding a costly duplication of facilities.

23. Under a communist system resources are owned by the government and everyone works for the government. Communist governments claim to achieve a more equal distribution of income than exists in free market or "capitalistic" economies.

24. Disadvantages of a communist system include the loss of individual freedom and private property, massive and harsh treatment of political dissenters, inefficiencies resulting from the inability of central planners to have access to the millions of pieces of information, lack of economic incentives for people, and a concentration of economic and political power in the hands of a few individuals.

25. Demand is defined as an inverse relationship between price and quantity; people buy more of an item when its price is low, and vice versa.

26. Supply is defined as a positive relationship between price and quantity; producers supply more of an item when its price is high, and vice versa.

27. Equilibrium price occurs at the point where buyers are willing to buy the exact amount that sellers are willing to sell. This corresponds to the intersection of the demand and supply curves.

28. If price is higher than the equilibrium, the quantity supplied will be greater than the quantity demanded, resulting in a surplus and downward pressure on price. If price is lower than the equilibrium, the quantity supplied will be less than the quantity demanded, resulting in a shortage and upward pressure on price.

29. An increase in demand means that buyers become willing to take a larger quantity off the market at any given price. This is illustrated by a shift to the right of the demand curve. The opposite is true for a decrease in demand.

30. When demand increases (shifts to the right), both equilibrium price and quantity increase. When demand decreases, both price and quantity decrease.

31. An increase in supply means that sellers become willing to place a larger quantity on the market at any given price. This

is illustrated by a shift to the right of the supply curve. The opposite is true for a decrease in supply.

32. When supply increases (shifts to the right), the equilibrium price decreases but quantity increases. When supply decreases, price increases and quantity decreases.

33. A shift in the demand for a good or service can occur as the result of changes in: *(a)* prices of related goods, *(b)* consumer incomes, *(c)* expectations of future prices and incomes, *(d)* tastes and preferences, and *(e)* number of consumers.

34. A shift in the supply of a good or service can occur as the result of changes in: *(a)* prices of resources, *(b)* prices of alternative goods or services that could be produced, *(c)* producer expectations of future prices, *(d)* technology, and *(e)* number of producers.

Questions for thought and discussion

1. Once upon a time a wise king instructed one of the most learned persons in his kingdom to teach him the most important concept in economics. The king's only condition was that the lesson had to consist of ten words or less (the king was a very busy man). After months of deliberation the sage approached the king and was heard to say: "There's no such thing as a free lunch." What did the sage mean by this statement?

2. Consider the following production possibilities schedule:

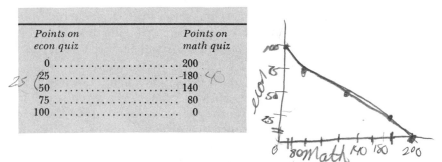

Points on econ quiz	Points on math quiz
0	200
25	180
50	140
75	80
100	0

   a. What is the opportunity cost of increasing econ points from 25 to 50? From 75 to 100? (Present your answer in terms of each econ point obtained.)

1.6
25 √40.0
  25
  150

for every econ point gained 2 lost 1.6 pts on the math quiz

  b. What is the opportunity cost of increasing math points from 80 to 140? From 180 to 200? (Present your answer in terms of each math point obtained.)

  c. Does this example represent constant or increasing opportunity cost? Explain.

  d. Represent this production possibilities schedule by a production possibilities curve.

 3. Would you expect increasing opportunity cost to be important in your allocation of time? Consider, for example, spending more and more of your time on economics and less and less on other subjects.

 4. In a market economy how do producers know whether they are producing too much or too little of each good?

 5. The desire on the part of business firms to maximize profits leads them to waste scarce and expensive resources such as energy. Therefore the government must closely monitor the actions of firms and, if necessary, order them to conserve on energy and use less expensive forms. True or false? Explain.

 6. Traditionally people in the United States have purchased larger, less fuel-efficient cars than Europeans. Why?

 7. Suppose your instructor announces that everyone in the class will receive a "C" regardless of his or her performance on examinations. How will your study effort be affected? (Be honest.) Now carry the analogy to the entire economy.

 8. The demand curve for a good generally is drawn as a downward sloping line.

  a. What does this mean in economic terms?

  b. Why do buyers behave in this manner?

 9. The supply curve for a good generally is drawn as an upward sloping line.

  a. What does this mean in economic terms?

  b. Why do sellers behave in this manner?

10. Under what conditions will there be a surplus of a product? A shortage?

11. According to the theory of demand, is it possible for consumers to want to buy less of a product at a given price? Explain.

12. According to the theory of supply, is it possible for producers to place a smaller quantity of a product on the market at a given price? Explain.

13. Explain how each of the following circumstances would effect the demand for running shoes made in the United States. Also indicate the effect on the equilibrium price and quantity.

    a. A decrease in the price of foreign-made shoes.

    b. An increase in the unemployment rate.

    c. The expectation of higher prices next year.

    d. An increase in the number of joggers.

14. Explain how each of the following circumstances would affect the supply of gasoline in the U.S. market. Also indicate the effect on equilibrium price and quantity.

    a. Drilling costs increase.

    b. There is an increase in the price that can be received in foreign markets.

    c. Producers expect prices to be higher next year.

    d. Environmental regulations require refiners to reduce emissions.

15. Using demand and supply, explain how it would be possible to observe the following phenomena.

    a. Price decreases and quantity increases.

    b. Both price and quantity decrease.

    c. Price increases and quantity decreases.

    d. Both price and quantity increase.

2

Consumer choice

Consumer sovereignty

It is fitting to begin the study of microeconomics with the individual consumer, because without consumption there would be no justification for production. The ultimate aim of all production is to satisfy the wants of consumers.

In the U.S. economy and in all other reasonably free market economies, the consumer is king (or queen). It is in the interest of producers to cater to the wishes of consumers because if they produce what is most highly demanded, they are rewarded by higher profits and a better standard of living for themselves and their families. Economists refer to an economic system where production is carried on to satisfy the wishes of consumers as one characterized by *consumer sovereignty*.

Society has found it necessary to restrict the sovereignty of the individual consumer somewhat, however. If consumption of a good is thought to be harmful to either the consumer or to others, society may pass a law against it. The use of habit-forming drugs is one example. Drug addicts, as well as harming their own health, may also harm others if they drive an automobile under the influence of these drugs or turn to crime rather than employment to obtain money for their purchase. Laws regulating the consumption of alcoholic beverages are another example of restricting consumer sovereignty to a certain degree. Although society might prefer that consumers have cornflakes for breakfast rather than bourbon, in general consumers are free to choose what they most desire, and producers respond to their wants.

In recent years, however, some people, including some economists, have begun to question whether the idea of consumer sovereignty accurately depicts our current economic system. They argue that today's giant corporations, with their multimillion-dollar annual advertising budgets, are able to persuade consumers to buy what the corporations want to produce, and this is not necessarily the same as what consumers would buy in the absence of such advertising. If the basic wants of consumers are in fact altered or determined by the advertising campaigns of corporations, it might be more accurate to refer to "producer sovereignty" rather than consumer sovereignty.

Economists who maintain that consumer sovereignty still reigns in our economic system argue that it would be unprofitable and, hence, irrational for corporations to spend millions of dollars to change the basic wants of consumers. Rather, they maintain, it is much more profitable for producers to discover the basic consumer wants, cater to these wants, and then advertise in order to expand the sales of their particular brand of that product.

The increase in demand by consumers for smaller automobiles that gave better gas mileage during and after the Arab oil embargo, and the consequent scramble by the auto manufacturers to satisfy this demand, is a case in point. When the abrupt increase in the price of gasoline prompted consumers to switch their purchases to smaller cars, the auto manufacturers did not mount a large advertising campaign in an attempt to convince consumers to continue buying large cars, while continuing to produce them in the same numbers as before. Instead the companies invested millions of dollars to retool some of their factories in order to increase their production of small cars. Then each company began to advertise in an attempt to convince consumers to buy its small cars instead of the small cars produced by competitors.

Tastes

Since consumers are such an important part of our economic system, it will be useful to study them in some detail. The first thing to recognize is that no two consumers are exactly the same in terms of their likes and dislikes. One may like to spend leisure time watching baseball on television while drinking beer and eating pretzels; another may prefer to attend the opera or a symphony concert or travel to far-off places.

Even though it is generally recognized that tastes differ among people, we have a tendency to forget this when we criticize others for liking things that do not appeal to us or for spending their income on a different mix of goods and services than we do. One person may place an expensive home high on the list of priorities, while another prefers to spend more on travel or a more expensive automobile. But who is to say which is the superior taste—the expensive home or the expensive auto? If a person were forced to sell the expensive auto and buy a higher-priced home, his or her total satisfaction might well be decreased considerably. For this person, the superior taste is represented by the automobile. The main point to remember about taste is that there is no absolute standard—each person decides what he or she likes best and then tries to satisfy these wants.

Utility

Although tastes and satisfaction are familiar ideas, it is difficult to express them in concrete terms. Suppose you had just eaten an apple and a candy bar. Could you tell someone how much satisfaction you received from each of these items? Possibly you could tell which item you liked best, but could you tell how much better you liked one than the other? You might say "quite a bit" or "just a little" or some such vague descriptive term. But how much is "just a little" or "quite a bit"?

It is evident, then, that we need a more quantitative measure of satisfaction. For this reason economists have developed the concept of utility. The word *utility* means about the same thing as satisfaction. For illustrative purposes, however, economists have created the concept of a "util," which is a unit measure of utility. In the previous example, suppose you agreed to arbitrarily assign 100 utils as the satisfaction or utility you received from the apple. If you liked the candy bar less, you would then assign it a number smaller than 100, or if you liked it more, you would give it a number greater than 100. If, for example, you assigned 50 to the candy bar, we could say that you liked the apple about twice as much as the candy bar.

Conceivably, if you wanted to take the time, you could assign utils to all the things you consume or might possibly consume, using one of the items as a reference point. The important thing in assigning utils to each item is not the absolute size of the util measure of each item but its size relative to the other items. Because tastes are an individual matter, utility is not something that can be compared from person to person. An individual might assign numbers to a partial list of the things consumed during one week in the following manner:

Items consumed per week	No. of utils
Two pounds of steak	100
One-fourth pound of coffee	30
Two quarts of milk	60
Shelter of house	300
Repair of auto	200

This example brings out two points that should be emphasized. First, consumption is measured as an amount per unit of time. In this example, we used one week. It does not make any sense to say two pounds of meat were consumed if you do not specify per day, per week, per year, or per lifetime. The time dimension is necessary in order to know how much is being consumed relatively. The second point is that we consume services as well as goods. In the above example, the repair of the automobile is a service. We could list many more, such as services purchased from a doctor, lawyer, dentist, barber, or beauty shop operator. In economics a service is treated just as if it were a good. For our purposes they are essentially the same; both yield satisfaction or utility to the buyer.

The marginal unit

A concept that is used a great deal in economics is the marginal unit. Perhaps the easiest way to grasp this idea is to think of "marginal" as being the same as "extra" or "additional." If you have ten units of something, say ten pencils, and you acquire one more, then the 11th one is the marginal pencil. The marginal unit is the one that is added to or subtracted from the top of whatever you have.

The idea of the marginal unit is one of the most important and useful of those employed in economics. This is because most economic decisions involve relatively small (or marginal) changes. For example, you do not decide whether to spend all your income on steak or none on steak. Rather you decide whether you should buy a little more steak and a little less hamburger, or vice versa. Thus the decisions you make generally involve the marginal or extra unit.

Marginal utility

Maraginal utility is the extra or additional utility you obtain by consuming one more unit of a good or service per unit of time. It can also be the utility you lose by reducing your consumption by one unit. In the utility example in a previous section, 100 utils were obtained by consuming two pounds of steak per week. Now suppose you were to increase your steak consumption to three pounds per week and receive 140 utils from this amount. The utility received from the third, or marginal, pound of steak in this case would be 40 utils. We could take the same example and subtract one pound of steak from weekly consumption. If, for example, we received 55 utils from one pound, then the marginal utility of the second pound is 45 utils. The following table summarizes what total and marginal utility might be for zero, one, two, and three pounds of steak consumed per week:

Pounds of steak consumed per week	Total utility (utils)	Marginal utility (utils)
0	0	—
1	55	55
2	100	45
3	140	40

You will note that the utility added by the marginal unit (the marginal utility) can be calculated by subtracting the total utility obained *before* the marginal unit is added from the total utility obtained *including* that unit. Another method of calculating marginal utility is to divide the *change* in total utility by the *change* in the number of units consumed:

$$\text{Marginal utility} = \frac{\text{Change in total utility}}{\text{Change in units consumed}}$$

You might also note that the total utility of any given quantity is the sum of all the marginal utilities up through and including that quantity.

Diminishing marginal utility

The preceding example also illustrates the idea of *diminishing marginal utility*. This means that as you increase your consumption of one good or service, say steak, holding constant the other things you consume, beyond some point the extra or marginal utility you obtain from the last unit will begin to decline. The intuitive appeal of diminishing marginal utility stems largely from our own personal experience. If we consume more and more of something, even steak, we soon tire of it and desire more variety.

The idea of diminishing marginal utility also is supported by lack of evidence of "monomania" among people, even among heroin addicts. If diminishing marginal utility did not prevail, there is no reason why some people would not spend all their income on one thing. In that case, you might as well choose an item that gives you the most satisfaction for the first dollar spent and then devote your entire income to it.

Marginal utility and price

The utility or satisfaction we receive from a good or service is, of course, a major reason we buy the things we do. Generally, if we do not like a product we do not buy it. But it is not quite this simple. For one thing, likes or dislikes are not all-or-nothing concepts. We all have varying degrees of likes and dislikes, as indicated by the diminishing marginal utility concept. And there is another problem we all have to face: the problem of price.

When faced with a choice between two or more items that we could buy, we often deliberately choose the item we like the least. Looking over a menu in a restaurant, for example, you may prefer the $10 T-bone steak to the $4 chopped beef, but you choose the latter. Or, when buying a car, you may like the $10,000 sports car better than any car in the showroom, but you end up buying the $5,000 sedan. Is your behavior irrational or inconsistent with the concept of utility? Not at all. In your purchasing decisions you must consider price as well as utility.

When you choose an item that is less desirable but also less costly, you are implicitly deciding that the extra cost is not worth the extra satisfaction it brings. You decide, for example, that the additional satisfaction from the steak over the hamburger is not worth $6 to you. There are other things you can buy with the $6 that will give you more utility. In deciding what things to spend your money on, you really look at marginal utility per dollar rather than maraginal utility alone. Using the chopped beef–T-bone steak example, suppose the marginal utility, price, and marginal utility per dollar (marginal utility divided by price) are as follows:

	Marginal utility (utils)	Price	Marginal utility per dollar
Chopped beef	60	$ 4	15
T-bone	100	$10	10

This example illustrates that choosing chopped beef over T-bone steak is indeed a rational choice. The marginal utility per dollar of the cheaper cut (15) exceeds the marginal utility per dollar obtained from the T-bone (10). Now, of course, this is only an example. We could have as easily created an example in which T-bone woud have been the best choice by raising its marginal utility or lowering its price. The point is that it is not always best to buy the cheaper item, but it can be.

Maximizing satisfaction: Marginal utility over price approach

So far we have considered choosing between only two items. We know, however, that life is more complex than this. During a normal shopping trip to the supermarket, for example, we have literally thousands of items to choose from. How do we decide what to buy?

The first thing we must realize is that our budget is limited; we just have so much to spend. Given this constraint, our objective is to maximize our satisfaction or utility. The basic rule is to equalize, as much as possible, the marginal utility per dollar for all the goods and services we buy. Recall that marginal utility per dollar is obtained by dividing marginal utility by price. For example, if the marginal utility (MU) of good A is 30 and its price is $5, then its marginal utility per dollar is 6. The general rule to follow for all goods and services A through Z is:

$$\frac{\text{MU of A}}{\text{Price of A}} = \frac{\text{MU of B}}{\text{Price of B}} = \cdots = \frac{\text{MU of Z}}{\text{Price of Z}}$$

Thus to maximize utility, we should try to make the marginal utility per dollar of good or service A equal to that of good or service B, and make these equal to all the other things we consume.

Why does an equalization of the marginal utility per dollar for all goods we consume result in maximum satisfaction for us? This is perhaps easiest to see if we look at a situation where they are not equal. Suppose the marginal utility per dollar you spend on housing per month is 50 but the marginal utility per dollar spent on your automobile per month is only 30. Consider what would happen if you spent one dollar less on your automobile and one dollar more on housing. Your total utility from the auto would decline by 30 utils, but your total utility from housing would increase by 50 utils. You would give up 30 but gain 50, for a net gain of 20 utils. Thus you could gain 20 utils per month simply by rearranging your purchases. This same idea applies to everything you buy. If certain goods or services are not giving you as much marginal utility per dollar as other goods or services are providing, reduce your purchases of the low-return items and increase your spending on those that give you a higher marginal utility per dollar. By doing so, you can increase your total satisfaction without spending an extra cent.

Some complications

Although the preceding rule for maximizing utility cannot be questioned from the standpoint of pure logic, one might question its practical usefulness. Surely, you might argue, no one takes the time to think of the utils obtained from consuming an item, much less writing them down and dividing by price. It might come as a surprise to learn that most people implicitly follow such a rule in their daily purchases. Most of us have felt at one time or another that an item was a "good buy" or that it "wasn't worth it." In doing so, we have indeed made an implicit calculation of the item's marginal utility per dollar. If we decide that an item is a "good buy," it is an indication that its marginal utility per dollar is large relative to other things we could buy. If an item "isn't worth it," its marginal utility per dollar for us is relatively low. We have also purchased items that we could not be sure were good buys; in these cases the items provided a marginal utility per dollar that was just about equal to that of the other things we buy.

Even though we may try to maximize our satisfaction by striving to equalize the marginal utility per dollar for all our purchases, we are not likely to ever reach that theoretical maximum and stay there. One main reason is that our estimates of utility or satisfaction from each good and service are likely to be changing all the time because of several factors. First, we may just grow tired of something that we have consumed for a long while; most of us like some variety in our lives. Thus the marginal utility of what we consume today depends somewhat on what we consumed yesterday. Second, new products or services may appear on the market that make old ones less desirable to us. This phenomenon is most evident in products that change in fashion or style. How many times have we admired a certain model of automobile only to have a new model come out that made our former dream car seem ugly and old-fashioned? Third, our tastes or estimates of utility may be changed by advertising. If a popular movie star or athlete uses a product, for example, it might become more appealing to some people.

A second major reason to change the mix of goods we consume is because prices are always changing. If the price of one item increases relative to those of other alternatives, its marginal utility per dollar will decrease relative to other things. We would then want to buy less of it.

As a final complicating factor, the marginal utility of each good or service we consume may well depend on the other things consumed along with it. Economists call this *interdependence of utilities.* Interdependence between goods can take the form of either a complementary or a substitute relationship. Two goods are *complements* to each other if consuming one enhances the marginal utility of the other. Bacon and eggs are a good example. Most people find eggs more appealing at breakfast when accompanied by a strip or two of bacon. Or, take the woman who has purchased a new dress; a new handbag, gloves, and shoes generally will make the dress more desirable, and the dress also complements the accessories. On the other hand, a *substitute* relationship between goods exist if consuming one good reduces the marginal utility of another. For instance, the marginal utility you obtain from consuming a glass of orange juice at breakfast probably would decline if you also had a glass of grapefruit juice at the same meal.

Because of the many complications that have the effect of changing the marginal utility of each good or service we buy or consider buying, the optimum bundle of goods and services that will maximize utility is constantly changing. Therefore it is necessary to continually reevaluate purchase decisions if we hope to get the most for our money.

Consumption versus saving

Although we must decide what mix of goods and services will give the most utility for a given expenditure, this does not imply that all income is spent. Most people attempt to save at least a small portion of their current income for various reasons. We may save "for a rainy day" in order to have something to fall back on in case we cannot work, or for retirement to supplement a pension. Most people save in order to make a large purchase, such as a car or a down payment on a house. Others may wish to leave an estate for their heirs or some institution.

The decisions to save or not to save and what to save for are very much like the expenditure decisions we have just considered. The marginal utility of saving is the satisfaction we can expect to obtain when we eventually spend that extra dollar, or the satisfaction we now obtain from knowing that someone else will be able to spend it.

The marginal utility obtained from an extra dollar saved varies among individuals. Some people like to spend what they earn relatively quickly and do not place a high value on saving. Economists would say that these people have a *high rate of time preference.* They prefer to consume now rather than later. The stereotyped soldier or sailor who epitomizes the "eat, drink, and be merry" attitude is a good example of someone with a high rate of time preference. His marginal utility of future consumption is low relative to that of current consumption.

Other people, being perhaps more patient, are willing to devote a relatively large share of their current income to saving, with the idea of adding to their consumption in the future. These people could be said to have a *low rate of time preference.* The miser represents the extreme case of a person with a low rate of time preference, although it is doubtful that most misers ever envision spending the entire amount of their savings at some future date. Of course, even the miser has some degree of time preference. No one can postpone all consumption for the future; if a person tried, there would be no future!

Most of us fall somewhere between the spendthrift and the miser with regard to time preference. Those who have a low rate of time preference tend to obtain relatively more utility from future consumption than their counterparts with a high time preference. Hence they will be likely to save a larger fraction of their income, other things equal.

In estimating the marginal utility of future consumption, it is also necessary to take into account the interest or dividends received on savings. If the rate of interest received on savings is, say, 5 percent, $1.00 saved today will be worth $1.05 one year from now. Assuming no increase in prices,[1] the extra dollar saved will buy somewhat more in the future than it will buy today. Hence the interest return on savings compensates us for waiting to consume in the future. The higher the interest or dividend returns on our savings, the more each dollar saved at the present will buy in the future. In other words, a higher interest rate increases the price of present consumption compared with future consumption.

The price of present consumption

The basic idea that the combination of goods we presently consume depends on both marginal utility and price also applies to decisions to consume now or in the future. The price or opportunity cost of present consumption is what must be given up in the future. The higher the rate of interest, the more a dollar saved will buy in the future, and consequently the higher the cost or price of present consumption.

We can therefore consider the price of one dollar in present consumption as the dollar plus the interest return. If we specify the marginal utility that an extra dollar of present consumption will provide, we can divide this by price to obtain marginal utility per dollar. As an example, consider two individuals, one a spendthrift and the other a miser. In Situation 1 both receive a 5 percent rate of interest on their savings; in Situation 2 the rate is 10 percent. The two situations are shown in Table 2–1.

Because the spendthrift in this example enjoys spending money in the present more than does the miser, whatever the rate of interest, the marginal utility per dollar of present consumption is higher for the spendthrift than for the miser. But at higher rates of interest the price of present consumption rises, which results in a reduction in marginal utility per dollar of present consumption for both individuals.

---

[1] A stable price level is assumed to simplify the example. But the rule still holds; the higher the interest rate, the higher is the price of present consumption for any given rate of inflation. The effect of inflation on the interest rate is discussed in Chapter 10.

TABLE 2–1
Price of present consumption and marginal utility

	Marginal utility of an extra dollar consumed at present	Interest rate	Price of present consumption	Marginal utility per dollar
Situation 1				
Spendthrift	20	0.05	$1.05	19.05
Miser	10	0.05	1.05	9.52
Situation 2				
Spendthrift	20	0.10	1.10	18.18
Miser	10	0.10	1.10	9.09

The decision to save or to consume at the present, therefore, is very similar to the decision on what mix of goods to buy, also depending on taste and price. Theoretically a low rate of time preference and a high price (high interest) should be associated with a high rate of saving, and vice versa. Empirically, however, economists have found it very difficult to measure the relative importance of each of these factors in people's decisions to save or to spend. For one thing an independent, quantitative measure of time preference is lacking. Although there seems to be general agreement that the rate of time preference does affect the proportion of income saved, there is much less agreement on the importance of the rate of interest. The measurement of the impact of the interest rate on saving is complicated by a number of other factors that also are expected to influence saving. These include the level of income, changes in the general price level (mainly inflation), and expectations of future economic conditions. The probable impact of these factors on saving is discussed more thoroughly in the macro book that supplements this text.

Short-run versus long-run saving

The rate at which an individual saves can fluctuate a considerable amount over time. Suppose you want to purchase a new car next year. During the present year you will probably attempt to save enough at least for the down payment and possibly for the entire car. During the time you save for the car, the proportion of your income saved may be quite large—say 40 percent. But as soon as you buy the car, all this is spent. Thus the length of time for saving generally influences the rate of saving.

The important point is that saving during a short period such as a month or even a year may not at all reflect long-run saving habits. The seafaring man may save almost 100 percent of his wage during a six-month voyage but spend every cent when he arrives in port. It would be very misleading to measure the sailor's saving during the voyage and assume this is what he will save in the long run.

A similar situation exists with people whose incomes fluctuate a great deal; farmers are a good example. It is sometimes argued that farmers are thrifty folk who save much of their income. But the real reason might well be that farm incomes tend to fluctuate more than other people's, and when farm income is high much of it is saved to provide for times when it is very low or even zero.

With college students it is not unusual to find a negative rate of saving; they consume more than their income. The difference is made up by consuming out of past saving, borrowing, or using gifts from relatives, friends, or benevolent institutions. There is nothing wrong with this behavior, indeed it is to be expected. In the long run (a decade or more) the percentage of income saved by these same people may well be substantial.

Indifference curves

We have shown that consumers maximize utility, or obtain the most for their money, by equalizing as much as possible the marginal utility per dollar of all goods and services they consume, as well as their saving. A slightly different approach utilizes the concept of the indifference curve, which is another way of representing consumer choice. Indifference curves are useful in that they allow us to talk about the degree of substitution of one good for another in rather specific terms. As we will see, the ability to substitute one good for another is an important dimension of consumer behavior. But let us first develop the concept of the indifference curve.

Assume that you are given a collection of two different goods, say ten tickets to see your favorite football team and ten tickets to the theater of your choice. We can represent this combination by point *A* in Figure 2–1. Now ask yourself this question: If two football tickets were taken away from me, how many additional theater tickets would I have to be given in order to remain equally satisfied? Assume there is no chance to sell the tickets, so you cannot exchange the extra theater tickets for football tickets. Also do not be concerned, at least for the moment, about the price of the tickets. Assume they are being given to you or taken away without charge or compensation.

FIGURE 2–1
An indifference curve

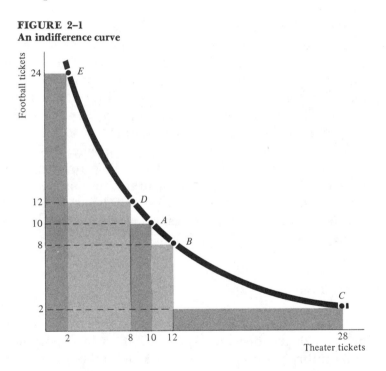

Your answer to this question will depend, of course, on how well you like football and the theater. Suppose you decide that two additional theater tickets would compensate you for the loss of the two football tickets. In other words, you are indifferent between the combination of ten football and ten theater tickets and the combination of eight football and 12 theater tickets. Let this second combination be point *B* in Figure 2–1.

We might go through the same procedure again, this time taking away a total of eight football tickets. Now you only have two football tickets left. How many theater tickets would you have to be given to remain as satisfied as you were with the original combination of ten of each kind of tickets?

According to the idea of diminishing marginal utility, additional nights at the theater will provide less and less satisfaction. Moreover, the closer you come to no football tickets, the loss of football tickets will mean increasingly less satisfaction. It seems reasonable to believe, therefore, that you will require more than eight additional theater tickets to compensate for the loss of eight football tickets. Suppose you want 18 more theater tickets. We could say that you are indifferent to the following combinations:

Combination	Theater	Football
A	10	10
B	12	8
C	28	2

Thus we are tracing our alternative combinations that would make you equally well off. We could also trace out points on the upper part of the curve by taking away theater tickets in exchange for football tickets. For example, you might choose eight theater and 12 football, or two theater and 24 football tickets as additional combinations, labeling these points *D* and *E*, respectively.

Assuming that the general relationship holds between the points as on them, we can connect points *A* through *E*. We have now constructed what economists call an *indifference curve*. From the standpoint of total satisfaction, you are indifferent at all points along this curve.

Of course, any number of curves can be drawn, as shown in Figure 2–2. We started out with ten tickets of each, but we might have started with six. If you prefer more tickets to less, then the smaller combination would be on a lower indifference curve, such as I_0 in Figure 2–2. Similarly, a larger combination, such as 14 of each, would be on a higher curve, say I_2. Economists call many such curves on a single diagram an *indifference map*. In a sense the in-

FIGURE 2-2
An indifference map

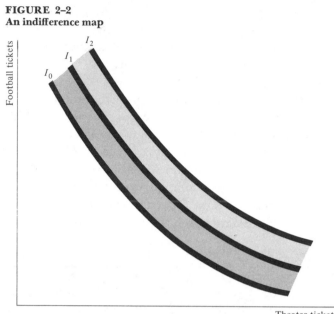

difference map is a picture of your preferences, much like a contour map is a picture of the landscape. Curves farther from the origin represent higher levels of satisfaction.

SUBSTITUTION POSSIBILITIES

1. Imperfect substitutes. The shape of a person's indifference curves tells us the degree of substitution that exists between the two goods represented on the axes of the diagram. In the preceding example, the indifference curves are drawn with a slight curvature, convex to the origin. An indifference curve of this shape implies that the two goods represented on the axes are substitutes for one another but that they are imperfect substitues. This means that as you move down along the curve, more and more units of the abundant good must be obtained in order to make you willing to give up each successive unit of the relatively scarce good. This is illustrated by Figure 2–1. Moving from point A to point B, you are willing to give up two football tickets if you gain two theater tickets. In other words, one theater ticket is enough to compensate you for giving up one football ticket. Now move from point *B* to point *C*. By giving up these six football tickets, you insist on 16 additional theater tickets. In other words you now require nearly three theater tickets to compensate you for the loss of one football ticket. Under these conditions we say that the two goods are imperfect substitutes. It is possible to substitute between them but as one moves to the extremes, it takes more and more of the abundant good being added to substitute for each unit of the scarce item being given up.

2. *Perfect substitutes.* Two items are defined as perfect substitutes if the amount of one good that is necessary to compensate for giving up each unit of another good remains constant at all possible combinations. For example, under most conditions a person should be willing to give up one dozen white shell eggs for one dozen brown shell eggs of comparable size and quality, regardless of the combination being consumed. Indifference curves depicting perfect substitutes are drawn as straight, downward sloping lines as illustrated by Figure 2–3. Notice here that one brown shell egg will compensate for one white shell egg regardless of where one happens to be on the curve.

FIGURE 2–3
Indifference curves for perfect substitutes

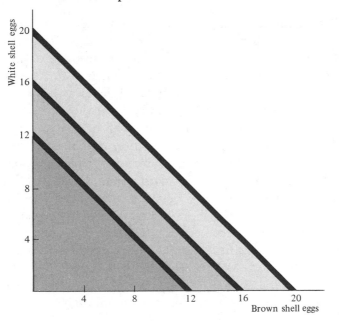

It should be pointed out, however, that the ratio between the two items does not have to be one for one in order to have perfect substitutes. It may be that a person who had a preference for brown shell eggs would have to be given two white shell eggs to compensate for each brown egg given up. Or it could be that the size of the eggs are different. If the brown shell eggs are large and white eggs are small, the ratio may have to be two white for one brown. The distinguishing characteristic of perfect substitutes is that the ratio remains constant at various combinations, not that the ratio is always one for one.

3. Perfect complements. The third possible kind of substitution relationship that may exist between two items is zero substitutability. These items often are called *perfect complements* because they always must be used in a certain ratio or proportion in order to yield any utility. The best examples are right and left shoes. Presumably a two-legged person would not be any better off with one left shoe and two right shoes than with one left and one right. In other words the individual would be on the same indifference curve with the one left and one right shoe combination as with one left and two right shoes. The indifference curve reflecting this situation turns out to be rectangular in shape as illustrated by Figure 2–4.

Bear in mind that a person is on the same level of utility or satisfaction at all points along an indifference curve. Thus adding more right shoes to the one left shoe does not, in this example, give the person any more satisfaction. Moreover, it is not possible to stay on the same level of satisfaction by taking away left shoes and adding right shoes. In other words, two right shoes are not as good as one left and one right. Thus the indifference curve runs parallel to each axis after the exact combination that makes the two items useful is attained. More units of one or the other good are just redundant and add nothing to satisfaction. These goods are perfect complements because they must be used in the fixed ratio to be useful. Again the ratio does not necessarily have to be one for one, although most pairs of perfect complements seem to occur in this ratio. The main point is that the ratio cannot be altered.

Note in the case of perfect complements that the indifference curves are parallel (Figure 2–4). In the cases of imperfect and perfect substitutes, however, the curves do not have to run parallel to

FIGURE 2–4
Indifference curves for perfect complements

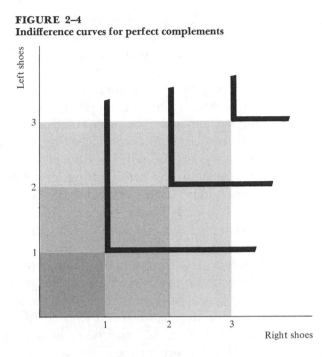

each other. The only restriction is that they do not cross, for if they did they could not be indifference curves. (Think about it.)

In the area of consumer behavior economists have not been very interested in perfect substitutes or perfect complements. For all practical purposes, pairs of perfect substitutes or perfect complements can be looked upon as just one good. For example, white and brown shell eggs can be considered as eggs, or right and left shoes as pairs of shoes. The most interesting case is that of imperfect substitutes, in which various alternative combinations of two goods can provide the same level of satisfaction. Does this mean, therefore, that it doesn't make any difference to the individual which combination is selected? No. We will soon see that only one combination will give the individual the most for his or her money.

The budget line

In order to determine which of the many possible combinations of imperfect substitutes will give the individual the most for his or her money, it is necessary to add or superimpose a budget line on the indifference curve diagram. The budget line shows the various possible combinations of two goods that cost a given amount of money.

Perhaps the easiest way to gain an understanding of a budget line is to construct one from a simple example. Let us continue to use the football and theater ticket example discussed in the preceding section. In the construction of a budget line, two pieces of information are necessary: (1) the person's budget, or how much money he or she can spend on the two items under consideration, and (2) the price of each item. In this example, suppose you decide to spend $60 on football and theater entertainment for the upcoming season. Also suppose that the price of football tickets is $4 while theater seats cost $6.

All that is necessary to construct a budget line is to determine where the line intersects the two axes. This can be accomplished by asking a couple of questions. First, how many football tickets could be purchased if you decided to spend your entire $60 entertainment budget on football if the price of each ticket were $4? Correct—15 tickets. Now let us pose the same question for theater tickets. How many theater tickets could you purchase if you spent

FIGURE 2–5
A budget line

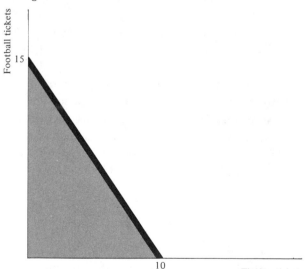

your entire $60 entertainment budget on the theater if the price of theater tickets were $6? In this case, the answer is ten. We now have the two points where the budget line intersects the two axes. It intersects the football axis at 15 tickets and the theater axis at ten tickets. To complete the budget line we just draw a straight line between the two points that we have identified on the axes, as shown by Figure 2–5. The budget line is always a straight line regardless of the degree of substitution that exists between two goods. This is because of the way the budget line is defined. All points on the line represent a given expenditure. At the point where the line intersects the football axis $60 is being spent on 15 football tickets. At the 12 football–2 theater combinations, $48 is being spent on football and $12 on the theater. Moving down the line, you spend more and more on the theater and less and less on football, but you always spend $60.

Maximizing satisfaction: Indifference curve– budget line approach

We are now ready to combine indifference curves with the budget line to find out what combination of tickets would give you the most satisfaction for your $60. In Figure 2–6 we have imposed an indifference map on the budget line from Figure 2–5. As a first step let us choose any combination of tickets that totals $60, for example 12 football and two theater tickets. Will this combination give you the most satisfaction for your money? This question can be answered by looking at Figure 2–6. You will note that the highest indifference curve that can be reached with the 12 football–2 theater combination is I_0. But you will note also that a higher indifference curve can be reached by moving down the budget line, that is, by choosing a different combination of tickets that will be worth $60 (say, nine football and four theater tickets). As you move down the budget line you reduce your purchase of football tickets and increase the number of theater tickets you buy.

Keep in mind that your overall objective is to reach the highest possible indifference curve within the constraint of the $60 you have to spend. The highest possible indifference curve you can

FIGURE 2–6
Budget line on indifference map

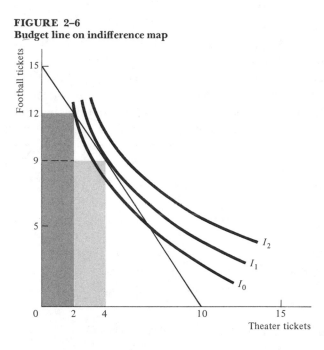

reach is the one just tangent to the budget line, I_1 in Figure 2–6. Indifference curve I_2 could not be reached unless you wanted to spend more than $60. Thus the general rule to bear in mind is that your satisfaction will be maximized when you select that mix of goods on the budget line that enables you to reach the highest possible indifference curve.

In the example above, the combination that maximizes your satisfaction is nine football and four theater tickets. The cost of this combination, $60, is the same as any other combination on the budget line, such as 12 football and two theater, or three football and eight theater, but your level of satisfaction is the greatest only at the nine football–four theater ticket combination.

Thus we see that even though we may be able to purchase any one of a number of different combinations of goods and services for a given expenditure, there is only one combination that will maximize our satisfaction. That is the combination that corresponds to the point of tangency between the budget line and the indifference curve.

Of course, it should be understood that the indifference curves drawn in Figure 2–6 are an arbitrary representation of a person's tastes. The nine football–four theater combination that happens to maximize satisfaction for the $60 resulted from the way in which the indifference curves were drawn. We could have as easily drawn the curves to illustrate a tangency point at any other combination. For example, an avid football fan who has little time for the theater likely would exhibit a different configuration of indifference curves, causing the tangency point to occur at a combination that weighed more heavily in favor of football, such as the 12 football–2 theater combination illustrated by Figure 2–7(A). On the other hand, a theatergoer would exhibit a set of indifference curves that would give rise to a tangency point favoring relatively more theater, such as the three football–eight theater combination illustrated by Figure 2–7(B). As mentioned at the beginning of the chapter, each person has unique tastes and therefore exhibits a unique set of indifference curves between any given pair of goods.

In the preceding examples we considered only one budget level —$60. The position of the budget line is determined in part by how large the budget is; the larger the budget, the farther to the right the budget line will be. For example, a $120 entertainment budget would cause the budget line to intersect the football and theater axes at 30 and 20 tickets, respectively. As a result, more of both items would be purchased, allowing one to reach a higher indifference curve, i.e., a higher level of satisfaction. We will see in the next chapter that the price of each item also influences the position of the budget line and therefore affects the utility–maximizing combination, that is, the tangency point.

Although we have been dealing with an example of imperfect substitutes (football and the theater), the same procedure applies to perfect substitutes and perfect compelments. In the case of perfect substitutes, the utility-maximizing point will occur at one axis or the other if the slope of the budget line is different than the slope of the indifference curve. This means that the individual would buy only one of the two items, whichever is cheapest. This is reasonable to expect. If one item is just as good as the other in satisfying one's tastes, why purchase any of the good that is more expensive? In reality, two goods that are perfect substitutes generally sell for the same price, otherwise no one would buy the good that offered less for the money. As you might expect, we will not be

FIGURE 2–7
Illustrating differences in tastes

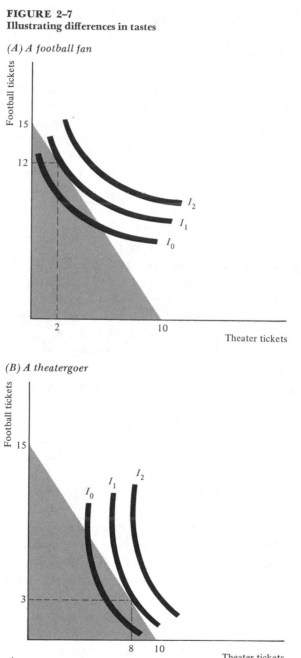

(A) A football fan

(B) A theatergoer

very interested in two goods that are perfect substitutes and sell for the same price; essentially they are just one good. In the case of perfect complements, the utility-maximizing combination will occur at the corner of the indifference curve.

To summarize briefly, in this chapter we considered two approaches to the analysis of consumer behavior: (1) the marginal utility over price approach, and (2) the indifference curve-budget line approach. Actually both approaches yield the same results. In the first approach utility is maximized for a given expenditure when the consumption pattern is such that the marginal utility per dollar is equalized across all purchases. In the second approach utility is maximized when the combination that is consumed corresponds to the tangency point between the budget line and highest possible indifference curve. Although we will not do so here, it can be shown with the aid of mathematics that the marginal utilities per dollar of the two goods represented on the indifference curve–budget line diagram are equal for both goods only at the point of tangency.

Both approaches have their place. The marginal utility over price approach is most useful for showing why additional utility can be gained by rearranging purchases until the marginal utilities per dollar of all items are equal. The indifference curve–budget line also brings out this point, but in addition it is useful for illustrating differences in the degree of substitution between goods, as reflected by the shape of the indifference curves. It also turns out to be useful for deriving a demand curve, as we will see in the next chapter.

Main points of Chapter 2

1. In a free market economy, production is carried on solely to satisfy the wants of consumers. This is known as a system of consumer sovereignty.
2. Since each person has unique tastes, one should talk about "different" tastes rather than "good" or "bad" taste in regard to a person's choice of goods and services.
3. Utility is a measure of satisfaction. Utils enable us to rank

goods or services according to the satisfaction they provide.

4. The marginal unit is the last unit added to or subtracted from the top of whatever we are measuring.

5. The marginal unit is especially important in economics because most economic decisions involve small, or marginal, changes rather than all-or-nothing situations.

6. Marginal utility is the utility or satisfaction provided by the marginal unit consumed.

7. Diminishing marginal utility means that as you consume more and more of a good or service, holding constant the consumption of other goods and services, the amount of satisfaction obtained from each additional unit consumed will, after a point, begin to decline.

8. When considering whether or not to buy an item, we should consider both its marginal utility and its price.

9. In order to maximize satisfaction for the money we spend, we should equalize as much as possible the marginal utilities per dollar of all the things we consume. Marginal utility per dollar is obtained by dividing marginal utility by price.

10. The combination of goods and services that maximize our utility for a given expenditure is constantly changing for a variety of reasons. These include: (*a*) changes in how much we like the things we presently consume because of what we consumed in the past, what others are consuming, advertising, and new products appearing on the market, and (*b*) changes in the prices of goods or services.

11. The decision to consume now or save for future consumption depends on both a person's utility of present consumption (time preference) and the price of present consumption.

12. The price of present consumption increases with an increase in the interest rate, because with higher rates of interest, each dollar saved at the present will buy more in the future providing prices remain unchanged.

13. The true picture of a person's saving habits is best reflected by long-run behavior, because much short-run savings may just be an accumulation of money to spend in a large lump sum.

14. An indifference curve traces out alternative combinations of two goods, all of which would make you equally satisfied.

15. An indifference map is a collection of indifference curves. Curves farther from the origin represent higher levels of satisfaction.

16. Indifference curves for imperfect substitutes are represented by downward sloping curved lines, convex to the origin. In this case more and more of the abundant good must be obtained to compensate for the loss of each successive unit of the scarce good.

17. Indifference curves for perfect substitutes are represented by straight, downward sloping lines. In this case the amount of one good that must be received to compensate for the loss of another good remains constant on all possible combinations.

18. Indifference curves for perfect complements are rectangular. In this case, the two items must be used in a fixed proportion; adding more of one good without the other does not add anything to the level of satisfaction or utility.

19. A budget line traces out alternative combinations of two goods that cost a given amount.

20. To maximize satisfaction for a given expenditure, it is necessary to move along the budget line until you reach the highest possible indifference curve. This is the curve that is tangent to the budget line.

21. The configuration of a person's indifference curves depends on that person's tastes. Each person has unique tastes and unique indifference curves.

Questions for thought and discussion

1. It has been argued that consumer sovereignty is a thing of the past in the United States because the advertising media in large part determine what consumers want to buy. What does this argument imply about the behavior of firms?

2. How would people behave if the law of diminishing marginal utility did not exist?

3. "The more the merrier" contradicts the law of diminishing marginal utility. True or false? Explain.

4. How should consumers allocate expenditures in order to maximize the utility from a given amount of money?

5. The marginal utility of a steak and a fish dinner for an individual is given below. Under the following prices, is the individual maximizing utility for a given expenditure? Why or why not?

	MU	Price
Steak dinner	100	$10
Fish dinner	75	5

6. It is likely that more people would prefer a Cadillac or Mercedes over a Ford or Chevrolet, but more people buy Fords and Chevrolets than the more expensive makes. This just shows that most people are irrational. True or false? Explain.

7. After returning home from a shopping trip and contemplating one's purchases, it is common to regard some items as "good buys" and other items as things you wonder whether you should have bought or not. What do these thoughts imply about the marginal utility per dollar of the items you purchased?

8. Suppose you are in the market for a new bicycle. A salesperson shows you a "cool" ten-speed model for $185. You say the bike is very nice, but you cannot afford such an expensive model. What do you really mean when you say you cannot "afford" this bicycle? Surely you should be able to put your hands on $185 from either your savings or a small loan.

9. Let's say that the combination of food that maximizes your satisfaction for lunch consists of one cheeseburger, one slice of apple pie, and one cup of coffee. According to the marginal utility over price approach to making consumer decisions, you should continue to consume this mix of foods for lunch the rest of your life. True or false? Explain.

10. It is a common practice in restaurants for customers to be given as much coffee as they desire free of charge when they purchase a meal. Under these circumstances what should be the marginal utility of the last cup of coffee; that is, what should be the marginal utility of the last unit consumed of goods received "free."

11. On the scale of time preference, where would you place a miser? A spendthrift? A college student?

12. An increase in the rate of interest on savings increases the price of present consumption. True or false? Explain.

13. Draw indifference curves for the following pairs of products and explain why you have drawn them in a certain shape.
    a. Paper and pencils.
    b. Pens and pencils.
    c. Beef and pork.
    d. Fords and Chevrolets.
    e. Automobiles and bicycles.

14. A person is equally well off at any point along a budget line. True or false? Explain.

15. Consider a sailor on shore leave who has $300 to spend. He decides that he will spend $200 on wine and women and the remainder foolishly.
    a. Draw the sailor's budget line for wine and women, assuming the price of wine is $5 and the cost of a "night on the town" is $40.
    b. Add some indifference curves to the budget line diagram to indicate the mix of goods (or services) that will maximize his satisfaction. Assume in this case that the sailor considers wine and women as very imperfect substitutes but is more of a "ladies' man" than a "wine connoisseur."
    c. Next assume that the sailor considers wine and women as good substitutes for each other, and if given a choice he prefers alcohol to romance. Now draw his indifference curves showing the utility-maximizing combination of goods (or services) for the $200 budget.

3

Product demand

The concept of demand

Because *demand* is a word that most everyone has used to convey one meaning or another, there tend to be many interpretations of it. It will be useful at this stage, therefore, to define rather rigorously the concept of demand as used by economists. You will probably find that the economist's concept of demand differs at least somewhat from the way it is used in everyday conversation.

Demand is defined as a *relationship* between price and quantity. In keeping with this definition, the first and perhaps most important thing to recognize about demand as used by economists is that it is not a set or fixed quantity but a relationship between price and quantity. In order to know what quantity a person or group of persons will demand, we must first know what price they will have to pay. For example, if you were asked what your demand is for football tickets, you would probably be reluctant to answer unless you knew what price you had to pay. The number of tickets you buy likely would be quite different if you had to pay $20 per ticket than if the price were $4. In this chapter we will organize our thinking about the relationship between the price of an item and the quantity people buy. We will begin by using the football ticket example established above.

FIGURE 3–1
The concept of demand (football ticket example)

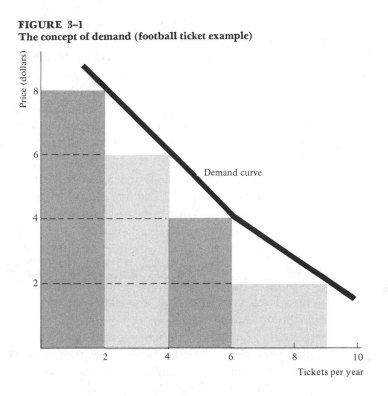

Figure 3–1 provides an example in which only two football tickets are demanded per season if the price is $8 per ticket; at a $4 price, six tickets are demanded; and at the bargain price of $2, nine tickets are demanded per season. By connecting the series of points on the graph, we obtain a curve that is known as a *demand curve*. Essentially a demand curve describes a relationship between price and quantity. If we establish a price, the demand curve tells us what quantity will be demanded. Or if we specify a quantity, the curve tells us what price will be paid.

It is important to distinguish between demand and quantity demanded. Demand, as we have noted, refers to the relationship between price and quantity. However, quantity demanded refers to a particular quantity or point on the demand curve. Thus when you wish to stipulate a particular quantity you can avoid confusion by calling it "quantity demanded" rather than "demand."

A second important characteristic to note about the concept of demand is that it reflects *wants*, not *needs*. If you tell me that you need six football tickets if the price is $4 per ticket, it would be easy to take issue with your statement. That is, it could be argued that you do not need *any* football tickets because watching football is not necessary to sustain life.Or you might say you need a new car or a vacation trip to a distant city. Again, neither is necessary to sustain life. On the other hand, if you said you *wanted* six football tickets or a vacation trip, this could not be disputed. Only you can determine what you want, and these wants are at least partly satisfied by the things you buy.

A third point to note about a demand curve is that it reflects what people actually would do if faced by certain prices rather than what they would like to do. Your favorite make of automobile may sell for $12,000, and you might like a new one every year, but that does not mean you would actually purchase one of these cars every year or even one in a lifetime. Demand is useful only if it reflects the actions of people, not what they would *like* to do. In other words, demand reflects wants that are translated into action, not mere intention or desire.

A fourth item to note about demand is that quantity is measured as an amount per unit of time. In Figure 3–1, the quantity of football tickets is measured in the number of tickets per year. However, there is no set time period that is always used. We can measure quantity as amount per week, per month, per year, and so forth. The time dimension that is chosen is often the one that is most useful in analyzing the problem at hand. It must be recognized that when you change the time period, you also change the scale on the quantity axis.

It should be kept in mind, as well, that the demand curve shown in Figure 3–1 is only an example. In this diagram the demand curve is drawn with a slight curvature. This is not meant to imply that demand curves for all products look this way. Some may be straight, downward sloping lines; others may have more curvature. For the present our main concern will be with the downward sloping characteristic rather than with the extent of curvature of the line.

Marginal utility and demand

Although the downward sloping nature of a demand curve has a certain intuitive appeal, we can establish this characteristic in a more rigorous fashion using what we learned about marginal utility and price in the previous chapter. Recall that a consumer maximizes satisfaction when the marginal utilities (MU) per dollar are equal for all the goods and services available. The following expression summarizes this idea:

$$\frac{\text{MU of good A}}{\text{Price of good A}} = \frac{\text{MU of good B}}{\text{Price of good B}} = \cdots = \frac{\text{MU of good Z}}{\text{Price of good Z}}$$

Recall also that marginal utility per dollar depends on both marginal utility and price. For a given marginal utility, the higher the price, the lower is the marginal utility per dollar. As a very simple example, suppose a consumer is initially maximizing utility, as is illustrated in the expression above. Now consider that just one of these goods, say good A, changes in price as shown below:

	Initial situation	*Price of A rises*	*Price of A falls*
Marginal utility of A	20	20	20
Price of A	$4	$5	$2
Marginal utility per dollar	5	4	10

In the initial situation, all goods consumed by this person yield a marginal utility per dollar of five utils. When the price of good A rises, this good only yields four utils per dollar. In this case it will pay the consumer to reduce the amount of good A purchased. One dollar less spent on A will reduce the person's satisfaction by four utils, but spending this dollar on something else that has not risen in price will yield close to five utils. Thus the consumer can gain one util of net satisfaction by spending one dollar less on good A and one dollar more on one or more other goods.

As the consumer continues to reduce the consumption of A, the marginal utility of A will increase (increasing the marginal utility per dollar of A). Also as more other goods are consumed, the marginal utilities of these goods will decrease. Eventually the consumer will reach a new equilibrium where the marginal utilities per dollar are again equal for all goods. The important thing to note here is that as the price of a good rises, marginal utility per dollar declines, and this creates an incentive for the consumer to reduce purchases of the good in question. The end result, then, is consistent with the idea of a downward sloping demand curve, such as that constructed in the preceding section, in which a higher price leads to a decreased rate of purchase.

Exactly the same reasoning applies for a decrease in the price of A. Here marginal utility per dollar increases, which in turn provides an incentive for the consumer to increase purchases of A at the expense of other goods. Again this is consistent with the concept of demand.

Indifference curves and demand

So far we have shown that the downward sloping nature of a demand curve is consistent with the marginal utility over price approach of maximizing utility. In this section we will go one step further and derive a demand curve using the indifference curve–budget line approach. It is necessary first to understand what happens to the budget line when the price of one of the two items changes. Recall from the preceding chapter that the intersection of the budget line with each axis is determined by dividing the dollar value of the budget by the price of each respective good. In terms of the football–theater ticket example, the 15- and 10-unit intersection points were obtained by dividing the $60 entertainment budget by $4 and $6, respectively.

What happens to the budget line if we change the price of theater tickets from $6 to $4? At the $4 theater price, the budget line intersects the theater axis at 15 tickets. If we hold the price of football tickets constant at $4, the budget line continues to intersect the football axis at 15 tickets. By drawing the budget line between the original point on the football axis and the new point on the theater axis, you will notice that a decrease in the price of theater tickets causes the budget line to rotate in a counterclockwise fashion, as illustrated by Figure 3–2. A further reduction in the price of theater tickets to $3 causes the budget line to rotate further, intersecting the horizontal axis at 20 theater tickets.

By superimposing the indifference curves that are tangent to these three budget lines, we obtain the utility-maximizing combination for each set of prices, as denoted by points *A, B,* and *C* on

FIGURE 3–2
Indifference map and budget lines illustrating changes in the price of theater tickets

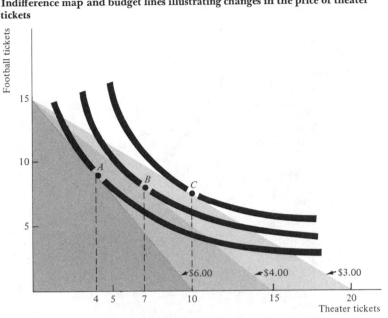

Figure 3–2. Notice that as the price of theater tickets declines, the optimum number of theater tickets purchased increases. By selecting three different theater ticket prices, we have determined three different quantities of theater tickets that will be purchased, given these indifferent curves and the $60 budget. If this relationship between price and quantity looks familiar, it should, because it is none other than the information shown by a demand curve. (Recall that a demand curve is a relationship between price and quantity.) By plotting the quantity of theater tickets that goes along with each price, we obtain a demand curve for theater tickets as shown by Figure 3–3. At the $6 price, four tickets are demanded; at the $4 price, seven tickets are demanded; and so on. Thus we have derived a demand curve for theater tickets from the indifference curve–budget line diagram.

This procedure brings out one additional characteristic of a demand curve: Each point on a demand curve corresponds to a point of tangency between an indifference curve and a budget line, meaning that the individual is maximizing utility for the given

FIGURE 3–3
Demand curve for theater tickets, as derived from Figure 3–2

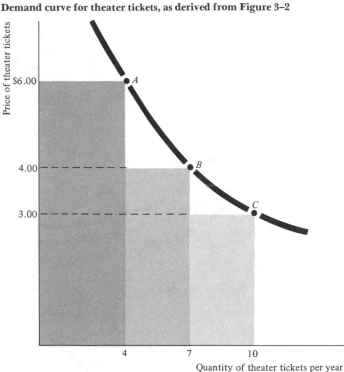

expenditure. Notice also that this demand curve is drawn for a given income or budget and a given price of the good represented on the vertical axis. We could easily derive a demand curve for football tickets by going through the same procedure. Only now we would hold the theater ticket price constant while changing the price of the football tickets. Notice that a decrease in the football ticket price causes the budget line to rotate in a clockwise fashion.

Income and substitution effects

It is somewhat reassuring to see that the downward sloping nature of the demand curve that we obtained first by appealing to our intuition also is obtained by the somewhat more rigorous procedure we have just used. It will be useful to probe deeper into the relationship between price and quantity in order to more fully understand why people buy more of a product when its price declines, or less when its price increases.

Economists have identified two major factors or effects that help explain why people behave this way: (1) the income effect and (2) the substitution effect. The income effect accounts for the fact that a change in the price of a good you buy changes the purchasing power of your income. It has the same effect as if you had experienced a change in income. For example, as the price of theater tickets declines, your $60 entertainment budget can buy a larger number of tickets. It is as if your income had been increased. The opposite occurs, of course, if the ticket price rises; then the $60 buys fewer tickets, so it is just like a decrease in your budget or income. The substitution effect occurs because when the price of one good changes *relative* to another, there is the incentive to buy more of the lower-priced good and less of the higher-priced one. In other words, you try to substitute the good that is relatively inexpensive for the one that is relatively more expensive.

The income and substitution effects can be defined in more specific terms by means of the indifference curve–budget line diagram. In Figure 3–4 we illustrate, using the theater ticket example, the effect of a decrease in the price of tickets from $6 to $3. Because of this price decline, the quantity of theater tickets demanded increases from four to ten. We will now determine what part of this increase in tickets demanded is due to the income effect and what part is due to the substitution effect.

Probably the most common procedure is to measure the substitution effect first. This is done by drawing a hypothetical budget line parallel to the new budget line but tangent to the original indifference curve. The hypothetical budget line is illustrated by the downward sloping broken line in Figure 3–4. It is tangent to the original indifference curve at point *B*. The horizontal distance between point *A* and point *B* (four theater tickets in our example) represents the substitution effect. Because of the lower price of theater tickets, illustrated by the flatter budget line, people substitute theater for football in their entertainment budget. The remaining two additional theater tickets are due to the income effect. This is shown by the movement point from *B* to *C* in Figure 3–4. These two additional theater tickets are purchased because the $60

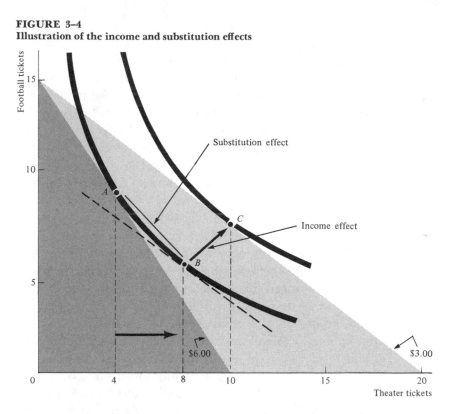

FIGURE 3–4
Illustration of the income and substitution effects

entertainment budget goes further due to the decrease in the theater ticket price. It is like having an increase in income, hence the name *income effect*. The substitution effect is always found by moving along an indifference curve, whereas the income effect is determined by moving from one indifference curve to another.[1]

Market demand

While we have been concerned with the demand curve of an individual consumer, the concept of demand is most useful when

---

[1] It is possible, and equally correct, to show the substitution effect along the new indifference curve rather than the original curve as explained above. This is accomplished by drawing the hypothetical budget line parallel to the original budget line and tangent to the new indifference curve. In this case the income effect is measured first and the remainder is the substitution effect.

applied to a market situation—an entire group of consumers. We began our discussion of demand at the level of the individual consumer, however, in order to derive the concept of a demand curve from the closely related concept of consumer indifference curves.

It is relatively simple to develop the idea of a market demand from the demand of individual consumers. First, suppose that every consumer has a demand for every product. For some consumers, of course, the demand will be large at a given price; for others, the demand might be zero at the same price. No two consumers have the same demand for a given product. All we need to do to visualize the idea of market demand is to add up, at each possible price, the quantity demanded by all consumers in the market. In other words, we obtain a horizontal summation of the demand curves of individual consumers. Figure 3–5 provides an example of how this can be done.

FIGURE 3–5
Constructing market demand from individual demand (theater ticket example)

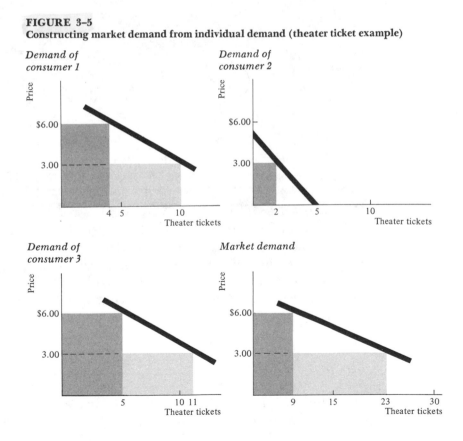

You might recognize the demand of consumer 1 in the first diagram as the same demand as constructed in Figures 3–3 and 3–4. At $6 per ticket, consumer 1 demands four tickets per season, whereas at $3 per ticket, this person will buy ten tickets. Consumer 2 is less of a theater fan. At $6 per ticket, consumer 2 would not attend the theater at all, and at the $3 price, this individual will buy two tickets. Consumer 3 is a more ardent theatergoer than both 1 and 2. This person demands five and 11 tickets at the $6 and $3 prices, respectively.

To keep the example simple, assume that the market consists of these three demanders. The market demand curve is found by adding at each price the quantities demanded by all the consumers in the market, as shown in the following table. The market demand curve is plotted in the lower right frame on Figure 3–5.

Notice in the above example that the increase in quantity de-

Price	*Quantity demanded by consumer*				*Market demand*
	1	*2*	*3*		
$6	4 +	0 +	5	=	9
3	10 +	2 +	11	=	23

manded by the market as price declines comes from two sources: (1) the increase in quantity by the existing demanders in the market, and (2) the entrance into the market of new demanders when the price declines, as illustrated by consumer 2. Thus we can expect that the response to a price change will be greater for the entire market than for the average individual buyer because of new people coming into the market when price declines, or people leaving the market as price increases. Unless one takes into account the entrance and exit of buyers as the price changes, the response of the market to price changes is likely to be underestimated.

Response to price changes

Our interest thus far has centered mainly on the downward sloping nature of the demand curve, meaning that people buy more of an item when its price decreases and less when its price increases. It is necessary, however, that we become somewhat more specific than this. In this section we will consider the *responsiveness* of consumers to price changes. Even if we know that consumers buy more of a good when its price decreases, it is equally important to know whether they buy a lot more or just a little bit more.

The shape of the demand curve can tell us something about the responsiveness of consumers to price changes. A demand curve that is relatively flat, as illustrated by Figure 3–6(A), reflects that consumers are relatively responsive to a price change. In this example, the individual increases the quantity of tickets from 12 to 18 when the price declines from $6 to $4. On the other hand, a demand curve that is relatively steep implies that consumers are relatively unresponsive to price changes. This is illustrated in Figure 3–6(B), where the consumer buys only one more ticket per year when the price declines from $6 to $4.

Gauging the responsiveness of consumers to price changes by the shape or slope of the demand curve can be misleading, however, because it is possible to change the shape of the curve simply by changing the scale along one or both axes. For example, the market demand curve represented in Figure 3–5 can be made to appear relatively flat by expanding the units of measure on the quantity axis while squeezing together the price axis scale as illustrated by Figure

FIGURE 3–6
Differences in response to price changes

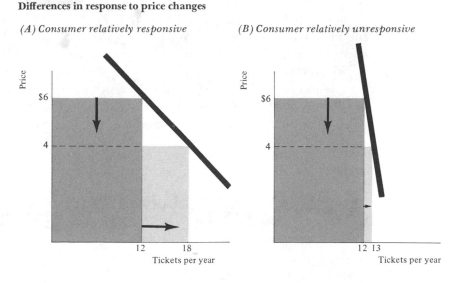

(A) Consumer relatively responsive   *(B) Consumer relatively unresponsive*

FIGURE 3–7
The same response to a price change by different shaped demand curves

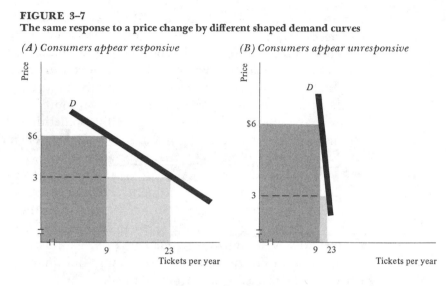

(A) Consumers appear responsive   *(B) Consumers appear unresponsive*

3–7(A). In viewing the demand curve drawn in Figure 3–7(A), a person might conclude that consumers are relatively responsive to changes in ticket prices. By the same token it is possible to represent the same price-quantity relationship as a relatively steep demand curve by contracting the scale on the horizontal axis while expanding the price axis scale as shown by Figure 3–7(B).

Whenever viewing statistical phenomena presented by a graph or diagram, it is a good idea to be aware that the message conveyed may to a certain extent be influenced by the scale on the two axes. Although economists frequently use a flat demand curve to convey the idea that consumers are relatively responsive to price changes and a steep curve to indicate the opposite tendency, they are aware of this shortcoming and consequently supplement the diagramatic representation with another measure of price response that is not dependent on the scale used. In fact it does not even require a diagram. This measure is called price elasticity of demand.

Price elasticity of demand

Price elasticity of demand is defined as the percent change in quantity demanded resulting from each percent change in price. A formula for computing price elasticity is:

$$E_d = \frac{\dfrac{Q_0 - Q_1}{Q_0}}{\dfrac{P_0 - P_1}{P_0}}$$

where E_d is an abbreviation for price elasticity of demand, Q_0 and P_0 are the beginning quantity and price, respectively, and Q_1 and P_1 are the ending quantity and price. In order to become somewhat more familiar with the formula, let us compute the price elasticity of demand for the change shown in Figure 3–6(A). In this example the Q_0 is 12, Q_1 is 18, P_0 is \$6, and P_1 is \$4. Thus we have

$$E_d = \frac{\dfrac{12 - 18}{12}}{\dfrac{6 - 4}{6}} = \frac{\dfrac{-6}{12}}{\dfrac{2}{6}} = \frac{-0.50}{0.33} = -1.5$$

In this example, a 1 percent decrease in price is associated with a 1.5 percent increase in quantity. You will note that the price elasticity of demand is a negative number. This occurs because as we move along a demand curve, quantity and price change in opposite directions; when price goes down, quantity goes up, and vice versa.

Although the price elasticity measure is a negative number, when economists refer to a specific elasticity measure they often drop the negative sign and designate the number as an absolute value. For example, a price elasticity measure of -1.5 generally is referred to as 1.5. Once one is aware that the negative sign is implicit in the discussion, it is redundant to keep repeating it.

In order to further facilitate discussion, economists have grouped the price elasticity measure, or *coefficient*, as it is often called, into three categories. Generally the groupings are made according to the absolute size of the coefficient (minus sign dropped). These categories of elasticity coefficients are:

Less than 1 = Inelastic
Equal to 1 = Unitary elastic
Greater than 1 = Elastic

When the demand for a product is inelastic to price, we say that consumers are relatively unresponsive to a price change. In this case the percentage change in quantity is smaller than the corresponding percentage change in price. If demand is elastic, on the other hand, we say that consumers are quite responsive to a price change. Here the percentage change in quantity is greater than the percentage change in price. In the intermediate case of a unitary elastic demand, price and quantity both change in the same proportions.

The smallest possible value of the elasticity coefficient is zero. If E_d is zero, a change in price will not result in any change in quantity whatever. In this case demand is said to be perfectly inelastic. Demand that is perfectly inelastic is represented by a demand curve that is perfectly vertical (Figure 3–8).

The largest possible value of the elasticity coefficient is infinity. Here a very slight change in price corresponds to an infinitely large change in quantity. In this situation demand is said to be perfectly elastic and is characterized by a demand curve that is perfectly horizontal (Figure 3–9).

Two characteristics of the elasticity coefficient ought to be mentioned at this point. Both stem from the fact that elasticity deals with percentage changes. The first is that the size of the elasticity coefficient becomes larger as we move higher up on a downward sloping, straight-line demand curve. This phenomenon occurs because the base or beginning values change at different points along the demand curve. At points high on the curve, the beginning price is high. Thus for a given dollar change in price, the percentage change is relatively small. For example, a $1 change in price will be only 10 percent if the beginning price is $10, whereas the same $1 change in price would represent a 100 percent change if the beginning price is only $1. The same reasoning applies to different points along the quantity axis. The beginning or base quantity is small at points high on the demand curve (small quantity demanded), which in turn results in large percentage changes for a given absolute change in quantity. The effect of a change in base values on E_d is illustrated in the following elasticity formulas. Consider the absolute change in quantity ($Q_0 - Q_1$) and the absolute change in price ($P_0 - P_1$) to be the same in each case, so that the only things changing are the base values.

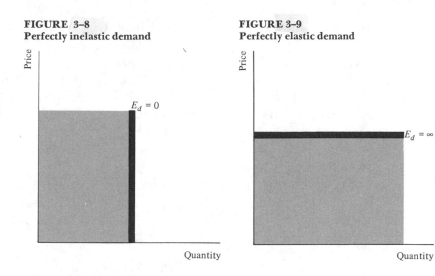

FIGURE 3–8
Perfectly inelastic demand

FIGURE 3–9
Perfectly elastic demand

Points high on a demand curve: $-1 \times \frac{15}{5}$

$$E_d = \dfrac{\dfrac{\overset{5}{\cancel{Q_0}} - \overset{10}{\cancel{Q_1}}}{\underset{5}{\cancel{Q_0}}}\ \overset{-1}{\underset{\text{small}}{}}}{\dfrac{\overset{}{P_0 - P_1}}{\underset{15}{P_0}}\ \overset{\frac{5}{15}}{\underset{\text{large}}{}}}$$

large

$\frac{15}{5}$ large E_o

small

$\frac{15}{5} = 3$

Points low on a demand curve:

$$E_d = \dfrac{\dfrac{\overset{20}{Q_0} - \overset{30}{Q_1}}{\underset{20 Q_0}{}}\ \overset{\frac{-10}{20}}{\underset{\text{large}}{}}}{\dfrac{P_0 - P_1}{\underset{5}{P_0}}\ \overset{\frac{1}{5}}{\underset{\text{small}}{}}}$$

$\frac{-10}{20} \times 5$

small

large

$\frac{-10}{4} = 2\frac{1}{2}$

small E_o

A second characteristic of elasticity that occurs because it is measured in percentage terms is that the coefficient depends on the direction of a given absolute change in price and quantity. In the example for computing price elasticity of demand used above, the beginning or base quantity and price were 12 and $6, respectively. But if we had started at the $4 price and moved up along the demand curve, the elasticity coefficient obtained would have been different. This is because the base values would have changed to 18 and $4 for quantity and price. The larger base value for quantity would have made the percentage change in quantity smaller (−33

Chapter 3

percent), whereas the percentage change in price would have increased to 50 percent. The overall elasticity coefficient would have declined to 0.66.

Because different answers are obtained for different directions of movement, the elasticity coefficient is accurate only if it is computed over relatively small changes in price and quantity. Economists measuring price elasticity of demand for actual products use statistical tools that measure only very small movements in price and quantity.

For teaching purposes, economists have modified the elasticity formula slightly, using both beginning and ending values of price and quantity for the base in the numerator and denominator. The formula becomes:

$$E_d = \frac{\dfrac{Q_0 - Q_1}{Q_0 + Q_1}}{\dfrac{P_0 - P_1}{P_0 + P_1}}$$

This formula measures the "average" elasticity between two points, and it results in the same answer regardless of the direction of movement.[2] The formula discussed first is sometimes known as the "point elasticity" formula, whereas the second expression has come to be known as the "arc elasticity" formula. Notice that the elasticity coefficient for the example we have been working with is 1.0 using this second formula.

In an effort to master the mechanics of price elasticity, one should not lose sight of its economic meaning. Keep in mind that price elasticity of demand measures the responsiveness of consumers to changes in price. An inelastic demand means that consumers are not very responsive to price, whereas an elastic demand means that they will be quite responsive to price changes. The elasticity co-

---

[2] The above formula also can be expressed as $\dfrac{\dfrac{Q_0 - Q_1}{(Q_0 + Q_1)/2}}{\dfrac{P_0 - P_1}{P_0 + P_1)/2}}$ and referred to as the "midpoints" formula. In this case the base values are taken as halfway between the beginning and ending quantities and prices. However, because the 2s cancel, the same answer is obtained as in the above expression.

efficient tells us the percentage change in quantity demanded for each percent change in price.

Price elasticity and total revenue

One of the most valuable uses of the price elasticity concept is that it enables us to predict what will happen to the total expenditure on a product by consumers, or the total revenue going to the sellers of the product, when its price changes. To understand how elasticity is related to changes in total expenditure or revenue, it is necessary to first understand that a price change has two offsetting effects on total revenue or expenditure. Consider the case of a decline in price. Before the price falls, total revenue is given by:

$$TR = P_0 \times Q_0$$

Where TR is total revenue and P_0 and Q_0 are beginning price and quantity. After the price falls, total revenue is given by:

$$TR = P_1 \times Q_1$$

where P_1 and Q_1 are the new price and quantity, respectively.

The reduction in price, of course, has the effect of reducing total consumer expenditures or revenue. If the demand curve is downward sloping, however, the reduction in price will lead to an increase in quantity sold, and the increase in quantity will have the effect of pulling total revenue back up. If demand is elastic, quantity increases by a larger percentage than price decreases; in this case total revenue will increase with a price reduction. The opposite occurs when demand is inelastic. In that case, a price reduction results in a decrease in total revenue because quantity increases by a smaller percentage than price decreases.

Figures 3–10 and 3–11 illustrate the relationship between price elasticity and total revenue or expenditure by means of demand curves. The area denoted by a minus sign represents a pulling down of total revenue, whereas the plus area represents the augmentation of total revenue due to the price fall. In Figure 3–10, a representation of an inelastic demand, the minus area outweighs the plus area, resulting in a reduction in total revenue. The opposite occurs

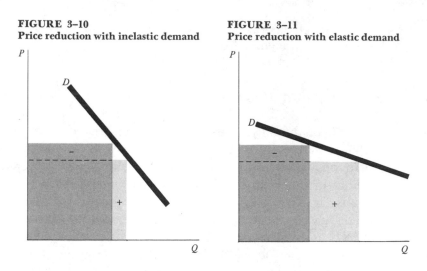

FIGURE 3–10
Price reduction with inelastic demand

FIGURE 3–11
Price reduction with elastic demand

in Figure 3–11, where the plus area outweighs the minus area because of the elastic demand.

Of course, we would observe just the opposite change in total revenue if we considered a price increase. Here an inelastic demand would give rise to an increase in total revenue because price would increase more than quantity would decrease. By the same token, a price rise with elastic demand results in a decrease in total revenue. The relationship between price elasticity of demand and total revenue is summarized in the following table.

	Change in total revenue or expenditure
Elastic demand	
Price fall	Increase
Price rise	Decrease
Inelastic demand	
Price fall	Decrease
Price rise	Increase

Notice that for an elastic demand, price and total revenue or expenditure change in opposite directions, whereas for an inelastic demand they change in the same direction.

Economic factors affecting price elasticity of demand

We have seen that price elasticity is affected by the point we happen to choose along a demand curve. But this is strictly an algebraic phenomenon that occurs because of the way we calculate price elasticity. We now want to explore briefly the economic factors that affect the size of a product's price elasticity of demand. The demand for some goods is elastic, and the demand for other goods is inelastic. Why?

The first, and perhaps most important, factor influencing the price elasticity of a good is the degree of substitution between it and other goods. The larger the number and the better the substitutes that exist for a good or service, the more elastic will be that particular good or service.

To understand the economic rationale of this generalization, consider a product that has many substitutes, pork chops, for example. When the price of pork chops goes up, consumers have many other alternative products to choose from—other cuts of pork; all other meat, such as beef, poultry, and fish; as well as other protein foods that can be eaten in place of meat, such as cheese or the new meat analogs. A rise in the price of pork chops, then, will provide an incentive for consumers to reduce pork chop consumption and increase their consumption of these alternative products. When pork chop consumption declines, it is an indication that consumers are being responsive to the rising price of pork chops. You will recall that this is the meaning of an elastic demand.

Products that have few or very poor substitutes, on the other hand, tend to have an inelastic demand. Salt is the classic example of such a good. If the price of salt should rise, consumers would still have to buy it in about the same amounts, since it has no satisfactory substitute. This means that consumers are not very responsive to a change in the price of salt, which is just another way of saying that salt has an inelastic demand.

It is important to recognize as well that the definition of a product influences its elasticity. In general, the more broadly we define a product, the lower will be its price elasticity. This is because there are fewer substitutes for a broadly defined product than for one that is narrowly defined. For example, the price elasticity for all pork would be smaller (less elastic or more inelastic) than it is for only pork chops. The substitutes for pork chops include pork loins and pork roasts, as well as the pork substitutes, whereas the substitutes for all pork include only the other meats or meat substitutes. Similarly, the demand for a particular brand of salt would be more elastic than for all salt, because brand X, for example, has substitutes in the form of the other brands of salt on the market.

The second major factor influencing the elasticity of a product is the proportion of the consumer's budget accounted for by the product. Products that take up a very small proportion of the budget tend to be less elastic than those that rank relatively large in the budget. For example, if the price of paper clips doubles, the impact on your budget would be imperceptible; hence there would not be a strong incentive to reduce your use of paper clips. Yet if something like dormitory room rent rises considerably, you might be forced to find an alternative place to stay, such as an apartment or in a private home, and you might even have to leave school. Thus we would expect the demand for dormitory rooms to be more elastic than the demand for paper clips.

A summary of the effect of these two factors on the price elasticity of demand is presented in the following table.

Factor	*Effect on price elasticity*
Many good substitutes	Increase
Large item in budget	Increase

It is not unusual to find cases, however, where each of these two factors has an opposite influence on the elasticity of a product. That is, a product may have many good substitutes, making for an elastic demand, but at the same time it may be a small item in the budget, which makes for an inelastic demand. The resulting price elasticity, therefore, is a summation of these two factors; both must be considered when attempting to assess the elasticity of such a product.

You might have noticed that the two factors named above as

influencing the price elasticity of a product closely parallel the two effects, discussed previously in this chapter, that account for the downward sloping characteristic of the demand curve—the substitution and income effects. This is not just a coincidence. The first factor, the degree of substitution possible, assesses the strength of the substitution effect; and the second factor, the importance of the item in the budget, assesses the strength of the income effect. The stronger or more significant these two effects are, the more responsive consumers are to a price change, which in turn implies a more elastic demand.

A change or shift in demand

Thus far the discussion has focused primarily on the relationship between price and quantity along a given demand curve. Demand is said to be elastic if the percentage change in quantity demanded is greater than the percentage change in price, and inelastic if the quantity demanded changes by a smaller percent than the change in price. An elastic demand reflects a greater responsiveness on the part of consumers to a price change than does an inelastic demand.

It is important to remember, however, that whenever a demand curve is conceived of or drawn, everything that might influence the given relationship between price and quantity is assumed to remain unchanged. This restriction is necessary because we are dealing with a two-dimensional diagram; in other words, only two items can be considered at a time. With demand these two items are price and quantity. The world, of course, is never so kind as to hold everything constant other than the two items we are interested in. There are a number of factors that influence the price-quantity relationship by shifting the entire demand curve from one position to another. Before we consider these factors, it will be useful to illustrate the two possible shifts in demand.

Think of D_1 in Figure 3–12 as a demand curve for a good or service during some time period. Then suppose, for some reason (which we will explain shortly), the demand changes position, say to D_2. This represents an increase, or an upward shift, in demand. One way of interpreting this shift is that buyers will take more off the market at any given price. For example, with the original de-

FIGURE 3–12
Shifts in demand

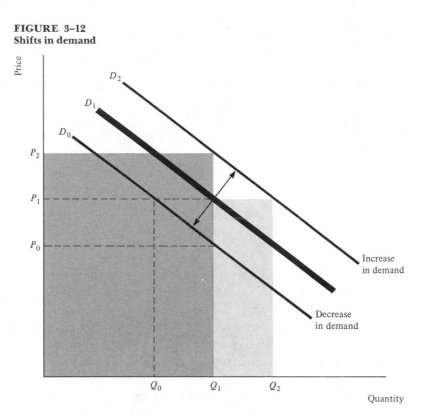

mand, D_1, quantity Q_1 is demanded at price P_1. Now with D_2, demanders will buy a larger quantity, Q_2, at price P_1. A second way of looking at an increase in demand is that buyers are willing to pay a higher price for a given quantity. With the increase in demand, buyers will pay price P_2 for quantity Q_1. At the original demand, buyers would pay P_1 for this quantity.

The meaning of a decrease in demand, as illustrated by D_0, is strictly parallel to an increase. At a given price, say P_1, the quantity demanded declines from Q_1 to Q_0. Or, looking at it the second way, the price buyers will pay for quantity Q_1 declines from P_1 to P_0.

Demand shifters

There are five major factors, or demand shifters, that can cause the demand curve to shift from one position to another.

1. CHANGE IN PRICES OF RELATED PRODUCTS

A. Substitutes. As we saw in Chapter 2 on consumer choice, most products or services have one or more substitutes. We know also that the quantity of substitutes consumed depends on their price relative to the price of the good or service in question. For example, if the price of margarine declines relative to that of butter, people tend to shift their purchases away from the relatively expensive butter to the relatively inexpensive margarine. Therefore, a decrease in the price of a substitute good decreases or shifts downward the demand for the good in question, as illustrated by D_0 in Figure 3–12. Conversely, of course, an increase in the price of a substitute increases (shifts upward) the demand for the good in question, as shown by D_2 in Figure 3–12.

B. Complements. Not all pairs of goods are substitutes for each other. There are certain pairs of products, which we call complementary goods, that are consumed together. Bacon and eggs are an example. If the price of eggs increases, people tend to have eggs for breakfast less frequently, and as a consequence the quantity of bacon sold decreases. Thus the demand for bacon decreases, to D_0 in Figure 3–12, because of the increase in price of eggs, a complementary product.

2. CHANGE IN MONEY INCOMES

An increase in money incomes of consumers results in an increase in the demand for many products. Some of the increase can come from using the product more frequently, such as having eggs more times per week, or from additional consumers coming into the market. For example, people tend to enter the Cadillac market as their incomes approach the $50,000 to $60,000 per year bracket. The more people there are in this income bracket, the greater is the demand for Cadillacs. Economists refer to goods that increase in demand with higher incomes as *superior goods*. This name does not necessarily imply that such goods are made better or last longer than other goods. It is just a name for the category of goods or services that exhibits an increase in demand as incomes increase.

There are examples of other goods or services that decrease in demand as incomes increase. For example, people tend to buy less of starchy, high-calorie foods as their incomes grow. With higher incomes they buy more steak, fruit, and fresh vegetables. Thus the demand for starchy foods declines, or shifts to the left, as incomes increase. Economists refer to these goods or services as *inferior goods,* again without any intention to describe the durability or quality of the good.

It is possible to name goods whose demand does not change at all with an increase in consumer incomes. One example is the aggregate demand for all food in the United States. Because of the relatively high incomes enjoyed by a large part of the U.S. population, food consumption for most people is already at a maximum. Thus with continued increase in incomes people tend to buy about the same quantity of food, while increasing their purchases of the other amenities of life.

In order to measure the response of consumers to a change in income, economists have developed the concept of income elasticity. *Income elasticity* is defined as the percentage change in quantity demanded at a given price resulting from each percent change in the money income of consumers. Notice that income elasticity bears some resemblance to price elasticity presented earlier. The difference is that with income elasticity, we are dealing with the response to changes in income, whereas with price elasticity, we measure the response to changes in price. The formula for calculating income elasticity is:[3]

$$E_I = \frac{\dfrac{Q_0 - Q_1}{Q_0}}{\dfrac{I_0 - I_1}{I_0}}$$

It may be helpful to insert some actual numbers in the above formula to illustrate how income elasticity can be computed. Suppose a family increases its purchases of beef steak from 200 to 225 pounds per year as a result of an increase in annual income from $14,000 to $15,000. In the above formula, Q_0 would be 200, Q_I 225, I_0 $14,000, and I_1 $15,000. In this example income elasticity turns out to be 1.76, as shown by the following computations. The 1.76 means that this family increases its beef steak consumption by 1.76 percent when its income increases by 1 percent.

---

[3] The arc elasticity, or midpoints, formula also can be applied to the computation of income elasticity.

$$E_I = \frac{\dfrac{200 - 225}{200}}{\dfrac{14{,}000 - 15{,}000}{14{,}000}} = \frac{\dfrac{-25}{200}}{\dfrac{-1{,}000}{14{,}000}} = \frac{-0.125}{-0.071} = 1.76$$

Because, with changes in income, demand can increase, decrease, or remain the same, income elasticity can be a positive number, a negative number, or zero. If demand increases, or shifts to the right, with an increase in income, income elasticity is positive. Thus a superior good has a positive income elasticity. The opposite is true for an inferior good. Here demand shifts left with an increase in income, and the resulting income elasticity is negative. If there is no change in quantity with a change in income, E_I is zero.

3. CHANGE IN CONSUMER EXPECTATIONS REGARDING FUTURE PRICES AND INCOMES

Since no one knows the future with certainty, our actions at the present are influenced a great deal by what we expect the future to bring. This is quite important in the case of product demand. If, for example, you expect a product to be scarce and high-priced in the future, you will likely increase your purchases (demand) now in order to avoid the higher future price. An expected higher price will likely result in a shift to the right in demand, as illustrated by D_2 in Figure 3–12. Expecting a lower price in the future will, of course, have the opposite effect; present demand will decrease, such as D_0 in Figure 3–12, as buyers wait for more favorable prices.

Anticipated changes in income also tend to affect present demand. If you expected a rich uncle to leave you $1 million dollars in one or two years, you would likely be a little more liberal in your spending habits even now, well in advance of the date you actually receive the money. Thus your demand for many products or services would shift to the right, as shown by D_2 in Figure 3–12. Or, if you expected your present source of income to dry up, you no doubt would become more frugal, meaning that your demand for some items would shift to the left.

It is important to realize that current demand depends heavily on your long-run expected income. College students illustrate this idea very well. They tend to enjoy a considerably higher standard of living while going to college than people with similar incomes who do not have much hope of substantial raises in the future.

4. CHANGE IN TASTES AND PREFERENCES

There are a few products or services whose demand is influenced by the changing whims or fancies of consumers. Mainly these are the fads or items that often change in fashion or style. For example, there is not much demand nowadays for high-button shoes. On the other hand, there seems to be a resurgence in demand for narrow neckties. In economic terms, the demand for goods that are no longer "in" shifts to the left, as in D_0, whereas the demand for items that are now "in" shifts to the right, D_2 in Figure 3–12.

When attempting to explain changes in consumer purchasing behavior, it is tempting to ascribe too much importance to a change in tastes and preferences. Except for fads or fashions, tastes of large groups of people (markets) tend to be relatively stable. Before falling back on changes in tastes and preferences to "explain" consumer behavior, it is always a good idea to exhaust all other possibilities first. Be particularly careful to include changes in price that result in a movement up or down the demand curve as a possible reason for changes or differences in consumer behavior. For example, it is sometimes stated that Europeans have different tastes than North Americans regarding their preference for small cars. Yet if Americans had to pay $1.50 to $2.00 per gallon for gasoline as Europeans have been doing for years, we would likely see small cars as often in the United States as in Europe. In this case the difference in items purchased is better explained by a difference in price rather than a difference in tastes.

5. CHANGE IN POPULATION

Since the market demand for a good or service is made up of the sum of all individual demands, the greater the number of individuals in the market, the greater will be the market demand. Population growth, therefore, is an important factor in shifting the demand to the right, such as D_2 in Figure 3–12. It is about the only factor shifting the demand for all food to the right, for example. In fact, the demand for most goods and services is being shifted steadily to the right because of growth in the size of the population.

Although these five demand shifters are the major economic factors that influence the position of the demand curve, there are other special circumstances that also can shift the demand curve. For example, as will be discussed in Chapter 6, the enactment of a law that restricts or forbids the purchase of an item can be expected to have the effect of decreasing the demand for that good or service.

In order to fully understand the concept of demand and the behavior of consumers, it is as important to be aware of the possible shifts in demand as it is to know about the downward sloping nature of the demand curve itself. Without a knowledge of these shifts and the factors that can cause them to occur, it is not possible to understand consumer behavior. For example, if the demand curve for an item shifts to the right, consumers will increase their purchases of it at the same price or even at a higher price. (We will see how the latter can occur in Chapter 6.) To the uninformed it may appear that price has no relationship to quantity demanded. But if one knows why the demand curve has shifted, the observed changes in price and quantity will be reasonable and expected.

Main points of Chapter 3

1. Demand is a relationship between price and quantity rather than a fixed amount. Quantity demanded, on the other hand, refers to a fixed amount—a point on the demand curve.
2. Demand reflects the wants of consumers, not their needs. Demand also reflects what consumers actually do when faced with specific prices rather than what they would like to do.
3. The downward sloping characteristic of a consumer's demand curve for a product is consistent with diminishing marginal utility because with an increase in the price of a product, the marginal utility per dollar declines. This in turn makes it

worthwhile for the consumer to reduce consumption of the product.

4. A downward sloping demand curve is also obtained when it is derived from an indifference map and alternative budget lines. Each point on a demand curve represents a tangency point between an indifference curve and a budget line.

5. Consumers change their purchases of products with changes in prices because of the income and substitution effects. The income effect occurs because a price change has the effect of changing the purchasing power of an individual's income. The substitution effect reflects the consumer's desire to obtain the most for his or her money by purchasing the "best buys." These two effects constitute the economic explanation for the downward sloping characteristic of a demand curve.

6. The market demand curve is obtained by adding the demand curves of all the individual consumers in the market. This is done by adding all the quantities demanded by the individuals at each possible price.

7. Changes in the quantity demanded by the market are due to changes in the quantity demanded by individual buyers and by the movement of people in and out of the market.

8. A relatively flat demand curve is frequently used to denote a situation where consumers are relatively responsive to price changes. However, one should be aware that the slope of a demand curve can be changed by changing the scale along either axis.

9. The responsiveness of consumers to price changes is measured by price elasticity of demand. Price elasticity of demand is defined as the percentage change in quantity demanded resulting from each percent change in price.

10. Demand is elastic if E_d is greater than one, indicating that the quantity changes by more than 1 percent when the price changes 1 percent.

11. The elasticity coefficient can range from zero to minus infinity. Demand is perfectly inelastic if E_d is zero and perfectly elastic if E_d is minus infinity.

12. The elasticity coefficient becomes larger at points high on a downward sloping, straight-line demand curve and smaller

points farther down the curve. This is a mathematical phenomenon explained by changes in the base values that are used to calculate percentage changes.

13. Whether consumers spend more or less on a product after its price changes depends on the product's price elasticity of demand. If demand is elastic, a price rise reduces total revenue or expenditure, whereas total revenue increases with a price rise if demand is inelastic.

14. This relationship between total revenue and elasticity is explained by whether quantity changes by a larger or smaller percentage than price. If price rises 1 percent, total revenue or expenditure on the product will decrease if quantity declines more than 1 percent (elastic demand), whereas total revenue increases if the quantity declines less than 1 percent (inelastic demand).

15. The two economic factors that affect price elasticity of demand are the number and acceptability of substitute products available and the importance of the product in the budget. A product with many good substitutes tends to be elastic. Elasticity is increased if the product accounts for a sizable portion of consumers' budgets.

16. A demand curve is drawn under the assumption that everything that can affect the price-quantity relationship is held constant. When one or more of these factors change, the demand curve shifts from one position to another.

17. An increase in demand (shift to the right of the demand curve) means that consumers will take a larger quantity off the market at a given price, or that people will be willing to pay a higher price for a given quantity.

18. A decrease in demand (shift to the left of the demand curve) means that consumers will take a smaller quantity off the market at a given price, or that people will be willing to pay a lower price for a given quantity.

19. The five major factors that shift the demand curve are changes in: (*a*) prices of related products, (*b*) consumer incomes, (*c*) consumer expectations regarding future prices and incomes, (*d*) tastes and preferences, and (*e*) population.

20. Income elasticity of demand measures the responsiveness of

consumers to changes in income and is defined as the percentage change in the quantity demanded resulting from each percent change in income.

Questions for thought and discussion

1. Suppose two of your friends are having an argument. One says that the demand curve shows what quantities people will buy at various possible prices. The other argues that a demand curve shows the prices people will pay for various possible quantities. Which of your friends is correct? Explain.
2. An increase in price causes a decrease in demand. True or false? Explain.
3. Is the utility-maximizing rule consistent with the downward sloping nature of a demand curve? Explain.
4. Derive a demand curve from the indifference curve–budget line diagram.
5. Do the income and substitution effects have anything to do with why people buy more of a good when its price decreases? Explain.
6. Using the table below:
   a. Plot the market demand curve on a diagram.
   b. What are the two sources of the increase in quantity demanded in the market as price declines?

	Quantity demanded by consumer		
Price	*1*	*2*	*3*
$40	0	5	10
30	5	8	12
20	10	12	20

7. *a.* How does the slope of the demnad curve describe the responsiveness of consumers to changes in price?
   b. How might a person be misled by the slope of the demand curve in gauging the responsiveness of consumers to price changes?

8. Compute the price elasticity of demand from the following diagram and explain what the coefficient means.

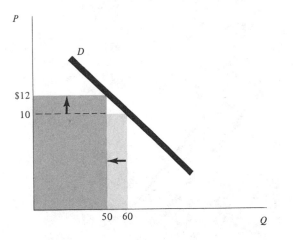

9. Would you expect the demand for the following goods to be elastic or inelastic? Explain why.
   a. Paper clips.
   b. Student housing on campus.
   c. This textbook.
10. a. Which would likely be more elastic, the demand for all cars as a group or the demand for Volkswagens? Explain.
    b. Which would likely be more elastic, the demand for coffee at a student coffee shop or at the most exclusive restaurant in town? Explain.
11. On most weekdays during the baseball season, professional baseball teams tend to play to less than sell-out crowds. Assuming, as is reasonable, that the demand curve for baseball tickets is downward sloping, wouldn't the baseball teams take in more money by lowering their ticket prices in order to fill up their stadiums? Explain.
12. Suppose two of your friends are having an argument. One argues that an increase in demand means that people will buy a larger quantity at any given price. The other argues that it means that people will be willing to pay a higher price for a given quantity. Who is right? Explain.
13. Income elasticity of demand is the percent change in the purchasing power of a person's income resulting from each percent change in price. True or false? Explain.

14. Compute the income elasticity of demand from the information on the accompanying diagram and explain what the coefficient means. (Assume D_0 corresponds to a $10,000 annual income and D_1 to $12,000.)

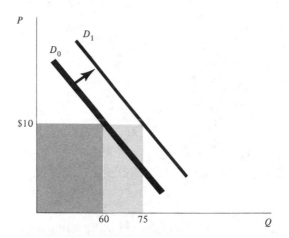

    a. What is the meaning of the elasticity coefficient?
    b. Is this a superior or inferior good? Explain.

15. State whether each of the following circumstances would *increase* or *decrease* the demand for new American-made cars. Provide a brief explanation with each answer.

    a. An increase in the price of foreign-made cars. (Consider American-made and foreign-made cars as substitutes.)
    b. An increase in the price of gasoline, a complement to new cars.
    c. An increase in consumer incomes. (Assume new cars are a superior good.)
    d. Potential car buyers begin to feel more optimistic about keeping their jobs; that is, fewer of them believe they will be laid off in the future.

4

Producer choice

To recap briefly, in Chapter 2 we developed the criterion that must be met for consumers to maximize utility for a given expenditure or budget. Then in Chapter 3 we developed the concept of demand using the utility-maximizing behavior set forth in Chapter 2. In this and the next chapter we will follow a similar format in studying the decisions made on the production and supply side of the market. In this chapter we will focus our attention primarily on how to produce a given level of output at the least possible cost. In the next chapter, we will focus on how to determine the level of output that will maximize profits. In so doing, we will derive product supply. Before we turn to the question of minimizing costs, it is necessary first to define production and develop the basic concepts that are useful in making production decisions.

The concept of production

Production can be defined as any activity that creates present and/or future utility. This all-inclusive concept of production, of course, includes the activities of conventional business firms. The output of the automobile manufacturer yields utility because of the transportation services it provides. The auto dealer provides utility by making the product more accessible to car buyers. If a business firm did not produce as much utility as its consumers thought it was worth, the firm would soon go out of business. A little reflection will reveal that most other activities also involve production as it is defined above. The dentist in filling a tooth may not create present utility but does create future utility by preventing a toothache. The artist in painting a picture creates present utility for himself or herself and future utility for others who view the work. The symphony orchestra and vocalist create utility by the production of harmonious sound. The author creates future utility for others who learn from and/or enjoy reading his or her works. The typist creates utility by making the words readable for others.

The activities of homemakers represent a large and important form of production. Utility is created by the preparation of meals, the rearing of children, and the many other activities homemakers perform that enhance their lives and those of their families. Students take part in a production process by studying and attending classes. The knowledge and experience that are acquired or produced impart both a present and a future utility. Present utility is created by the satisfaction of learning something new or gaining new experiences. Future utility stems from an increased awareness and understanding of the world, as well as from widened economic opportunities made possible by increased earning power. Teachers also perform a production activity by facilitating the assimilation of knowledge by students. Even sleeping creates utility and as a result is a production activity. By now it should be clear that production characterizes just about every activity of our lives.

While it is not correct to limit the concept of production to only items we can package, pile up, or count, there are certain activities that should not be classified as production as far as society is concerned. The arsonist, for example, may derive some satisfaction from burning down a building, but such an activity usually reduces the utility for other people. The same is true for the "mugger" or thief. Activities that destroy property or human beings or forcibly transfer wealth from one person to another are better described as destructive rather than productive.

Inputs in production

In any production activity there must be inputs that are either transformed or utilized in some way to produce an output. In economics, inputs are also referred to as resources or factors of production. All three names apply to the same thing.

In a modern, economically developed economy, most inputs are themselves the product of some other production activity. For example, the steel in automobiles is itself an output of the steel industry. Even the human input in virtually all production has been modified or improved by some past training, whether it be formal schooling or informal knowledge gained from family, fellow workers, or experience. Knowledge itself also is the output of a production activity, as we will see in Chapter 11.

Most production utilizes several inputs at the same time or in some time sequence. In fact, it is rather difficult to think of an example where production is carried on with just one input. One that comes close is the production of sound by a vocalist. But even this is not strictly correct, since the singer utilizes energy obtained from food, which should also be considered an input.

For descriptive purposes inputs can be grouped or classified in a number of ways. One common classification is that of land, labor, and capital. Land can be looked upon as the resource provided by nature, including the minerals, petroleum, and water found therein. It is recognized, of course, that land is seldom used in its so-called natural state, except perhaps in the production of utility as a wilderness area. Labor is the services provided by human beings. Capital generally is defined as durable, man-made resources such as buildings, machines, and tools. It is important to recognize, however, that both land and labor also include considerable capital or man-made improvements. We will see in Chapter 11 that education involves the production of human capital. And we all know that land may have to undergo considerable change such as clearing, leveling, or draining before it can be used as an input. In the production of nonagricultural products land is often treated as a capital input, resulting in just two main types of inputs: labor and capital.

It will be useful for future discussion to group inputs into two other categories: fixed and variable inputs. In most production processes it is possible to identify certain inputs that contribute to production but that, for the time period under consideration, cannot be increased or decreased in order to change the level of output. These are called *fixed inputs. Variable inputs,* as the name implies, can be varied according to the desired level of output. For example, in manufacturing, the building is considered a fixed input because it cannot be readily changed to a different size, and variable inputs include such things as labor, materials, and fuel. Now, of course, over a long period, the building can be changed in size or a new one constructed, so eventually even a fixed input can become variable. We will emphasize the distinction between fixed and variable inputs as well as the importance of the time dimension to this classification in the discussion that follows.

Production with one variable input

In developing some of the basic concepts of production, it will be easiest to begin with the simplest possible case: production with one variable input. As noted, it is just about impossible to visualize a realistic example of production using just one input. But it is possible to imagine a situation in which one or more *fixed* inputs such as land or some physical facility are combined with one *variable* input such as labor in the production of an output.

As a specific example of such production, let us assume that you decide to grow some tomatoes in your spare time on a small plot of land, either for home consumption or for sale to a vegetable market. To begin we will assume that only two major inputs are used in your tomato production: land, the fixed input, and your labor, the variable input. Of course you will need some seed and a spade or hoe at the very minimum as additional inputs, but these are relatively minor. If you like, they can be considered fixed inputs along with land. The variable input we will be concerned with is your labor. Specifically, we will be interested in the relationship between the amount of effort you devote to your tomato plants and the resulting output of tomatoes.

A PRODUCTION FUNCTION

As you begin your tomato-growing endeavor, one of the first decisions you will have to make is how much time you will spend on this activity. Without any previous experience in tomato culture, it would be difficult to predict how many tomatoes could be produced and harvested with a given input of labor. To obtain some reasonable estimates of what you might expect from your labor, suppose you consult an experienced tomato grower. You tell the grower some possible amounts of time you might spend in your tomato patch and he or she tells you how many bushels of tomatoes you could reasonably expect, as shown in columns (1) and (2) of Table 4–1. (You might consider each day as equivalent to eight hours. Each eight-hour day of labor does not have to be applied all at one time.) Of course, these numbers would be only estimates, but in actual situations production decisions must often be made on estimates no more accurate than these. The more experience or knowledge a producer has, of course, the more accurate the estimates will be.

TABLE 4–1
Hours of labor input and resulting output of tomatoes

(1) *Labor input (days)*	(2) *Tomato output (bushels)*	(3) *Marginal physical product of labor (bushels per day)*	(4) *Average physical product of labor (bushels per day)*
0	0	—	—
1	1	1	1.0
2	8	7	4.0
3	20	12	6.7
4	29	9	7.3
5	36	7	7.2
6	42	6	7.0
7	46	4	6.6
8	48	2	6.0
9	48	0	5.3
10	45	−3	4.5

$$P = f(L)$$

In a production process the relationship between input and output is often referred to by economists as a *production function*. In the example here, the output of tomatoes depends on, or is a function of, the quantity of labor used. By knowing the production function, I can tell you how many tomatoes to expect if you tell me how much labor is put in. With zero labor, for example, we would expect zero output. As labor input increases, output increases.

Additional labor input enables you to plant and harvest a larger portion of the tomato patch, as well as to do a better job of controlling the weeds, and so forth.

TOTAL PHYSICAL PRODUCT

Notice in column (2) of Table 4–1 that output increases at an increasing rate at first, then increases at a decreasing rate after the third day of labor, and finally begins to decline after the ninth day of labor. Although the production of every good or service is governed by its own unique production function or relationship, the general relationship described above is fairly typical of most production processes. When there is just a small amount of an input used in relation to other inputs (land in this case), additional amounts of that input are likely to have a significant impact on output. The most important and highest-payoff tasks are likely to be done first. As a result output increases rather rapidly at the initial levels. Then as more and more of the output is added, holding constant the quantities of other inputs, fewer high-payoff tasks remain to be done and much of the activity takes the form of refining the initial tasks. In the case of tomato growing, the initial tasks might be planting and harvesting. Additional tasks might be preparing the soil and removing the largest weeds. As more and more time is added, the tasks might take the form of removing the small or occasional weeds, which may not have much effect on total product or output. Eventually it is possible for total output to even decline as more of the variable input is added. In the tomato patch this could be due to "tramping down" tomatoes as an excessive amount of time is devoted to growing tomatoes.

The relationship between the variable input and total output is perhaps most easily seen by means of a diagram such as Figure 4–1 (A). In this diagram the numbers from columns (1) and (2) of Table 4–1 are plotted against each other. The labor input is represented on the horizontal axis and total tomato output is measured along the vertical axis. The resulting line is called the *total physical product* (TPP) *curve*. (The curve is smoothed out slightly from the actual points in order to illustrate the general input-output relationship more clearly.) Notice that total output increases at an increasing rate up to three days of labor input and then increases

FIGURE 4–1
Physical product curves

(A) Total physical product

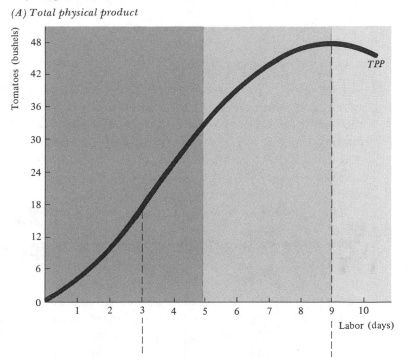

(B) Marginal and average physical product

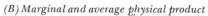
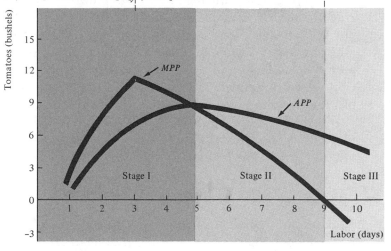

at a decreasing rate. At nine days of labor, TPP reaches a maximum and then begins to turn down. In this case the ninth day adds nothing to output.

MARGINAL PHYSICAL PRODUCT

Let us examine this relationship, or production function, between labor input and tomato output in more detail. We noted that each additional day of labor brings forth additional bushels of tomatoes. The first day (eight hours) brings forth one bushel. The second day adds seven bushels (eight minus the one produced by the first day's labor). The third day adds 12 bushels over the second, and so on.

The numbers we have been deriving here represent the *additional* output brought forth by an *additional* unit of input. Economists refer to this additional output as the *marginal physical product* (MPP) of the particular input that is being increased, labor in the example. This is shown in column (3) of Table 4–1. You recall from the discussion in Chapter 2 that the marginal unit is the additional or last unit either added to or subtracted from something. Hence, the marginal physical product of labor is the additional product obtained by adding one more unit of labor, or the loss of product by reducing labor by one unit.

In the tomato example it is fairly easy to calculate the marginal physical product because the labor input increases by only one unit at a time. In many kinds of production, however, it is not always possible to add or subtract just one unit of an input. If General Motors added only one person to its labor force, for example, the growth in output would be too small to measure.

It is useful, therefore, to have a formula that will make it possible to calculate the MPP of an input even if it is not added one unit at a time. The formula is:

$$MPP = \frac{\text{Change in output}}{\text{Change in input}}$$

This formula gives the MPP of any input, regardless of whether it is changed (increased or decreased) by one unit or by several units at a time. In the preceding example, increasing labor by one unit, from one to two days, results in an increase in output from one to eight bushels (a seven-unit change). Thus the denominator in the formula is 1 and the numerator is 7. In writing the MPP column you will often see the MPP figures written opposite the input that has been added, for example the 7 is written opposite the second unit of input in Table 4–1. You might try calculating the MPP of labor when it is increased from one to three units at one time. (The answer is 9.5.) Economists have estimated the MPP of the inputs used in producing many products by the same statistical techniques used to estimate the price elasticity of demand.

THE LAW OF DIMINISHING RETURNS

You probably noticed the change in size of the marginal physical product of labor [column (3) in Table 4–1] as we move down the column. At first it increases from 1 to 7 to 12, and then it begins to decline, eventually becoming zero and negative. This simple example depicts fairly well what one might expect in any production process.

At very low levels of use of the variable input, its efficiency is low because it is spread too thinly across the fixed input. For example, an input of only eight hours (one day) might not enable you to adequately prepare the soil, plant, and harvest even a portion of the quarter-acre of land. But an additional input of two or three days would make it possible to weed and care for the tomatoes so that output would increase significantly.

The region where MPP is increasing is known as the *region of increasing returns.* It extends up to and includes the third unit of the variable input in this example. Increasing returns need not be present in every production process, but at very low levels of variable input use, it is reasonable to expect such a region.

The region that is of most interest to us here begins at the point where the MPP of labor starts to decline at each successive increment of labor. This is commonly known as the *region of diminishing returns,* and the declining characteristic of MPP is referred to as the *law of diminishing returns.* This principle states that beyond some point the output resulting from each additional unit of a variable begins to decline. Notice in Figure 4–1 that MPP starts to decrease at the point where TPP begins to increase at a decreasing rate and that MPP becomes negative when the TPP curve begins to turn down.[1]

The economic logic underlying the idea of diminishing returns is fairly simple and reasonable. As more and more of the variable input is added to the fixed input, the productivity of the variable input begins to decline because of crowding and inefficient use of the variable input. Applying more labor to the tomato patch, for example, may increase production because of better preparation of soil, more careful weeding, and so forth. But there is only so much you can do in a tomato patch; eventually the added output from more labor becomes negligible. Indeed, if diminishing returns did not materialize, you could continue to add labor until you produced the world's supply of tomatoes on this one small plot of land. In fact, it is not unreasonable to believe that after some point is reached, additional labor input to this fixed land area will have a detrimental effect and will actually reduce output. As mentioned, you may just tramp down plants by adding the tenth day of labor.

Basically the same rationale can be used to explain the existence of diminishing returns in any production activity. As more and more of a variable input is applied, holding constant the quantity of other inputs, at some point the crowding that occurs results in a decrease in the MPP of that input.

The law of diminishing returns is also known by two other names: (1) diminishing marginal physical product and (2) the law of variable proportions. The first term is rather self-explanatory. The second stems from the fact that the proportion of total inputs that are variable changes as more and more of the variable input is added.

AVERAGE PHYSICAL PRODUCT

Another concept stemming from the production function is *average physical product* (APP). The average physical product of labor, for example, is calculated at each level of labor input by dividing the total output by the units of labor employed:

---

[1] For those who have had calculus, MPP is the first derivative of TPP.

$$APP = \frac{Output}{Input}$$

Notice that this formula is similar to the one used to calculate MPP, except that the absolute amount of output and input is used, rather than changes in output and input.

The APP of labor in the tomato production example is shown by column (4) in Table 4–1. We see that APP increases for a time and then begins to decline, just as we observed for MPP. One difference between the two measures, however, is that APP never becomes negative. It may approach a very small number, but as long as output is positive, APP must be positive. It will be helpful to use a diagram, such as Figure 4–1(B), in understanding the relationship between MPP and APP.

STAGES OF PRODUCTION

Economists have found it useful to classify the levels of input use into three states of production. As shown in Figure 4–1(B), Stage I is defined to include the area of increasing returns and extending up to the point where the MPP curve intersects the APP curve. At this point APP is at a maximum. Notice that Stage I includes a portion of the MPP curve that is declining. The distinguishing characteristic of Stage I is that MPP is greater than APP. As long as the marginal unit is greater than the overall average, the average will always increase.

It is easiest to understand the relationship between the average and marginal measures with a simple example. Suppose your overall grade point average in college is 3.0 (out of a possible 4.0). Now suppose during the current quarter you work extremely hard and earn a 3.5. When your overall grade point average is recalculated with the current quarter included, you will, of course, observe an increase in your overall average. The grade from the current or marginal quarter has pulled the overall average up. Or, if you had earned only a 2.5 for the current quarter, your overall average would have declined.

The distinguishing characteristic of Stage II in Figure 4–1 is that MPP is everywhere less than APP. This results in the continual decline of APP. Stage II ends at the point where MPP becomes negative. Stage III begins where the MPP curve crosses the horizontal axis and extends to the right indefinitely as the negative MPP continues to pull APP down lower and lower, approaching zero but never reaching it.

The significance of the three stages of production will become clearer when we relate them to the concept of supply in the next chapter. For now we will have to settle for an intuitive explanation of their importance. It can readily be seen that no producer would ever want to be in Stage III. This is evident from the example in Table 4–1. By adding the tenth day of labor, total tomato output actually declines. A person would be better off to go fishing or stay in bed than to put in a day of work that brings negative results.

It is also true that no producer would ever want to operate in Stage I, although the reason why is less clear than that for Stage III. Consider the region of increasing returns. If it paid to produce any quantity at all, it would always pay to increase the level of the variable input until the product was past the level of increasing returns. As long as a producer is in the region of increasing returns, each additional unit of input adds more and more to output. Thus the more input that is added, the more efficient production becomes, and the cheaper it is to produce the added output. Consequently it would be foolish to stop adding the variable input when in the region of increasing returns.

We have established that a rational, profit-maximizing producer would add enough of the variable input to go past the region of increasing returns but would stop adding before entering Stage III, the region of negative marginal physical product. Thus a producer will always produce in the region of diminishing returns. Moreover, if it pays to produce at all, a producer will always avoid Stage I, even though this stage may contain a small region of diminishing returns (as shown in Figure 4–1). For the moment we will just assert this and wait until Chapter 5 to show why it is true.

Production with two variable inputs

Although the example of production with one variable input serves as a useful starting point to develop the basic concepts of production, virtually all production activities involve the use of two or more variable inputs. Because our main interest in this chapter is on choosing the mix of inputs that will yield a given output for the least possible cost, it is necessary that we expand the original example a bit in order to focus on this decision. We can retain the tomato production example by assuming that labor is combined with another variable input. It would be reasonable to assume that even in this small-scale production of tomatoes, the use of some kind of equipment, such as a garden tractor and its various attachments, would be feasible. Suppose we measure the use of a specific size of garden tractor by machine-days.

We will assume as well that it is possible to use various alternative combinations of labor and machine-hours. For example, if little or no machine-hours are utilized, a relatively large amount of labor would have to be used to produce a given amount of output, whereas with more machine inputs the same output could be obtained with less labor. Having two or more variable inputs that can be used in different proportions brings us face to face with the main question of this chapter: What mix of inputs will produce a given level of output at the least possible cost?

Cost-minimizing rule

In order to answer the above question, we need two pieces of information: (1) the MPP of each input at the various input levels, and (2) the price of each input. As you recall, the MPP of an input is the units of output resulting from the use of one more unit of that input. Because of the law of diminishing returns, the MPP of each input eventually becomes smaller and smaller as more of the input is added. In measuring the MPP of an input when there are two or more variable inputs, it is necessary that the quantity of all other inputs is held constant execept the one being varied. For example, in the tomato-growing case, the MPP of labor would be measured holding the number of garden tractor–hours constant at a given level. Similarly the MPP of the garden tractor would be determined by varying the machine-hours while holding the number of hours of labor constant. It is true that the MPP of one input will likely be influenced by the level at which the other input is held constant, however. We will come back to this point in Chapter 9.

The decision of how much of each input to use to produce a given level of output will depend also on the price of each input. As you might expect, even if an input contributes a lot to output (has a high MPP), it may cost so much that it does not pay to use much of it. Thus a producer must consider both the MPP of each unput and its cost in deciding how much of each to use in producing a given level of output. Intuitively it makes sense to utilize a relatively large amount of an input that exhibits a high MPP (for a given input and output level) and is relatively cheap. This commonsense notion is made somewhat more specific when placed in the context of the *cost-minimizing rule*. To minimize costs at any given level of output, the inputs should be used such that the ratio of the price of each input to its MPP is equal for all inputs, as indicated below:

$$\frac{P_a}{\text{MPP}_a} = \frac{P_b}{\text{MPP}_b} = \cdots = \frac{P_z}{\text{MPP}_z}$$

It is easiest to see why the cost-minimizing rule holds true if we choose a situation where the above equality is not met. Returning to the tomato production example, suppose the MPP of labor at a given output level is seven bushels of tomatoes and the price (or cost) of a day of labor is $28. Dividing the price of labor ($28) by its MPP (7 bushels) yields a figure of $4 per bushel. This means that it costs $4 to produce an extra bushel of tomatoes by adding one more unit (day) of labor. Adding the extra day of labor adds seven bushels to output and adds $28 to the total cost of producing tomatoes. Hence each of these seven bushels costs $4 to produce.

Now consider the price and MPP of the garden tractor. Suppose you are able to rent the garden tractor for $30 per day and an extra day of using the garden tractor results in ten extra bushels of tomatoes. In other words the MPP of the garden tractor is ten bushels of tomatoes. Dividing the $30 cost by 10 bushels yields a figure of $3 per bushel. This means that it costs $3 to produce an extra bushel of tomatoes by adding an extra unit (day) of the garden tractor. The labor and garden tractor ratios are summarized below.

Labor	Garden tractor
$\frac{\$28}{7} = \$4$ per bushel	$\frac{\$30}{10} = \$3$ per bushel

You will notice here that the two ratios are not equal, which according to the cost-minimizing rule means that costs are not being minimized; that is, you are wasting money. Why? Suppose you reduce the amount of labor used just slightly and produce one less bushel of tomatoes. Assuming that labor can be hired (or paid) by a fraction of a day, this small reduction in labor used saves $4. Of course, you are producing one less bushel of tomatoes now than before. To offset this one bushel loss of output, let us assume you can add just enough extra garden tractor time to produce one additional bushel of tomatoes, so that you are producing the same level of output after this slight rearrangement of inputs as before. Of course, adding the extra bushel of tomatoes by means of adding more garden tractor time adds $3 to total cost. (Recall that the P/MPP ratio for the garden tractor is $3.) But by rearranging the inputs slightly you saved $1. The results of rearranging the inputs are summarized below:

Producing one less bushel by labor saves $4
Producing one more bushel by machine adds $3

Net saving = $1

As long as all the P/MPP ratios are not equal, it will always be possible to reduce costs by using slightly less of the input(s) that exhibit the highest ratio(s) while making up the loss of output with the input(s) that have the lowest ratio(s). Only when all the ratios are equal will it no longer be possible to rearrange inputs and reduce costs for a given level of output. Once they are equal, then the reduction in cost resulting from a one-bushel reduction in output by using slightly less of one input will exactly be matched by the added cost of making up that bushel of output by some other input. When this occurs the cost-minimizing rule is being fulfilled.

One might ask: How are the relatively high P/MPP ratios reduced and the relatively low ratios increased when rearranging inputs to meet the condition set forth by the cost-minimizing rule? The answer is found in the law of diminishing returns. In the above example labor exhibited a relatively high $4 per bushel ratio. By subtracting units of labor, we move up labor's MPP curve, which means that the MPP of labor becomes larger and larger. This in turn causes the P/MPP for labor to decline. By the same token the addition of machine-hours causes the MPP of the garden tractor to decline as we move down along its MPP curve. This in turn causes the P/MPP ratio for the garden tractor to increase. Eventually the two ratios should equalize. When ratios become equal, the cost of producing the given level of output is minimized.

Isoquants

In the process of moving toward an equality of the P/MPP ratios, we assumed that it was possible to substitute one input for the other so as to continue producing a given level of output with different combinations of the two inputs. Although the ability to substitute one input for another is a common characteristic of inputs, it is not a universal condition. Because of differences in substitution possibilities among inputs, economists have found it useful to represent this relationship with a diagram. They call it an isoquant.

An *isoquant* is a line showing the various possible combinations of two inputs that can be used to produce a given level of output. Since *iso* means equal, a more literal translation of the term is equal-quantity. Returning once again to the tomato-growing example, consider the possible ways of producing a given level of output, say 40 bushels. At one extreme you might utilize much labor and a small amount of machine services. This possibility is illustrated by the six labor–one machine combination in Figure 4–2. Or one could visualize the other extreme of using a large amount of machine services with a relatively small amount of labor, as indicated by the one labor–seven machine combination. The first situation would be described as a labor-intensive method of production while the second would be called capital-intensive. Of course, there may well be many other possible combinations of

FIGURE 4–2
Isoquants of labor and machines input (tomato production example)

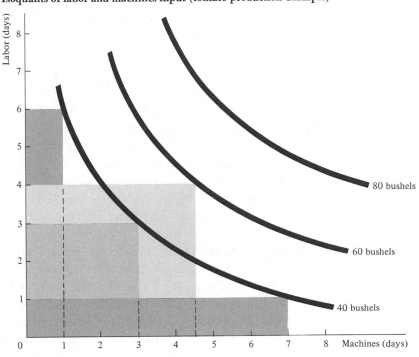

inputs for producing the 40 bushels, such as the three labor and three machine-day combination.

Choosing a higher level of output such as 60 bushels would require larger amounts of one or both inputs. As shown by Figure 4–2, 60 bushels could be produced by four days of labor and 4½ machine-days. Still larger levels of output, such as 80 bushels, would of course require still higher levels of one or both inputs. Whatever the level of output, each isoquant in Figure 4–2 tells us the various possible combinations of the two inputs that can be used to produce that output.

SUBSTITUTION POSSIBILITIES

The particular shape of the isoquant is what interests us most at this point. Notice in Figure 4–2 that each isoquant is drawn convex to the origin. This implies that the two inputs are imperfect substitutes for one another in the production of tomatoes. They are called imperfect substitutes because it takes more and more of the abundant input to compensate for the loss of each successive unit reduction of the scarce input. As you move down along the labor axis, more and more machine-days are required to compensate for the loss of each unit of labor. Moving from six to five days of labor requires only about one-half extra machine-day to compensate for the loss of one day of labor. But moving from two to one day of labor requires about 2½ extra machine-days. The same relationship holds true when increasing labor and decreasing machine time. You might try this on your own.

The necessity of using more and more of the abundant input to substitute for the loss of each unit of the relatively scarce input has a certain intuitive appeal. The abundant input must be pressed into service on tasks for which it may not be well suited. Hence it takes a larger amount of the input to do the job. The distinguishing characteristic of inputs that are imperfect substitutes is the progressively increasing amount of the abundant input required to substiute for the loss of each unit of the scarce input. You will notice that the isoquant is a close relative of the indifference curve presented in Chapters 2 and 3. Also the meaning of imperfect substitutes is similar. The one deals with goods and utility, the other with inputs and output.

Before leaving the case of imperfect substitutes, it might be helpful to explain in more detail just how it is possible to substitute machines (capital) for labor, or vice versa. At first glance one might argue that machines and labor have to be used together in a one-to-one ratio because it always takes a person to operate a machine. Although machines do require operators, there are still two ways that a substitution can occur. First, it is possible to utilize machines for more and more tasks. In the tomato-growing example, the garden tractor might only be used as the primary tillage machine with all other jobs done by hand. But as long as there are other tasks that can be done at least in part by the machine, such as cultivating the weeds, it is possible to produce a given output by utilizing more machine-hours and less labor-hours. A second way that machines or capital can substitute for labor is to adapt larger models that can do a given task in less time. For example it might take ten hours to plow the tomato patch with an eight-horsepower tractor but only six hours with a 12-horsepower model. Hence less labor is used because of the utilization of more capital.

So far we have considered only the case of imperfect substitutes among inputs. There are two other cases that should be mentioned, however. The first is that of perfect substitutes. In this situation, the amount of one input necessary to compensate for the loss of the other remains constant at all possible combinations. Isoquants depicting perfect substitutes are straight downward sloping lines as illustrated by Figure 4–3. As you move down the vertical

FIGURE 4–3
Isoquants illustrating perfect substitutes

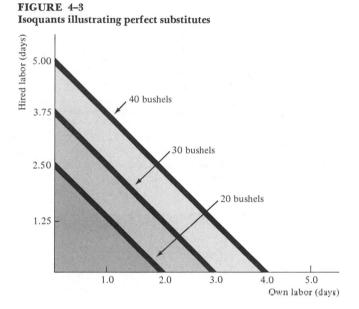

axis by equal increments, the distance you move out along the horizontal axis remains the same. Examples of perfect substitutes are relatively rare. In the context of tomato growing, one might argue that hired labor is a perfect substitute for your own labor, at least within a certain range. In this example 1¼ days of hired labor substitutes for one day of your own labor at all possible combinations. Economists have not been very interested in cases of perfect substitutes because the two inputs together can be thought of as just one input. For example, hired labor and your own labor can be considered as labor.

Another possible case occurs when two inputs must be used in fixed proportions. In other words, there is no chance to substitute one for the other. You will recognize this as the same general idea as the case of perfect complements on the consumption side (rectangular indifference curves). Inputs that must be used in fixed proportions are sometimes called perfect complements. Isoquants that depict fixed proportions or perfect complements are rectangular, as illustrated by Figure 4–4. In this example, we assume

FIGURE 4–4
Isoquants illustrating fixed proportions

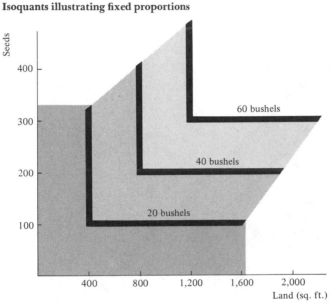

seeds and land must be used in fixed proportions, although in reality this may not be strictly true. At any rate, the diagram indicates that 100 seeds and 400 square feet of land are required to produce 20 bushels of tomatoes. Increasing the seeds without more land (moving up the isoquant) or increasing land without more seeds does not result in any greater output. Beyond the required proportion, extra units of one input without more of the other are redundant. Probably the most common examples of fixed proportions occur in manufacturing where products require certain materials or ingredients. For example, a cotton shirt of a given size requires a certain amount of material, a certain number of buttons, etc. Of course, in a broader context one can visalize substitution between different types of material, different buttons, and so on. The fixed proportion case generally applies to inputs that are narrowly defined, or in relatively short-run situations where it may not be possible or economically feasible to substitute one input for another.

You might have recognized that perfect substitutes and fixed proportions are the extreme or limiting cases of the more general case of imperfect substitutes. In the more general case, isoquants can vary in shape from a very gentle curvature to a very sharp curve. The less curvature of the isoquant, the closer it comes to the limiting case of perfect substitutes. Thus an isoquant that exhibits a relatively small amount of curvature represents the case of two inputs that can be readily substituted for each other. On the other hand, a sharply curved isoquant comes close to the case of fixed proportions, meaning that the possibility for substitution is quite limited. You might try drawing isoquants that show different degrees of substitution on your own.

Isocosts

Although the isoquant is a useful device for representing the degree of substitution that exists between two inputs, it also can be used to demonstrate the cost-minimizing rule. To do so, however, requires that we first construct the isocost line. An *iso-cost* line shows various combinations of two inputs that can be purchased for a given amount of money. As the name implies, it is a line showing equal costs.

In order to construct an isocost line, two pieces of information are required: (1) the price of each input, and (2) the total amount of money to be spent on the inputs. Utilizing the tomato production example, suppose the price of labor is $40 per day and the machine price (say, rental cost) is $60 per day. As a place to start, suppose that $200 will be spent on labor and machines. The point where the isocost line intersects the labor axis can be found by dividing the $200 by the cost of labor, $40. The answer (five days of labor) means that you could buy five days of labor if the entire $200 were spent on labor. Similarly the intersection of the isocost and the machine axis occurs at 3⅓ units ($200 divided by $60). By connecting the two end points we construct the $200 isocost line

FIGURE 4–5
Isocosts and isoquant illustrating an optimum input combination

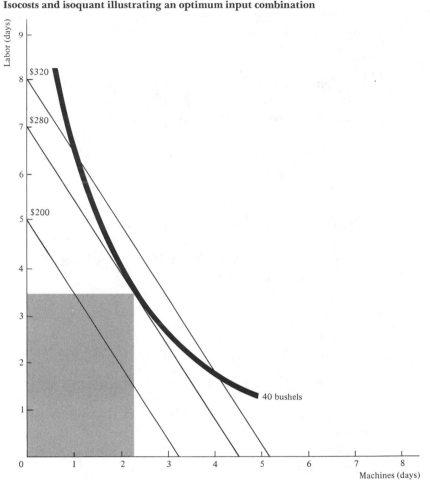

as shown by Figure 4–5. Different points along the line shows different combinations of labor and machines that cost $200. For example, four days of labor plus ⅔ of a machine-day cost $200, and so on down the line. The higher $280 and $320 isocost lines shown on Figure 4–5 are constructed in the same way.

Least-cost input combination

By utilizing both the isoquant and the isocost concepts, we can determine the least-cost combination of inputs that will produce a given output. Consider as an example the output of 40 bushels of tomatoes. This is shown on Figure 4–5 by the 40-bushel isoquant. Note first that the $200 isocost line does not touch the 40-bushel isoquant in any place. This means that there is no way 40 bushels can be produced for $200. Look next at the $320 isocost line. It intersects the isoquant at two places: at about 6½ days of labor and slightly more than one machine-day, and about 1⅔ days of labor and four machine-days. This means that 40 bushels could be produced by either of these combinations or any other combination on the isocost line between these two. But it would be wasteful to produce the 40 bushels with any of the input combinations shown on the $320 isocost. There is another lower isocost line exhibiting a combination of inputs that also will produce 40 bushels: the $280 line. The point where the $280 line is tangent to the 40-bushel isoquant denotes the least-cost combination of inputs that will produce 40 bushels. This is shown by the 3½ labor-days and 2⅓ machine-days on Figure 4–5. All other combinations will cost more than $280. Thus the tangency point between the lowest possible isocost line and the isoquant tells us the least-cost combination of inputs to produce a given output.

Earlier in the chapter we derived the cost-minimization rule using the P/MPP ratios. Recall that costs are minimized when each input is used such that the P/MPP ratio is the same for all inputs. This cost-minimization rule also holds true with the isoquant–isocost technique. Although we will not do so, it can be shown mathematically that the P/MPP ratio for both labor and machines are equal at the point of tangency. Thus we have essentially shown the same thing by two different techniques. The isoquant–isocost technique allows us to be somewhat more precise regarding the specific combination of inputs to be used, and it makes it possible to specify more clearly the degree of substitution that exists between the two inputs.

Changing input prices

Another important use of the isoquant–isocost technique is to show what happens to the least-cost combination of inputs when the price of one of the inputs changes relative to that of the other. To see what happens in this case, suppose the price of labor in the tomato-growing example increases from $40 to $60 per day, while the price or rental cost of the machine stays the same. (We will explain in the next chapter how to price your own labor.) At a $60 per day labor price, the $280 isocost line intersects the labor axis at about 4⅔ units. As a result the isocost line rotates in a clockwise fashion. (In this diagram we represent labor on the horizontal axis instead of on the vertical axis as in Figure 4–5. Once accustomed to working with price changes along the horizontal axis, it is best to continue in this manner.)

The relative increase in the price of labor and the consequent rotation of the isocost line gives rise to two changes. First the $280 isocost line no longer touches the 40-bushel isoquant. This means it is now impossible to produce 40 bushels at the $280 cost. The isocost line that is tangent to the isoquant, denoted by the dashed line in Figure 4–6, represents a cost greater than $280, about $325 in this example.

FIGURE 4–6
Illustrating the effect of an increase in the price of labor

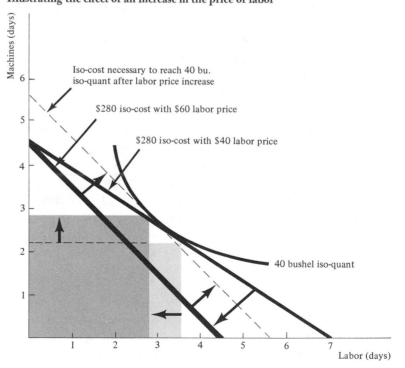

A second change that comes about as a result of the labor price increase is the movement of the tangency point up along the isoquant. Notice now that the least-cost combination of inputs weighs somewhat more heavily in favor of machines, with somewhat less labor being utilized to produce the 40 bushels than in the initial situation. Intuitively this is reasonable. When labor becomes relatively more expensive, it pays to conserve on this input, replacing some labor with the now relatively cheaper machine. Essentially this is what has been happening in the United States and other developed nations over the years. Wage rates have increased relative to the cost of capital, thus prompting producers to conserve on labor by using more capital-intensive methods of production.

It is important to recognize also that the amount of substitution that will take place in response to an input price change depends on the substitution possibility between the two inputs. If labor and machines are fairly good substitutes for each other, the isoquant will not exhibit much curvature and the tangency point will change by a relatively large amount. On the other hand, if the inputs are poor substitutes for each other, the isoquant will be sharply curved, and the tangency point will not move very much. (You might demonstrate this by drawing a number of diagrams similar to Figure 4–6, keeping the price change the same in each diagram but varying the shape of the isoquant from nearly fixed proportions to nearly perfect substitutes.)

Regardless of the shape of the isoquants, however, an increase in the cost of one of the inputs will increase the total cost of producing a given level of output. By substituting away from the more expensive input, the cost increase can be kept to a minimum, but it cannot be escaped entirely.[2]

The same general conclusion is reached by using the P/MPP ratio approach. As the price of labor increases, the labor ratio becomes larger, meaning that it costs more to produce an extra unit of output by adding labor. If the ratios were equal before the labor price increase, they now become unequal. As a result it pays to cut back on the higher-priced labor by substituting the relatively cheap capital. As relatively less labor and more capital are used to pro-

---

[2] An exception may occur if the two inputs are perfect substitutes and the isocost and isoquant exactly coincide before the price increase. After the price increase, the more expensive input would not be used at all. However, this would probably be a relatively rare occurrence.

duce the given output, the MPP of labor increases while that of capital decreases. Eventually they change enough to restore the equality. When this happens, it is equivalent to being at the new tangency point.

Notice the similarity between the material in Chapter 2 (Consumer Choice) and that of this chapter. The consumer maximizes utility for a given budget by arranging his or her purchases such that the MU/P ratios are equalized, or the combination of goods consumed corresponds to the tangency point between the budget line and the highest possible indifference curve. The producer minimizes cost for a given level of output by utilizing inputs such that the P/MPP ratios are equalized, or the combination of inputs corresponds to the point of tangency between a given isoquant (given level of output) and the lowest possible isocost line. Both sets of decisions are similar.

Main points of Chapter 4

1. Production can be defined as any activity that creates present and/or future utility. This all-inclusive concept of production includes household activities as well as many others outside of conventional business firms.
2. Most kinds of production utilize several inputs either at once or in some time sequence. Many inputs are themselves the product of some former production activity.
3. Inputs can be grouped into three large categories: land, labor, and capital. In nonagricultural production, land is often included as capital.
4. Inputs also can be classified as fixed or variable. Fixed inputs cannot be varied with the level of production, whereas variable inputs can be varied according to the desired level of output.
5. A production function is a relationship between inputs and output. The quantity of output depends on, or is a function of, the amount of inputs used.
6. The total physical product (TPP) curve shows the level of

output obtained from alternative levels of a variable input. Typically the TPP curve slopes upward, first at an increasing rate, then at a decreasing rate, and finally turns down.

7. Marginal physical product (MPP) of an input is the additional output obtained by adding one more unit of variable input.

8. According to the law of diminishing returns, the marginal physical product of a variable input will at some point begin to decline as more and more of the variable input is added to one or more fixed inputs.

9. The level of average physical product (APP) of an input will increase as long as MPP is greater than APP. The level of APP declines when MPP is less than APP.

10. Economists have divided production into three stages. During Stage I, MPP is greater than APP. In Stage II, MPP is less than APP, but MPP is positive. In Stage III, MPP is a negative quantity. Production should always be carried on somewhere within Stage II, which includes the region of diminishing returns.

11. To minimize costs for a given level of output, the P/MPP ratios for all inputs should be equal.

12. The P/MPP ratio for an input tells us how much it costs to produce one more unit of the output by using slightly more of that input.

13. If the P/MPP ratios for all inputs are not equal, the cost of producing a given level of output can be reduced by decreasing the input(s) with the highest ratio while increasing the input(s) with the lowest ratio.

14. The P/MPP ratios eventually are equalized by the increase in MPP of the inputs that are decreased and the decrease in MPP of the inputs that are increased.

15. An isoquant is a line showing the various possible combinations of two inputs that will produce a given level of output.

16. The shape of the isoquant reflects the extent that one input can be substituted for another.

17. Two inputs that are imperfect substitutes will exhibit an isoquant convex to the origin. This means that more and more of the abundant input is required to compensate for the loss of each unit of the scarce input.

18. Capital can substitute for labor by using machines to perform more tasks and by using larger machines to do a given task in less time.

19. Two inputs that are perfect substitutes will exhibit an isoquant that is a straight, downward sloping line. This means that the amount of one input required to compensate for the loss of another remains constant at all possible combinations. Perfect substitutes are relatively rare.

20. Two inputs that must be used in fixed proportions (perfect complements) will exhibit an isoquant that is rectangular. This means that adding more units of one input without more of the other will not increase output after the exact proportion has been reached.

21. An isocost is a line showing the various combinations of two inputs that cost a given amount.

22. The least-cost combination of inputs corresponds to the tangency point between the isoquant and the lowest possible isocost line.

23. An increase in the price of the input on the horizontal axis causes the isocost line to rotate in a clockwise fashion. This results in an increase in the cost of producing a given level of output and causes the tangency point to move up the isoquant and changes the least-cost combination away from the relatively higher-priced input toward the one that has become relatively cheaper.

Questions for thought and discussion

1. In each of the following activities, identify what is being produced and the major inputs:
   a. Baking a cake.   d. Providing taxi service.
   b. Cleaning an apartment.   e. Eating.
   c. Cutting a lawn.   f. Sleeping.
2. In what units is the marginal physical product of labor measured in the production of:
   a. Wheat   c. Houses
   b. Haircuts   d. Dental services

3. If the law of diminishing returns did not exist, the world's supply of wheat could be grown in a flower pot. True or false? Explain.

4. Increasing a variable input in its region of diminishing returns leads to a reduction in total output. True, false, or uncertain? Explain why.

5. Stage II of the three stages of production is defined as the region where MPP is declining but positive. True or false? Explain.

6. How should a firm allocate resources in order to produce a given level of output at the least possible cost?

7. Consider the following information:

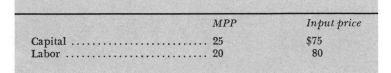

	MPP	Input price
Capital	25	$75
Labor	20	80

    a. Is the given level of output being produced at the least possible cost? Why or why not?

    b. How much, if anything, could be saved by producing one more unit of output by capital and one less by labor?

8. By what means are the high *P*/MPP ratios reduced and the low ratios increased when inputs are rearranged to satisfy the cost-minimizing rule?

9. Draw isoquants for the following pairs of inputs in the production of automobiles and explain why you have drawn them in a given shape.

    a. Capital and labor.

    b. Wheels and tires.

    c. Steel and aluminum.

    d. Plastic and cloth.

10. How is it possible to substitute capital for labor if each machine must have an operator?

11. Draw the isocost line that corresponds to the following information. (Be sure to indicate where the line intersects each axis.)

Total cost	$200
Price of capital	50
Price of labor	25

12. Every point on an isoquant represents an equal cost of producing a given level of output. True or false? Explain.

13. In the United States production in the manufacturing sector takes place under capital-intensive techniques, whereas in the less developed countries production in this sector is much more labor-intensive. Why?

14. For two inputs that are imperfect substitutes, an increase in the price of one input must increase the cost of producing a given level of output. True or false? Explain.

15. Does the shape of the isoquant have any bearing on how much a given change in the price of an input changes production costs? Explain.

5

Product supply

In Chapter 4 we were mainly interested in the least-cost combination of inputs for producing a given level of output, along with the substitution possibilities that exist between inputs. In this chapter we will focus our attention on determining the level of output that will maximize profits. We will see that by determining the most profitable level of output at various output prices we in effect are deriving a supply curve for the individual producer.

The classification of costs

1. EXPLICIT AND IMPLICIT

Because supply is closely related to production costs at various levels of output, it is necessary to gain a somewhat better understanding of what is included in costs. For descriptive purposes production costs are commonly grouped into two categories: explicit and implicit. *Explicit costs* include all cash or out-of-pocket expenses incurred in carrying out production. Some examples of explicit costs are wages paid to hired labor, interest paid on borrowed money, rent on buildings, and the cost of supplies and raw materials purchased. These are the costs that are paid for purchased inputs, whether they are fixed or variable.

Implicit costs, however, tend to be less obvious. These are the costs that should be charged to inputs that are provided by the firm or whoever is carrying out the production. A good example of implicit costs can be taken from the tomato-growing example in the preceding chapter. In this small-scale enterprise, it is reasonable to believe that you would provide much of the labor yourself. It is necessary to include a charge for your own labor in calculating the total cost of growing a certain output of tomatoes; otherwise you will grossly underestimate the cost of your production. By not including the value of your own labor you could easily make the wrong decision about whether or not to grow tomatoes in the first place or what is the most profitable quantity to produce.

A simple example will help make this clear. Suppose you anticipate that your cash or explicit cost of growing 20 bushels of tomatoes is $40 and that you will be able to sell the tomatoes for $5 per bushel. Thus you anticipate spending $40 and taking in $100. Will it pay you to grow tomatoes? On the surface it seems to be a profitable venture; you are left with $60 after paying your bills. But you still have not paid yourself. How much is your own labor worth?

The best way to determine the value of your own labor in a self-employed enterprise is to determine the wage you could have earned in the best alternative open to you. For example, you might have been able to work part-time at a checkout counter in a grocery store for $4 per hour. If you put in three eight-hour days of labor to grow these 20 bushels of tomatoes, the implicit cost of your labor is $96. In this case we could summarize your total income from and expense for growing 20 bushels of tomatoes as follows:

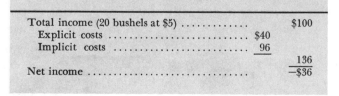

Total income (20 bushels at $5)		$100
Explicit costs	$40	
Implicit costs	96	
		136
Net income		−$36

Including the implicit cost of your own labor reduces the attractiveness of this venture considerably. One way of looking at the outcome is that you paid $36 for the privilege of growing tomatoes. Or, looking at it from another viewpoint, you were able to sell your labor for only $20 per day ($60/3) as a tomato grower, whereas you could have sold your labor for $32 per day in the grocery store. Of course, this is only an example; it is not meant to convey the idea that tomato growing is a losing proposition. The main point is that it is necessary to consider all costs, not just explicit costs, when deciding to produce or not to produce.

Thus the total cost (explicit plus implicit) to you of producing something is very dependent on your alternative employment opportunities. If your only alternative to tomato growing is doing nothing, the implicit cost of your labor would be zero. In this case, the tomato venture reaps a $60 net income over costs. You would still have to decide, however, whether $60 is enough to compensate you for the three days (24 hours) of leisure you forgo.

If the grocery store employment, or any other job, is open to you, it is necessary to decide whether the additional income of this job would be sufficient to compensate you for any disadvantages it may have compared with tomato growing. For example, you may be the type of person who puts a high value on independence; you like to be your own boss. In this case, you might be willing to sacrifice $12 a day for the privilege of doing what you like best. There is nothing irrational or wrong with choosing work that does not maximize your salary. It is important, though, that you realize how much it will cost you to work in more agreeable surroundings. You may decide that the cost of doing what you like best is too high and as a result decide to make a living doing something that is not first on your list of desirable occupations. A great many people have made this decision.

2. FIXED AND VARIABLE

Costs can also be classified according to whether they are fixed or variable. As mentioned in the preceding chapter, inputs are commonly grouped according to these two categories. Since the purchase of inputs (including one's own time or facilities) is what gives rise to costs, it is reasonable to also classify by these same categories. As the name implies, fixed costs are those that do not change at various levels of output. Examples of fixed costs include depreciation on capital that occurs regardless of whether it is used, rent on property that must be paid, again regardless of use, and real estate taxes. Variable costs are defined as those costs that vary with the level of output. Examples include the cost of raw materials, fuel, and hired labor.

The items included in each category depend to a large extent on the time period allowed for adjustment. In the short run, a greater proportion of all costs will fall in the fixed category than will be the case when taking a longer-run view. In the tomato-growing example, the rent paid for the land would be considered a fixed cost during the growing season, once it has been paid. But over a longer period, say several growing seasons, rent would be considered a variable cost because a person could decide to rent more or less land depending on how much output was planned. In general, the longer the adjustment period allowed, the greater is the proportion of costs that will be variable. As soon as enough time is allowed to be able to change any or all inputs according to the desired level of output, all costs become variable. We will have more to say about fixed and variable costs as we go along.

Profits

Profits is a word that tends to be used rather loosely and as a result often means different things to different people. Because profits play an extremely important role in the areas of production and supply, it is necessary to define what is meant by profits. In the field of accounting, profits are generally defined as income minus expenses. (Depreciation on buildings and machines is included in expenses.) Most people probably think of profits in this way. Economists, however, have found it useful to define profits in a slightly different manner. They begin by dividing profits in two categories: (1) normal profits and (2) pure profits.

Normal profits are defined as the minimum return to the labor, capital, or other inputs contributed by the owner(s) of the firm that is necessary to keep the inputs in a given production activity. By and large, normal profits are the same thing as implicit costs. Just because certain inputs happen to be contributed by the owner(s) of a firm does not mean that they should not be paid a wage or some kind of compensation just like hired inputs. In the tomato-growing costs and returns example presented in the preceding section, we saw that income minus expenses (explicit costs) netted a $60 return. In accounting or layman's terms the $60 would be thought of as profits. But when we subtract a charge for your own labor, the picture changes drastically. Now there is $36 loss rather than a $60 profit. Thus the accounting or layman's definition of profits can provide a misleading picture of the so-called profitability of a firm. By including a return to the owner's resources (normal profits), a more accurate picture of true costs and profits is obtained. There probably would be less misunderstanding about profits if normal profits were not called *profits* at all but rather *implicit costs,* which is really what they are. Normal profits happen to exist because the owners of most firms contribute a part of the firm's resources. If all resources were hired from outside the firm, there would be no implicit costs or normal profits.

Normal profits (implicit costs) are particularly important for corporations because a large share of the capital utilized by these firms is contributed by stockholders. Stockholders are the owners of corporations. The reported "profits" of corporations generally include the dividends paid to stockholders. But a major part of dividends is implicit costs because they represent a payment to the resources contributed by the owners of these firms. Hence much of what is considered profits of corporations is really a cost. We will present a couple of measures of corporate profits in the next section.

Pure profits, the second category of profits mentioned above, are defined as the return above all costs (explicit plus implicit). Pure profits exist because no one has perfect knowledge or knows the future with certainty. If knowledge were perfect and the future were known with certainty, resources would gravitate to where they could earn the highest returns. This movement of resources would result in a competing down of the earnings in high-return areas as resources became more plentiful in these areas, and a bidding up of their earnings in low-return areas as they decreased in supply. As a consequence earnings of each resource would equalize in all activities (given the skill requirements and working conditions for labor). When the earnings of each resource became equal in all activities, every resource would be earning what it could earn in the next best alternative. Hence there would be no pure profits.

Because knowledge is imperfect and the future uncertain, the possibility of pure profits provides the incentive for entrepreneurs and investors to take risks. Whenever there is risk, the possibility of loss exists as well as the possibility of gain. If there were no possibility of gain (pure profits) there would be no incentive to risk a possible loss. Pure profits also provide a source of funds to invest in order to increase output when an endeavor turns out to be successful. In such cases it pays producers to increase output. Serving as a source of investment funds, pure profits benefit society by making it possible to increase the output of goods and services that are most highly demanded.

Although pure profits have suffered from a "bad press" in recent years, they do play a beneficial role in society by providing an incentive to bear risk and by serving as a source of investment funds. This is not to say that entrepreneurs and investors should be relieved of paying their "share" of taxes out of pure as well as normal profits. But generally it is not in the best interest of society to regard pure profits as unnecessary and as a result confiscate a major proportion through taxes, as England decided to do in the early to mid–1970s.

In the discussion on business firms in Chapters 7 and 8 normal profits will be included in total production costs unless otherwise stated. When we refer to profits in these chapters it will be in reference to pure profits—any earnings in excess of explicit plus implicit costs.

Profit rates of U.S. corporations

There are two commonly used methods of measuring and presenting profits. One is to divide the firm's annual accounting profits by its net worth (equity capital) to derive a rate of return on equity capital. This figure has the same interpretation as the rate of return on a savings account or government bonds. The second way is to divide accounting profits by the firm's sales. The resulting figure (multiplied by 100) indicates how many cents "profit" are earned on each dollar of sales. The after-tax profit rates computed under both methods are presented in Table 5–1. Bear in mind that these are accounting profits which in part at least represent a payment to the firm's own resources, mainly capital.

During the 1949–78 period, the rate of return (after income

TABLE 5–1
Profit rates of U.S. manufacturing corporations after income taxes, 1949–1978

Year	Rate of return on equity capital (percent)	Profits per dollar of sales (cents)
1949	11.6	5.8
1954	9.9	4.5
1959	10.4	4.8
1964	11.6	5.2
1969	11.5	4.8
1970	9.3	4.0
1971	9.7	4.1
1972	10.6	4.3
1973	12.8	4.7
1974	14.9	5.5
1975	11.6	4.6
1976	13.9	5.4
1977	14.2	5.3
1978*	14.6	5.3
Average 1949–78	11.6	4.9

* First three quarters.
Source: *Economic Report of the President,* 1979, p. 280.

taxes) on equity capital earned by U.S. manufacturing corporations averaged 11.6 percent. These firms earned on the average 4.9 cents per dollar of sales. One should bear in mind too that not all "profits" are paid out as dividends to stockholders. Part are "plowed back" into the firms to finance new investment. During the 1968–78 period, more than half the funds used for new investment came from undistributed profits, or *retained earnings* as they are called.[1]

Rates of return on equity capital by industry groups for 1978 are presented in Table 5–2. Although there are substantial differences in the profit rates for industry groups at this time, one should not conclude that such differences will persist year after year. Demand and cost conditions change, which in turn changes profit rates. Even if these market conditions did not change, profit rates would begin to equalize because capital would move out of low-profit industries and into those industries that offer more attractive returns. As capital moved out of low-return industries, profit rates would

---

[1] *Economic Report of the President,* 1979, p. 282.

TABLE 5–2
Rates of return on equity capital after income taxes, U.S.
manufacturing corporations, 1978*

Industry	Rate of return (percent)
Iron and steel	8.8
Nonferrous metals	8.9
Fabricated metal products	16.2
Machinery, except electric	16.7
Motor vehicles and equipment	16.7
Aircraft, guided missiles, and parts	16.7
Instruments and related products	17.7
Food and kindred products	13.4
Tobacco manufacturers	18.3
Textile mill products	11.3
Paper and allied products	12.6
Printing and publishing	17.6
Industrial chemicals	13.7
Drugs	19.5
Petroleum and coal	12.7
Rubber products	10.8
Other nondurable products	14.7

* First three quarters.
Source: *Economic Report of the President*, 1979, p. 281.

begin to increase because of the decrease in output and the resulting increase in price. Similarly, as capital moved into the high-return industries, their output would increase, thereby causing price and profit rates to decline.

Marginal cost

Before we can derive a supply curve, it is necessary to define several other types of cost. *Marginal cost,* the object of our interest in this section, is defined as the additional cost of producing and selling one more unit of output. Or it can be thought of as the reduction in total cost (explicit plus implicit) by reducing output one unit.

To gain a better understanding of marginal cost it will be helpful to compute some actual marginal cost figures. Let us continue to use the tomato production example of the preceding chapter. Also it will be simplest to begin the case of one variable input—your labor.

The marginal cost of producing an extra unit of output at various levels of output can be computed from the change in total cost at each level of output. Total cost, you recall, is made up of two categories: fixed and variable. Assume that the fixed cost of the tomato production endeavor is $40. Consider this to be mostly land rent, although it could well include the cost of seeds as well as some small garden tools. Assume also that the implicit cost of your own labor is $4 per hour, or $32 per day. We now have the necessary data to calculate the marginal cost (MC) for alternative levels of output.

Columns (1) and (2) in Table 5–3, showing tomato output and labor inputs, respectively, are taken from Table 4–1. Total variable cost (TVC) of the labor input, obtained by multiplying days of labor times $32, is shown in column (3). Total cost (TC), obtained by adding the $40 fixed cost to each level of variable cost, is shown in column (4).

TABLE 5–3
Total and marginal cost

(1) Tomato output (bushels)	(2) Labor input (days)	(3) Total variable cost	(4) Total cost	(5) Marginal cost per unit
0	0	$ 0	$ 40	—
1	1	32	72	$32.00
8	2	64	104	4.58
20	3	96	136	2.66
29	4	128	168	3.56
36	5	160	200	4.58
42	6	192	232	5.34
46	7	224	264	8.00
48	8	256	296	16.00

Marginal cost, shown in the last column, is our main interest at the present. Recall that MC is the additional cost of obtaining one more unit of output. Note that even at zero units of output, total cost is $40. Increasing output to one bushel increases total cost to $72. Thus the MC of this bushel is $32 ($72 − $40).

As is often the case in actual production situations, however, it may not be possible to increase output by just one unit. In this illustration, for example, the second day of labor results in eight bushels of output, or an increase in seven bushels over the output at one day of labor. All we can do in this case is to estimate the "average" marginal cost of the output in the range of one to eight bushels. This is obtained by using a formula very similar to the one used to calculate marginal physical product (MPP). The formula for MC is:

$$MC = \frac{\Delta \text{ total cost}}{\Delta \text{ output}}$$

in which the Δ symbol is an abbreviation for "change in."

Using this formula, we see that the change in total cost from one to eight bushels is $32 ($104 − $72), and the change in output is seven (8 − 1), so the "average" marginal cost of an extra bushel in this range of output is $4.58 ($32 ÷ 7) per bushel. (You might try to calculate MC at the other levels of output to acquaint yourself with the calculation procedure.)

It is interesting to notice that it is possible to calculate MC using either the TC or TVC figures. Using the TVC figure, the MC of the first bushel is $32 − 0, or $32, just as it was using the total cost figure. Comparable answers are also obtained at the other levels of output. Thus an alternative formula for MC is

$$MC = \frac{\Delta \text{ total variable cost}}{\Delta \text{ output}}$$

It is not difficult to understand why the use of either TC or TVC results in the same MC when it is recalled that fixed cost remains the same at all levels of output; thus changing output does not change fixed costs. In other words, the only cost that changes when output changes is TVC. As a consequence, fixed cost does not enter into the MC calculation.

Marginal cost and marginal physical product

As shown in Table 5–3, marginal cost varies considerably over the range of output considered. It begins at a relatively high figure, $32, declines as output increases, and reaches a minimum at 20 bushels of output or three days of labor. After that, MC increases with larger levels of output. The behavior of the MC figures is similar to that of the MPP figures in Chapter 4 (Table 4–1), although with MPP the direction of movement is just opposite; MPP begins as a relatively small number, increases to a maximum, and then declines.

The relationship between MPP and MC is shown more clearly in Figure 5–1. The line representing MPP is the same as shown in Figure 4–1, whereas MC is derived from the last column in Table 5–3. The most important characteristic of Figure 5–1 is that MPP reaches its peak just at the exact level of input, or output, where MC reaches its lowest value. This correspondence between MC and MPP is not a mere coincidence. Both are derived from the variable input—labor, in this example. It is reasonable to expect, therefore, that the more productive labor is, the higher is its MPP and the less costly it will be to obtain an additional unit of output.

Average costs

In order to derive the concept of product supply it is necessary also to be familiar with the idea of average costs. We shall consider three types of average costs: (1) average fixed costs (AFC), (2) average variable costs (AVC), and (3) average total costs (ATC). As their names imply, each of these average costs is calculated by dividing the corresponding total cost figure by output. Specifically, average fixed cost is found by dividing total fixed cost by the level of output, and average variable cost is obtained by dividing total variable cost by output. Average total cost can be calculated in two ways: (1) dividing total cost by output or (2) summing AFC and AVC.

Again it is easier to understand these measures of cost by looking at a specific example. In the tomato production example, recall that total fixed costs (land rent mainly) were $40 and labor costs (variable cost) were $32 per day of labor input. The resulting average cost figures for this example are presented in Table 5–4.

Looking briefly at these average costs, we see first that AFC becomes smaller at larger levels of output. We might expect this, since fixed cost is spread across more units at larger output levels so each unit bears a smaller share of the cost. Perhaps most interesting is

FIGURE 5–1
Relationship between marginal physical product and marginal cost

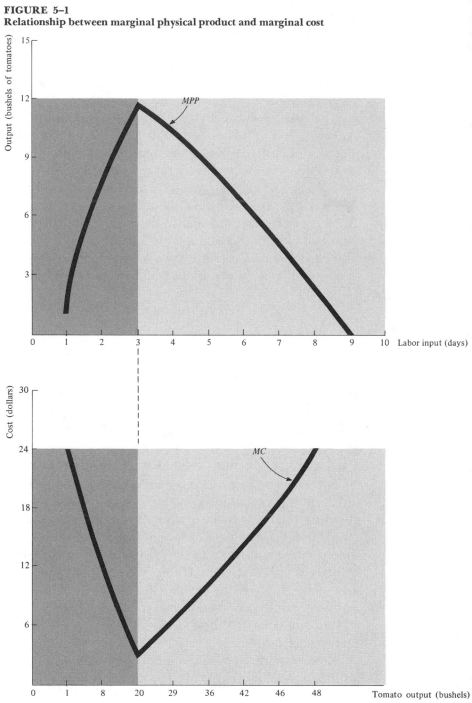

TABLE 5–4
Average fixed, variable, and total cost (tomato production example)

Tomato output (bushels)	Labor input (days)	AFC	AVC	ATC
1	1	$40.00	$32.00	$72.00
8	2	5.00	8.00	13.00
20	3	2.00	4.80	6.80
29	4	1.38	4.42	5.80
36	5	1.12	4.44	5.56
42	6	0.96	4.58	5.54
46	7	0.88	4.88	5.76
48	8	0.84	5.34	6.18

the behavior of AVC and ATC. Note first that AVC declines over a range of output or inputs, reaches a minimum point, and then begins to increase. The same pattern is observed for ATC, only these figures continue to decline until a slightly larger output is reached before they begin to increase.

Average variable cost and average physical product

We will be able to understand the average variable cost figures more thoroughly if we compare them with average physical product (APP), which was developed in Chapter 4. Recall that APP is total output (tomatoes, in the example) divided by the variable input (labor). The relationship between AVC and APP is most easily seen in a diagram.

In Figure 5–2, the line representing APP is the same as shown in Figure 4–1, whereas AVC is derived from the numbers in the fourth column of Table 5–4. The most important characteristic of Figure 5–2 is that APP reaches its peak at the exact level of inputs, or output, where AVC reaches its lowest value. Like MC and MPP, the correspondence between APP and AVC is not a coincidence. Both are derived from the variable input—labor. The more productive the average unit of labor, the higher is its APP and the lower will be the variable cost of an average unit of output.

FIGURE 5–2
Relationship between average physical product and average variable cost

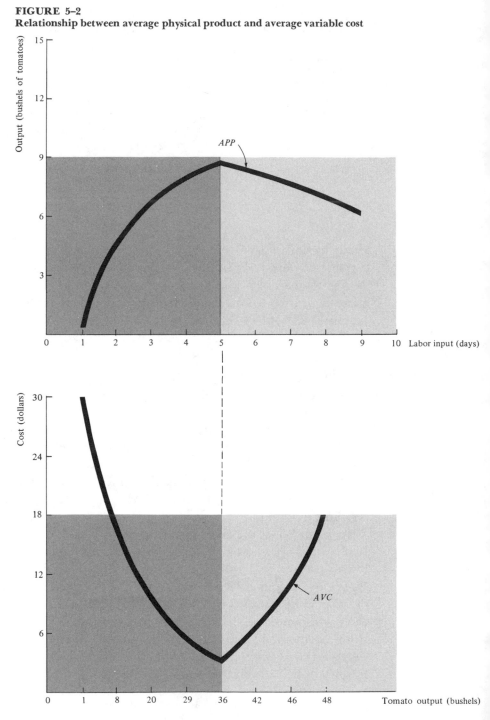

A glance back to Figure 4–1 will serve as a reminder that Stage II of the production process begins at the point where APP starts to decline. From Figure 5–2 we see that this also corresponds to the point where AVC begins to rise. Thus Stage II begins at the minimum point of AVC. Keep this in mind, because it will provide in part the reason why a rational, profit-maximizing producer will choose to produce only somewhere in Stage II. It is best to defer the explanation, however, until after we derive product supply.

Because the total cost (TC) curve is not used in deriving the supply curve, it is not shown on a diagram. But if this curve is plotted, it turns out that the TC curve is a mirror image of the TPP curve. In other words, the TC curve rises at a decreasing rate when the TPP is going up at an increasing rate. Then TC starts to increase at an increasing rate when TPP is increasing at a decreasing rate. You may wish to draw the two curves on your own with diagrams similar to Figures 5–1 and 5–2. (In the TC curve diagrams, plot dollars of total cost on the vertical axis and bushels of output on the horizontal axis.) One should also be aware that the MC curve is closely related to the TC curve. When TC is increasing at a decreasing rate, MC is declining; when TC is increasing at an increasing rate, MC is increasing.[2]

Marginal and average costs

To fully understand the concept of supply it is also necessary to understand the relationship between marginal and average costs. As in the previous relationships examined, these are easiest to see when represented by a diagram. In Figure 5–3, the three average cost curves and the marginal cost curve are superimposed on the same diagram.

Perhaps the most important characteristic to note is that MC intersects both AVC and ATC at their minimum points. The explanation of this characteristic is essentially the same as that set forth for MPP intersecting APP at its maximum point: If the marginal unit is below the average, it will pull the average down; if above the

---

[2] For those who have had calculus, the MC curve is the first derivative of the TC curve.

FIGURE 5–3
Relationship between marginal and average costs

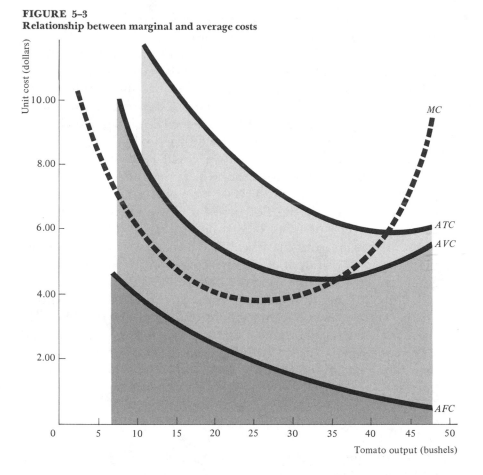

average, the average will be pulled up. The effect of this quarter's or semester's grade point average on your overall grade average was used as an example. If this quarter's grade average (the marginal quarter) is above the overall average, the overall average will improve, and vice versa.

Exactly the same reasoning applies to marginal and average costs. Marginal costs will continue to pull AVC and ATC lower as long as MC is below the averages. Notice that MC can be increasing during this time, as it is just left of the intersections with AVC and ATC. To the right of the intersections, MC is above the averages and hence pulls them up. It follows also from this reasoning that MC must intersect AVC and ATC at their minimum points.

Perhaps the most important thing to note about the AFC curve is that it is not very important. When it is necessary to consider fixed costs they can be found in the ATC figure. Recall that AFC equals ATC minus AVC. Or AFC at any given output is equal to the vertical distance between ATC and AVC at that level of output.

You might have noticed that all the cost curves, with the exception of AFC, are drawn in a ∪-shaped configuration. This common shape of the marginal and average cost curves stems from the law of diminishing returns. At the point where MPP begins to decline, MC turns upward, and when APP turns down, the AVC curve swings upward. And when AVC turns upward, the point where ATC begins to increase is not far behind.

The profit-maximizing rule

One of the more important concepts in economics is the idea that a producer will maximize profits (or minimize losses) by producing that quantity of output at which the additional cost of the marginal unit is just equal to the additional returns from that unit. Marginal cost, you recall, is the additional cost of producing and selling one more unit. For a small, individual producer, such as you would be in the tomato production example, the additional income you receive by selling one more unit of output would be equal to the price of the output. For example, if price is $4 per bushel, selling an extra bushel adds $4 to your total revenue or sales.

It is perhaps easiest to see why you would want to produce that level of output where marginal cost is equal to price if we pick a quantity where price is *not* equal to marginal cost, and then see what happens. Consider quantity Q_0 in Figure 5–4. (In this diagram we only need the MC curve, so we delete the three average cost curves.) Notice that at Q_0 the additional cost of producing one more bushel is equal to $4.

However, if the price of tomatoes happened to be $6, as is assumed here, you could increase your profits by increasing output. By producing the $Q_0 + 1$ unit, you spend roughly $4 but obtain $6 back, leaving a net gain of $2. Anytime you can spend $4 and obtain $6

FIGURE 5–4
Maximization of profits where price equals marginal cost

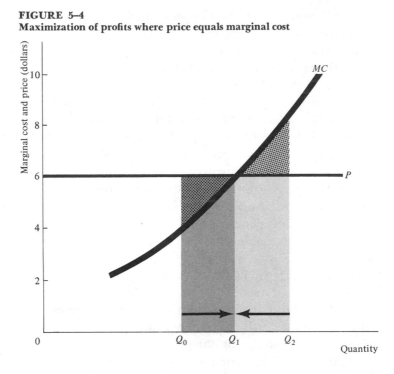

back, you would be foolish not to produce that extra unit, so you definitely would want to produce $Q_0 + 1$ units. If you ask yourself if $Q_0 + 2$ units should be produced, you would obtain a similar answer, only now the difference between price and marginal cost would be somewhat less than $2. Since you would obtain a net gain, nevertheless, you would not want to stop short of quantity Q_1. If you did stop short at Q_0 you would give up profits equal in value to the area of the shaded triangle to the left of Q_1.

If you produced a quantity greater than Q_1, say Q_2, then MC would be greater than price. Here the marginal unit adds more to total costs, roughly $8, than it does to total revenue, $6, so you would definitely not want to produce the marginal unit at output Q_2. Nor would you want to produce $Q_2 - 1$ units, because the added cost still would outweigh the added gain. The same would hold true for any output beyond Q_1. Thus you would be forced back to Q_1. If you insisted on producing the level of output denoted by Q_2, you would give up profits equal to the shaded triangle to the right of Q_1.

Thus we see that profits will be maximized (or losses minimized) if output corresponds to the point where the price of the product equals the marginal cost. In formulating this rule, namely that price must equal marginal cost to maximize profits, we will see shortly that we have derived product supply.

Derivation of supply: One variable input

Supply is defined as a relationship between price and quantity. Intuitively we would expect an individual producer to increase the level of output in response to higher and higher prices. Thus supply, like demand, is not a fixed quantity but rather a relationship between price and quantity.

It is not possible, therefore, to stipulate what level of output will be forthcoming until price is brought into the picture. Given the fact that you decide to produce tomatoes, for example, the number of bushels you produce would likely be different if you could sell each bushel for $10 than if a $4 price prevailed. Quite likely, at the $10 price you would treat your tomato plot with a great deal more tender loving care than at the lower $4 price. But the question remains: How much care?

The derivation of product supply is easily accomplished with a familiar diagram. Figure 5–5 is essentially the same as Figure 5–3, except that AFC has been deleted and some alternative prices have been added. All we have to do now is apply the rule that price equals marginal cost to find out how much output will be forthcoming at various prices.

At the relatively high $8 price, the horizontal line intersects the MC curve at 46 bushels of tomato output. Thus, at $8, the quantity supplied is 46 bushels. At a lower price, say $6, the intersection of the line representing this price and MC corresponds to a smaller level of output—approximately 43 bushels. As we continue to lower price, the intersection between the price line and MC continues to move downward and to the left, corresponding to smaller and smaller levels of output. We see, therefore, that our intuitive idea of supply—larger quantities at higher prices—is consistent with the more rigorous concepts of economics.

As we continue to move down along the MC curve with lower

FIGURE 5–5
Deriving product supply

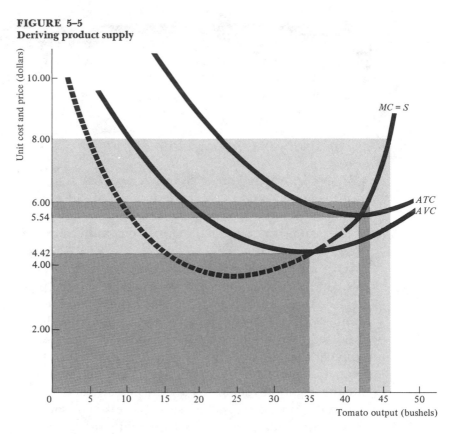

prices we soon reach the intersection of MC and ATC. Recall that this intersection corresponds to the lowest point of the ATC curve. As the name implies, average total cost is the average cost per unit of output of all output produced up to that point. For example, at 42 bushels of output the total cost per bushel averages $5.54 for these 42 bushels. Thus if price falls below $5.54, the total income received from the total output will be less than the total cost of producing it, and a loss will be incurred.

It is reasonable to believe, therefore, that in planning future output, no production will take place if price is expected to be below a minimum point on the ATC curve. In the tomato production example, you would decide not to rent the land and, in so doing, would avoid the fixed costs.

Thus, in planning future output, the most profitable level of output at any given price corresponds to that output where price equals MC. In other words, the MC curve above the ATC curve is really the product supply curve (S) for an individual producer. All we have to do is label the vertical axis "price" instead of "cost," and we have the supply curve.

It is not unusual, however, to find situations where the producer either underestimates cost or overestimates price in planning future output. In making a commitment to anticipated future production, a producer might have to incur a fixed cost that must be paid regardless of how much is produced. For example, the land rent for the tomato plot might have to be paid well in advance of the planting date. If the anticipated price falls below the minimum point on the ATC curve after the fixed cost is incurred, will it pay to still produce and take a loss? The answer might well be yes, for in producing it might be possible to lose less than in not producing at all, paying the fixed costs.

If fixed costs are incurred that cannot be avoided (sometimes called *sunk costs*), it will pay to produce and take a loss as long as price is at least equal to or above the minimum point of the AVC curve. If this is the case, then we are at least making back all our variable costs plus some of the fixed costs, depending on how much price is above this minimum point. Keep in mind that AFC at any given output level is equal to the vertical distance between ATC and AVC. Thus if price is higher than AVC at the optimum level of output (price equals MC), some of these fixed costs are being made back.

In view of the preceding discussion regarding fixed or sunk costs, it is necessary to revise slightly the definition of product supply. If it is impossible to avoid the fixed costs, the product supply will consist of the MC curve down to the minimum point on the AVC curve. In Figure 5–5, we see that this is represented by the continuous portion of MC above ATC, as well as the broken-line portion of MC that lies between AVC and ATC.

In no case will the supply curve extend below AVC. If price is below AVC, all the fixed costs are being lost as well as some of the variable costs. If it is not possible to make the variable costs back, you will lose less by doing nothing.

Stages of production and supply

In Chapter 4 we defined three stages of production and asserted that production should take place only in Stage II. At that time we gave fairly convincing reasons why it would not be rational to produce in the area of increasing returns (the beginning of Stage I) or the area of negative MPP (Stage III). But it was not possible to explain adequately then why the last part of Stage I (MPP decreasing but APP still increasing) was not a rational production area. The reason can now be seen by looking at Figure 5–6.

FIGURE 5–6
Relationship of stages of production and cost curves

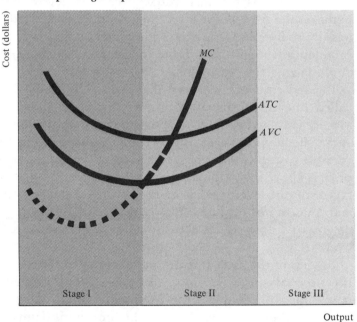

Recall that Stage I ends and Stage II begins at the point where MPP intersects APP. Since MC and AVC are mirror images of MPP and APP, Stage II begins at the intersection of MC and AVC. If price is so low as to intersect MC below AVC, it will not pay to produce at all because the firm will not even be making back its variable costs. It would be like paying $5 per bushel to pick to-

matoes that were selling for $4. Product supply, therefore, is mean-
ingful only in Stage II. Here price intersects MC above the AVC
curve. Moreover, unless there are fixed costs that cannot be avoided,
production will be forthcoming only above the ATC curve, which
in turn means that we are well into the region of diminishing
returns before it becomes profitable to produce.

Derivation of supply: Two or more variable inputs

In our discussion of supply, we have assumed the simplest case
of one variable input. However, in most situations, production is
carried on using two or more variable inputs. It is necessary to
explain, therefore, how a supply curve can be derived under these
more realistic conditions. Recall from the preceding chapter that
when two or more inputs are utilized to produce a given level of
output, costs are minimized when the inputs are combined such that
the P/MPP ratios for all inputs are equal. Also recall that the
P/MPP ratio for an input refers to the dollars required to produce
one more unit of output by adding slightly more of that input. If
this definition seems familiar, it should be; for it is none other
than marginal cost. Recall that marginal cost is the cost of producing one more unit of output. Granted the P/MPP ratio for an
input is the cost of producing one more unit of output by that
particular input, but when costs are minimized, all the P/MPP
ratios are equal. Thus a marginal cost (supply) curve can be derived
using two or more variables in the same way that it is derived with
one variable input. The only condition for doing so is that the
P/MPP ratios of all the variable inputs are kept equal.

We should expect to obtain the same ∪-shaped marginal cost
curve with two or more variable inputs as with one. At very small
levels of output, the several variable inputs may well experience a
region of increasing returns, resulting in progressively higher MPPs
and a progressively lower MC as inputs and output are increased.
At some point, as the increasing quantities of variable inputs begin
pressing against the fixed input(s), diminishing returns set in and
the MC begins its upward journey. For example, in the tomato-
growing case, more and more labor- and machine-hours applied to

a given land area (the fixed input) will eventually result in diminishing returns (lower MPPs) to both labor and machines, and at
this point marginal cost (P/MPP) will begin to increase. One should
bear in mind, of course, that in order to talk about a marginal cost
curve with two or more variable inputs, it is necessary to assume
that costs are being minimized for any given level of output;
that is, the P/MPP ratios are all equal.

The rest of the story as far as deriving the supply curve is the
same as for the one variable input case. To maximize profits (or
minimize losses) the supplier will choose to produce that output
corresponding to the point where product price equals marginal
cost. Hence the MC curve is in reality a supply curve. The supply
curve slopes up and to the right because the MC curve slopes up
and to the right. Recall that the MC curve slopes up and to the
right because of the law of diminishing returns.

Market supply

Although it is necessary to focus on the individual producer or
firm in order to derive supply, the concept is most useful when applied to the entire market. *Market supply* is obtained by summing
the quantity supplied by all producers in the market at the various
possible prices. Taking a simple example, suppose there are three
producers in the market, each having a specific supply curve as
shown by the first three frames of Figure 5–7. To obtain the market
supply curve shown in the fourth frame, we sum the three quantities
at each price as indicated in the following table.

	Quantity supplied by producer:				Market
Price	1	2	3		supply
$4	30 +	40 +	0	=	70
8	40 +	60 +	30	=	130

Notice that the increase in quantity placed on the market when
price increases comes from two sources. First there is an increase in
the quantity supplied from existing producers in the market as
illustrated by producers 1 and 2. Second, the increase in price is

FIGURE 5–7
Deriving market supply

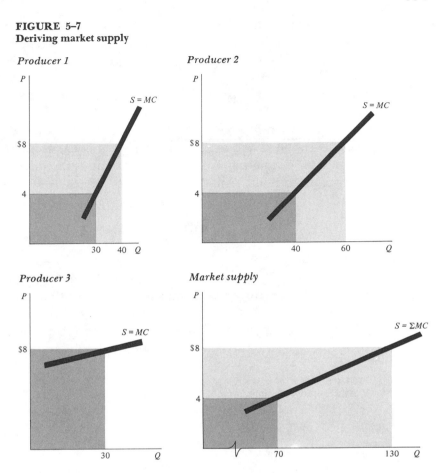

likely to bring new producers into the market as illustrated by producer 3 in this example. The relatively high $8 price of tomatoes entices this producer to produce tomatoes. Although an example cannot be used to prove a point, in general an increase in price will bring forth an increase in market output that is greater than that forthcoming from existing producers because of new producers coming in to "get a piece of the action."

Elasticity of supply

Thus far we have indicated only that product supply is an upward sloping line, meaning that producers are willing to produce larger amounts when they expect higher prices. We have not considered how responsive producers are to a price change. Economists use a concept known as *elasticity of supply* to measure the responsiveness of producers to a price change. We will see that this concept is very similar to price elasticity of demand presented in Chapter 3.

Elasticity of supply (E_s) is defined as the percentage change in quantity supplied resulting from each percent change in price. The formula for computing E_s is exactly the same as the price elasticity of demand formula, namely:

$$E_s = \frac{\dfrac{Q_0 - Q_1}{Q_0}}{\dfrac{P_s - P_1}{P_0}}$$

In computing E_s, however, the quantities Q_0 and Q_1 refer to the beginning and ending quantities supplied rather than quantity demanded.

A simple example can be worked out by inserting the numbers in Figure 5–8 into the E_s formula. Let \$4 be the initial price, P_0;

FIGURE 5–8
Elasticity of supply computation

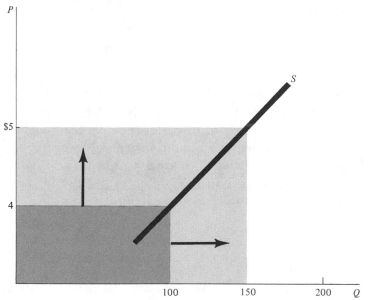

$5 the new price, P_1; 100 the initial quantity, Q_0; and 150 the new quantity, Q_1.

$$E_s = \frac{\frac{100 - 150}{100}}{\frac{4 - 5}{4}} = \frac{\frac{-50}{100}}{\frac{-1}{4}} = \frac{-0.5}{-0.25} = 2$$

The elasticity coefficient of 2 in this example means that quantity changes by 2 percent for each 1 percent change in price.

Since the formula for computing E_s is the same as the formula for finding the price elasticity of demand, it suffers from some of the same problems. First, it is a "point" elasticity formula, so it should be applied to only very small changes in price and quantity. In measuring E_s for actual products, economists use a statistical technique that measures very small changes. This technique is studied in intermediate level statistics courses and also in a specialized area of economics known as *econometrics*.[3]

Also, E_s varies in size along the supply curve, again because the base values change, although in the case of supply both price and quantity base values (P_0 and Q_0) change in the same direction. As you move up and out along the supply curve, the value of E_s approaches 1. At points low on the supply curve, E_s approaches zero if the curve intersects the quantity axis and approaches infinity if it intersects the price axis. You may want to convince yourself of this by working out a few examples.

Economists also classify E_s similar to E_d. If E_s is less than 1 it is considered inelastic, whereas a supply elasticity coefficient greater than 1 is said to be elastic. And as E_s approaches zero, a vertical supply curve, E_s is described as highly inelastic. Similarly when it approaches infinity, a horizontal supply curve, E_s is described as highly elastic.

Unlike E_d, however, the size of E_s, whether it be elastic or inelastic, does not influence the direction of movement of total income ($P \times Q$) when price increases or decreases. That is, when price increases quantity also increases, so total income must go up. Similarly, total income declines when price declines because quantity also declines.

---

[3] The "arc elasticity" or "midpoints" formula used to calculate the price elasticity of demand also can be applied to the elasticity of supply computation.

FACTORS INFLUENCING ELASTICITY OF SUPPLY

All products or producers do not exhibit the same elasticity of supply. Some products exhibit a highly elastic supply; a slight change in price brings forth a relatively large change in quantity. For others, supply is highly inelastic; a price change has relatively little effect on quantity supplied. Why do we observe these differences in the size of E_s?

There are two major factors that influence the size of the elasticity of supply of a product: (1) the availability of substitute inputs that can be drawn away from other uses, and (2) the time allowed for adjustment to take place. Regarding the first factor, if the production of a product utilizes inputs that are commonly used to produce other products, it will tend to have a more elastic supply than if it uses specialized inputs suited only for its production. For example, the supply of all agricultural products in the aggregate is believed to be relatively inelastic because there is only so much agricultural land. If all agricultural prices increase, farmers can increase output somewhat by using land substitutes, such as fertilizer, and more intensive care. But the increase in output would be much larger if additional land could be drawn from other uses into agricultural production.

For an individual agricultural product such as wheat, supply tends to be much more elastic because land and other inputs can be drawn away from other types of agricultural production. In fact, for most individual products or services, it is hard to imagine examples of any input that does not exist in some form in another line of work. Even the number of people with highly specialized training, such as economists or heart surgeons, could be increased substantially if the prices of their services increased and there was freedom of entry into the field. This has, of course, happened in the case of economists, although the number of heart surgeons has not exhibited as large an increase because of restricted entry into the medical profession. It is a mistake to underestimate the latent talents of people or the adaptability of resources to many different uses. Our experience during national emergencies such as World War II bears this out.

The second factor, time for adjustment, is important because most production activities cannot be changed in scale "overnight."

If price should increase, for example, some additional output will likely be forthcoming from increasing the amount of variable inputs; for instance, more labor can be hired and machines and facilities used more intensely by operating two or three shifts. However, relatively large changes in output usually cannot be attained until the level of fixed inputs can be changed, and it takes time to construct facilities and manufacture machines.

It should be recognized that the ability to adjust output is likely to differ among industries. For example, changes in retail trade where temporary facilities can be set up are likely to take less time than changes in the output of heavy industry where specialized plants and equipment are required. At any rate, in any given industry, the longer the time that elapses after a price change, the greater the change in output that is physically possible and the more elastic the supply is likely to be.

In addition to the purely physical constraints on changing output, particularly increasing it, the economic aspects are very important. Even if it is physically possible to adjust output, it may not be profitable to do so immediately after a price change. The major consideration here is the length of time the price change is *expected* to remain in effect. If the price change is expected to be only temporary, there is little incentive for a rational producer to change the level of output substantially because changes in output usually involve additional expense. To increase output it may be necessary to purchase new equipment, buildings, and so forth; or to decrease production one might have to let fixed inputs remain idle but still bear the fixed cost. Unless producers expect the price change to remain in effect for a time, it may not pay to incur the expense necessary to adjust output. As an analogy, you generally do not bother to put on a heavy coat to pick up the morning paper on your doorstep on a cold day, but when you expect to be out for an hour the bother of putting on a heavy coat is worth the effort.

Of course, no producer has a crystal ball to accurately predict whether a price change is going to be temporary or long-run in nature. Most producers probably have an opinion on the duration of a price change based on information about the market, but none can be absolutely sure. The longer a price change remains in effect, the more information producers will have and the more certain they will be as to the duration of the change. As a result, we should not expect to observe much change in output resulting from short-run, month-to-month fluctuation in output price. Rather we would expect producers to respond mainly to changes in the overall average level of prices that exists over a period of time. We will illustrate the effect of time for adjustment on the supply curve at the end of Chapter 6.

A change or shift in supply

Although it is important to be aware of the upward sloping nature of the supply curve and the responsiveness of producers to price changes, it is equally important to understand that the supply curve itself can shift from one position to another, the same as happens to demand. Representing the supply curve by a two-dimensional diagram makes it necessary to hold constant the other factors that can affect supply. If these factors do not remain constant, which is usually the case, there will be a shift in the supply curve from one position to another. Both an increase and decrease in supply are illustrated by Figure 5–9.

An increase in supply, illustrated by a shift from S_1 to S_2 in Figure 5–9, can be interpreted in two ways. First, at a given price, say P_1, producers will offer a larger quantity on the market: Q_2 instead of Q_1. A second way of interpreting an increase in supply is that producers will supply the same quantity, say Q_1, at a lower price. Both ways of looking at an increase in supply have the same meaning.

The meaning of a decrease in supply, as illustrated by S_0 in Figure 5–9, is strictly parallel to an increase. At a given price, say P_1, the quantity supplied declines from Q_1 to Q_0. Or, looking at it the second way, the price suppliers will require for quantity Q_1 increases from P_1 to P_2.

Supply shifters

There are five major factors, or supply shifters, that can cause a shift (increase or decrease) in the supply curve from one position to another.

FIGURE 5–9
Shift-in-supply

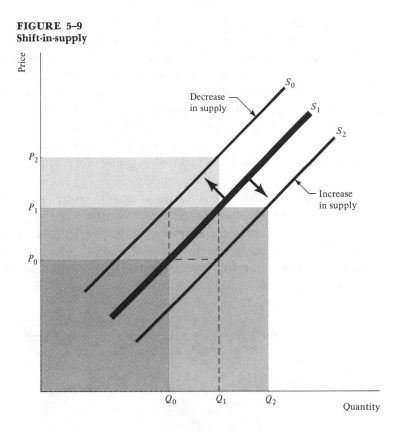

1. CHANGE IN PRICES OF INPUTS

As noted earlier in the chapter, product supply is really the same thing as marginal cost. Thus anything that changes production costs should eventually change supply. If, for example, there is an increase in the price of labor, the total variable cost of a given output will increase, which in turn will have the effect of increasing the marginal cost—the added cost of an extra unit of output. Thus an *increase* in input prices or cost has the effect of *decreasing* supply, shifting it upward and to the left, as shown by S_0 in Figure 5–9. Conversely, a decrease in input prices will increase supply, or shift it to the right (S_2 in Figure 5–9).

Keep in mind, too, that marginal cost includes implicit as well as explicit costs. Thus any change in wages or employment opportunities in other lines of work will tend to affect the supply of a given product. For example, the supply of tomatoes in the example used in preceding chapters probably would decline if wages in the alternative supermarket job rose substantially or some other kind of work became available that was more attractive than growing tomatoes. If you took advantage of these opportunities, you would devote less effort to growing tomatoes, which in turn would result in a decrease in the supply of tomatoes. When wages or the prices of other inputs change in one industry, it is a good idea to inquire what effect this will have on the costs and supply of related industries.

The effect of a change in wages (implicit costs) is illustrated by the following table. Notice that the marginal cost of growing any given level of tomatoes increases when the wage that could be earned in the grocery store increases from $4 to $5 per hour. This means that the marginal cost curve shifts upward and to the left (decreases).

| Output | Marginal cost when hourly wage is: | |
(bushels)	$4	$5
0	—	—
1	$32.00	$40.00
8	4.58	5.71
20	2.66	3.33
29	3.56	4.44
36	4.58	5.71
42	5.34	6.66
46	8.00	10.00
48	16.00	20.00

An increase in the wage rate also increases the minimum point on the ATC curve. For example, the increase in the wage rate from $4 to $5 per hour increases the minimum point on the ATC curve from $5.54 to $6.66. Producers who have a minimum ATC higher than $6.66 eventually will drop out of the market and find something more profitable to do if the market price is not at least this high.

It is interesting to note that an increase in the price of a fixed input will not shift the MC curve and as a result does not shift the firm's short-run supply curve. (Recall that marginal cost is derived only from variable costs.) However, an increase in fixed costs does have the effect of increasing the minimum point on the ATC curve. As a result, those firms that begin to incur losses because of the minimum point on the ATC rising above price will eventually drop out of the market. With fewer firms producing, the market supply curve then will shift to the left. (Recall that the market supply curve is the summation of all individual firm supply curves.) Of course, a decrease in the price of an input (variable or fixed) will tend to have the opposite effect, namely, to increase or shift the market supply curve to the right.

2. CHANGE IN PRICE OF OTHER PRODUCTS

Most inputs, including labor, can be used in any one of a number of production activities. If the price of an alternative product that can be produced increases, there is an incentive for producers to shift out of former lines of production into the production of the good that has risen in price. Not to do so would mean that producers deliberately forgo higher incomes. For example, in the tomtao-growing endeavor, the decision to grow tomatoes would depend on the price of sweet corn, strawberries, beans, and so forth. If you could sell your labor for $6 per hour growing sweet corn, why should you grow tomatoes if this activity returns only $4 per hour? Thus an increase in the prices of other products tends to decrease, or shift to the left, the supply of the product in question. Of course, the converse is also true.

3. CHANGE IN PRODUCER EXPECTATIONS OF FUTURE PRICES

Since producers are human beings and therefore cannot know the future with certainty, many of their present production decisions are based on what they believe will happen in the future. If producers have a reason to expect changes in future prices, either in the prices of the product they presently produce or in prices of products they could produce, they will likely begin to adjust their production capacity accordingly. However, it is not possible to generalize across all situations the effect of, say, an expected increase in price. Each situation must be analyzed separately. For example, if the product can be stored, an expectation of higher future prices may well lead to a reduction in the present supply as producers build up their inventories in order to have more to sell when they expect prices to be higher. Of course, the expected price increase must at least compensate for storage costs. For products that cannot be stored, such as tomatoes, the expectation of higher future prices may lead to an increase in the present supply as producers begin to expand capacity for the future.

Another important item to keep in mind is the expected duration of a price change. If producers expect only a temporary rise in future prices, they will be less willing to make extensive changes in productive capacity than if they expect higher prices to prevail for many years. Thus the magnitude of the supply shift will depend on the length of time the expected price change is expected to stay in effect. If the expected duration is short, the supply shift will be small, and vice versa.

4. CHANGE IN TECHNOLOGY

In general, new technology has the effect of making presently used inputs more productive by improving their quality or by creating new inputs that are more productive than the old ones; both result in higher productivity. Proceeding one step further, we can define higher productivity as decreasing the cost of a given level of output, say Q_1 in Figure 5–9, or increasing the level of output for a given cost, such as P_1 in Figure 5–9. You will recognize that both these changes describe an increase in product supply. Thus new technology always has the effect of increasing supply. If new technology did not reduce costs, producers would have no incentive to adopt it. We will discuss the economic effects of new technology in more detail in Chapters 7 and 12.

5. CHANGE IN NUMBER OF PRODUCERS

As mentioned earlier, the market supply of a good or service is the summation of the supplies of all individual producers. Thus the more producers there are of a given size, the greater will be the supply. As the population and the economy grow, the growth in the number of firms shifts the product supply for many goods and services to the right. Of course, if the average size of firms increases substantially, there can be an increase in supply even with a reduction in number of firms. A good example of this phenomenon is agriculture in the United States.

In conceptualizing market supply for items already in existence, such as used cars, previously owned homes, and land, it is important to distinguish between the existing *stock* and the *supply*. For these items the supply is the quantities that owners will place on the market at various possible prices. At low prices owners can be expected to place smaller quantities of these items on the market than at higher prices. Thus their market supply curves still can slope up and to the right even though the quantity of each item in existence is fixed at a given point in time. It is not correct to assume that just because the item is not currently being produced, its supply curve will be vertical. Owners of such items are not likely to place the same quantities on the market at low prices than they would at high prices.

Although these five supply shifters are the major economic factors that influence the position of the supply curve, there may be other shifters that are important for certain kinds of products. For example, a change in the weather or growing conditions is an important supply shifter for agricultural products. A period of adverse weather is likely to decrease the supply of certain products, while unusually good weather should increase their supply. Also, as will be discussed shortly, a law that prohibits the production or sale of an item can be expected to decrease its supply, particularly if the penalty is severe.

In order to fully understand the concept of supply and the behavior of producers, it is as important to be aware of the possible shifts in supply as it is to know about the upward sloping nature of the supply curve. Without a knowledge of these shifts and the factors that cause them, it is not possible to understand producer behavior. For example, if the supply curve shifts to the right, producers will increase the quantity they place on the market at the same price or even at a lower price. (We will see how the latter can occur in Chapter 6.) To the uninformed it may appear that price has no relationship to quantity supplied. But if one knows why the supply curve has shifted, the observed changes in price and quantity are reasonable and expected.

Main points of Chapter 5

1. In measuring the cost of producing an item, both explicit and implicit costs should be included. Explicit costs are the normal cash expenses incurred in production, whereas the implicit cost of an input is the wage that this input could have earned in the best alternative employment available.

2. A rational person may willingly choose not to work at a job that maximizes his or her salary. It is important, however, to know how much income is sacrificed to work in a more agreeable occupation.

3. Fixed costs (explicit or implicit) are those incurred by the purchase of fixed inputs. By definition fixed costs do not change as output changes. Variable costs (explicit or implicit) are incurred by the purchase of variable inputs; these costs change at different levels of output.

4. Normal profits are defined as the minimum return to inputs owned by the firm necessary to keep them in a given production activity. Normal profits in reality are implicit costs because they are payments to the resources owned by the firm. They exist because most firms utilize some of their own inputs, mainly capital but also some labor, as opposed to purchasing all inputs from outsiders.

5. Pure profits are defined as earnings in excess of all costs, explicit plus implicit. Pure profits exist because knowledge is imperfect and the future uncertain. They provide an incentive to bear risk and serve as a source of investment funds.

6. Profits are commonly presented in terms of a rate of return on equity capital or in terms of cents per dollar of sales. During the 1949–78 period, after-tax profit rates of U.S. manufacturing corporations averaged 11.6 percent on equity capital and 4.9 cents per dollar of sales. These figures are accounting

profits which include a payment to the firm's own resources.

7. Marginal cost is the additional cost (explicit plus implicit) of producing and selling one more unit of output. It is derived exclusively from variable cost.

8. Marginal cost and marginal physical product are mirror images of each other. In other words when MPP reaches its peak, MC bottoms out.

9. Average variable cost and average total cost exhibit the same ∪-shaped pattern as marginal costs. Both decline if MC is below them, and both increase if MC is above. MC intersects AVC and ATC at their minimum points.

10. The same relationship exists between AVC and APP as between MC and MPP. AVC reaches a minimum point at the exact location where APP is at a maximum. Thus Stage II begins at the minimum point of AVC.

11. For a small, individual producer the additional income derived from selling one more unit of output is equal to the price of the unit. Thus if MC is less than price, there is an incentive to produce more because the additional income exceeds the additional cost. On the other hand, if MC exceeds price, there is an incentive to reduce output because the additional expense exceeds the additional income. Thus a producer maximizes profits (the difference between income and expense) at the point where MC equals price.

12. If a producer is not committed to any fixed costs, the supply curve of a firm is the same as the MC curve above the point where it intersects ATC. If there is a commitment to pay fixed costs, however, the supply curve is the same as the MC curve above the point where it intersects AVC.

13. Comparing supply with the stages of production, we see that the supply curve lies entirely in Stage II, which is characterized at all points by diminishing returns.

14. To minimize cost for a given level of output using two or more variable inputs, the inputs are combined such that the P/MPP ratios for all inputs are equal. The P/MPP ratio is the cost of adding one more unit of output by each respective input. This also turns out to be the definition of marginal cost. Hence the same rule for deriving supply for one variable input also holds for two or more variable inputs, namely, to produce

that level of output corresponding to the point where output price equals MC.

15. Market supply is the summation of the supply of all individual producers at given prices.

16. Elasticity of supply is defined as the percentage change in quantity supplied resulting from each percent change in price.

17. An increase in supply means that producers are willing to place a greater quantity on the market at a given price or will take a lower price for a given quantity. This is illustrated by a shift to the right of the supply curve.

18. A decrease in supply means that producers will place a smaller quantity on the market at a given price or must be paid a higher price to place the same quantity on the market. This is illustrated by a shift to the left of the supply curve.

19. The five main supply shifters are a change in: (*a*) input prices, (*b*) the prices of alternative products that can be produced, (*c*) producer expectations regarding future prices, (*d*) technology, and (*e*) the number of producers in the market. In addition there may be other factors that shift the supply of certain products. For example, a change in weather can shift the supply of agricultural products.

Questions for thought and discussion

1. Implicit costs are fixed, whereas explicit costs are variable. True or false? Explain.

2. How might you estimate the implicit cost of your own labor if you were in business for yourself?

3. An increase in wages in nonfarm occupations will increase the cost of producing food. True or false? Explain.

4. *a.* Some people choose to work in an occupation that does not provide them with the greatest monetary reward. Are these people irrational? Explain.

   b. Some people choose to work in an occupation that does not represent to them the most desirable way of making a living. Are these people irrational? Explain.

5. What are profits and why do they exist?

6. The average and marginal cost curves generally are U-shaped. Why?
7. If a firm wishes to maximize profits, how much should it produce?
8. In order to talk about a supply curve, it is necessary to assume that firms maximize profits. True or false? Explain.
9. Will it ever pay a firm to produce at a loss? Explain.
10. If it pays to produce at all, why does it always pay to use each variable input past the point of diminishing returns?
11. If the price of a product increases, what are the two sources of the increase in output coming on the market?
12. Compute the elasticity of supply from the following data.

	Price	Quantity supplied
Initial situation	$10	1,000
New situation	15	2,000

13. The market supply of items that are no longer being produced such as land, Rembrandt paintings, and 1955 Chevrolets will be perfectly inelastic. True of false? Explain.
14. According to the theory of supply, is it possible for producers to place a larger quantity on the market at a lower price? Explain. How about a smaller quantity at a higher price?
15. Indicate how each of the following circumstances would affect the supply of beef.
    a. An increase in the price of feed.
    b. An increase in the price of wheat (an alternative product).
    c. The expectation of higher prices over the next several years.
    d. An increase in the number of beef producers.

6

Demand and supply in the product market

In developing the concepts of demand and supply, we noted that rational, utility-maximizing behavior by consumers implies a downward sloping demand curve. Profit-maximizing behavior by producers, on the other hand, is reflected in an upward sloping supply curve, subject, of course, to an upward sloping marginal cost curve.[1] We also saw that the demand and supply curves can shift from one position to another in response to several factors referred to as demand and supply shifters. Although demand and supply taken individually are useful concepts for understanding the behavior of consumers and producers, they become even more useful when used in conjunction with each other. In a sense, they are like two blades of a scissors. Taken separately they are of limited value, but when combined they become a useful tool. In this chapter, then, we will combine demand and supply to see, among other things, how the prices of goods and services are established in product markets, and how and why prices change.

---

[1] Recall too that the upward sloping MC curve is derived ultimately from the downward sloping MPP curve, which reflects diminishing returns to the variable inputs.

Equilibrium price and quantity

The first order of business is to superimpose the demand and supply curves on the same diagram, as shown by Figure 6–1. This is possible because both have price on the vertical axis and quantity on the horizontal axis. When the two curves are superimposed, you will notice that they intersect. The price that corresponds to the point of intersection is referred to as the equilibrium price, while the corresponding quantity is known as the equilibrium quantity. *Equilibrium* can be defined as a state of stability or balance where there are no forces causing movement, or there are equal opposing forces. If price is not at equilibrium, forces will exist in the market that will push price toward the equilibrium. This can be seen most

FIGURE 6–1
Demand and supply, showing equilibrium price and quantity

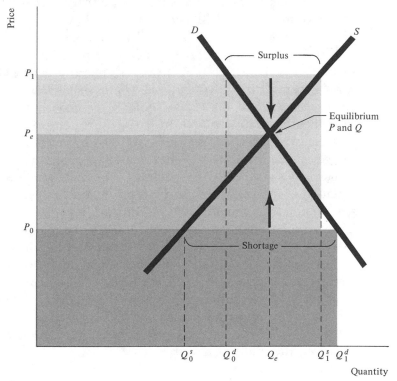

easily if we choose a price that is not equilibrium and see what happens. Consider price P_1 in Figure 6–1. At this relatively high price you will note that a relatively small amount is demanded, Q_0^d in the diagram. On the other hand, a relatively large amount is supplied, Q_1^s in the diagram. Thus at price P_1, the quantity supplied is greater than the quantity demanded. Hence there will be a surplus in the market; more goods or services are offered for sale than are bought, and inventories pile up or people who offer the services remain underutilized. The inevitable result of this situation is a downward pressure on price. Sellers, in an attempt to dispose of this surplus, are forced to take a lower price. After all, in order to make any money suppliers must be able to sell what they produce. Some sellers, therefore, will begin to cut price in order to entice buyers to buy from them rather than from other sellers. When some sellers cut price, others must follow to remain competitive. Of course, buyers also are likely to exert pressure, reminding those sellers who are reluctant to cut their price of the existing surplus and price reductions taking place. Thus we can see that if price is above the equilibrium, the resulting surplus causes downward pressure on price and pushes it toward the equilibrium.

Next let us see what happens if price is below the equilibrium, such as P_0 in Figure 6–1. At price P_0, quantity demanded, Q_1^d, is greater than the quantity supplied, Q_0^s. At such a low price there is an incentive for people to buy more of the good, but at the same time there is relatively little incentive for producers to supply it. As a consequence there is a shortage; the product disappears from shelves, inventories are drawn down, or people who provide the services are swamped with customers. The inevitable result of this situation is an upward pressure on price. Some buyers will not be able to obtain as much of the product as they would like and are likely to offer sellers a somewhat higher price if they will sell to them rather than to someone else. Other buyers, in order to remain competitive, must also offer higher prices. Of course, sellers, seeing the shortage and realizing they can sell all they produce at a higher price, are likely to be more than happy to cooperate in the process by asking for higher prices. Thus we see that if price is below the equilibrium, there will be an upward pressure on price caused by the resulting shortage.

Demand shifts

As explained in Chapter 3, an increase in demand means that people wish to buy a larger quantity for any given price or will pay a higher price for a given quantity. An increase in demand is illustrated by an increase or shift to the right by the demand curve, as shown by the shift from D_1 to D_2 in Figure 6–2. Notice in this case

FIGURE 6–2
The effects of shifts in demand on equilibrium price and quantity

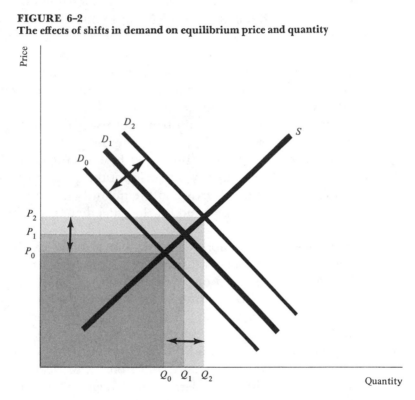

that both the equilibrium price and quantity increase. A decrease in demand, illustrated by the shift in demand from D_1 to D_0 in Figure 6–2, results in a decrease in the equilibrium price and quantity. Also recall from Chapter 3 that there are five main demand shifters. Let us now consider each in turn to see how they affect price and quantity in the product market.

1. CHANGE IN PRICES OF RELATED GOODS

A. Substitutes. As explained in Chapter 3, an increase in the price of a substitute has the effect of shifting the demand curve for a good to the right, as illustrated by the shift in demand from D_1 to D_2 in Figure 6–2. For example, if the price of Volkswagens increases, car buyers begin to substitute lower-priced Japanese- and American-built cars in their place. As a result there will be an increase in the demand for Japanese and American autos. Consequently, the equilibrium price and quantity of the goods in question both increase. As people switch away from the higher-priced substitute toward the good depicted in Figure 6–2, the demand for the good increases and as a result consumers end up paying somewhat more for it while they increase the amount purchased. The increased demand for the good is what causes its price to increase.

The opposite occurs if a substitute decreases in price. As people turn to the lower-priced substitute, the demand for the good in question decreases. This is illustrated by the shift from D_1 to D_0 in Figure 6–2. Consequently, the price of the good in question decreases along with the decrease in the quantity exchanged. In this case it is the decreased demand for the good that causes the price to decline.

It is interesting to note that shifts in demand resulting from changes in the price of a substitute cause the price of the good to move in the same direction as the substitute. Thus the prices of two or more goods that consumers regard as close substitutes tend to rise and fall together.

B. Complements. An increase in the price of a complementary good causes the demand for the good in question to decrease, as illustrated by the shift in demand from D_1 to D_0 in Figure 6–2. The increase in the price of the complementary good causes people to buy less of it and as a result they also buy less of the good depicted in Figure 6–2. For example, an increase in the price of gasoline, which can be considered a complement to automobiles, can be expected to decrease the demand for automobiles, especially those that offer the lowest gas mileage. In this case the price of the good in question (gas-guzzlers in this example) decreases along with a decrease in quantity exchanged.

As expected, the opposite occurs when the price of a complement decreases. This prompts people to increase their purchases of the complement, and in so doing they increase their purchase of the good in question. The increase in demand, illustrated by the shift from D_1 to D_2 in Figure 6–2, causes both the price and quantity of the good to increase.

2. CHANGE IN MONEY INCOMES

As explained in Chapter 3, an increase in income causes an increase in demand for so-called superior goods. The shift, depicted by the increase in demand from D_1 to D_2 in Figure 6–2, causes both price and quantity to increase. For example, an increase in incomes can be expected to increase the demand for luxury cars such as Cadillacs, Lincoln Continentals, and Mercedeses. For inferior goods such as old-fashioned washboards, the opposite occurs. In this case the increase in income causes demand to decrease, which in turn causes both price and quantity to decrease.

A decrease in money incomes such as occurs under conditions of increased unemployment has the opposite impact on demand. In this case, the demand for superior goods decreases, causing a decrease in both price and quantity, whereas the demand for inferior goods increases, resulting in an increase in both price and quantity. Hence during periods of generally depressed economic conditions, not all industries are likely to suffer a decrease in sales. Those that supply inferior goods may enjoy an increase in demand, such as experienced by washboard makers during the 1975 recession. When washing machines broke down some people decided to get along temporarily with the more labor-intensive washing technique until the employment picture brightened.

3. CHANGE IN CONSUMER EXPECTATIONS

Circumstances that cause people to expect higher prices and/or incomes in the future will in turn cause demand to increase and have the effect of increasing both price and quantity. It is interesting to note that the mere expectation of a price increase, which causes consumers to step up their purchases (increase demand), may be enough to cause the increase to occur. By the same token, circumstances that prompt people to expect lower prices or incomes in the future have the effect of decreasing demand, causing current price and quantity to decline.

4. CHANGE IN TASTES AND PREFERENCES

By now it is probably evident that a change in tastes or preferences that prompts people to increase the demand for a good or service will result in an increase in both price and quantity. For example, the resurgence in popularity of blue denim clothing in the late 1960s and early 1970s resulted in an increase in demand for this good, causing an increase in both its price and quantity exchanged. Conversely, a change in tastes away from a good will have the opposite effect of decreasing its demand, causing a decline in both price and quantity.

5. CHANGE IN POPULATION

As noted in Chapter 3 an increase in population causes demand to increase. As a result price and quantity both will increase as long as supply does not increase along with the increase in demand. Under normal conditions of long-run population growth, both demand and supply are gradually increasing due in the latter case to an increase in the number or size of firms. Probably the most noticeable effect of an increase in population growth alone is in an area of rapidly increasing population such as occurred near the Alaska pipeline or in the rapidly expanding coal mining areas of the West. Of course, it is not unheard of for certain areas or regions to experience a decline in population because of migration, or in other times and places because of plagues and famines. In this situation price and quantity decline as a result of the decrease in demand.

These five demand shifters are those most common to goods and services. As mentioned in Chapter 3, however, there may be other shifters that also cause demand to change, thereby influencing price and quantity. An important one is a change in the legal status of a good or service. We will consider the market for illegal goods and services later in this chapter.

Supply shifts

As explained in Chapter 5, an increase in supply means that producers are willing to place more on the market at any given price or are willing to sell the same quantity for a lower price. An increase in supply is illustrated by the shift from S_1 to S_2 in Figure 6–3. Notice in this case that the equilibrium price decreases but the quantity increases. A decrease in supply, illustrated by the shift in supply from S_1 to S_0 in Figure 6–3, results in an increase in the equilibrium price and a decrease in quantity. Also recall from Chapter 5 that there are five main supply shifters. Let us now consider each in turn to see how they affect price and quantity in the product market.

1. CHANGE IN INPUT PRICES

We know from the discussion in Chapter 5 that an increase in the prices of inputs increases the cost of production and decreases product supply. Because of the increase in costs producers will supply a given quantity only if they receive a higher price to cover the increase in costs. The result is to decrease supply or shift it to the left as illustrated by the shift from S_1 to S_0 in Figure 6–3. As a result, the equilibrium price increases while quantity decreases. In this case consumers respond to the higher production cost and price by reducing their purchases. For example, in the early 1970s the supply of beef shifted to the left (decreased) in response to an increase in the price of feed grains. Because of the increase in the price of beef, consumers reduced their purchases of this product by substituting other types of meat or protein sources for it. Conversely a decrease in the price of an input results in an increase in supply, as shown by the shift from S_1 to S_2 in Figure 6–3. In this case, the product price decreases and quantity increases. It is interesting to note in both these cases that the price of the product changes in the same direction as the price of the input. When an input becomes more costly, so do the products it helps to produce.

2. CHANGE IN THE PRICE OF OTHER PRODUCTS

Most firms can and do produce more than one product or at least one type of product. When the price of strawberries increases,

FIGURE 6–3
The effects of shifts in supply on equilibrium price and quantity

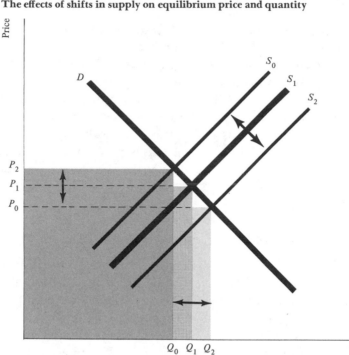

for example, some tomato producers may switch to strawberries, causing a decrease in the supply of tomatoes. The shift to the left of the tomato supply curve, as shown by the shift from S_1 to S_0 in Figure 6–3, causes the price of tomatoes to increase and the quantity to decrease. Conversely a decrease in the price of strawberries would cause an increase in the supply of tomatoes. Notice that prices of goods that are substitutes in production also tend to rise and fall together, as was true on the demand side of the market.

3. CHANGE IN PRODUCER EXPECTATIONS OF FUTURE PRICES

For goods that can be stored, an expected increase in price is likely to result in a decrease in the current supply placed on the market. Understandably, producers will hold back part of their output, hoping to obtain a higher price for it in the future. The decrease in current supply will in turn cause the current price to increase, while the quantity exchanged declines. The opposite occurs when producers expect a future decline in the price of the product. As is evident, the mere expectation of a price increase is enough to precipitate an increase, or vice versa. For example, if a forecaster predicts higher wheat prices in the future and a sizable proportion of producers believe the forecast, some price increase is likely to occur. This is known as a *self-fulfilling prophecy.*

4. CHANGE IN TECHNOLOGY

As pointed out in Chapter 5, a change in technology, if it is adopted, always has the effect of increasing supply because it reduces production costs. If costs were not reduced from what they would otherwise be, producers would have no incentive to adopt the new technology. The increase in supply as a result causes the price of the product to decline and the quantity exchanged to increase. Bear in mind that in this case we are talking about the output of a given quality. If the new technology results in an increase in quality of the product, the price may not decrease. But in any event, consumers are getting more for their money than before the change in technology.

5. CHANGE IN NUMBER OF PRODUCERS

Other things being equal, an increase in the number of producers of a given size at any given price causes the supply curve of a product to increase. The same phenomenon can occur if the average size of the firms in the market increases. As more firms come into the market, supply shifts to the right, price declines, and quantity increases. The opposite occurs when the number or size of firms decreases. In Chapters 7 and 8, we will see that changes in the number of firms in response to pure profits, or losses, play a key role in either competing away pure profits or restoring at least normal profits.

These five supply shifters are those most common to goods and services. As noted in Chapter 5, there may be other factors that cause supply to shift. In agricultural production, weather represents an important supply shifter. As expected, unfavorable weather causes supply to decrease, resulting in a higher price and smaller quantity, whereas unusually good growing conditions have the opposite effect.

Simultaneous shifts in demand and supply

To simplify the discussion in the preceding two sections, we considered only one shifter at a time. We have no guarantee, of course, that actual market situations will be so simple. One or more of the demand shifters may be operating in the market at the same time as one or more of the supply shifters. For example, an increase in money incomes may cause an increase in demand at the same time as an increase in wage rates results in a decrease in supply. You may recognize this condition as what takes place during inflation. Other combinations of demand and supply shifts also are possible. Therefore, it will be useful to list and illustrate the various possible combinations of demand and supply shifts in order to observe what happens to price and quantity under each circumstance. There are four possible combinations of demand and supply shifts: (1) demand increases, supply increases; (2) demand increases, supply decreases; (3) demand decreases, supply increases; and (4) demand decreases, supply decreases. Each of these shifts can, of course, be caused by any one (or more) of the five demand shifters and by any one (or more) of the five supply shifters. These four possible combinations are illustrated by Figure 6–4.

Looking first at panel A of Figure 6–4, note that an increase in both demand and supply causes quantity to increase. However, in this example the upward pressure on price caused by the increase in demand is exactly offset by the downward pressure exerted by the increase in supply. Consequently, price remains constant. Of course it would be possible to construct the example so that price either increases or decreases. If demand increased more than supply increased, the price would rise, whereas price would decline if supply increased more than demand. Thus we can say only that the direction of price movement in this case is uncertain; it may stay the same, increase, or decrease. This example depicts the long-run behavior of most goods. Demand for most items, at least large categories of goods, tends to increase over time because of the growth

FIGURE 6-4
**The effects of simultaneous shifts in demand and supply on equilibrium price
and quantity**

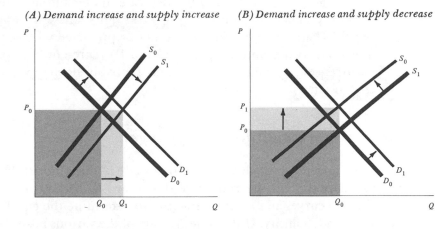

(A) Demand increase and supply increase

(B) Demand increase and supply decrease

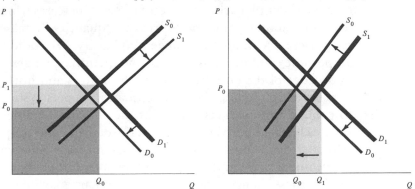

(C) Demand decrease and supply increase

(D) Demand decrease and supply decrease

in income and population. Supply tends to increase because of the growth in the number or size of firms.

The same general idea applies to the other three combinations. In panel B the demand increase and supply decrease both exert an upward pressure on price so that price increases. But they exert offsetting pressure on quantity, so it is not possible to say how quantity will change, if at all. As mentioned, this example depicts the behavior of markets during inflationary times because of the increase of money incomes and input prices.

In panel C the decrease in demand and increase in supply both exert a downward pressure on price, causing a certain decrease in price. But these shifts exert offsetting pressures on quantity, so it is not possible to say what happens to quantity; perhaps there will be no change as shown. Finally the decrease in demand and decrease in supply shown by panel D cause a certain decrease in quantity, but the change in price (if any) cannot be predicted with certainty. These last two examples (panels C and D) represent less common occurrences, although they can and probably do happen in specific instances.

Summary of price and quantity changes

By now it is probably evident that there is much more to demand and supply than the respective downward and upward slopes of the two curves and their interaction to determine the equilibrium price and quantity. Unless one is aware of the various possible shifts that can and do take place in demand and supply, there may appear to be no order to markets. Sometimes price increases while quantity decreases; at other times both price and quantity increase. Or price may increase without any change in quantity. We could go on with all possible combinations of price and quantity changes. But with a knowledge of the demand and supply shifters and how they affect demand and supply, and price and quantity, a person should be able to explain why markets behave as they do and be able to predict future changes for given changes in the demand and supply shifters. Although it is better to utilize a diagram each time you wish to determine a price and/or quantity change rather than just memorizing these changes, the following summary may be of some help in drawing together material from the preceding two sections.

Change in:		Resulting change in:	
Demand	*Supply*	*Price*	*Quantity*
Increase	None	Increase	Increase
Decrease	None	Decrease	Decrease
None	Increase	Decrease	Increase
None	Decrease	Increase	Decrease
Increase	Increase	Uncertain	Increase
Increase	Decrease	Increase	Uncertain
Decrease	Increase	Decrease	Uncertain
Decrease	Decrease	Uncertain	Decrease

Government in the market

Our discussion thus far on the determination of price and quantity and their changes has focused largely on market-oriented factors. It is well known, of course, that government at all levels has seen fit to intervene in markets either through direct action such as setting price or through legal regulations that affect buyers and/or sellers. It is no secret either that a great deal of disagreement exists regarding the optimum amount of government intervention. People with a fairly conservative political viewpoint tend to believe that markets are capable of running themselves within, of course, the legal framework of our society. Those with a more liberal viewpoint tend to prefer a greater amount of government intervention in markets. We will not argue one point of view over the other; instead we will attempt to identify the major types of government intervention and briefly evaluate their effects.

ESTABLISHING THE "RULES OF THE GAME"

Alhough we will not dwell at length on the legal aspects of markets, it is important to note that in order for any market to function properly, both buyers and sellers must obey certain rules. An important function of the government in any market is to establish basic rules of behavior and enforce them.

Perhaps the most basic rule is the law requiring buyers to pay sellers for goods purchased or services rendered. For many people this rule would not be necessary; payment of one's debts is a matter of personal integrity. But for others, payment would not be forthcoming without the threat of legal action and punishment. A few, of course, still attempt to gain ownership without payment; we call these people thieves. Without reasonable assurance of payment for goods or services, sellers would find it virtually impossible to remain in business. Those that did remain would be required to charge higher prices so that the people who paid would cover the loss from those who did not. Needless to say, a market characterized by gross nonpayment by buyers would soon break down. Honest people would quickly grow tired of paying for the goods and services consumed by their dishonest neighbors.

A second important role of government in the operation of the market is to provide information about products to buyers or to require that this information be made available. As noted in Chapter 2, a consumer maximizes utility by equating the marginal utilities per dollar for all goods purchased. If information about the product or its price is lacking or wrong, it is not possible to compare the marginal utility per dollar of the product with the possible alternatives. Most of us have purchased goods or services that we would not have bought had we known their true characteristics or price. The recent truth-in-packaging and truth-in-lending legislation is an attempt to improve buyer information in the market. As a rule it is much easier and more successful to provide buyers with correct information and let competition take its course than to attempt to regulate sellers closely.

Government also is active in setting standards and testing products before they are put on the market. This is particularly important for potentially harmful products such as drugs and food. Harmful products would eventually come to the attention of buyers and be forced off the market, but needless injury or death can be avoided if these products are identified beforehand.

The increase in awareness about pollution and society's attempts to do something about this problem require some additional rules of the game. Each firm operating independently tries to produce at the lowest possible cost in order to maximize profits and compete with other firms. As a result each firm cannot afford to spend much money on pollution control devices unless all other firms do likewise. There will likely be some firms that choose not to invest in pollution control equipment in order to gain a competitive advantage. Therefore, if society wishes to clean up the environment, it is necessary for the government to intervene in the market and require that all firms meet certain clean air and water standards. We will see in the following two chapters that such action increases the prices of the industries affected, but this is the choice that society must make. In an industrialized society, clean air and water are not free goods.

CEILING PRICES

There are times, generally during war, when society believes that the prices of certain goods or services are too high. This belief probably stems from the idea that excessive pure profits are being earned in the production or supply of these items. As a consequence the government may enact legislation that establishes maximum prices of certain goods or services, making it illegal for suppliers to sell any of the regulated items for a higher price.

The prices that are established are known as *ceiling prices* because the selling price is not supposed to rise above this maximum. The ceiling price is, of course, below the market equilibrium price, otherwise it would not be a ceiling or have any effect on the market.

The consequences of a ceiling price can be most easily illustrated by the use of the traditional demand-supply diagram, as in Figure 6–5, where P_c represents the ceiling price, which is below the market equilibrium price, P_e. You will note at P_c that the quantity demanded, Q_d is greater than the quantity supplied, Q_s. At price P_e, people want to buy more than is being offered for sale. Thus some buyers will have to settle for less than they would like. How should the available supply be allocated?

One option open to the government is to allocate the available quantity on a first-come, first-served basis. The problem with this

FIGURE 6–5
Ceiling price in a market

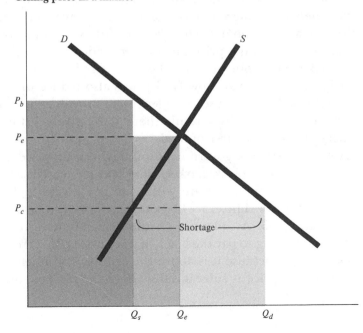

approach is that it is very wasteful. Countless hours are spent by people standing in line in order to obtain a portion of the scarce item. The total output of goods and services to society could be increased if people devoted their energies to production rather than to standing in line or attempting to bribe the distributors of the product.

An alternative and more efficient method of allocating the available output is to issue ration stamps more or less equally among the population. Although many people cannot buy as much as they would like under this scheme, at least there is a little for everyone, and it eliminates a large part of the wasted effort mentioned above. At any rate, it is important to recognize that a ceiling price inevitably creates a shortage in the market and, as a consequence, makes it necessary to impose some sort of rationing scheme.

A second important side effect of a ceiling price is that it reduces the quantity produced of the already scarce commodity. As you can see in Figure 6–5, before the ceiling price, output is at Q_e, whereas after the ceiling is imposed, output declines to Q_s. This happens because the lower price provides an incentive for suppliers to reduce their production of the good or service in question, perhaps increasing their output of nonregulated items.

Because of food shortages and subsequent high food prices, the governments of numerous developing nations have set ceiling prices on food as a way to hold down inflation. However, from our analysis of the effect of ceiling prices, it is quite evident that such a policy only makes the problem worse, because it reduces even more the meager output of food. Low food prices also reduce the incentive for public and private research agencies to provide new technology for agriculture, and as a result there is relatively little increase (shift) in the supply curve of food.

A third effect of a government-imposed ceiling price is the creation of a so-called black market, where people who desire a larger amount than their quota are willing to pay a very high price in order to obtain it. The exact black-market price can be determined from Figure 6–5. At quantity Q_s the demand curve tells us that people are willing to pay the black-market price (P_b). Of course, this price is illegal because it is above the ceiling. You might notice as well that this price is substantially above the market equilibrium price, P_e. Thus the black-market price is not a valid indicator of the price that would prevail without the price ceiling.

SUPPORT PRICES

In other situations society has decided that the prices of certain items are too low, and as a result government action is undertaken to keep prices above the market equilibrium. The motivation for this action generally stems from a belief that producers of the supported products suffer from low incomes and that raising the price of the products they sell will in turn raise their incomes.

FIGURE 6–6
Support price in the market

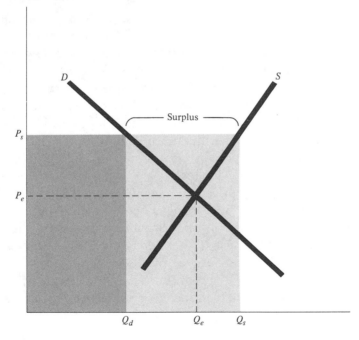

The effect of a support price in the market can also be seen by use of the demand-supply diagram in Figure 6–6. At the support price, P_s, the quantity supplied, Q_s, exceeds the quantity demanded, Q_d. As a result there is a surplus in the market amounting to the difference between Q_s and Q_d. The only way the government can maintain the support price, therefore, is to buy up this surplus and keep it off the market. Otherwise the excess output will exert a downward pressure on price and drive it down toward the equilibrium.

The best example of support prices and their effects can be seen in U.S. agriculture as well as that of many other developed nations. The clusters of grain bins that used to be seen along the highways of the country were visible evidence of this surplus. In the early 1970s, the large increase in agricultural exports, particularly to the Soviet Union, virtually eliminated the surpluses that had built up during the 1950s and 1960s.

The existence of a support price provides an incentive for producers to produce even more of the already overabundant product. At the equilibrium price, P_e, Q_e is supplied, whereas at the higher support price, P_s, Q_s is offered for sale. In an attempt to reduce this surplus, the government restricted the use of land by those producers who wished to sell at the higher support price. Unfortunately, restricting land has not been a very successful means of restricting output because producers have been able to increase output by increasing the use of inputs that substitute for land, particularly fertilizer, herbicides, and improved varieties of crops.

The ability of support price programs to substantially raise the income of producers who really need help is increasingly being questioned. Support price programs in general have not been effective as an income-supporting scheme because the low-income producers tend to be the small producers. Doubling the price of wheat from $2 to $4 per bushel adds only $1,000 per year to the income of a 500-bushel-per-year producer, but it adds $40,000 per year to a 20,000-bushel producer. Thus price support programs have a tendency to help high-income producers more than their low-income counterparts.

SALES AND EXCISE TAXES

A common method of obtaining revenue utilized by governments, both state and federal, is sales and excise taxes. By and large these taxes are levied as a percentage of the selling price of the goods or services they cover. Some items, particularly those that society regards as luxuries or nonessentials, such as liquor or jewelry, may be covered by more than one such tax. Other items, such as food and clothing, may be taxed at a lower rate or not at all.

The effect of sales and excise taxes can also be evaluated by the simple demand-supply diagram. A convenient way of thinking about a sales or excise tax is that it increases the price of a given quantity of the item taxed. In other words, we can think of a sales or excise tax as decreasing the supply or shifting the market supply curve upward and to the left. Because of the tax, a given quantity will cost more to buy. The imposition of such a tax is illustrated in Figure 6–7, in which the supply curve after the tax is represented by S_0.[2]

FIGURE 6–7
Effect of a sales or excise tax

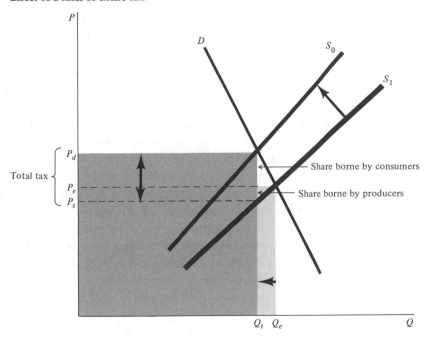

Notice, first, that the market equilibrium price increases from P_e to P_d after the tax is imposed. But it is also important to recognize that with a downward sloping demand and an upward sloping supply, the price rise to consumers is less than the amount of the tax. Figure 6–7 shows that the total tax at quantity Q_t is the same as the distance from P_s to P_d on the vertical axis. This is the amount that the supply curve has been shifted up because of the tax.

However, it can also be seen that the price that producers obtain after the tax is reduced by the distance between P_e and P_s. Although producers (sellers) collect price P_d from buyers, they must relinquish an amount equal to the tax, leaving them with a lower net price than before the tax, as long as the demand curve is downward sloping. Producers are left with a lower net price after the tax than before because they do not decrease quantity enough to push the selling price up by the full amount of the tax. Even though producers suffer a reduction in profits due to the lower net price received, they would suffer an even greater reduction in profits by forcing the price up by the full amount of the tax. The reason for this result is the large decrease in quantity sold that would occur if the price were increased by the full amount of the tax. Profits depend on both price and quantity. We will see this more clearly in the next two chapters.

Because of the increase in price to consumers and the decrease in the net price received by producers, it is sometimes said that consumers bear part of the burden of the tax according to the increase in the price they must pay, while producers bear a part of the burden according to the decrease in the net price they receive. In the particular example depicted by Figure 6–7, consumers bear a slightly greater share of the burden than producers. Over the long run, however, supply is likely to become more elastic, resulting in a greater share of the tax being borne by consumers. In this case the more elastic long-run supply curve shifts up by the amount of the tax and raises the price paid by consumers by almost as much as the tax.

Because of the reduction in the quantity of a taxed item demanded and supplied, the use of selective sales or excise taxes has the effect of distorting the output mix of goods and services produced in an economy. The quantities of nontaxed or less heavily taxed items increase at the expense of those items taxed at higher rates. This outcome has been of some concern to economists because it causes a reduction in the value of output to society from a given amount of resources used. An intuitive explanation for this outcome is that resources are pushed into lines of production whose products are valued less highly by society than the taxed items. We will have more to say about the effect of resource allocation on total value of output in Chapter 7.

Sales and excise taxes also have been criticized for being "regressive" in nature, that is, for falling most heavily on low-income people. This will occur if low-income people spend a larger share of their income on the taxed items than their higher-income counterparts do over the long run. An attempt is made to mitigate this problem by taxing "nonessentials," such as alcoholic beverages, tobacco, and luxury items, at relatively high rates and not taxing such "necessities" as food and clothing, or taxing them at lower rates. However, this differential in tax rates still causes a distortion in the output mix of goods and services mentioned above.

ILLEGAL GOODS OR SERVICES

Most societies enact laws that forbid the use of certain goods or services. Laws of this kind generally stem from the belief that consumption of the illegal items harms either the individual who consumes them or the people with whom the person comes in contact. Examples of illegal goods and services in the United States at the present time include such things as mind-distorting drugs, pornographic literature, prostitution, and certain kinds of gambling. Unfortunately, passing a law against the use of a good or service does not eliminate the demand for it. Indeed, there would be no need for such a law in the first place if the demand for the good or service did not exist.

Just as for any other good or service, we can visualize both a supply and demand for the illegal item. We have no reason to believe that its demand curve will not slope downward and to the right, like any other market demand curve. There probably will not be as many demanders in such a market because most people do not buy illegal items. Moreover, as the equilibrium price increases we would expect the number of people who buy in these markets to decline, as well as the quantity demanded per person.

Regarding the market supply of illegal goods, there is no reason to believe that higher prices would not bring forth additional quantities. As long as there is a demand for the item, there will always be entrepreneurs ready to supply it for a profit. And as prices increase, so do profits; this provides even more incentive for the illicit suppliers to do their thing.

Although the market demand and supply of illegal goods and services can be represented by the traditional downward sloping and upward sloping lines, respectively, there is one important consideration with such goods and services that is not present for their legal counterparts—the penalty for getting caught. We can think of the penalty as a demand shifter if it applies only to the person consuming the good or service. If the penalty applies only to the supplier, it will be primarily a supply shifter. And if it applies to both parties, we would expect the penalty to shift both demand and supply.

In general, the imposition of a penalty or an increase in the harshness of the penalty will decrease (shift to the left) the demand, the supply, or both. For example, imposing a "slap on the wrist" or a suspended sentence will not decrease the demand for marijuana nearly as much as a definite five-year prison term. Thus we can expect that increasing the harshness of the penalty on buyers will shift demand to the left, reducing the market price and the quantity exchanged, as illustrated in Figure 6–8.

On the other hand, if there is an increase in the penalty on suppliers, we can expect a decrease in supply. For example, many "ladies of the evening" likely would find alternative ways of making a living if the penalty for practicing this trade consisted of a $10,000 fine compared with a $100 fine. The effect of a penalty on suppliers is illustrated in Figure 6–8(B).

Although a penalty on either the demander or supplier will decrease the quantity of an illegal good or service, the price change will depend on who is penalized. Goods or services for which only the supplier is penalized will tend to have a higher price than would exist in a free market. Most illegal goods or services fit this description. It is not clear why most societies have penalized suppliers more harshly than demanders for dealing with illegal goods and services. Imposing a more severe penalty on consumers will lower the market price from what it would be in a free market, or from what it would be if only suppliers were penalized.

FIGURE 6–8
Effects of penalties in the market for illegal goods and services

(A) Penalty on the consumer

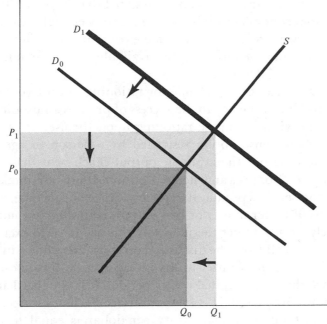

(B) Penalty on the supplier

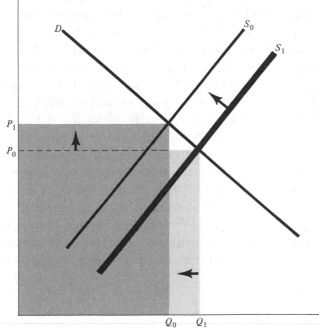

The rationing function of price

At the beginning of this book we stated that scarcity is the major reason for economics to exist. There is rarely enough of anything to bring everyone to a state of complete contentment. Thus there has to be a scheme for rationing the available output among all who want a piece of the pie.

The most successful scheme for rationing output yet devised is price. No doubt the key to the success of price as a rationing device is that individuals impose rationing upon themselves rather than having their consumption restricted by a person or agency with power to dole out the available output. Each of us has a limited capacity to produce, and hence we must limit our intake of the goods and services produced in society. Since our income, measured in terms of either money or real output, is limited, we must spend it wisely, trying to get the most for what we have to exchange.

As you recall from the discussion on consumer choice in Chapter 2, each person maximizes utility or satisfaction by allocating purchases so that the marginal utility per dollar is equalized among all the things purchased. If a good or service becomes scarce, its price will rise. Since marginal utility per dollar is equal to marginal utility divided by price, a rise in price decreases the marginal utility per dollar, which in turn provides an incentive to reduce its use and look for other things that will yield more marginal utility per dollar. No one has to tell us or order us to do so; we do it of our own accord. Moreover, there is no incentive for us to cheat by attempting to consume more. Even though we are free to consume a relatively large quantity of a scarce item, it is irrational to do so because it would just reduce our overall satisfaction.

Thus market price is an effective rationing device. It rations available output efficiently and automatically, and scarce resources do not have to be devoted to rationing the available output. This is a serious mistake made by some developing nations that have decided to use too many of their meager resources to ration what little they have. Letting market prices accomplish the rationing task, and freeing resources to produce goods and services, has proved to be a wiser policy. If government agencies do the rationing, it can also be very profitable for those who obtain the goods to spend a great deal of time and resources attempting to obtain a larger slice of the pie. Market price, being impersonal, does not respond to favor or bribe.

The fact that price rations the available output automatically and efficiently does not imply, however, that everyone is happy or satisfied with the prevailing price or resulting allocation. Indeed, it is likely that most sellers would like the price to be higher and most buyers would like it to be lower. When there is extreme dissatisfaction with price, by either buyers or sellers, the government may step in and establish a ceiling or support price. It is important to remember, though, that establishing a ceiling price takes away the rationing function of price, generally leaving it in the hands of government agencies.

The allocating function of price

In addition to rationing the available output, market price serves to allocate the available resources to their most valuable use. For example, if buyers reduce their demand for a product, its price will fall as demand shifts left and intersects supply at a lower level. The lower price serves as a signal to producers, telling them that consumers no longer desire as much of a certain product. Producers, seeing their profits decline as the price falls, begin to search for other things to produce that consumers might desire more. This action on the part of producers does not have to be motivated by any love or empathy for consumers but rather by a desire to improve their own incomes and purchasing power.

Since market price serves to allocate resources between alternative goods and services, it might be expected that government policies that change market prices, such as ceiling or support prices on selected items, would also change the pattern of resource allocation in the economy. Consider a ceiling price. If the price of a good or service is maintained at an artificially low level, producers have an incentive to look for more profitable items to produce, and there is a tendency for resources to leave these areas in search of more profitable opportunities elsewhere.

Unfortunately, this outcome is just the opposite of what we would like to happen. If the price of an item is relatively high, it is an indication that the item is scarce relative to the demand of consumers. But the imposition of a ceiling price has the effect of driving some resources away from its production, making the item even more scarce than it was before the ceiling. An example of the effect of ceiling prices is provided by rent controls in New York City. Not only has a "shortage" been created for apartments, particularly in the central part of the city, but landlords also have had little incentive to maintain their buildings, thus hastening the deterioration of living units in the inner city. Resources that otherwise would have gone to the repair and upkeep of these rent-controlled buildings have gone elsewhere in search of higher returns. A similar phenomenon occurred in the petroleum industry during the 1970s due to the ceiling price on this product. In this case, however, the shortage was made up by the increase in imports from other countries.

A parallel but opposite problem occurs when the price is set artificially high, that is, when there is a support price. In this case the equilibrium price is low because the supply is large relative to the demand of consumers. The existence of a support price that is higher than the equilibrium price serves to draw even more resources into the production of an already abundant good. Again the result is just the opposite of what we would like to see.

Sales and excise taxes also have an impact on the allocation of resources. By "driving a wedge" between the prices that consumers pay and producers receive, a sales or excise tax has the effect of reducing the profitability of producing the taxed item, and thus it has a tendency to drive some resources away from the production of the item to which it is applied. The higher price that consumers pay also tends to discourage its use.

Of course, market prices in general do not allocate resources to the production of public goods and services. Many such products, such as roads, police protection, and the military, do not even have a market price. The allocation of resources to public goods, then, has to be done mainly "by hand." The objective of those in charge of this allocation should be to produce the amount and mix of public goods and services that maximize the welfare of society, given the wishes of people for private goods and services. This is a very difficult job, not only because no one really knows what such an optimal allocation is, but also because it is likely to differ for different people. For example, the more politically conservative members of society tend to prefer a smaller proportion of all output to be public goods, or at least goods and services provided by government, than do their more liberal counterparts. The anticipated benefits from public goods in relation to the amount of taxes one has to pay also can be expected to influence a person's desire for such goods. Few people like to pay for public goods and services that do not appear to be a "good buy" in relation to the private goods and services available. Of course, people who receive public goods without having to pay substantial taxes for them are not as likely to call them a "bad buy."

As we saw earlier, market prices provide the signals that enable producers to decide upon the amount and mix of private goods and services produced in the economy. The signals that guide the action of public decision makers who are faced with the task of allocating resources to public goods and services are much more varied and complex in nature. Sometimes a "shortage" of such goods can be directly observed, as in the case of crowding in our national parks or congestion on our streets and highways. In other cases the representatives of citizen groups, such as the Sierra Club or Common Cause, may petition public decision makers to reorder their priorities. Professional lobbyists who represent special-interest groups are also likely to influence the amount and mix of public goods produced. It is also common for people with a special interest to demonstrate or picket an agency of government in an attempt to change the allocation of resources. Sometimes the demonstrations become violent and turn into riots. Needless to say, riots tend to be a destructive way to reallocate resources.

In communistic economies, most of the resources used in the production of both public and private goods are allocated by direct orders of the government. One drawback of allocating resources by political decree as opposed to price signals is that it often forces people to act against their own self-interests, which, to put it mildly, tends to dampen incentives. As an extreme example, you would not likely be very happy if a government official ordered you to quit college or your current job and take a job in the coal mines because of a shortage of fuel. Nor would you likely be very happy if you were ordered to use coal rather than fuel oil or gas to heat your dwelling. On the other hand, if the wages of coal miners rose substantially relative to other occupations, many people would voluntarily enter this occupation in order to increase their own incomes. Similarly, if the price of oil and gas increased relative to that of coal, there would be a tendency for people to voluntarily increase their use of coal while conserving on oil and gas.

Time for adjustment

When dealing with prices and markets it is important to realize that change is seldom instantaneous. On the demand side of the market, we know from experience that a change in price may not precipitate an immediate response. For example, if the price of our favorite toothpaste increases, it may take us a certain amount of time to even find out about it. The first time we buy another tube the price may seem a bit high, but not having considered another brand, we go ahead and buy it. By the time we are ready for the next tube, however, we might well compare the prices of various brands; if our favorite brand is out of line with the others, we might try a lower-priced alternative.

The same process can go on in the event of a price decrease of a good or service. If we are not already buying it, the lower price will not likely come to our immediate attention. After we have had time to find out about the lower price and something about the good itself, we may give it a try. It is reasonable to believe, therefore, that the longer time consumers have to adjust to a price change, the more responsive they will be.

This idea can be represented by demand curves with differing slopes or elasticities. If only a short time is taken for adjustment to a price change, the demand curve will be relatively steep, or less elastic, than if a long period of time is considered. This is illustrated in Figure 6–9, where D_s represents a demand with only a short time to adjust, whereas D_l represents a demand where adjustment by consumers takes place over a longer period. If supply shifts from S_1 to S_0 (decrease) and price increases, some consumers begin to decrease their purchases. The quantity sold then begins to decline, approaching Q_{s0} rather quickly. However, as more and more consumers adjust to this price increase, the quantity decreases further, eventually reaching Q_{l0}.

FIGURE 6–9
Effect of time for adjustment on product demand

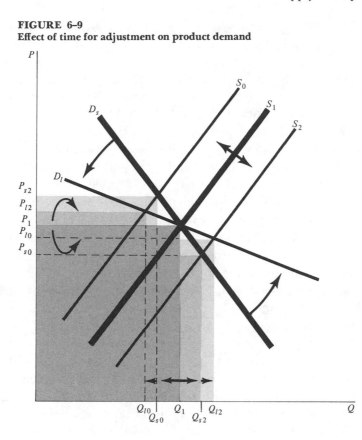

Figure 6–9 also can be used to represent a price decrease that might take place following an increase in supply, as illustrated by supply shifting from S_1 to S_2. Here a few consumers increase their purchases soon after the price fall, so that the quantity increases to Q_{s2}. Then, as more consumers adjust, the quantity continues to increase, eventually approaching Q_{l2}.

It is interesting to note as well the pattern of price changes that take place. With a decrease in supply, the price moves upward rather rapidly. Then, as consumers are able to adjust their purchases toward other products, the price levels off and even decreases somewhat. With an increase in supply, the price falls rather abruptly, but as consumers take note of this and adjust their purchases toward this product, the price reaches a minimum and begins to ease upward slightly.

Time for adjustment is perhaps even more important for supply than demand. There are two reasons producers do not adjust immediately to a price change. First, from a technical standpoint, it generally is not physically possible either to acquire fixed inputs rapidly or, because of contractural commitments, to dispose of them quickly. Second, from an economic standpoint, changing the level of production to a sizable extent generally requires additional expense. To increase output, new facilities and equipment will have to be bought and additional personnel hired. Thus producers want to be sure that a price increase will stay in effect for a fairly long period of time before they incur this expense. Similarly, producers who dispose of machines or structures before they have been substantially depreciated may have to bear a substantial loss. Thus producers may try to ride out a period of low prices, hoping for higher prices in the future.

Because of these factors, the elasticity of supply that allows a long period of time to adjust is higher (more elastic) than is elasticity that allows little time to adjust. This is illustrated in Figure 6–10, where price is assumed to change because of shifts in demand. If demand declines, say to D_0, the quantity produced will at first decline relatively little, to Q_{s0}. But if the price remains low for a time, more adjustment will take place, reducing the quantity supplied even more, to Q_{l0}. The same rationale applies to an increase in demand where the quantity supplied increases first to Q_{s2} and later to Q_{l2}.

Notice also, as with demand, that the process of moving to a longer time for adjustment affects the price of the good or service. For example, there is a rather abrupt decline in price as demand decreases, but after producers adjust their production downward, the price eases back up slightly. The same phenomenon can be observed for an increase in demand, only here the price rises rather abruptly and then eases back down a little as producers adjust their production upward.

One important point that should be kept in mind when thinking about this process of adjustment by either producers or consumers is that not every producer or consumer needs to change the quantity produced or consumed when the price changes. All that is required to obtain a market response to a price change is that some people change the quantities they buy or sell. The fact that not

FIGURE 6–10
Effect of time for adjustment on product supply

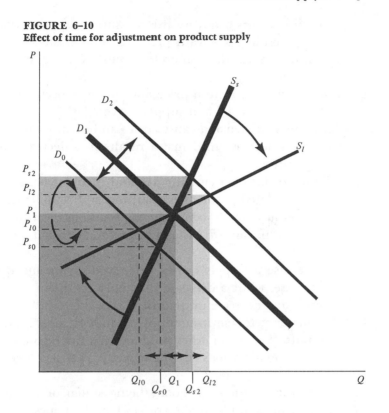

everyone may change the quantity demanded or supplied with a price change has led some people to the erroneous conclusion that price has little effect in the market. Indeed, if everyone reacted to a price change, there would tend to be relatively large changes in the quantities exchanged in markets in response to just minor changes in price.

Main points of Chapter 6

1. Equilibrium price and quantity correspond to the intersection of the demand and supply curves.
2. There will be a surplus in the market if price is above the equilibrium and a shortage if price is below equilibrium.

3. A surplus exerts a downward pressure on price, whereas a shortage results in upward pressure. The existence of either a surplus or shortage therefore pushes price toward the equilibrium.

4. Changes in equilibrium price and quantity occur because of shifts in the demand and supply curves.

5. An increase in demand causes price and quantity to increase, whereas a decrease in demand results in a decrease in price and quantity.

6. The major factors that shift demand include changes in: (*a*) prices of related products (substitutes and complements), (*b*) consumer incomes, (*c*) consumer expectations regarding future prices and income, (*d*) tastes and preferences, and (*e*) population.

7. An increase in supply causes price to decrease and quantity to increase, while a decrease in supply results in an increase in price and decrease in quantity.

8. The major factors shifting supply include changes in: (*a*) price of inputs, (*b*) price of other products that can be produced, (*c*) producer expectations of future prices, (*d*) technology, and (*e*) number of firms.

9. Losses that result from goods being stolen or not paid for must be made up by higher prices paid by honest people.

10. Simultaneous changes in demand and supply can result in a change in price with no change in quantity, or a change in quantity with no change in price.

11. In order to explain and predict market behavior it is necessary to recognize the existence of demand and supply shifts.

12. Ceiling prices create shortages in the market, which makes it necessary for the government to impose some kind of rationing scheme. Black-market activities also result from ceiling prices and rationing.

13. Support prices create surpluses in a market, making it necessary for the government to buy up the surplus and keep it off the market in order to hold price up.

14. In the short run sales and excise taxes on products increase the price paid by consumers and decrease the price received by the producers, but in the long run consumers bear most of the tax.

15. Penalties on buyers of illegal goods or services tend to decrease the demand for these items and lower their price. Penalties on sellers tend to decrease supply and increase market price.

16. Price is a relatively efficient rationing device. Individual consumers voluntarily reduce their purchases of a scarce item as its price rises in order to maximize their utility for a given budget.

17. Price also allocates resources to the goods or services most desired by consumers, since a rising price tends to increase profits for producers and thus provides them with an incentive to produce more of the most wanted items. By the same token a decrease in the desirability of a good or service leads to a fall in its price, which tends to lower the profits of producers and provides them with an incentive to produce things that are more appealing to buyers.

18. The process of adjusting to a price change is not instantaneous. Both buyers and sellers require time to adjust their purchases or production after a price change. Thus demand and supply curves that allow for adequate time to adjust are more elastic than those that do not allow sufficient adjustment time.

Questions for thought and discussion

1. Equilibrium price is the price that makes both buyers and sellers happy. True or false? Explain.

2. Water, one of the basic necessities of life, is in most places very cheap, if not free. Diamonds, on the other hand, very nonessential items in our lives, are very expensive. Can you explain this rather perverse behavior of price?

3. An increase in demand leads to an increase in price, but an increase in price leads to a decrease in demand. What, if anything, is wrong with this statement?

4. State whether each of the following demand shifters would increase or decrease the price of used cars and briefly explain why.
   a. An increase in the price of new cars.
   b. An increase in the price of gasoline.

    c. An increase in incomes (assume used cars are an inferior good).

5. It is common to observe the prices of goods that are close substitutes in consumption rising and falling together. Is this behavior consistent with the principles of demand and supply? Explain.

6. For some goods, such as rooms at summer resorts, both price and quantity increase during certain times of the year. For other products, such as fresh strawberries, price is negatively correlated with quantity. Why does price *increase* when quantity increases for one good while price *decreases* when quantity increases for the other?

7. State whether each of the following supply shifters would increase or decrease the price of tomatoes and briefly explain why.
    a. An increase in wage rates (explicit or implicit).
    b. A decrease in the price of sweet corn, an alternative crop.
    c. The availability of new higher-yielding varieties of tomatoes.

8. It is common to observe the prices of goods that are close substitutes in production rising and falling together. Is this behavior consistent with the principles of demand and supply? Explain.

9. *a.* Is it possible for the equilibrium price of a good or service to change without a change in the equilibrium quantity exchanged in the market? (Assume that neither the demand nor supply curve is perfectly inelastic.) Explain.
    b. Is it possible for the equilibrium quantity of a good or service to change without a change in the equilibrium market price? (Assume that neither the demand nor supply curve is perfectly elastic.) Explain.

10. It is generally believed that the demand for mind-distorting drugs is inelastic. If so, should the mafia be in favor of tighter or looser controls over drug traffic? Explain.

11. The government has the capability of creating either a shortage or a surplus of any good at any time. True or false? Explain.

12. A 10-cent-per-gallon increase in the tax on gasoline will increase the price paid by consumers by the same amount. True or false? Explain.

13. The black-market price of a product is a good indication of its market equilibrium price in the absence of price controls. True or false? Explain.

14. Price controls prohibit price from performing its rationing and allocating functions. True or false? Explain.

15. Long-run demand and supply are more elastic than short-run demand and supply. True or false? Explain.

7

Perfect competition in the product market

Our discussion thus far has focused largely on the fundamentals of demand and supply and the use of these concepts to explain and predict market behavior. In this and the following chapter we will take a closer look at the kinds of business firms that operate in a market economy. As you probably are aware, there is a great deal of diversity among business firms. Some are small, one-person enterprises such as family farms or retail shops. Others are giant corporations employing thousands of people and selling their products throughout the world. To create some order out of this diversity, we will study the characteristics and behavior of different types of firms, beginning in this chapter, with the type of market situation that economists have labeled perfect competition. Agricultural production probably provides the closest example of perfect competition today. Imperfect competition will be the topic of Chapter 8.

The perfectly competitive firm: A price taker

A *perfectly competitive* firm can be defined as one that has no power to alter the price it receives for its product. For this reason, the perfectly competitive firm is sometimes called a *price taker*. The firm takes the price of its product as determined in the market. There are two basic reasons that a perfectly competitive firm must accept the price that is determined by the market: (1) it sells a product that is undifferentiated from the product of all the other firms in the market, and (2) it sells a very small proportion of the total market.

The fact that a perfectly competitive firm sells a product that is indistinguishable from that produced by the other firms in its market means that buyers have no preference for the product of one firm over any other. Thus every firm must sell its product at the price all the other firms are obtaining. Why should buyers pay $4.25 per bushel for wheat from farmer Jones if 10,000 other farmers are selling exactly the same product for $4.00 per bushel? In other words, each producer must conform to the market price.

We know also that because of the downward sloping nature of market demand curves, market price can be changed only if the quantity sold is changed; quantity must decrease to obtain a higher price, or any increase in the quantity demanded must be accompanied by a reduction in price. But because the perfectly competitive firm sells just a minute fraction of the market, each firm cannot alter market price by producing more or less. For example, suppose farmer Jones decides that the market price of wheat is too low. What can he do about it? If he reduces his production by half (a drastic measure for any firm), the total market supply would remain virtually unchanged, because taking a few hundred bushels or even a few thousand bushels from a market in which millions of bushels are traded would have an inperceptible effect; it would be something like taking a handful of sand away from a beach. Thus no matter what quantity the firm decides to produce, within reason, the market price remains the same.

Thus, the characteristic of an undifferentiated product requires each perfectly competitive firm to sell at the same price as all other firms, that is, the market price, and the characteristics of producing just a small fraction of the market means that each perfectly competitive firm has no power to alter the market price.

Demand facing a perfectly competitive seller

We can obtain a better understanding of the relationship between a perfectly competitive firm and the market in which it sells by means of diagrams. The traditional market demand and supply curves are depicted in Figure 7–1(A). These are the curves developed in Chapters 1 through 6. The equilibrium price and quantity that will prevail in this market are denoted by P_e and Q_e. The price that each firm will face, therefore, is P_e if the market is allowed to reach an equilibrium.

FIGURE 7–1
Relationship between the market and the perfectly competitive firm

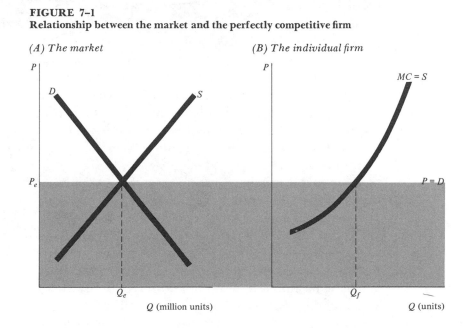

(A) The market   *(B) The individual firm*

The individual perfectly competitive firm operating in this market is represented by Figure 7–1(B). Its supply curve, as we know, is simply the marginal cost (MC) curve above the point where it intersects the average variable cost curve if it is already committed to its fixed costs. The price that the firm can expect to receive for its product is P_e, as determined by market supply and demand. This price, P_e, can be thought of as the demand facing this firm. The price line, P_e in this example, is a demand curve in the sense that it tells the firm what price it will receive for its product. The fact that the demand curve is a perfectly horizontal line (perfectly elastic) means that the firm can produce and sell any output within reason at this price. In other words, the market stands ready to buy any reasonable quantity from this firm at price P_e. Thus the line showing the price is in reality the demand-curve facing this firm.

We should bear in mind, of course, that in an actual market situation, the market price that prevails at any time need not be the equilibrium price. For example, if market demand had recently shifted to the right and the market price had not yet adjusted to the new higher equilibrium level, the actual market price probably would be less than the equilibrium. However, as explained in the preceding chapter, forces then would come into play that would tend to push the actual price up toward the new equilibrium. During the process of adjustment, the price line facing the individual firm would rise in accordance with the market price that happened to exist at the time. In other words, we would not expect the price line to shift instantaneously from one equilibrium position to another.

From our discussion relating to product supply we know that a producer of this nature maximizes profits by producing a quantity that corresponds to the point where price equals marginal cost. This quantity is represented by Q_f in Figure 7–1(B). Notice, of course, that the units of measure on the quantity axis differ greatly between the market and the firm. The market quantity might be measured in terms of millions of units, whereas the firm's quantity might be measured just in number of units. The units of measure on the price axes are, of course, the same for the market and the firm.

We might pause at this point to summarize the different kinds of demand curves we have studied. There are three. The first is the demand of an individual consumer, represented by a downward sloping line indicating that quantity increases as price decreases, and vice versa. The second demand curve is market demand—the sum of all the individual demanders in the market. This is also represented by a downward sloping line, as in Figure 7–1(A). The third is the demand curve facing an individual seller. For the perfectly competitive seller this demand curve is a perfectly horizontal line, indicating that the market will take any reasonable quantity the seller wishes to produce at the market price.

Price, costs, and profits

The perfectly competitive firm takes the price as determined in the market and decides whether or not it should produce, and if so, how much. Recall from the discussion on product supply in Chapter 5 that pure profits are earned only if price is greater than the average total cost at the quantity the firm chooses to produce. We also know that the profit-maximizing quantity will correspond to the point where marginal cost equals price.

FIGURE 7–2
Possible profit or loss positions of perfectly competitive firms

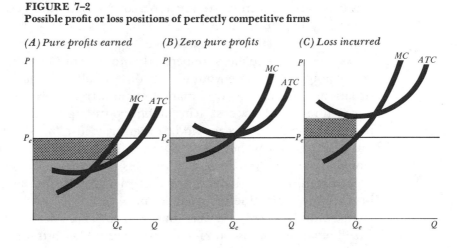

(A) Pure profits earned *(B) Zero pure profits* *(C) Loss incurred*

The three diagrams in Figure 7–2 illustrate the three possible profit positions for perfectly competitive firms. The price, P_e, that is shown is determined by market demand and supply, as illustrated in Figure 7–1(A). A firm that is earning pure profits in its business is illustrated in Figure 7–2(A). The resources (inputs) used in this production activity are earning more than they could in other kinds of work. The total pure profits for the firm are represented by the shaded area. Notice that total profits are maximized at a level of output beyond the point where profit per unit is the largest, that is, the point where the distance between price and average total cost (ATC) is the greatest. Such an outcome is reasonable because the firm is interested in maximizing its total profits rather than profit per unit.

The situation depicted in Figure 7–2(B), zero pure profits, is one in which the resources employed by this firm are earning just what they could earn in some other alternative occupation. This situation is the only one of the three shown in which the firm will produce a quantity corresponding to the minimum point on its ATC curve. The case of a firm that is not covering its costs (implicit plus explicit) is shown in Figure 7–2(C). In this example the resources employed by the firm are earning less than what they could in other occupations. This does not necessarily mean, however, that this firm's cash expenses are greater than its total sales because, as noted in Chapter 5, the ATC curve includes a charge for the resources owned by the firm as well as its cash expenses.

If we were able to measure perfectly the costs of individual firms at any point in time, we would likely observe all three of the above situations existing in a given market or industry. There would be a few well-managed low-cost firms making pure profits, as illustrated in Figure 7–2(A). There would be other firms just "breaking even" but doing as well as they could in any other occupation. And there would likely be a few firms making less than they could in other occupations, perhaps looking for a chance to sell their assets and begin some other line of production.

It should be noted, however, that Figure 7–2(C) need not depict a badly managed, slipshod kind of enterprise. The costs for this firm might be high because it has better alternatives than the other firms in the market. For example, the owner of the firm might be a highly educated wheat farmer who has the opportunity of working in a nearby bank at a salary much higher than his neighbors could obtain in their best alternative occupations. Thus a firm's cost might be high either because the owner is a bad manager or because the person has superior talents that are in demand elsewhere. It is not valid to conclude, therefore, that an industry in which the number of firms is decreasing is losing its least productive people. It may well be losing some of these, but at the same time it can be losing its most productive people because they have superior opportunities elsewhere.

Long-run adjustment

Economists have given rather precise definitions to the terms *short run* and *long run* as they apply to production and supply. The short run is defined as the length of time that is too short to change the level of fixed inputs used or the number of firms in the industry but long enough to change the level of output by means of changing variable inputs. Essentially, the marginal physical product curve and its mirror image, marginal cost, reflect short-run changes in production.

The long run is defined as a period of time long enough to change either the level of fixed inputs used by firms or the number of firms. Unfortunately it is not possible to designate a period of time that constitutes the long run for all different types of firms or even for different situations. The length of this period differs among types of firms, depending on how difficult or costly it is to change fixed inputs. If production requires extensive fixed inputs, say extensive irrigation or drainage facilities, the length of time to reach a long-run adjustment will be much longer than will be the case for firms that carry production in small rented facilities, say barber shops.

The length of time to reach a long-run adjustment also will depend on how profitable it is to adjust. If it is very profitable for a firm to expand its fixed inputs or for new firms to enter, the adjustment time will generally be shorter than if it just barely pays to change the level of output or to enter or leave the industry. For example, if it is very profitable to expand facilities most contractors will step up the completion date if they are paid to do so. A higher fee will enable them to pay their employees for overtime work in order to finish the job more quickly.

In looking at this process of long-run adjustment for a perfectly competitive industry in somewhat more detail, we will start where the market is in equilibrium, that is, where price corresponds to the intersection of supply and demand, as shown in Figure 7–3(A). Suppose that the typical firm in the industry in making substantial pure profits, as shown in Figure 7–3(B). Assume as well that each firm is maximizing its profits by producing an output that corresponds to the point where price is equal to marginal cost, Q_f in

Figure 7–3(B). These two conditions—market price is at the point where the quantity demanded equals the quantity supplied and price equals marginal cost for each firm—constitute a short-run equilibrium for an industry. This situation is illustrated in the two diagrams in Figure 7–3.

FIGURE 7–3
Short-run market equilibrium with pure profits made by the average firm

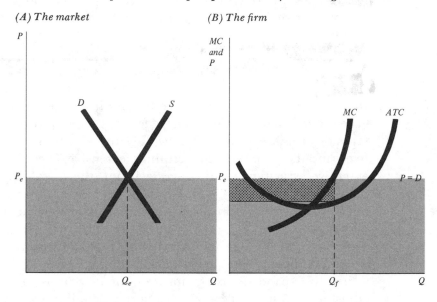

(A) The market   *(B) The firm*

If each firm is making pure profits, however, it is reasonable to expect that existing firms will expand their facilities (increase their fixed inputs) and/or additional firms will enter this industry to "get a piece of the action." We need not assume that all firms are making substantial pure profits for this to happen. In fact, some might be characterized by Figures 7–2(B) and (C). All that is necessary is that a sizable portion of existing firms is making pure profits.

Recall from the discussion on product supply that an increase in the number of firms or an increase in the size of firms has the effect of shifting the market supply curve to the right, as shown in Figure 7–4(A). The effect of an increase in supply, of course, is a reduction in market price. As the market price falls, so does the

FIGURE 7–4
Long-run adjustment to pure profits by entry of additional resources or firms

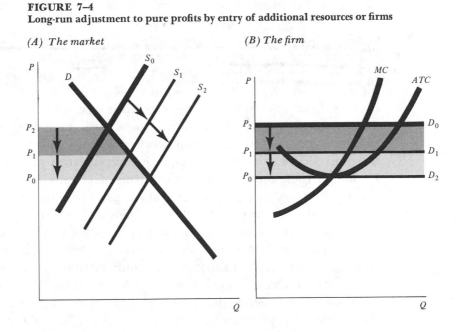

(A) The market

(B) The firm

price that faces each firm. Thus as the supply shifts right and market price falls, the pure profits that each firm is making are competed away. This process is illustrated in Figure 7–4(A) and (B).

This process of new resources coming into an industry to compete away pure profits probably will be most noticeable at relatively high levels of pure profits. Then, as price falls closer and closer to the zero profit point (P_0 in Figure 7–4), it is to be expected that the entry of additional resources will slow down as the prospects for pure profits diminish, although it is not uncommon to observe situations where firms have built up optimism over a period of time and continue to expand until price falls below the zero pure-profit point. As soon as this happens, of course, some firms find more profitable opportunities elsewhere, move out of this industry, and contribute to a decrease in supply, which eventually pulls price back up toward the zero pure-profit equilibrium.

A similar but opposite process of adjustment would take place if a large share of the firms in a market or industry is suffering losses or negative pure profits. Here we would see firms moving to more profitable opportunities, decreasing the market supply, and raising market price. (You may want to illustrate this process with diagrams of your own similar to Figure 7–4).

Thus the existence of pure profits or losses results in a long-run adjustment characterized by the corresponding entry or exit of resources or firms. It is also possible to observe adjustments on the cost side. In the production of tomatoes, for example, there may be a few firms that enjoy some special advantage, such as very productive soil. The entry of new firms might push price down to the zero profit position for just about every firm in the industry except these privileged few. They might continue to reap pure profits. Eventually these unusually profitable firms will be sold to new owners; and it is reasonable to expect that the price paid for these firms would reflect the pure profits that can be expected in the future; the new owners would be willing to pay more for productive land than for poor land. With an increase in the land price there will be an increase in the cost of production, mainly because of the increase in the interest charge (explicit or implicit) and taxes. If the sellers of these very productive firms are shrewd bargainers, they will obtain a price that pushes average total cost (ATC) just about up to the expected future price, as illustrated in Figure 7–5.

This phenomenon of cost adjusting to price has been particularly important in U.S. agriculture. As pointed out in Chapter 6, the government has attempted to increase incomes by establishing support prices of various products. In this situation the price is fixed, but over the years pure profits have been eroded away because of the bidding up of land prices. Eventually producers are forced back to the same zero pure-profit position that existed before the support prices came into being. Of course, the people who owned the land during its price rise enjoyed a capital gain. One should also bear in mind that for this phenomenon to occur, a necessary condition is that the product price be maintained at the artificially high level, as done by price supports. Without the price support, competitive forces would tend to drive the product price down to the zero pure-profit level, as illustrated by Figure 7–4.

Again we should caution that adjustment is not likely to be instantaneous. Pure profits or losses are likely to exist for different firms at any point in time. But if pure profits or losses exist, we can expect to observe an adjustment toward a long-run zero pure-profit position in a perfectly competitive industry.

FIGURE 7–5
Long-run adjustment to pure profits by increases in cost of resources to the individual firm

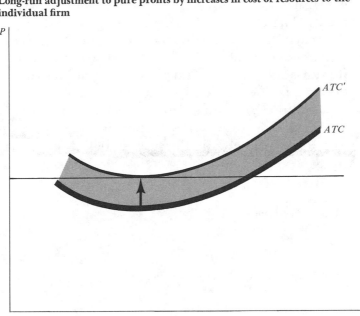

The continual search for lower costs

Even though all firms in a perfectly competitive industry face a common market price, there are likely to be substantial differences in *costs* among firms. High costs may be due to low productivity resulting from inept management, or they may be high implicit costs stemming from high-paying opportunities in other lines of work. It has been established that a perfectly competitive firm has no control over the price of its product. It is also true that such a firm cannot alter the opportunities that exist elsewhere. In fact, high implicit costs stemming from superior opportunities elsewhere would be welcomed because they represent opportunities to increase income.

However, most perfectly competitive firms can do something about the efficiency of their production processes. The more efficient a firm is in transforming inputs into output, the lower will be its production costs and the higher will be its profits. Thus most firms, at least those managed by alert people, are continually search-ing for new cost-reducing inputs or techniques in order to increase profits. The effect of achieving a cost reduction in production is illustrated by Figure 7–6. Average total cost (ATC) is shifted down-ward, and marginal cost (MC) is shifted downward and to the right. If price is at P_0, then the firm can move from a zero pure-profit posi-tion to a position of positive pure profits after the cost reduction.

In addition to creating pure profits for the firm in this example, a second effect of a cost reduction is the shift downward and to the right of the MC curve. Essentially this tells us that the firms now can produce an additional or marginal unit more

FIGURE 7–6
Effects of a cost reduction

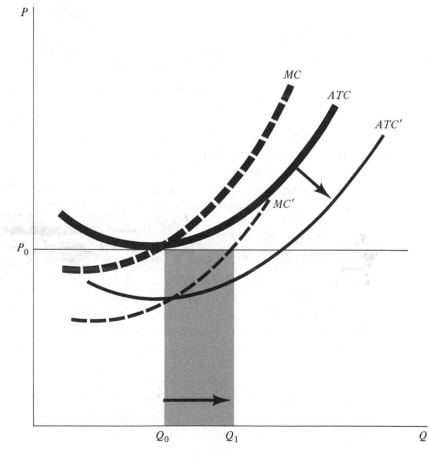

cheaply than before. But we should keep in mind that the MC curve is also the supply curve of the firm. At the original MC, Q_0 is produced by this firm, whereas at the new lower MC', Q_1 is produced. Of course, if just one or a few firms find a way to reduce costs and shift their supply curves, there will be no perceptible effect in the market. Increasing the production of wheat by 1,000 bushels, for example, will not be noticed in a market where millions of bushels are traded.

Although the increased production by a single firm has no appreciable effect on the market, similar action by many such firms will shift the market supply curve to the right, which has the effect of reducing the market price. Furthermore, the lowering of market price has the effect of squeezing the newly created pure profits out of the firms that have achieved lower costs.

Once a significant proportion of firms adopts a new cost-reducing input or technique and the market price begins to fall, the firms that have not reduced their costs find their profit positions eroding, and consequently they have no choice but to also adopt these inputs or techniques so they will not suffer losses or, eventually, be forced to leave the industry. This process of the early adopters reaping pure profits and the subsequent erosion of these profits to these firms (and losses to the remaining firms) is somewhat like being on a treadmill; each firm must run faster and faster (decrease costs more and more) just to stay even. Although each firm may not appreciate this continuous struggle, consumers and society in general gain from it, because more output is obtained from the nation's scarce resources.

The planning curve

There comes a time in the life of every firm when it must make decisions that affect its long-run future. This might come when it first starts in business or at any point when it decides to change the level of its fixed inputs, such as land, buildings, or equipment. A perfectly competitive firm, which by itself cannot affect the market price, might reasonably be expected to be interested in finding the level of fixed inputs that will minimize its average total costs, because only by achieving a size that will minimize per unit cost can it hope to compete in the long run with other firms that are also searching for the most efficient size.

Ideally a firm would like to utilize experts, such as engineers, architects, cost accountants, and economists, to estimate the potential average total costs (ATC) for various levels of ouput at various levels of fixed inputs. In other words, it would like to know the short-run ATC curves for various sizes of plants or facilities. One possible configuration of short-run ATC curves is represented by Figure 7–7.

FIGURE 7–7
Planning curve or long-run average total cost curve

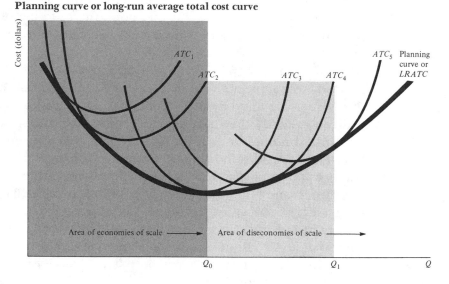

In this example the level of ATC is relatively high at relatively small levels of fixed inputs and output, as illustrated by ATC_1. As the size of fixed inputs is increased, the ATC curves shift downward and to the right, reaching a minimum of ATC_3. Further increases in the size of fixed inputs still shift the short-run ATC curves to the right, but at the same time they shift them upward, indicating that per unit costs increase for larger firms.

Although only five alternative sizes are illustrated in Figure 7–7, many more could be estimated and drawn in. The individual firm may not wish to consider an excessive number of alternatives, however, because of the cost of estimating the various ATC curves. At any rate, it would be possible with only the number of ATC curves shown in Figure 7–7 to estimate what economists call a planning curve or long-run average total cost (LRATC) curve. Such a curve is constructed by tracing out an "envelope" of all the short-run ATC curves.

Essentially, the planning curve, or the LRATC, shows the lowest possible cost of obtaining a given output. For example, at output Q_1 the level of fixed inputs represented by ATC_5 would be most efficient. Producing Q_1 by a smaller level of fixed inputs, ATC_4, for example, would result in higher unit costs. The planning curve also shows the level of fixed inputs that would result in the overall lowest possible ATC—represented here by ATC_3. Thus a firm that wanted to minimize ATC in the future would utilize this level of fixed inputs and produce output Q_0: Producing Q_0 by any other level of fixed inputs, say ATC_2 or ATC_4, would result in higher unit costs.

In reality, of course, a small firm, may not wish to incur the expense of estimating in detail many possible short-run ATCs. Instead the firm may simply try to estimate the lowest possible point on a few possible ATC curves and, in so doing, attempt to obtain a rough idea of what its planning curve or LRATC might look like. At least, rough information of this kind is helpful in deciding on the size that comes close to minimizing ATC over the long run.

Economies and diseconomics of scale

The planning curve or LRATC brings out a concept long used by economists—economies and diseconomies of scale. As the name implies, the concept of economies of scale means that the long-run average total cost declines as the size or scale of the firm increases, as illustrated by the decreasing portion of the planning curve. Perhaps the greatest source of economies of scale is the more efficient utilization of fixed inputs in large firms compared with small firms. For example, the equipment depreciation charge per bushel is likely to be higher on a 100-acre wheat farm than on a 1,000-acre farm. Perhaps even more important, the implicit cost of the farmer's own labor would have to be covered by fewer bushels on the small farm, hence the average total cost per bushel would be higher on the small farm.

Diseconomies of scale implies the opposite, namely, that unit costs increase in larger firm sizes, as illustrated by the increasing portion of the planning curve. Management problems appear to be the major factor causing diseconomies of scale. As a firm increases in size, the task of management becomes more and more complex. One reason management becomes more difficult as the firm size increases is the problem of accessibility and accuracy of information. Managers of small firms can know firsthand what is going on, while those who manage large firms have to rely on reports from subordinates for information. If the information is incomplete or inaccurate, there is a greater chance of making bad decisions, thereby causing costs to increase or sales to decline.

Because people differ a great deal in management ability, it is reasonable to expect that diseconomies of scale set in sooner for some firms than for others. This probably explains why some firms grow larger and larger, continuing to prosper, while others stay about the same size for the life of the owner or manager. Indeed, a relatively poor manager might go bankrupt at the level of production that minimizes costs for a good manager. Thus it is important for the owner or manager of the firm to assess his or her management skills in estimating the firm's LRATC curve.

Although a ∪-shaped LRATC curve is plausible, economists attempting to obtain an empirical measure of economies and diseconomies of scale rarely find evidence of the upward sloping portion of the curve, that is, diseconomies of scale. A more frequent finding is a curve that may reflect some scale economies at small firm sizes but fairly constant costs for a large share of the observed firms. In other words, the observed shape of the LRATC curve is more likely to reflect the shape of a ski jump, with a long flat portion rather than the traditional ∪.

One possible explanation for the relative rarity of an upward sloping portion of the LRATC curve is that firms that find their LRATC increasing as they expand, or those that anticipate that costs will increase, may decide to stop growing before they incur significant diseconomies of scale. Or a firm that mistakenly grows to a size that results in high costs may simply cut back its output in order to compete with firms operating in the relatively flat portion of their LRATC curve. A third possibility, of course, is that large high-cost firms are forced out of business and therefore are not observable.

We might expect the relatively small firms that operate on the downward sloping portion of their LRATC to attempt to expand in order to realize the lower unit costs obtainable at larger sizes. In fact, a relatively simple way to detect whether the firms in an industry are able to capture scale economies is to observe changes in their average size over time. If the average size of the firm is increasing, we can conclude that large firms are more efficient than small firms in the industry, that is, scale economies exist.[1]

Production costs: The firm versus the industry

Although the preceding discussion of economies and diseconomies of scale focused on the individual firm, it should be kept in mind that a firm's production costs can be affected by what the other firms in the industry do. One way that this can happen is through the price of resources. If just one or a few perfectly competitive firms expand or contract, there is not likely to be any change in the price of resources because they most likely use a very small part of the industry total. A change in output by all firms in the industry or a substantial change in the number of firms, however, might well change the price of the resources used in this industry. A substantial contraction by the industry, for example, releases resources that must find alternative employment. To do this, they might be required to accept lower prices. On the other hand, if there is interest in attracting a substantial quantity of additional resources, their price might be bid up in order to draw them away from other industries.

From the discussion of product supply, we know that an increase in the price of resources shifts the cost curves for the individual firm upward and to the left. Thus, in the case of industry expansion, two offsetting forces are operating: The increase in size or number of

---

[1] This simple test, often called the *survival technique,* is presented by George Stigler, in *The Theory of Price,* 3rd ed. (New York: Macmillan Co., 1966), pp. 158–60.

firms shifts the product supply to the right, but an increase in resource prices has the opposite effect, so that the net shift is smaller than without the resource price rise.

In addition to resource price increases, expansion by the entire industry can affect the individual firm's cost curves through what economists call "technical or nonpecuniary" diseconomies. The most common example of these is waste disposal. If the industry is small and its firms are scattered, disposing of waste tends to be less costly than if the industry is large and highly concentrated. For example, one or a few small firms may pipe their wastes into a stream or body of water without causing public alarm. But with growth of the industry, each firm may have to construct costly waste disposal facilities, which has the effect of increasing the cost curves of all the individual firms.

Economists refer to industries that experience a rise in costs, either through resource price increases or through technical diseconomies, as increasing-cost industries. As this kind of industry expands, the minmum point on each firm's LRATC curve increases so that the zero pure-profit price rises higher and higher. Thus, as the industry grows larger, the long-run equilibrium price for the industry increases. The situation is illustrated in Figure 7–8(A), in which it is assumed that the industry expands by adding additional firms.

Although increasing costs can reasonably be expected in many industries, it is possible to visualize one that can expand its output without incurring increasing costs. This could happen if the resources used by the industry make up a small proportion of the total employment of these resources. Tomato production might be a possible example because this industry employs only a small proportion of the total land, labor, and other resources that can be used to produce tomatoes. Also, no technical diseconomies can be present. Economists refer to such an industry as a constant-cost industry because each firm's cost curves and the long-run equilibrium price do not change as the industry expands to large levels of output, as in Figure 7–8(B).

There is a third possibility, a decreasing-cost industry, in which costs decline as the industry grows. This is less common than the first two cases but still possible. Decreasing costs can occur if the price of the industry's resources declines as the industry grows. This

FIGURE 7–8
Long-run average total cost curves for a typical firm in industries in which costs are increasing, constant, and decreasing

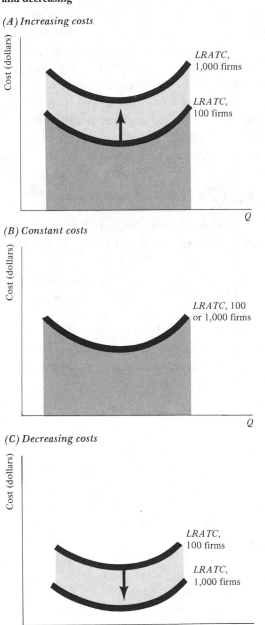

(A) Increasing costs

LRATC,
1,000 firms

LRATC,
100 firms

(B) Constant costs

LRATC, 100
or 1,000 firms

(C) Decreasing costs

LRATC,
100 firms

LRATC,
1,000 firms

phenomenon would be most likely to occur in new or developing areas. If only a few firms are present, many of the resources it uses will have to be shipped in from distant places or produced locally on a small scale at high costs. If the industry is small and insignificant, there will likely be no public effort to establish institutions to serve it or to train people to work in it if special skills are required. On the other hand, an industry that becomes a significant part of an area's or a nation's economy can expect to enjoy some special advantages. Supporting industries that can supply resources at a minimum cost will emerge, financial institutions will consider it a better risk and will loan money at a lower rate of interest, and public schools might offer special training to young people who want to find employment in the industry. Economists refer to these circumstances as *external economies*. In this case, the entrance of additional firms lowers costs for all firms. It is not totally unexpected, therefore, that industries tend to concentrate in specific areas rather than spreading out excessively. Decreasing costs are illustrated in Figure 7–8(C).

Bear in mind, however, that an industry might exhibit all three situations at different stages of its development. When an industry is young and becoming established, it might enjoy decreasing costs. Then for a time, when it is moderate in size, it might expand with constant costs. Finally, as it becomes a major industry using a significant proportion of the resources it employs, it may run into increasing costs.

Long-run supply

We know that in a long-run equilibrium, price will tend to adjust to the minimum point of the typical firm's LRATC curve. If each firm's LRATC curve shifts upward as the industry expands or increases output, as illustrated by Figure 7–8(A), then of course this minimum point also will rise. In this situation an increase in output will be forthcoming only with an increase in price. In other words, the long-run supply curve for the industry in this case would slope upward, as illustrated in Figure 7–9(A).

In the case of a constant-cost industry, output can expand with-

FIGURE 7–9
**Long-run supply curves for increasing-cost, constant-cost, and decreasing-cost
industries**

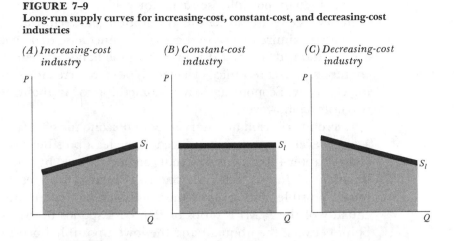

*(A) Increasing-cost
industry*

*(B) Constant-cost
industry*

*(C) Decreasing-cost
industry*

out any change in the level of the firms' LRATC curves. Hence a
larger output will be forthcoming at the same price as that for
a small output. The long-run supply curve in this case will be
perfectly elastic, as shown in Figure 7–9(B). The third case, where
the minimum-cost point declines as the industry expands, would
result in a downward sloping industry long-run supply curve, as in
Figure 7–9(C).

Economic efficiency

A perfectly competitive industry frequently is used by economists
as a standard by which to judge other industries. The reason is that
a perfectly competitive equilibrium (short-run or long-run) results
in maximum economic efficiency. At this point resources are allocated such that the value of output of society is maximized. Three
criteria are required to obtain economic efficiency. First, there must
be maximum technical efficiency. This means that a physical output
obtained from a given level of inputs is at its maximum. In other
words, resources are not being wasted. For example, a given amount
of labor and capital might produce only 20 bushels of tomatoes if
time were wasted or the machine used inappropriately. But if the
inputs were fully utilized in the correct manner, 30 bushels might
be produced. Technical efficiency also can be visualized as being

on the highest possible isoquant for a given input mix. In economics we generally make the assumption that technical efficiency is being maximized because there is not much else that economists can say about this topic. It is mainly in the hands of managers and engineers. In fact technical efficiency is often referred to as engineering efficiency. Economists do have something to say about the other two criteria, however.

A second criterion necessary to obtain economic efficiency is that a given level of output is produced at the least possible cost. Recall from Chapter 4 that a given output can be produced by various combinations of inputs, but only one combination will result in the lowest possible cost. This is the combination that results in the equality of the P/MPP ratios or that corresponds to the tangency point between the isoquant and the lowest possible isocost line. As you recall, this is the cost-minimizing condition. Actually any firm, whether it is perfectly competitive or not, can meet these first two conditions, namely, the attainment of maximum technical efficiency and the cost-minimization condition.

The third criterion necessary for maximum economic efficiency is that the level of output of each good corresponds to the point where the marginal cost of producing an extra unit is equal to the price of the good. You will note that this is the profit-maximizing level of output for each perfectly competitive firm. In the next chapter we will see that an imperfectly competitive firm will not produce this level of output. Hence only perfect competition meets the three criteria required to reach maximum economic efficiency, i.e., the maximum value of output. The next question is: Why does the $P = \text{MC}$ equality result in the maximum value of output given the amount of resources available to a country? To understand why, it is first necessary to understand what price and marginal cost represent.

We can think of the price of a product as the value that society assigns to marginal unit. For example, if the price of tomatoes is \$4 per bushel, we can infer that society values an extra bushel of tomatoes at \$4 or it would not choose to buy it for this price.

Marginal cost (MC), on the other hand, represents the cost to society in terms of other products given up to obtain an extra unit of this product. For example, if the MC of tomatoes is \$4, then in order to produce an extra bushel of tomatoes, $4 worth of some other good or service must be given up, assuming that these other things are produced in an industry in which price and MC also are equal.

It is perhaps easiest to understand why the equality of price and MC results in a maximum value of output if we first look at situations in which price does not equal marginal cost. Suppose that, for some reason, the price of a bushel of tomatoes is $4 and its MC is $3. This means that society values an extra bushel of tomatoes at $4 and values the goods or services given up to produce this extra bushel at $3. Now if one extra bushel of tomatoes is produced, society gains $4 and gives up $3, leaving a net gain of $1. Thus it behooves society to increase the production of tomatoes under these circumstances, because the value of total output is increased using the same amount of resources. In other words, there is a underallocation of resources to the production of a good or service if its price is greater than its MC.

Taking the opposite situation, say price is still $4 but MC is $5, we can see that by decreasing the production of tomatoes by one bushel, society gives up $4 worth of tomatoes but gains $5 worth of other goods and services, resulting in a net gain of $1. Thus if MC is greater than price, there is an overallocation of resources to the production of this product because by reducing its production, the total value of output is increased with a given amount of resources. Now it is possible to see that the value of output is maximized only if price equals marginal cost because only when this is the case is it impossible to reallocate resources to increase the total value of output. As mentioned, perfectly competitive firms attempt to produce at the point where price equals MC. Thus an advantageous characteristic of perfect competition, at least from society's point of view, is that producers attempting to maximize their own profits by equating price and marginal cost also maximize the value of output to society.

It should not be concluded from this discussion, however, that perfect competition is the ultimate goal to be strived for in all industries. We will see in the following chapter that the nature of most products precludes perfect competition in their production. However, the further removed an industry is from the perfectly competitive model, the greater is the chance that society will suffer a significant reduction in the value of output for a given amount of resources.

We ought to mention at this point that the idea of competitive forces working for the good of society was first introduced by the 18th-century Scottish economist and philosopher Adam Smith, in *The Wealth of Nations* published in 1776. He called this phenomenon the "invisible hand." Each firm that is attempting to maximize its own profits also maximizes the value of output to society, as though guided by some "invisible hand."

Economics of pollution and other social costs

Society has become very concerned of late with the problem of pollution. When the population was smaller and more dispersed and industrial output was considerably smaller, much of our waste material was disposed of by dumping it into water or the atmosphere. Little thought was given to the cost of waste disposal, probably because it was relatively cheap to let nature do the disposing, and relatively few people—at least few with any influence—complained about the effects of waste materials in the environment.

Society is becoming increasingly aware, however, that the cost of disposing of wastes by dumping them into the environment is much greater than that borne solely by the one doing the dumping. For example, the cost of piping waste material into a stream far exceeds the cost of the pipe, at least from society's point of view.

Economists have long been aware that certain production costs are not taken into account by the individual firm but nevertheless represent a cost to society. These are sometimes called *social costs* or *externalities*. Pollution represents a rather significant social cost at the present. Accidental destruction of life and property because of alcohol or drugs also is a social cost that has concerned society for some time.

We can obtain a somewhat clearer picture of the economic effects of social costs such as pollution by use of a diagram. Suppose MC in Figure 7–10 represents the traditional implicit and explicit marginal costs of producing a product. Also suppose that the production

FIGURE 7–10
Divergence of private and social marginal cost because of pollution

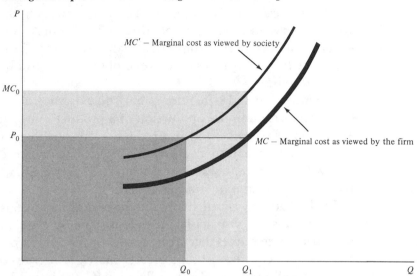

of this product results in certain waste materials that are disposed of by dumping them into a river. These waste materials, however, represent an additional cost to society, either because they must be taken out downstream in order for the water to be reused or because people living downstream suffer the cost of viewing unsightly water and are not able to use it for other purposes. For example, if pollution prohibits recreational uses of water, people must bear the cost of traveling to alternative areas where the water is not polluted.

If the firm were required to bear the full cost of disposing of its waste material, then the true or full MC curve would be somewhat higher for a given output, such as MC' in Figure 7–10. If the firm does not have to pay the full cost of waste disposal, it will base its production decisions entirely on MC rather than MC'. In other words, MC is the firm's marginal cost and MC' is society's marginal cost. The latter includes the private marginal cost of the firm plus the social cost of pollution.

Assuming, as is reasonable, that the firm tries to maximize its profits, it will produce quantity Q_1 if faced by price P_0. However, you will note that if all costs are taken into account, the additional cost to society of one more unit of the product is given by MC_0 on the vertical axis. In other words, MC_0 represents the value of goods or services given up to obtain one more unit of this product —say, tomatoes. Since consumers value an extra bushel of tomatoes at P_0, society gives up more to obtain this extra bushel than it gets from it.

We must conclude, therefore, that the existence of a social cost such as pollution in the production of a product results in an over-allocation of resources to this product, even though production is carried on by perfectly competitive firms. The "correct" amount that will maximize the value of output to society is Q_0, where price is equal to the true or full marginal cost.

In the future we will likely see more and more legislation requiring firms to construct facilities to dispose of waste materials or to stop using resources that create wastes or residue. In other words, they will be required to bear a greater share of the true costs of producing their products. As they do so, MC as viewed by the firm will move up and toward the true marginal cost, MC' in Figure 7–10. We know, however, that an upward shift in the marginal cost for each firm also will have the effect of shifting the market supply curve of the product upward and to the left, as shown in Figure 7–11. And the inevitable consequence of this shift is a rise in the market price of the product.

We should not be surprised, therefore, if our efforts to control pollution result in higher prices for the products affected. This is not to say that pollution control is undesirable, because we will be buying cleaner air and water along with these products. The main point is that clean air and water are not free goods in an industrialized society.

The perfectly competitive buyer

In discussing perfect competition, we have considered only the selling side of the market. It is necessary, however, to realize that there are two sides to every market: the selling side and the buying side. In the product market, the buying side is made up mainly of ordinary consumers such as yourself. There is only one character-

FIGURE 7–11
Effect of pollution control in the product market

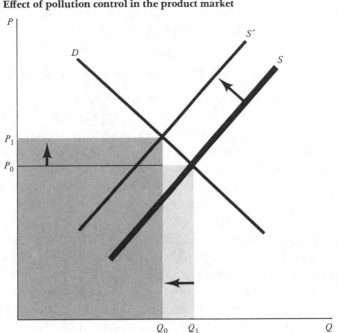

istic that we need to consider on the buying side, and that is the amount that each buyer purchases relative to the total market. Economists classify a market in which each buyer is small and purchases only a small proportion of the item traded as perfectly competitive on the buying side.

Because the perfectly competitive buyer buys only a minute proportion of the market, he or she alone has no influence over the market price. For example, if you decide that the price of a textbook is too high and therefore refuse to buy it, your decision not to buy will have virtually no effect on the quantity exchanged in the market, and hence no effect on market price. If you wish to double or triple your usual purchases of an item, say football tickets, your decision alone will not cause an increase in the price of the tickets.

In practice, a perfectly competitive buyer faces a situation very similar to that faced by a perfectly competitive seller: Neither can influence the price of the product bought or sold. The distinguishing characteristics of a perfectly competitive buyer is that he or she buys only a minute fraction of the market. The same is true for a perfectly competitive seller, only here the additional characteristic of selling a homogeneous product is required.

SUPPLY FACING A PERFECTLY COMPETITIVE BUYER

The fact that a perfectly competitive buyer has no control over the market price of a good or service implies that the supply curve facing the individual buyer of this item is represented by a perfectly horizontal line, as in Figure 7–12(B). The meaning of this supply curve is that the individual buyer can purchase any reasonable amount without having to pay a higher price for larger quantities. Essentially, this supply curve reflects the price of the item as determined in the market.

The market supply and demand, which determine price, are illustrated by Figure 7–12(A). If there were no further services involved between the producer and the buyer, Figure 7–12(A) would be exactly the same as Figure 7–1(A). The market price would be P_e, and the total quantity exchanged would be equal to Q_e. Each producer or firm would supply Q_f, as shown in Figure 7–1(B), and

FIGURE 7–12
Relationship between the market and the perfectly competitive buyer

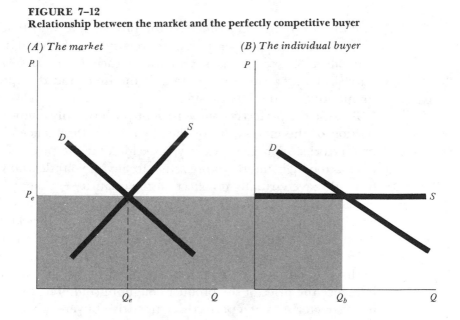

(A) The market   *(B) The individual buyer*

each consumer would buy Q_b, as shown in Figure 7–12(B), on the basis of individual demand for the items. Of course, the so-called going price facing the individual buyer need not necessarily be the equilibrium price, as shown in Figure 7–12. However, if the actual price is different from the equilibrium, we would again expect market forces to drive price toward the equilibrium.

To summarize, three different kinds of supply curves have been presented: (1) the supply of the individual firm (really its MC curve), (2) the market supply, which is just a summation of the individual firms' supply curves, and (3) the supply curve facing the individual buyer. You might recognize that these three supply curves run parallel to the three demand curves that were summarized at the beginning of this chapter. With a total of six different demand and supply curves, it is necessary to be careful not to confuse one with another. You should be aware as well that a perfectly competitive seller does not have to be a perfectly competitive buyer, and vice versa. In fact, most goods and services are purchased by perfectly competitive buyers but produced by imperfectly competitive sellers. The latter group will be the topic of Chapter 8.

Main points of Chapter 7

1. The perfectly competitive firm must take the price as determined in the market because it sells a product that is indistinguishable from other firms in the market, and its sales represent a very small proportion of the total market.

2. We have studied three different kinds of demand curves: (a) the demand of an individual consumer, (b) the market demand, and (c) the demand facing an individual producer or seller.

3. The demand facing a single perfectly competitive firm is perfectly elastic, meaning that the firm can sell any reasonable amount at the going market price.

4. A perfectly competitive firm maximizes profits (or minimizes losses) by producing up to the point where price equals marginal cost.

5. At any point in time, there will likely be some perfectly competitive firms that are making pure profits, others making zero pure profits, and still others incurring negative pure profits (or losses).

6. If a substantial share of the firms is making pure profits, existing firms will likely increase in size and/or new firms will enter, leading to an increase in the market supply, a decrease in price, and a competing away of the pure profits.

7. If a substantial share of the firms is incurring negative pure profits (they are earning less than they could in other lines of work), there will be a decrease in the size or number of firms, leading to a decrease in supply, an increase in price, and a restoration of at least zero pure profits.

8. Long-run adjustment to zero pure profits also can occur because of changes in the price of resources owned by the firm and hence changes in the firm's costs.

9. It is in the interest of each firm to search for cost-reducing techniques or resources in order to increase profits. Firms that do not adopt these eventually incur losses or are forced out of business.

10. The planning curve or long-run average total cost (LRATC) curve represents an envelope of all possible short-run average total cost (ATC) curves. From the planning curve the producer is able to determine the size of fixed inputs that will minimize the unit costs of a given output, as well as the size that will minimize unit costs overall.

11. The downward sloping portion of the planning curve represents the range of economies of scale. Scale economies generally result from a more efficient utilization of fixed inputs.

12. The upward sloping portion of the planning curve represents the range of diseconomies of scale. This phenomenon generally results from management problems brought on by increasing firm size.

13. An increasing-cost industry is one in which the production costs of all firms in the industry increase as the industry expands. This takes place because of an increase in the price of resources or because of technical diseconomies that increase production costs for all firms as the industry grows.

14.   In a constant-cost industry the expansion of the industry does not affect the cost curves of the individual firms.

15.   A decreasing-cost industry is characterized by a reduction in firm costs as the industry grows. This phenomenon is most likely to occur in developing areas.

16.   The long-run industry supply curve is upward sloping in an increasing-cost industry, perfectly elastic in a constant-cost industry, and downward sloping in a decreasing-cost industry.

17.   Economic efficiency is defined as obtaining the maximum value of output from a given level of resources. Three criteria are required to obtain economic efficiency: (*a*) technical efficiency is maximized, output is on the highest possible isoquant for a given amount of resources; (*b*) a given output is produced at the least possible cost; and (*c*) the output of each good corresponds to the point where the marginal cost of producing another unit is equal to its price. While any firm can meet the first two criteria, only a perfectly competitive firm meets the third.

18.   The existence of social costs such as pollution results in an underestimation by the firm of the true or full marginal cost of producing a good or service. Since the true MC will be greater than the price, there will be an overallocation of resources to goods or services that entail social costs, even though production might be carried on in perfect competition.

19.   Laws that require polluting firms to bear a greater share of the cost of pollution likely will shift the MC and product supply of their goods or services upward, thus increasing their market price.

20.   On the buying side of the market, perfect competition results if each individual buyer purchases only a small fraction of the total market. Most individual consumers are perfectly competitive buyers.

21.   Three different kinds of supply curves have been introduced: (*a*) the supply of an individual producer, (*b*) the market supply, and (*c*) the supply facing an individual buyer.

22.   The supply curve facing a perfectly competitive buyer is perfectly elastic, meaning that the individual buyer can purchase any reasonable amount at the going market price.

Questions for thought and discussion

1. Perfectly competitive firms are sometimes called *price takers*. Why; what makes them price takers?

2. In Chapter 1 demand was drawn as a downward sloping line. In this chapter there is a demand "curve" drawn as a horizontal line. Which is correct? Explain.

3. Beef production in the United States is carried on by many firms, each selling a product undifferentiated from that of other firms in the market. Explain how the price of beef is determined at any given time and how this price relates to the individual producer.

4. Plant breeders are developing new hybrid varieties of wheat that are expected to yield nearly twice as much as the old varieties.
   a. Explain the effect that the new varieties will have on the costs and profits of the alert, early-adopting farmer.
   b. Explain the long-run adjustment of the wheat-producing industry to this new development.
   c. Explain what would happen to producers who do not adopt a new variety.

5. In a perfectly competitive industry, an increase in the market supply of a product leads to a decrease in the demand facing the individual firm. True or false? Explain.

6. An increase in support prices on agricultural products guarantees that at least some farmers should be able to reap pure profits as long as the increase stays in effect. True or false? Explain.

7. Diminishing returns to an input do not set in until the firm is in the region of decreasing returns to scale. True or false? Explain.

8. In the region of economies of scale, large firms always can produce a given level of output at a lower cost than smaller firms? True or false? Explain.

9. What effect, if any, has the substantial increase in nonfarm wages had on the average size of farms in the country? Explain.

10. Is it possible for the long-run industry supply curve to be downward sloping? Explain.

11. Is it possible for the long-run industry supply curve to be perfectly elastic? Explain.

12. An increasing-cost industry will exist only in cases where the individual firm must pay higher prices when it wishes to purchase additional inputs. True or false? Explain.

13. Society could obtain a greater value of output from its scarce resources if business firms did not try to maximize profits. True or false? Explain.

14. Pollution in a perfectly competitive industry causes the output of that industry to be larger than that which would maximize society's welfare. True or false? Explain.

15. Students can be described as perfectly competitive buyers of textbooks. Why?

8

Imperfect competition in the product market

By far the largest proportion of goods and services in the United States is produced or sold in an environment that economists refer to as *imperfect competition.* Virtually all nonagricultural firms, ranging from small family-owned and -operated retail stores to the giant multinational corporations, fall into the category of imperfect competition. As we will see, the distinguishing characteristic of all imperfectly competitive firms is that they face a downward sloping demand curve. This means that each firm has some leeway over the price it can charge. We will see, however, that many imperfectly competitive firms have relatively little power over what price they charge, while other firms have more choice.

The imperfectly competitive firm: A price maker

As defined in Chapter 7, a perfectly competitive firm has no control over the price it receives for its product; it takes the price that is determined in the market. A perfectly competitive firm, it has been noted, is a price taker for two reasons: (1) each firm produces a small share of the market, and (2) each firm produces a product that is indistinguishable from those of the other firms in the market.

An imperfectly competitive firm can be defined as one that can exercise some control over the price it receives for its product. For this reason an imperfectly competitive firm is sometimes called a *price maker*. There are two main reasons a firm might have some control over the price it can charge: (1) each firm produces a sizable share of the market, and (2) each firm sells a product that can be distinguished from those of its competitors. Note that these two reasons are the opposite of those given for a perfectly competitive firm. We will see shortly that it is sufficient for a firm to fulfill either of these two requirements to be classified as imperfectly competitive. Some firms, of course, exhibit both characteristics.

In examining why these two characteristics make it possible for a firm to have some control over the price of its product, we will consider first a firm that sells a relatively large share of the total market, such as U.S. Steel. If U.S. Steel reduced its annual output by 10 to 20 percent, we would likely observe a noticeable decline in the total steel output in the United States and a resulting increase in the price of steel, providing the market demand for steel is downward sloping (which is reasonable). As a result of its production cutback, U.S. Steel could then raise the price of its product, at least by a small amount. By the same token a comparable *increase* in output by U.S. Steel would add a noticeable amount to total steel output and result in at least a small decline in the market price of steel. In this case, U.S. Steel would likely have to accept a slightly lower price for its product. The main point to note here is that such a firm can manipulate the price it receives for its product by changing its level of output.

A firm that sells a product that is somewhat different from those of its competitors is also able to exercise some control over the price of its product. In the above example we considered a firm that sells a relatively large share of the market but whose product is virtually the same as its competitors in order to keep the effect of product differentiation separate from share of the market. Now we will consider a firm that sells a small share of the market but whose product is slightly different from those of its competitors—say, the local Standard Oil station in your neighborhood. At first glance it might appear that such a firm's main product, gasoline, is the same as that sold by the other stations in the area, or at least the same as other Standard stations. However, as we will explain shortly, a retail firm's specific location and the kind of service it renders can result in some difference in its overall product. If some of the firm's customers prefer its product to those of competing stations, the station in question probably could raise its price at least a few cents a gallon over its competitors without having its gasoline sales go to zero. The people who found the station a convenient place to stop or for some reason liked the service probably would continue to patronize it, at least for a time. On the other hand, if the station lowered its price a few cents a gallon below its competitors, it would likely attract additional customers. The main point is that a firm that sells a product that is somewhat different from its competitor's products has some leeway in the price it can charge.

Demand facing an imperfectly competitive firm

The imperfectly competitive firm's ability to alter the price of its product is translatable to the demand curve facing such a firm. In Chapter 7 it was noted that the perfectly competitive firm faces a perfectly horizontal (perfectly elastic) demand curve, reflecting the fact that it has no control over the price it receives. In the case of an imperfectly competitive firm, its ability to raise the price and sell a smaller quantity, or lower the price and sell a larger quantity, means in effect that the firm faces a downward sloping demand curve. This is illustrated in Figure 8–1.

If the firm raises its price, say from P_1 to P_2, it is forced to reduce its sales from Q_1 to Q_0. Or if the firm wishes to increase its sales, say from Q_1 to Q_2, it must lower the price from P_1 to P_0. Thus the demand curve of all imperfectly competitive firms is downward sloping. Keep in mind, however, that even though this downward sloping demand curve facing the individual firm resembles the market demand curve for the product, it is not the same thing as the market demand. (Pure monopoly is an exception, to be discussed later.) As long as there is more than one firm selling in a market, the demand curve facing each firm is considerably more elastic than the market demand curve.

FIGURE 8-1
Demand curve facing an imperfectly competitive firm

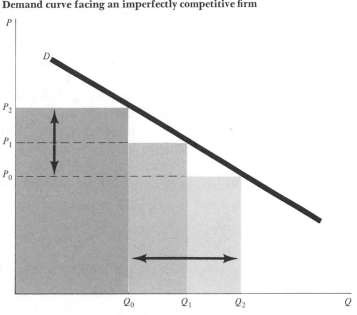

The concept of marginal revenue

The phenomenon of an individual firm facing a downward sloping demand curve makes it necessary to introduce a new concept—marginal revenue. *Marginal revenue* (MR) is defined as the additional revenue obtained by producing and selling one more unit of a good or service or, conversely, the reduction in revenue caused by a one-unit reduction in sales.

As pointed out in Chapter 4, it is not realistic to believe that a firm can change its production or sales by just one unit. For this reason, economists generally refer to a change in production and sales over a small range of output and compute MR for a unit change of output within this range. The formula for computing marginal revenue is:

$$MR = \frac{\text{Change in total revenue}}{\text{Change in quantity sold}}$$

This formula will be easier to understand if we apply it to a specific example. Suppose Figure 8-1 depicts a demand curve facing a shoe manufacturer and that the firm charges $40 per pair for its shoes and sells 1,000 pairs per week. (For the moment we will not be concerned with how the firm arrived at this price.) This price and quantity would correspond to P_1 and Q_1, respectively, in Figure 8–1. Multiplying price times quantity results in a total revenue to the firm of $40,000 per week.

Now suppose the firm wishes to expand its sales to 1,500 pairs per week and in order to increase its sales by 500 pairs of shoes per week it must lower the price to $38 per pair. With the new lower price and larger quantity, total revenue becomes $57,000 per week. We now have enough information to compute the marginal revenue of an extra pair of shoes sold in this range of output.

$$\text{\textasteriskcentered} \quad MR = \frac{\overset{TR_1}{\$57,000} - \overset{TR_2}{\$40,000}}{\underset{Q_1}{1,500} - \underset{Q_2}{1,000}} = \frac{\$17,000}{500} = \$34$$

In this range of output, an extra pair of shoes sold adds $34 to total revenue.

Marginal revenue and price

Because of the downward sloping demand curve in the above example, the firm had to lower its price from $40 to $38 a pair to sell the additional 500 pairs per week. But we might ask a reasonable question at this point: If an extra pair of shoes sells for $38, why doesn't it add $38 to total revenue?

The reason marginal revenue is less than price is because the lower $38 price applies to all of the weekly sales, not just to the extra or additional sales that result from the lower price. It would not be reasonable to expect the firm to sell the initial 1,000 pairs for $40 per pair and the extra 500 pairs for $38. No one would want to buy any of the initial 1,000 pairs. Thus when price is reduced to sell more of the product, the lower price must apply to all units sold, not just to the marginal units. As a result, MR is even less than the new lower price because that price reduces the total revenue obtained from the original quantity sold from what it would otherwise be.

Keep in mind, however, that marginal revenue is less than price only if the firm faces a downward sloping curve. If, as in perfect competition, the firm faces a horizontal demand curve, MR will equal the price. In this situation, the firm does not have to reduce the price to sell additional units. So the addition to total revenue (MR) is exactly the same as the price that the marginal unit sells for.

If we were to graph MR at various levels of output, we would obtain for perfect competition a horizontal line that is equal to price, which in turn is equal to the demand curve facing the individual firm, as shown in Figure 8–2(A). For imperfect competition the MR line would be less than price at any given level of output. Thus the MR line would be lower than its corresponding demand curve and would slope downward more steeply as in Figure 8–2(B).

FIGURE 8–2
Marginal revenue and demand facing the individual firm

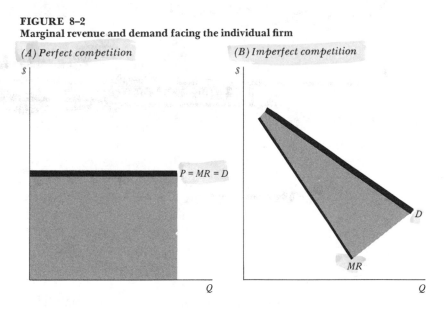

(A) Perfect competition

(B) Imperfect competition

Although all imperfectly competitive firms share one thing in common—they all face downward sloping demand curves for their good or service—there is a great deal of diversity among them. Economists have attempted to create some order out of this diversity by classifying imperfectly competitive firms into three categories: (1) monopolistic competition, (2) oligopoly, and (3) pure monopoly.

Monopolistic competition

As the name implies, monopolistic competition is similar in some respects to perfect competition. The two distinguishing characteristics of monopolistic competition are: (1) there are many firms, each selling a small proportion of the market, and (2) each firm sells a product that is slightly different from those of its competitors.

The characteristics of monopolistic competition that makes it very similar to perfect competition is that there are many firms, each selling a small proportion of the market. However, the fact that each firm sells a product that is slightly different from those of its competitors results in a downward sloping demand curve facing each firm. Because its product or service is slightly different from those of its competitors, the firm has some control over the price it charges.

The multitude of firms engaged in retail trade are the best examples of monopolistic competition. Service stations, barber shops, department stores, grocery stores, florists, and repair shops of all kinds are examples. In addition, most of the relatively small and medium-sized manufacturing firms fall into this category.

It may appear a bit strange to say that two retail outlets that sell the same brand of product, such as two Sandard Oil service stations, in fact sell a slightly different product. In the case of retail trade we should bear in mind that the location of the firm is in itself a part of the product sold. For example, a Standard Oil station located on a well-traveled, easily accessible location sells in a sense a different product from another Standard station in a remote location. Other things being equal, the product that is more accessible to us is more desirable, and most people are willing to pay a bit more for a more desirable product.

Another factor that distinguishes two seemingly identical products is service. Some people prefer to purchase their clothing in intimate little shops where the clerk is very friendly and instantly available for assistance. Others buy their clothes in large department stores with very little assistance and impersonal check-out counters. Even though the physical characteristics of the items sold in these two types of stores may be identical, the customer who wants to consume more service along with the item will buy from the small, intimate shop.

However, providing services involves a cost, so we should expect to pay a higher price where more service is provided. For example, gasoline is cheaper at self-service pumps because you are buying less services than at full-service pumps. As individual consumers we have to decide whether the marginal utility per dollar for these services is at least equal to the marginal utility per dollar of other things we buy.

PRICE DETERMINATION IN MONOPOLISTIC COMPETITION

The fact that the goods or services sold by monopolistically competitive firms differ in some respect, either physically or because of location or services, allows a particular firm some flexibility in the price it can charge. This does not mean, of course, that a service station, for example, could charge $1.50 per gallon for gasoline when other stations in the neighborhood are charging $1.00. To do so would be foolhardy because the station would soon lose many of its customers. But it might be able to charge somewhere in the range of $0.90 to $1.10 per gallon, without either causing a price war or losing most of its sales. If the station manager feels that the station can clear more net profit by a narrow-margin, high-volume operation, the manager will probably charge just a bit less than the competition. If the manager thinks the station can make more with a wider-margin, lower-volume business, the price charged will tend to be higher than average.

In monopolistic competition, the range of price within which the firm can operate is determined largely by the average price of its closest competitors. The individual firm may diverge slightly from the average market price, depending on the kind of business it wishes to operate. It is a mistake, however, to believe that just because a firm selling in monopolistic competition places a price tag on its product it can charge any price it pleases. Most firms in this kind of market are restricted to a rather narrow range of price. They have a bit more freedom, however, than the perfectly competitive firm, which has absolutely no leeway in the price it can charge.

In the case of perfect competition we were a bit more precise in determining the price and output for an individual firm. Recall that a perfectly competitive firm maximizes profits if it produces a quantity that corresponds to the point at which marginal cost is equal to market price. We were able to illustrate this with a diagram. We can utilize a similar technique for monopolistic competition, only in this case we must keep in mind that the firm faces a slightly downward sloping demand curve. Moreover, the marginal revenue of an additional unit sold is somewhat less than the price of this unit, because the new lower price must apply to all units sold. There is no difference in the way costs are derived between perfect competition and imperfect competition on the selling side, so we can continue to apply the average and marginal cost concepts utilized in Chapter 7.

As a general rule, an imperfectly competitive firm maximizes profits if it produces or sells a quantity that corresponds to the point at which marginal cost is equal to marginal revenue. Recall that marginal cost (MC) is the cost of producing or selling an additional unit of output, and marginal revenue (MR) is the additional revenue obtained from this extra or marginal unit sold. For example, if it costs a service station 90 cents to sell an extra gallon of gasoline, and the marginal revenue from this extra gallon is 95 cents, the station can increase its profits (or decrease losses) by 5 cents if it sells this extra gallon.

Moreover, it is to the firm's advantage to continue to increase output as long as MR is greater than MC. Why this is so is illustrated in Figure 8–3. Suppose we cut in at a quantity of output just short of the point where MC equals MR, call it Q_0. If we increase output by one additional unit past Q_0, our total costs increase by the distance from the horizontal axis up to the MC curve. However, our total revenue increase is shown by the distance between the horizontal axis and MR. The difference between these two distances represents the additional profit that the firm captures by producing this extra unit.

If we continue to increase output, we see that the distance between MC and MR continues to grow smaller, but as long as there is any distance between them at all, total profits can be increased by increasing output. Total profits are maximized (or losses minimized) at the quantity where MR equals MC, Q_1 in Figure 8–3. To stop producing short of this point, say at Q_0, means that the firm needlessly forgoes profits (or incurs unnecessary losses)

FIGURE 8–3
Profit-maximizing price and quantity for a monopolistically competitive firm

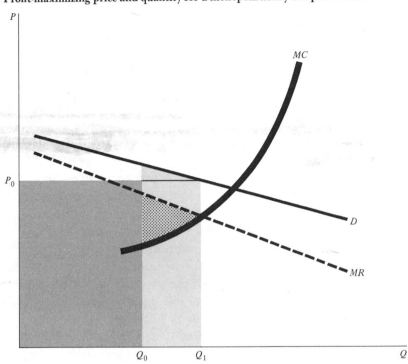

equal in value to the area of the shaded triangle in Figure 8–3.

We can use Figure 8–3 to illustrate the profit-maximizing price that a monopolistically competitive firm would charge. If the firm chooses to maximize profits and produce or sell Q_1, the demand curve facing this firm indicates that the price its customers are willing to pay is equal to P_0. The firm would not want to charge a lower price because in so doing it would just throw away profits. On the other hand it could not charge a higher price because its customers will pay only price P_0 for quantity Q_1.

In Figure 8–3 there is no indication, however, whether the firm is making a pure profit or incurring a loss. All we can tell from this diagram is that P_0 and Q_1 are the optimum price and quantity, respectively, meaning that either the firm's losses are minimized or its profits are maximized. In order to determine the extent of profit or loss, we must know the average total cost (ATC). If ATC is below the price at the optimum quantity, the firm reaps a pure profit; if ATC is above the price, the firm incurs a loss.

Figure 8–4(A) illustrates a situation where the firm is making a pure profit, meaning that the resources used by the firm are earning more than they could make in some alternative activity or occupation. The total dollar value of the pure profit is illustrated by the shaded area. A firm can find itself in this enviable position for one or both of two reasons: (1) the firm is managed very well so that its costs are low, or (2) the firm sells a desirable product so that the demand curve it faces is high relative to those faced by its competitors.

Figure 8–4(B) depicts a less fortunate firm that is incurring a loss. In this situation the resources used by the firm are earning less than they could in alternative employment. The total dollar value of the loss is illustrated by the shaded area. A firm can find itself in this circumstance if its costs are high because of either high-paying alternative employment for its resources or poor management. Or the firm can incur losses if the product it sells is not as desirable to consumers as the products sold by its competitors, so that the demand it faces for its goods is relatively low.

To summarize this procedure, we determine the profit-maximizing quantity for a monopolistically competitive firm by the intersection of the MR and MC curves. The profit-maximizing price is then determined by extending the vertical line drawn through the intersection of MR and MC up to the demand curve. The point where this vertical line just touches the demand curve corresponds to the profit-maximizing price on the vertical axis. Notice that the price line is not drawn over from the intersection of MR and MC, because the price is determined by the demand curve.

If price as determined by the demand curve is greater than the ATC at the profit-maximizing quantity, then the firm is making a pure profit. The average profit per unit is given by the distance between price and ATC at the profit-maximizing quantity. If we multiply this average profit per unit by the total units sold (the profit-maximizing quantity), we obtain the total pure profits. This is illustrated by the shaded rectangle in Figure 8–4(A). By the same token, if price is less than ATC at the profit-maximizing quantity, losses will be incurred. The average loss per unit is equal to the

FIGURE 8–4
Profit and loss situations for a monopolistically competitive firm

(A) Pure profit earned

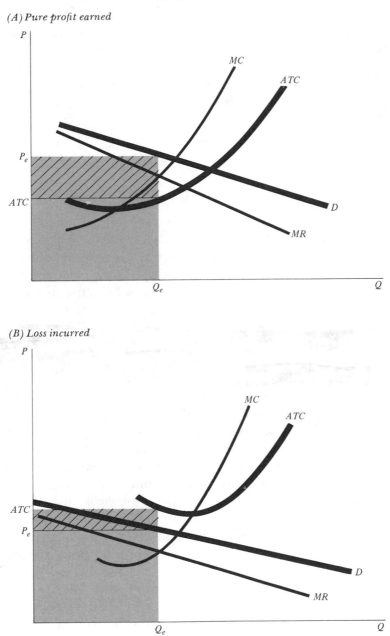

distance between price and ATC, and the total loss is then equal to the shaded rectangle, as illustrated in Figure 8–4(B).

In short, we use MR and MC to determine the quantity to produce and the demand to give us the profit-maximizing price at that quantity. The profit (or loss) is determined by the difference between price and ATC. This procedure holds true for any firm that faces a downward sloping demand curve, that is, any imperfectly competitive firm, including one that is monopolistically competitive.

LONG-RUN ADJUSTMENT IN MONOPOLISTIC COMPETITION

As we saw in the case of perfect competition, the existence of either pure profits or losses for a substantial number of firms in a monopolistically competitive market can be expected to give rise to adjustments by the industry. For example, if a substantial share of the firms is reaping pure profits, this is a signal for existing firms to enlarge their enterprises or for new firms to enter. In either case, the demand curve facing each firm begins to decrease, shifting downward to the left. A decrease in demand, you recall, has two meanings: (1) the firm's consumers will now buy a smaller amount at a given price, or (2) its consumers will buy a given amount only if the price is lower.

This phenomenon is somewhat easier to understand if you visualize yourself as the owner of a service station that is making substantial pure profits. Seeing a good opportunity, another firm builds a station across the street from yours and begins to take some of your customers, perhaps by selling at a slightly lower price. As some of your customers leave, the demand curve facing your firm begins to decrease. You lower your price somewhat in order to compete with this new firm and to adjust to the new lower demand and marginal revenue curves. As the demand curve facing your firm decreases (shifts left), the profit-maximizing price and quantity declines. As a result your pure profits decline and you approach a zero-profit position, as illustrated in Figure 8–5(A).

There is no reason, of course, why every monopolistically competitive firm has to end up at a zero pure-profit or tangency position. Some firms may be able to continue to reap pure profits

(A) Entry of new firms or resources

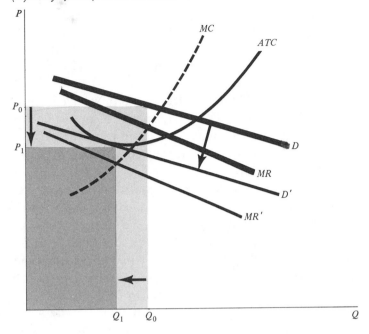

(B) Increase in asset value of profitable firms

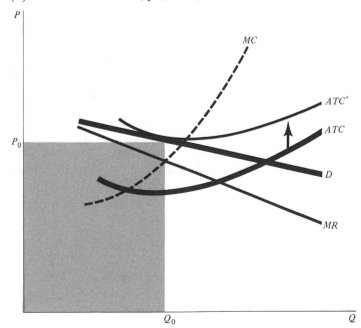

because they own or control certain specialized inputs that other firms cannot duplicate. In retail trade, each firm's location is unique, and some are likely to be more accessible to customers than others. The choice of a superior location may be due to the skill of the original owner or manager, to luck, or to circumstances beyond the control of the firm, such as the construction of a housing development nearby. In other cases a firm may have built up goodwill among its customers over the years, which cannot be duplicated by new entrants into the market. It is also likely that the owners of some firms possess superior entrepreneurial ability that cannot be duplicated by competing firms.

Will the owners of such firms continue to reap pure profits? In one sense yes, in another sense no. The fact that other firms cannot duplicate the firm's superior inputs means that the product price is not likely to be bid down any further, and that the firms can retain these profits. On the other hand, the market value of the profitable firm's assets will likely increase to reflect its superior profit position. We could expect potential buyers to be willing to pay more for the assets of a highly profitable firm than for the assets of a firm that earns normal profits or incurs losses. Economists would say that the pure profits are "capitalized" into the value of the firm. If the owner correctly calculates implicit costs, mainly forgone interest on the increased equity value in the firm, the average total cost curve will increase, as illustrated by ATC' in Figure 8–5(B). In this sense, the pure profits disappear into the increased capitalized value of the firm. However, the current owner still does not lose these profits because they have contributed to an increase in the value of the person's assets.

Since owners have finite life-spans, it is necessary for profitable firms to eventually change hands. If the original owner or the real estate person is a shrewd bargainer, it should be possible to obtain a price that will give the new owner just a normal profit or a normal return on the investment, as illustrated by Figure 8–5(B). The phenomenon is basically the same for corporations, only here the owners (stockholders) may number in the thousands, and the equity value of the firm is reflected in the value of its stock certificates.

It is important to keep in mind, of course, that in any industry circumstances are continually changing. Thus it is not likely there would ever be a situation in which every firm is at a zero-profit, long-run equilibrium. It is more realistic to visualize a situation where there is continual movement toward equilibrium but few instances where it is ever reached. We would expect to observe at any time a wide variety of profit positions by firms; some might be enjoying substantial pure profits, others just earning what might be earned in other industries, and still others incurring losses.

We could go through the same analysis for a case in which a substantial share of the firms in a monopolistically competitive market is suffering losses. Just the opposite would occur, compared with the pure-profit situation. Now firms would leave the industry, shifting the demand curve that faces the remaining firms to the right. [You might find it useful to illustrate this with a diagram of your own similar to Figure 8–5(A).]

Persistent losses also can change the asset value of a firm. As an example, consider a service station or restaurant that is built on a busy two-lane highway that gives way to a new expressway that takes most of the highway traffic. Needless to say, the firm is likely to suffer a major decline in sales and may even go out of business entirely. If the owner sells the structure, it is likely to bring considerably less than it would have in its original use. The new owners may turn the service station into a bicycle repair shop, or the restaurant may be converted to a mortuary. At any rate, if the new owners are shrewd bargainers, they will not pay any more for the structure than assures them a normal profit in the new business.

As an even more prevalent example, firms such as a service station, clothing store, or restaurant, that are realizing losses often go out of business. After a few months of remaining vacant, they may open up under new management but in the same kind of business. If the previous owner could not make a normal profit, how can the new owners expect to do any better? They may have some ideas on how to improve things, but in addition it is likely that they have been able to purchase the structure at a price that enables them to expect at least a normal profit. Or if the new owner is a shrewd bargainer, the person may be able to buy the property at a price low enough to yield pure profits, at least for a time.

It is interesting to note that a change in costs because of a revaluation of assets, either up or down, does not affect the price of the product sold or produced. Here we would say that costs are "price determined." In a case where costs are changed because of changes in production technology or input prices, we would expect the market price to change because of a change in supply. In the latter case, we would say that costs are "price determining."

Oligopoly

Oligopoly is derived from the Greek word *oligos,* meaning few. This definition provides a hint about the kind of industry that is characterized by an oligopoly. Basically an *oligopoly* is an industry in which a few firms, say three or four, produce the major share of the market. Oligopoly is commonly found in heavy industry or in products marketed nationally. Autos, steel, airplanes, drugs, farm equipment, minerals, petroleum, and computers are some examples of products that are produced by oligopolies.

Industries in which a few large firms produce the major share of the output come into being mainly because large firms are able to produce the product more efficiently than small firms, that is, because of economies of scale. For example, it is hard to visualize the auto industry consisting of several thousand or even several hundred firms. Each firm would be too small to utilize the most efficient mass production techniques.

Unlike monopolistic competition, the firms in an oligopolistic market do not necessarily produce a differentiated product. In fact, petroleum, steel, and minerals could all be classified as homogeneous products. A ton of steel produced by U.S. Steel is essentially the same product as a ton produced by Bethlehem or Jones and Laughlin. There are, of course, oligopolies that produce differentiated products such as automobiles or appliances. Thus the distinguishing characteristic of an oligopoly is the small number of firms in the market.

PRICE DETERMINATION IN OLIGOPOLY

The fact that each firm sells a substantial share of the market or sells a differentiated product makes it possible for each firm to influence to some degree the price of its product. For example, if one of the large steel companies reduced its output, there would likely be a noticeable decline in the amount of steel on the market, providing that imports of steel do not make up the difference. This would, in turn, result in an increase in the price of steel. Thus each firm has some control over the price of the product it sells, which is just another way of saying that each firm in an oligopoly faces a downward sloping demand curve.

We should note, however, that each firm's ability to influence the price of its product is limited by the substitute products available. Each firm, therefore, must sell its product at a price somewhere in line with the prices of its competitors. It is not likely that Ford would sell many cars if its price were several hundred dollars higher than that of comparable Chevrolet models. For homogeneous products produced in an oligopoly market, there is even less chance for price differentials to exist. Disregarding transportation charges, no one would want to buy steel from U.S. Steel if it charged just slightly more than the other companies.

We should not be surprised, therefore, when we observe all firms in an oligopoly market changing their prices at about the same time. This is an indication that consumers regard the products of the major firms in an oligopoly market as close substitutes. If a firm's price rises out of line with the prices of other firms, its customers soon discover substitute products that give them more for their money. If the products of firms in an oligopolistic market are close substitutes for one another, as in steel or petroleum for example, there will be virtually no difference in price between the products. For products such as luxury automobiles, which consumers regard as less perfect substitutes, wider differences in price between firms can be observed.

Also it should be recognized that all firms in a particular industry use about the same resources. Therefore if resource prices change, the MC and ATC curves for each firm will shift by about the same amount. Consequently the profit-maximizing price will change by about the same amount for each firm.

In dealing with the prices of oligopoly products, one ought to distinguish between the list price, the price on the window sticker for automobiles, for example, and the actual price that consumers pay. The difference between these two prices can be substantial for differentiated products. For example, the actual prices paid for new U.S.-made cars tend to be 15 to 20 percent lower than their list or "sticker" prices. For example, the actual selling price of a car with a $6,000 sticker price is likely to be in the range of $4,800 to $5,400. Just how much difference exists between the list price and actual price depends on a number of factors. The difference tends to be greatest for makes and models that are not selling as well as expected, causing inventories to accumulate. The difference also tends to be largest at the end of the model year. One should regard the actual price rather than the list price as the profit-maximizing (or loss-minimizing) price. No doubt all firms would *like* to obtain the higher list price, but in many cases the demand is such that firms would end up with large, unsold inventories at the end of the model year and as a result earn lower total profits, or incur greater losses, than if they cut the price and sold the extra units. Of course, if some models are in short supply, such as occurred for small cars during the period following the Arab oil embargo and again in 1979, firms may be able to sell all they produce of these models at the list price or close to it. Also most imported automobiles sell for about their list price.

Like monopolistic competition, oligopoly price determination can also be illustrated with a diagram (Figure 8–6). As a matter of fact, the same diagram used for illustrating the optimum price and quantity for a monopolistically competitive firm can also be used for an oligopoly. We might expect, however, that an oligopoly would face a slightly less elastic demand curve, because by definition it sells a larger share of the market. It is risky to generalize about this because of differences in the degree of product differentiation between the two types of firms and because of possible differences in the elasticity of the market demand for the general category of product, such as steel versus women's clothing. Also we would expect the demand facing an oligopolist selling a homogeneous product to be somewhat more elastic than would be the case for one selling a product different from that of its competitors.

At any rate, the two types of firms (monopolistic competitors and oligopoly) are similar in that the oligopoly attempts also to equate MC with MR to determine the most profitable output. The price charged by the firm is determined by the demand that faces the firm at this output. This profit-maximizing price shown in Figure 8–6 is actual price, not list price.

FIGURE 8–6
Profit-maximizing price and quantity for an oligopoly

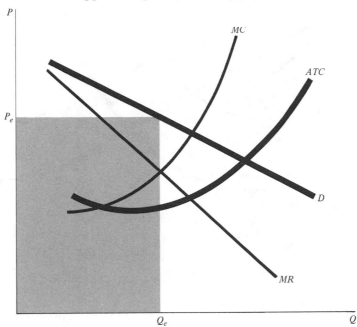

In this particular example, price is greater than average total costs, so the firm would be earning a pure profit. Of course, this is only an example. If the ATC curve was everywhere above the firm's demand curve, the firm would have no choice but to take a loss or shut down. (You might illustrate this situation by drawing a similar diagram.)

INTERDEPENDENCE OF FIRMS IN OLIGOPOLY

An inevitable result of the small number of firms in an oligopoly market is that the action of any one of the major firms has a significant effect on the sales and/or price of the other firms in the market. For example, suppose General Motors grants a wage increase to its employees, which in turn leads to an increase in the cost of production, as shown in Figure 8–7(A). We can see from Figure 8–7(A) that it would be in GM's interest to raise the price

FIGURE 8–7
**Effects of an increase in manufacturing costs of General Motors
automobiles**

(A) General Motors

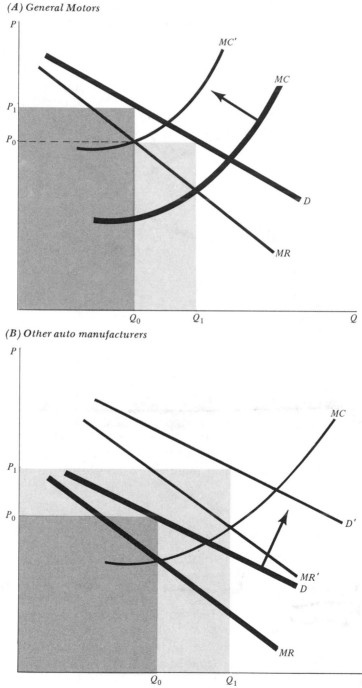

(B) Other auto manufacturers

of its cars from P_0 to P_1 and reduce the quantity sold from Q_1 to Q_0 in order to again equate MC and MR. If they continued to charge P_0 and sell Q_1, MC would be greater than MR, so they would be losing money on the marginal units produced.

Recall from our discussion of consumer demand that when the price of a good increases, there is an increase in demand for substitute goods. We can predict, therefore, that an increase in the price of GM cars will lead to an increase in demand for the other makes, as shown in Figure 8–7(B). Consumers will try to avoid the higher prices of GM cars by purchasing more of other makes. But an increase in the demand for other makes will in turn lead to an increase in both price and quantity of these cars, as the other firms attempt to equate MC with MR, as shown in Figure 8–7(B). We see, therefore, that an increase in the costs and price of products of just one of the major firms in an oligopoly market leads to an increase in price of products of the other firms as well. (You might also want to prove to yourself that a decrease in costs and price by one firm will also lead to a decrease in price of other firms by constructing diagrams of your own.) Of course, it is reasonable to believe that the other auto firms eventually will experience the same increase in labor costs as GM, so everyone's cost curves will end up at about the same level.

It should also be pointed out that the increase in demand and price shown in Figure 8–7(B) will in turn lead to a slight increase in demand for GM cars, resulting in a slightly greater increase in price for these cars than was originally specified in Figure 8–7(A). In fact, we could trace this process of cause and effect back and forth indefinitely. As a rule, however, the largest and most interesting changes come on the first round, so economists have not been greatly concerned with the second- or third-order effects.

THE KINKED DEMAND CURVE

Another apparent characteristic of an oligopolistic market is the relative "stickiness" of product price. Compared with perfectly competitive and monopolistically competitive firms, oligopolies tend to change the price of their products infrequently. For example, once an auto manufacturer announces the list prices of its new cars, it tends to stick with them, often for the entire model year except in periods of relatively high inflation. We should bear in mind, however, that these are list prices, not actual prices.

In an effort to formulate a theory that takes these characteristics specifically into account, economists have developed the idea of the "kinked" demand curve facing the firm. The basic assumption of this theory is that each firm attempts to retain its present customers or attract new ones. Let us see how the kinked demand curve is derived. Suppose General Motors raises its price. It is assumed in this case that the other auto manufacturers will hold to their original price in order to take GM's customers.[1] Thus GM experiences a substantial reduction in sales, as shown in Figure 8–8, where price increases from P_1 to P_2 and quantity declines from Q_1 to Q_0. On the other hand, if GM reduces prices from P_1 to P_0, it is assumed that other firms will also reduce their prices. Thus GM

FIGURE 8–8
Kinked demand curve

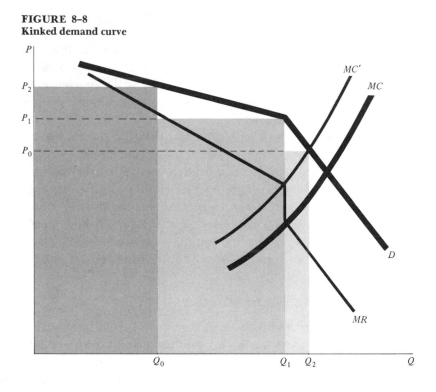

---

[1] Notice that this assumption implies that the other firms do not attempt to maximize profits by producing where MC equals MR.

is able to obtain only a modest increase in sales, say from Q_1 to Q_2, and we have a kink in the demand curve facing the firm.

Notice also that the kinked demand curve results in a discontinuous MR curve. The most elastic portion of the MR curve is derived from the more elastic segment of the demand curve, and the less elastic portion of MR is derived from the lower, less elastic portion of the total demand curve. The resulting two segments of the MR curve are joined by a vertical line. Now if MC should intersect MR at some point within this vertical section, a shift in MC, as shown in Figure 8–8, would not change the optimum price and quantity for the firm. That is, the profit-maximizing price and quantity would remain at P_1 and Q_1 respectively, for either MC or MC'. As a result, the kinked demand curve is sometimes used to explain why oligopoly prices do not exhibit a large amount of fluctuation.

The theory of the kinked demand curve has fallen out of favor among economists and is not used much any more for several reasons. For one thing, it is not possible to derive from the kinked demand curve how the going price and quantity come to be what they are. These magnitudes have to be assumed as given. Second, it is doubtful that oligopoly prices are as inflexible as generally assumed. Even though list prices might remain unchanged over a long period, actual prices may vary considerably. For example, the actual price of a new car tends to fall from the beginning to the end of the model year, even though the list price stays the same. The same is true for appliances. Or if an oligopolistic firm mistakenly produces more of an item than it thought would sell at the list price, price cuts are in evidence in order to get rid of the excess inventory. Finally, as pointed out in footnote 1, the assumptions imply that competing firms do not attempt to maximize profits.

PRICE SEARCHING

Although the diagrams developed in the previous sections are helpful in providing a framework for thinking about the operation of an oligopolistic firm and market, we should not lose sight of the complexities involved, particularly in reference to price determination by the individual firm. It is one thing to equate marginal cost with marginal revenue, follow the line up to the demand curve, and determine price and quantity. It is quite another thing to find out what these magnitudes actually are.

To be sure, each large oligopolistic firm is likely to have a staff of economists, cost accountants, market researchers, and the like to assess costs and market demand. But there is still a good deal of trial and error involved in price determination. This is particularly true for a new product or an entirely new firm. If there are similar products already on the market, the firm, of course, would want to set a price somewhere in line with that for the established items. The firm also would want to compare such a price with its unit production costs. It is likely to have a fairly good idea of average costs and may even have some idea of marginal costs.

Once a particular price is set and a production decision has been made, the firm will begin to receive information not only from the market but also from its own cost and profit figures. If the product is not selling and inventories are piling up, it may be an indication that the product is overpriced. When breaking in with a new product, it usually is necessary to offer consumers a bit more for their money than they receive from established items, or else they have little incentive to change. As time goes by and sales pick up (i.e., demand facing the firms increases or shifts to the right), the firm may want to adjust the price upward slightly, especially if production cannot keep up with sales. Of course, in times of inflation, with increased wages and prices of raw materials, product price will have to be increased, or the firm is likely to find its average total costs exceeding product price.

Naturally each firm must keep its eye on its major competitors. Indeed, if the firm is relatively small or new in the business, it might decide to play follow-the-leader. If the large, dominant firm increases price, the small firm follows suit; or if the large firm lowers price, so does the small one. This kind of behavior, quite common in oligopolistic markets, is referred to as *price leadership*. In addition to relieving the small firm of the task of periodically deciding on its product price, this practice reduces the likelihood that the small firm will provoke the large one into a price war, possibly wiping out the small firm.

Even with price leadership, at least one firm in an oligopolistic market must bear the responsibility of setting a price. One possible procedure for such a firm is to engage in what is sometimes called *average cost pricing.* Here the firm determines the average total cost of an item, adds a certain percent of that figure for profit, and uses this figure for its price. Of course, this does not guarantee the firm a profit regardless of its costs. If the firm becomes inefficient, other firms may decide that they can sell at a lower price and still cover their costs, including a normal profit. Thus even a so-called dominant firm has no guarantee of remaining dominant. In addition to contending with the up and coming firms on the home scene, it may have to contend with foreign competition. Competitive forces from foreign firms are especially evident in such industries as autos, steel, shipbuilding, shoes, radios, and textiles.

We should also point out that the potential competition of each firm is not limited to existing firms in its own industry. If excessive pure profits are evident in an industry, usually there is nothing to stop established firms in other industries from moving in to get a piece of the action. For example, if bicycle manufacturing should become very profitable, there is nothing to stop General Motors or Ford from getting into the bicycle business. Indeed many of the so-called conglomerates of today are involved in several industries simultaneously.

MERGERS AND CONGLOMERATES

Many firms find themselves in a situation where they must become larger in order to become more efficient (i.e., attain economies of scale) and remain competitive in their field. Since internal growth is often a relatively slow and difficult process, the merging of two or more firms has proved to be a popular vehicle for growth. A better appreciation for its popularity can be gained by looking at some of the advantages of a merger. Two or more firms that become one may be able to gain some advantages of specialization by devoting entire plants to the production of one or two components of their overall product. In the case of an auto firm, one plant might manufacture engines, another bodies, and so on. It may also be possible to gain some scale economies by sharing a common management and administrative structure. Instead of having two or three main offices and staffs, the merged firm may be able to get by with one. A larger firm may be able to take advantage of a more efficient advertising media, such as nationwide television, to borrow at a lower rate of interest, or to sell stock more easily.

In addition to pure scale economies, some firms have found it possible to obtain tax savings through merger. For example, if a firm that is incurring losses merges with one reaping pure profits, their overall tax bill may be reduced by writing off the one's losses against the other's profits. Another advantage is the possibility of easing the competitive pressure faced by each firm. It is evident that the merger of two intense rivals would likely make life considerably more pleasant for all involved. However, where the merger of two competing firms would result in a virtual monopoly, the Justice Department is likely to step in and forbid the merger.

Merger, of course, is not limited to firms in the same industry. When two or more firms in separate industries merge to become one, they form what is known as a *conglomerate*. A well-known conglomerate is International Telephone and Telegraph (ITT), which has holdings in numerous industries. Large firms such as this often have sufficient assets to simply acquire control of other firms and take over their management, as opposed to working out a mutual agreement, as in a merger. As a result some people have expressed concern over the large amount of "economic power" wielded by conglomerates and have called for tighter control over their actions.

COLLUSION AND ANTITRUST LEGISLATION

The small number of firms in an oligopolistic market opens up the possibility for two or more rival firms agreeing not to compete. Agreements of this nature can be informal in nature, with rivals agreeing to maintain a certain price or to divide up the market. There is the possibility also that participating firms will enter into formal, written agreements whereby they agree to a specified price that will be charged and the quantity of the product each will produce. This arrangement is commonly referred to as a *cartel*. In essence, a cartel, or even a binding informal agreement, results in a market situation resembling that of a monopoly. It is as though there were only one firm in the market. As a consequence we would expect a higher price than would exist if there were many firms competing in the market.

The two main legal tools that the government uses to fight non-sanctioned monopolies or cartels are the Sherman Antitrust Act of 1890 and the Clayton Antitrust Act of 1914. The Sherman Act makes "restraint of trade" or any attempt to monopolize trade a misdemeanor, that is, a criminal offense against the federal government. The Clayton Act essentially duplicates the Sherman Act but does spell out in a bit more detail the various illegal activities that might eventually lead to a monopoly or cartel. The intention of this act was to curb monopoly before it came into existence, rather than to just punish it after the fact. The Federal Trade Commission (FTC), also set up in 1914, was given power to investigate "unfair" business practices and to take legal action if required.

In addition to government action against monopolies or cartels, there is a market force that acts as a continual deterrent. This is the temptation by colluding firms to cheat on one another. As shown in Figure 8–9, an industry that becomes a monopoly or cartel must reduce its output in order to raise price. Thus each individual firm that agrees to collude must agree to reduce its output in order for the scheme to work. But if each firm is maximizing profits by equating MR with MC before the collusion takes place, as is reasonable to expect, then after they agree to reduce quantity and raise price, MR for each firm will be greater than MC, as shown in Figure 8–9. Before collusion, each firm maximizes profits by producing Q_1—the quantity that corresponds to the intersection of the MC and MR curves. During collusion, each firm reduces its output to Q_0. We cannot, however, illustrate the new higher price that will result from collusion on the diagrams in Figure 8–9 because these are the demand curves that face each firm, not the market demand. We can only assume that the new higher price will result in higher net profits for each firm, or else it would not pay to collude in the first place.

But the important point to note is that during collusion each firm is in a situation where MR is greater than MC. Thus it is in the interest of each individual firm to sell a few extra units of output "under the table." By doing so, the firm can increase its profits even more. But when all or most firms taking part in the collusion cheat in this manner, the market price must come down, otherwise the additional output cannot be sold. Unless the group of colluders can impose a penalty on the cheaters, there is a tend-

FIGURE 8–9
Effect on individual firms of colluding to reduce quantity and raise price

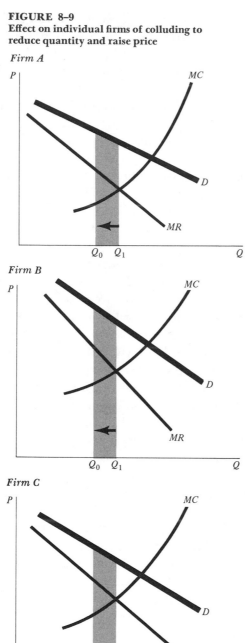

Firm A

Firm B

Firm C

ency for the collusive agreements to break down. And it is difficult to enforce any kind of penalty against a firm for refraining from an activity that is itself illegal.

Pure monopoly

At the other end of the spectrum of industry types is pure monopoly, which exists where there is just one firm providing a good or service in a market. This kind of market tends to exist only when the government has the exclusive right to supply a good or service, such as the post office, or when the government has given exclusive right for a firm to operate, such as a local light and power company.

The existence of a pure monopoly depends also on how broadly we define a good or service. For example, the post office has a monopoly on official mail service but not on all communications. Or the local light and power company has a monopoly on centrally generated electricity but not on factory- or home-generated electricity, or other sources of light and power such as gas or oil. It is not correct to assume, therefore, that consumers are forced to buy from a monopoly or else go without. In most instances there are substitutes for goods produced by a monopoly, albeit imperfect substitutes. As the price of the monopoly's good or service rises, these imperfect substitutes come into greater demand.

A monopoly is able to persist for any length of time only if entry into the industry is blocked. The most effective means of blocking entry into an industry is for the government to reserve exclusive right of production to itself or to firms that it designates by means of a license. Sometimes a firm can gain a temporary monopoly by discovering a new product or input and patenting it. Monopolies such as this, however, tend to be short-lived, or at least very narrowly defined, because patents usually can be circumvented by producing something just slightly different.[2]

The reason usually given for creating and nurturing government-sanctioned monopolies is to capture economies of scale, mainly by avoiding unnecessary duplication of facilities. For example, if

---

[2] There are, of course, exceptions, such as the Polaroid Land camera.

there were several telephone companies in your area, there would have to be as many sets of lines and switchboards. Moreover it would be inconvenient for people on one company's lines to attempt to call people who buy telephone service from a different company, unless there were some sort of central clearinghouse for calls.

In recent years an increasing amount of criticism has been directed at government-sanctioned monopolies. It is becoming less clear that the benefits of avoiding all duplication exceed the costs of such a policy. As long as a firm or an institution enjoys the exclusive right to operate free from competitors, there is little incentive for it to search for cost-reducing techniques or to provide better goods or services. There is nothing like a little competition, even one competitor, to keep the supplier of a good or service responsive to consumers. Complaints of bad service, protests, and the like tend to be not nearly so effective as the possibility of losing one's job to a competitor.

In the field of education, also, it can be questioned whether the monopoly held by the public school system is necessary or in the best interests of society. At the elementary and secondary levels of education, and to some extent at the college level, everyone must pay for public schools regardless of whether their children attend them or not. This tends to place the private and parochial schools at a competitive disadvantage in providing an educational service. Under the present system, public schools can become very bad before it pays parents to send their children to private schools. It has been suggested that a system of providing educational vouchers to students to "spend" at the school of their choice is one means of promoting more competition in the education "industry." It has been argued also that the general public would gain if public schools were allowed to compete with one another. Under the present setup a child is forced to attend a designated public school or no public school at all. Hence it is argued that improvements would be made in the poorer public schools if the children attending these schools were allowed to take their business elsewhere. By and large, public school officials and teachers' unions have not greeted the voucher idea with a great deal of enthusiasm. However, one should bear in mind that people who happen to enjoy monopoly privileges usually are against change and generally have an amply supply of reasons for keeping things as they are.

MONOPOLY PRICE DETERMINATION

Since government has created or at least sanctioned most present-day monopolies and therefore controls their prices, there is relatively little chance for a private monopoly to set a profit-maximizing price. We might, however, determine what this price might be and then determine the "socially optimum" price of a monopoly-supplied good or service.

The diagram for illustrating the price and output for a monopoly is essentially the same as those used to illustrate the price and output for monopolistic competition and oligopoly. The only difference for a monopoly is that the demand curve facing the firm is the same as the market demand curve for the good or service sold by the monopoly. Thus for a given good or service the demand facing a monopoly should be somewhat steeper (or more inelastic) than the demand facing an oligopoly firm, given the product sold.

As shown in Figure 8–10, the profit-maximizing price and quantity are P_m and Q_m, respectively. We should not take this to mean, however, that a monopoly is always assured of a pure profit. If the average total cost (ATC) curve is everywhere above the demand curve, the monopoly either takes a loss or shuts down. In fact, cases of monopoly losses are not uncommon in the public utilities. (You might illustrate a monopoly loss with a diagram of your own.)

Since present-day monopoly is generally regulated by the government, and since the government is supposed to represent the general public, at least in a democracy, we would expect it to set a price and quantity that would somehow maximize the general welfare of the people (i.e., consumers). To understand what this price and quantity might be, it is necessary to go back to what we said about perfect competition.

Recall that the value of output to society is maximized if each firm produces up to the point where the price of the marginal unit produced is equal to its marginal cost. Recall also that the price of the marginal unit is its measure of value to society, and its marginal cost (MC) is the value of goods given up to produce this extra unit.

FIGURE 8–10
Monopoly price and quantity

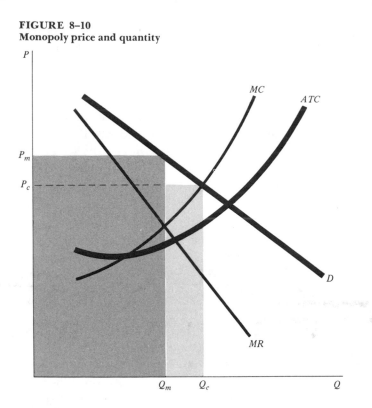

You will note in Figure 8–9, however, that price is greater than MC at the profit-maximizing price and quantity. This means, as we pointed out in Chapter 7, that there is an underallocation of resources to the production of this good or service.

It is fairly evident, then, that if the government wishes to maximize the total value of output to society for a given amount of resources, it should set a price that corresponds to the intersection of the MC curve and the demand curve, P_c in Figure 8–10. At this point, price is equal to MC, so that the value of the marginal unit is just equal to the value of the goods given up to produce it.

Notice that the socially optimum price, P_c is somewhat less than the profit-maximizing price, P_m, and the optimum quantity, Q_c, is greater than the profit-maximizing quantity, Q_m. It can also be seen that the monopoly firm is still making a pure profit at the regulated price and quantity, because price is still greater than

ATC. Because of this pure profit, you might suggest that the price be lowered still further to the point where ATC intersects the demand curve. But if this were done, we see that MC would be greater than the price, indicating an overallocation of resources to this production activity. If competing firms were allowed to enter this industry, there would be a decrease in the demand facing this firm and a gradual competing away of these pure profits. The government, however, in order to maintain the monopoly, prohibits entry of other firms.

Does the monopoly, then, continue to reap pure profits? Probably not indefinitely. The likely outcome of this situation would be an eventual bidding up of the value of the firm's assets, pushing the ATC curve upward. For example, over the years the value of New York City taxicab medallions, which represent an exclusive right to operate taxis in New York City, has increased substantially. The original or past owners enjoyed a capital gain, while new or future owners probably earn or will earn just a normal return on their labor and investment, taking into account the increased cost of operating a cab because of the interest charge (explicit or implicit) on the medallion.

In the case of government-regulated monopolies, there are some people who argue that the "regulator" soon becomes the "regulatee." They argue that monopolies develop powerful lobbies to influence the decisions of the government agencies that are supposed to regulate them. We see some evidence of this when the government either raises or lowers prices in response to pressure from regulated firms or industries. It is possible to argue, therefore, that a regulated price is not greatly different from a profit-maximizing price.

Moreover, we cannot be certain that a regulated price is always lower than the profit-maximizing price. If new technology comes on the scene and lowers MC, downward adjustments in the regulated price probably lag behind the adjustments that would automatically take place if the monopoly purposely tried to maximize profits. Also if firms are allowed to compete with each other, there is a stronger incentive to search for cost-reducing techniques and to offer better prices and services to consumers. It is interesting to note that interstate airline fares, which for many years were regulated by the government, averaged about twice (on a per mile basis) the fares of intrastate airlines, which were not government regulated.[3]

WHY MINIMIZE MONOPOLY?

We have seen that in some industries, mainly the public utilities, the government creates and maintains monopolies. However, in other industries the government attempts to discourage monopoly power and to maintain an atmosphere of competition. There are probably several reasons why this is so.

First, as discussed in the preceding section, any situation where price is greater than marginal cost causes a misallocation of resources, resulting in a smaller total value of output for society, given the resources available. Of course, the same criticism can be levied against any firm that faces a downward sloping demand curve (i.e., is imperfectly competitive). But economists have found that the loss of output in the U.S. economy because of a misallocation of resources stemming from monopoly power of firms is relatively small.[4] It is also true that politicians and the general public have not become very concerned about a misallocation of resources, probably because they are not able to envision the total value of output without the misallocation.

The general public does, however, have an idea of what is a reasonable or "just" level of profit. And it is assumed, probably correctly, that a firm that is able to monopolize an industry will reap excessive profits, resulting in an unjustifiable transfer of income from consumers to the owners of the monopoly. An atmosphere of competition is maintained, therefore, to keep profits down to what people consider a reasonable level.

A third reason for attempting to maintain competition is to encourage the adoption of cost-reducing technology or the development of new and better products. Again, if a firm has no com-

---

[3] For example the fare from Los Angeles to San Francisco, which was not regulated, was about half the regulated fare from Chicago to Minneapolis, which is approximately the same distance.

[4] See Arnold C. Harberger, "Monopoly and Resource Allocation," *American Economic Review* (May 1954), pp. 77–87.

petition, there is little incentive to risk and develop anything new.

MONOPOLY POWER

Although unregulated, private monopoly is illegal in the United States and therefore does not exist, it is common to refer to the degree of "monopoly power" held by firms, particularly large oligopolies. Monopoly power, however, tends to be a rather vague term. Probably the most precise measure of monopoly power is the ratio of the price of the product to the marginal cost of producing the last unit of the product. Recall from Chapter 7 that in a perfectly competitive industry each firm produces that quantity corresponding to the point where $P = MC$. In other words, the P/MC ratio for firms that have no monopoly power (perfectly competitive) is equal to one.

In the case of imperfect competition, each firm maximizes profits by producing the quantity that corresponds to the point where $MR = MC$. Because an imperfectly competitive firm by definition faces a downward sloping demand curve, its profit-maximizing price is greater than MC. Thus the P/MC ratio for all imperfectly competitive firms is greater than one. This ratio becomes larger, the steeper (less elastic) the demand curve facing the individual firm. Given the elasticity of the market demand for the product, the greater the share of the market enjoyed by each firm (the closer it comes to a pure monopoly), the steeper is the demand curve facing the firm and the higher is the P/MC ratio. Thus the size of the P/MC ratio is a rather precise measure of monopoly power. It also is a useful measure of the misallocation of resources resulting from monopoly power.

The main difficulty of using the P/MC ratio is the lack of information on marginal cost of firms. The lack of information on marginal cost tends to rule out the use of the P/MC ratio. The next best measure of monopoly power of the largest firms in a market or industry is the share of the market enjoyed by these firms. As mentioned, given the market elasticity of demand for the product, the larger the share of the market, the greater is the monopoly power of large firms. The market shares enjoyed by the four largest firms in selected U.S. industries are presented in Table 8–1. Although these figures do not give us the P/MC ratios, they can be helpful in identifying the industries where the potential for excessive monopoly power is present.

TABLE 8–1
Percent of total industry shipments accounted for by the four largest firms, selected U.S. industries, 1970

Motor vehicles	91%	Farm machinery	40%
Cigarettes	84	Metal stamping	40
Organic fibers	73	Petroleum refining	33
Tires	72	Periodicals	28
Soap	70	Shoes	28
Aircraft manufacturers	65	Pharmaceuticals	26
Radio and TV manufacturers	48	Meat packing	23
Malt liquors	46	Book publishing	21
Shipbuilding	46	Sawmills	16

Source: *Statistical Abstract*, 1974, pp. 720–23.

Bear in mind that these figures represent the share of the market accounted for by the *four* largest firms as a group. Even if the four firms' sales accounted for 100 percent of the market, on the average each firm would have 25 percent. Of course, it is possible that the largest of the four would have more than 25 percent. It should also be pointed out that these value of shipment figures include only U.S. firms. Consumers also have the option of buying imported goods. Imported products are especially important for automobiles, petroleum, steel, tires, shipbuilding, and radio and TV manufacturers. The added element of foreign competition causes the demand curves facing large U.S. firms to be flatter (more elastic) than they would otherwise be.

MONOPOLY POWER AND INFLATION

During times of increased inflationary pressure, there is a tendency for people to blame large business firms for the rising level of prices. Since business firms are the ones that are raising prices, it is understandable why people may come to such a conclusion. Although a full explanation for inflation is best left to a macroeconomics course, one ought to be reminded here that each imperfectly competitive firm, regardless of its degree of monopoly power, has one and only one profit-maximizing price for a given set of demand and cost curves. Recall that this price is that which is read off of the demand curve at the quantity corresponding to the intersection of MC and MR. If for some reason firms decided to raise prices higher and higher without a change in their demand and cost curves, they would experience a reduction in profits, which of course would be irrational. Thus we can be quite certain that the underlying cause of inflation is not due to a sudden increase in greed on the part of business people, for such behavior would lead to lower rather than higher profits. Indeed there is no reason to believe that the desire for profits is any greater during times of inflation than during periods of relatively stable prices.

The fact remains, however, that business firms do raise prices during periods of inflation. We may expect this behavior to be the result of the desire to maximize profits or minimize losses (the latter also occurs during inflation). Price increases are the result of an increase in the demand facing the firm and/or an increase in the cost of production. The demand facing the firm increases because of higher money incomes of consumers, although not necessarily higher real incomes. (Recall that a change in *money* incomes is a demand shifter.) In addition, higher prices paid for labor, capital, and raw materials increase the firms' marginal and average cost curves, shifting them up and to the left. Both shifts result in a higher profit-maximizing price. (You may want to illustrate the effects of these shifts on diagrams of your own.)

By and large, the shifts in the demand and cost curves that occur during inflation are out of the control of the individual firm. If the firm did have control over them, it would want to decrease costs rather than increase them in order to put more distance between price and ATC. The firm would, of course, like to experience an increase in demand for its product, but this desire is not limited to inflationary times. At any rate, the desired shifts in costs and demand, if the firm could control them, would not necessarily lead to an increase in product price. Thus we should look for a reason other than the monopoly power of business firms for the underlying cause of inflation. As mentioned, this is a major topic in the macroeconomics course.

Advertising

Advertising includes a wide range of activities. The homemade "For Sale" sign on an automobile, the want ads in the newspaper, roadside signs, and radio and TV commercials are all examples of advertising. Some advertising is done by buyers, such as help-wanted ads, though the majority probably is done by sellers.

Essentially advertising can be divided into two major types: informational and persuasive. Informational advertising, as the name implies, is intended to inform prospective customers about what is for sale, its characteristics, and its price. An example of informational advertising is the grocery store advertisements in the newspaper telling the prices of various items that can be bought at a particular store. Persuasive advertising, on the other hand, attempts to persuade people to buy one product rather than another. Most of the advertising we see on television or hear over the radio is in large part persuasive, although one might argue that such advertising also contains some information by making us aware of certain characteristics of the products.

All advertising attempts to accomplish one objective: increase the demand for the good or service being advertised. Of course, it must be realized that advertising costs money. Thus when a firm or group of firms decides to advertise, we can only assume that the marginal revenue obtained from the extra products sold due to advertising is at least as great as the marginal cost (including advertising expense) of the extra units sold; otherwise firms would not advertise.

A great deal of disagreement exists over the merits of advertising. Most people, including economists, probably would agree, however, that informational advertising is beneficial. In order for consumers to maximize utility, they must know what is for sale, something about the good or service being sold, and the selling price. In addition, it is likely that advertising increases competition between buyers and sellers and between different sellers of the same product. If buyers are informed through advertising that a given product is available at a lower price than is being asked by a particular seller, they can bargain with the seller to lower price or they will take their business elsewhere. Similarly, if sellers see other sellers offering lower prices, they are likely to follow suit in order to remain competitive. For example, it has been shown that the average price of eyeglasses in states where eyeglass advertising is banned was more than twice the average price paid in states where advertising is not restricted.[5]

Much less agreement exists, however, about persuasive advertising. The advertising industry argues that advertising stimulates the economy by enticing people to spend. Others, particularly those who have recently experienced a rather nauseating commercial, argue that persuasive advertising is pure waste because the effect of one firm's advertising just cancels out the advertising of other firms.

A truly objective appraisal of advertising, if such is possible, would likely rate it somewhere between these two extreme views. No doubt advertising stimulates spending on the item being advertised or it would not pay to advertise. But it is less clear whether advertising really makes people spend a larger share of their income. Expenditures on advertising have increased greatly during the past three or four decades, but on the average people spend about the same proportion of their income today as they did 40 or 50 years ago. Nor is it clear that it is even desirable for people to spend a larger share of their present income on consumer goods.

It has been suggested that the government ban advertising of the persuasive variety and allow only informational advertising. The problem, however, is to separate the two. One could argue, for example, that telling people that product A is superior to all competitive products is really informational advertising. It is likely that a ban on persuasive advertising also would result in much waste in the form of lawyers' fees and court costs. The cost of the litigation, of course, would be borne by consumers in the form of higher product prices and higher taxes.

Pollution by imperfect competition

In the chapter on perfect competition, the effects of pollution or social costs on the allocation of resources and prices were discussed. We should emphasize that this problem exists in the area of imperfect competition also. Undoubtedly a major share of the total waste material in the United States results from the pro-

---

[5] Lee Benham, "The Effect of Advertising on the Price of Eyeglasses," *Journal of Law and Economics,* 1972.

FIGURE 8–11
Effect of pollution control on the firm in imperfect competition

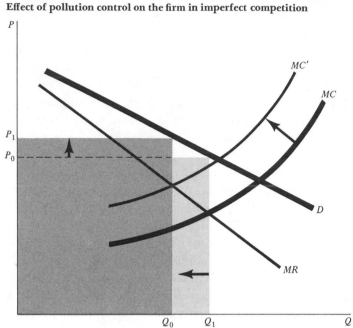

duction of firms that fall into the category of imperfect competition.

The same general analysis of social costs or externalities can be applied to the imperfectly competitive firm as was used for the firm in perfect competition. Recall that the existence of a social cost means that the true cost of producing a product is greater than the cost perceived by the firm. For example, the cost of getting rid of waste material exceeds the cost of the smokestack or the sewer pipe.

The effect of social costs for an imperfectly competitive firm is illustrated in Figure 8–11. The lower MC curve represents the cost as perceived by the firm, whereas MC' represents the marginal cost of production if the firm were required to install pollution control devices. If the firm bears this extra cost, the quantity produced declines from Q_1 to Q_0, while the price increases to P_1[6] Therefore if the firm is made to bear the full cost of dis-

---

[6] It is interesting to note that the existence of imperfect competition can result in a more optimum allocation of resources if pollution is occurring than if the market were perfectly competitive and polluting the same amount.

posing of its waste materials, there will be an inevitable increase in the price of the product produced. This is not to say that pollution control is undesirable. The main point is that in an industrialized society, a clean environment is not a free good. It appears that society is now becoming more willing than in years past to pay the price of pollution control; this is true especially of people in the upper income brackets.

As mentioned in Chapter 6, it is rather important to recognize that in order for society to reduce pollution, it is necessary to have some kind of government regulation. Even though a firm may desire to reduce its pollution, it will be prevented from doing so if competing firms are able to keep their costs and prices lower by continuing to pollute. Thus it is necessary to have regulation that forces all firms to play by the same rules of the game.

However, there is some evidence that the government may have gone overboard in its regulatory efforts. For example, a few years ago a large pharmaceutical firm reported that it spent more worker-hours filling out government forms than it devoted to its cancer and heart research combined.[7] There is evidence also that an increasing proportion of research is "defensive" in nature, aimed at keeping products on the market as opposed to developing new products. As another example, General Motors reported that in 1977 it took the equivalent of 24,500 full-time employees to meet federal regulations.[8] Not only do the nation's consumers pay for this regulation in the form of higher product prices, but taxes also must be higher to pay the salaries and expenses of regulatory personnel.

Marginal cost and supply

Throughout the discussion on imperfect competition, the use of the word *supply* has been deliberately avoided. This is because an imperfectly competitive firm does not have a supply curve as such. Recall in the case of perfect competition that the firm's marginal cost (MC) curve is essentially its supply curve. The firm, faced with a given price, maximizes profits by producing up to the point where price equals MC. The MC curve, therefore, is the

---

[7] *The Wall Street Journal,* November 11, 1976.

[8] *The Wall Street Journal,* March 29, 1979.

supply curve because it denotes the quantity that will be produced at a given price, or vice versa.

The MC curve of an imperfectly competitive firm, however, is not its supply curve, because for a given quantity the price charged will depend on the demand curve facing the firm. Thus we cannot determine both price and quantity from the MC curve alone. We have to know both MC and demand in order to determine the price and quantity for a firm operating in imperfect competition, as we have shown in this chapter's diagrams.

However, the same factors that shift the MC or supply curve of a perfectly competitive firm also shift the MC curve of a firm in imperfect competition. Moreover the result of a shift in MC is the same as a shift in supply. For example, a shift to the left, or an increase in MC, reduces the quantity and increases the price in imperfect competition, which is the same as a decrease in supply in perfect competition. Remember from our discussion of product supply that an increase in costs results in a decrease in supply, and vice versa.

Demand facing the firm: A summary

It will be useful at this point to summarize and compare the demand curve facing each of the four types of firms we have studied. We began in Chapter 7 with the perfectly competitive firm, that faces a perfectly elastic demand. In this chapter we looked at three types of imperfectly competitive firms: monopolistic competition, oligopoly, and pure monopoly. Each of these types of firms faces a downward sloping demand. In general, the smaller the number of firms and the more differentiated the product of each firm, the steeper or less elastic is the demand facing each firm. The demand curve facing the individual firm in each of the four market situations is illustrated in Figure 8–12.

It is best to think of these four types of firms as a continuous distribution, from perfect competition to pure monopoly, rather than four hard and fast categories. These categories are useful to the extent that they identify where in the distribution a given firm is located. Most firms in the U.S. economy fall somewhere between the two extremes of perfect competition and pure monopoly. As

FIGURE 8–12
Summary of demand curves facing the firms in the four major types of market situations

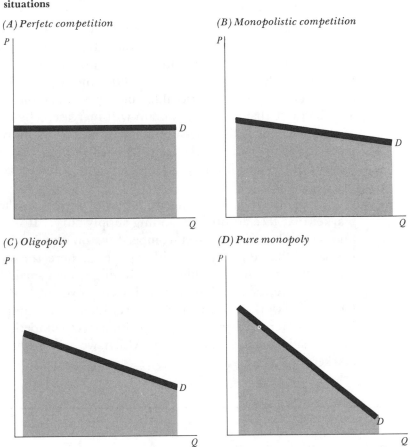

(A) Perfetc competition

(B) Monopolistic competition

(C) Oligopoly

(D) Pure monopoly

a result, economists often describe a firm by the degree of monopoly power it wields, instead of trying to decide whether it is a monopolistically competitive firm or an oligopoly.

The imperfectly competitive buyer

In this chapter we have been concerned exclusively with the selling side of the market. It is possible, although less common, to observe firms that are classified as imperfectly competitive buyers. Imperfect competition on the buying side of the market results if there is a relatively small number of buyers, each purchasing a significant share of the market.

An imperfectly competitive buyer is one that has some control over the price it pays for whatever it buys. If it reduces its purchases, there is a noticeable decline in the total market purchases, so the price that sellers can obtain tends to decline. Or if this buyer increases its purchases, a noticeable amount is taken off the market, and the price that sellers can obtain will increase. The implication of this behavior is that the supply curve facing the individual imperfectly competitive buyer is an upward sloping line. If it buys less, it can pay less; if it buys a larger amount, it has to pay a higher price per unit.

It is rather difficult to find examples of buyers in the product market that face an upward sloping supply curve. It is possible to find examples of imperfect competition on the buying side in the labor market, however, although even here the situation is relatively rare. One possible example might be a small "company town" where there is just one major employer of labor, particularly if the work is seasonal in nature, such as a canning factory. We will defer further discussion of imperfect competition on the buying side until Chapter 9, in which we will study the labor market.

Main points of Chapter 8

1. An imperfectly competitive firm is one that can exercise some control over the price it receives for its product. This occurs if the firm sells a significant share of the market or sells a product that is slightly different from those of its competitors.
2. The ability of a firm to have some control over the price of its product implies that the demand curve facing the firm is downward sloping.
3. Marginal revenue (MR) is the additional revenue obtained by selling an extra unit of output.
4. The downward sloping demand curve implies that MR is

less than price. MR is less than price for the firm in imperfect competition because additional units can be sold only if price is lowered, and the lower price must apply to all units sold, not just to the marginal units.

5. Monopolistic competition is characterized by a market in which there are many firms, each selling a small proportion of the market and a slightly differentiated product. Retail trade is a good example of monopolistic competition.

6. The firm in monopolistic competition is restricted to a price that is relatively close to those of its competitors. However, each firm attempts to maximize profits by producing up to the point where MC is equal to MR.

7. If a substantial share of the firms in monopolistic competition is reaping pure profits, there is a tendency for additional firms or resources to enter the industry. As a result, there is a decrease in the demand facing each firm. If a firm is able to reap pure profits over an extended time because of the ownership or control of some specialized resource, there is a tendency for the pure profits to be capitalized into the value of the firm's assets, thereby shifting the firm's ATC curve upward. Similarly, there is a tendency for the assets of a firm that is suffering persistent losses to be revalued downward.

8. An oligopoly is a market in which there are a few firms, each selling a substantial share of the market. An oligopoly may or may not sell a differentiated product. Oligopoly is common in heavy industry or nationally marketed products.

9. Products produced by oligopolies that have close substitutes must sell for about the same price as the substitutes. However, each oligopoly attempts to maximize profits by producing up to the point where MC is equal to MR.

10. Because of the small number of firms, the action of each firm in an oligopoly has a direct effect on its competitors. For example, an increase in costs and price for one firm results in an increase in demand and price charged by other firms.

11. The kinked demand curve is an attempt to describe the interaction of firms in an oligopoly market and to explain the apparent inflexibility of prices charged by oligopolies. It is derived under the assumption that each firm tries to hold its present customers or attract new ones.

12. Actual price determination by an oligopoly is likely to include considerable trial and error, in which price is adjusted up or down in response to new information that the firm receives. Price leadership and average cost pricing are two phenomena characteristic of an oligopoly market.

13. Growth obtained through merger can make it possible for firms to reduce costs by gaining some economies of scale. Merging can also result in tax savings and the easing of competitive forces. Conglomerates are firms that have resulted from the merger of firms in different industries.

14. The Clayton and Sherman Antitrust Acts provide the government with legislation to fight monopoly or restraint of trade. The temptation of colluding firms to cheat on one another also provides a check on cartels or collusion.

15. Pure monopoly exists when there is just one firm providing a good or service, although relatively imperfect substitutes generally are available for monopoly-produced products.

16. In order for a monopoly to persist for any length of time, entry into the market must be blocked. The most effective method of blocking entry is by government-issued licenses.

17. The U.S. postal service and the public utilities are the best examples of pure monopoly. The reason for creating monopoly is to avoid costly duplication of facilities.

18. The socially optimum price and quantity for a public monopoly corresponds to the point where the MC curve intersects the demand curve. At this point MC equals price. The profit-maximizing output for a monopoly corresponds to the point where MC equals MR, the same as is true for monopolistic competition and oligopoly.

19. The existence of private monopoly or monopoly power results in a misallocation of resources because the profit-maximizing price is greater than the marginal cost. Public condemnation of private monopoly, however, probably stems from fear of excessive monopoly profits, which would mean a transfer of income from consumers to the owners of the monopoly.

20. Monopoly power is measured by the P/MC ratio. The more this ratio exceeds one, the greater is the degree of monopoly power. Because of the difficulty of measuring marginal cost, a

proxy measure of monopoly power is the share of the market enjoyed by the largest firms in the industry.

21. During inflation the profit-maximizing price increases because of increases (shifts) in the demand facing the firm and/or because of increases in average and marginal costs. Because these shifts are in large part out of the control of individual firms, the underlying cause of inflation should not be attributed to the profit-maximizing behavior of firms. There is no reason to believe that the desire for profits is greater during inflation than during periods of stable prices.

22. The objective of advertising is to shift product demand to the right. However, advertising also increases costs, so the additional sales from advertising must outweigh the additional expense, or it will not be undertaken.

23. The existence of pollution by firms in imperfect competition means the cost as viewed by the firm is less than the true or full costs of production. Pollution control by firms will have the inevitable result of increasing the costs and prices of products.

24. The MC curve of an imperfectly competitive firm is not its supply curve, as is true for the perfectly competitive firm. In order for the MC curve to be a supply curve, it must show the quantity produced for a given price, or vice versa. For imperfect competition, demand and MR combine with MC to determine price and quantity.

25. Moving from perfect competition to pure monopoly, the demand curve facing each firm becomes less elastic.

26. The imperfectly competitive buyer faces a supply curve that is upward sloping. This is relatively rare because virtually all buyers purchase a relatively small share of the total market supply of a product or factor of production.

Questions for thought and discussion

1. What is the common characteristic shared by all imperfectly competitive firms? Why do these firms exhibit this characteristic?

2. *a.* What must happen to quantity if an imperfectly competitive firm decides to raise price, other things being equal?
   b. What must happen to price if an imperfectly competitive firm wants to increase the quantity sold, other things being equal?

3. Suppose by lowering its price from 94.9 to 92.9 cents per gallon, a service station can sell 15,000 gallons of gasoline per week as opposed to 10,000. Can we infer from these figures that the marginal revenue of an extra gallon sold in this range of output is 92.9 cents? Why or why not? What is MR in this case?

4. The higher the price charged by an imperfectly competitive firm, the greater will be its total profits. True or false? Explain.

5. Describe the process of adjustment that would be expected to occur if a grocery store in an expanding resort area is making pure profits.

6. Frequently we observe firms going out of business because of insufficient profits, only to be opened up again a month or two later by another owner. Can you explain why this should happen? If the original owner could not make a profit, how can the second owner expect to do any better?

7. Do costs determine product prices or do prices determine costs? Explain.

8. Comparable models of GM, Ford, and Chrysler cars sell for about the same price, and when one company changes its price, they all change prices by about the same amount. From these observations can we conclude that the Big Three auto makers are colluding to set price? Explain.

9. Why do collusive agreements have a tendency to break down?

10. Suppose you are hired as the manager of a newly established firm engaged in the manufacture of small fishing boats. One part of your job is to determine the price of your company's boats.
    a. What information would you attempt to obtain to help in making the initial decision on price?
    b. As time went by, what information would help you determine whether you set your price too high or too low?

11. Why are some industries such as autos and steel made up of a few large firms, while other industries such as agriculture and retail trade are made up of a large number of small firms? Would consumers enjoy lower prices if the government forced the largest firms in the country to break up into many small firms? Explain.

12. The socially optimum price for a regulated monopoly corresponds to the point where the demand curve facing the firm intersects the ATC curve so that there are no pure profits. True or false? Explain.

13. Who bears the cost of controlling pollution? Explain.

14. It is well known that large, imperfectly competitive firms raise prices during inflation. It follows that the action of these firms is the cause of inflation. True or false? Explain.

15. *a.* Why isn't the marginal cost curve of an imperfectly competitive firm a supply curve, as is true for a perfectly competitive firm?

    b. Does this prevent us from using an imperfectly competitive firm's marginal cost curve as if it were a supply curve? Explain.

9

The labor market

To this point we have been concerned with the market for consumer goods and services and the activities of individual firms within that market. In this and the next chapter we will study two other markets: those for the two primary factors of production, labor and capital. It is true, of course, that most production utilizes inputs in addition to labor and capital, such as fuel, light and power, and raw materials of all kinds. But these latter elements, often referred to as *intermediate inputs,* are themselves a product of some production activity. If we trace through the manufacture of these intermediate inputs we find that all are derived ultimately from labor and capital. In years past, when agriculture was the dominant industry, economists generally included land as a separate primary input, but in most cases land is now thought of as capital.

Labor as a factor of production

Economists at times have been accused of being callous or insensitive to the feelings of human beings by treating labor as an input or factor of production. It is argued that such treatment dehumanizes labor, making people equivalent to inanimate objects that are bought or sold.

In fact, economists are probably no more or less callous than any other group in society. Economists recognize that people are not bought and sold but their labor or services are. And economists have found that economic principles can be bought to bear in analyzing past behavior of the market for human services (labor) and predicting future behavior. Moreover, as we shall see, the special attributes of labor, such as the feelings of individuals, are reflected in the labor market.

We should also note that there is a certain amount of capital embodied (no pun intended) in labor because of the education and training that people receive. As we will see in Chapter 11, education or training of any kind can be thought of as an investment that results in the creation of human capital. In a modern society, there is relatively little demand for a person who does not possess some human capital but has only labor to sell. In this sense, workers have become capitalists.

The labor market, like the product market, is made up of demanders and suppliers. We will see that the price of labor (wage or salary) is determined by the interaction of demand and supply. Society, or at least certain groups in society, may not like the wage that the market determines and as a result may attempt to change the wage. But let us first see how the market functions before we study attempts to modify it.

Input demand with perfect competition in the product market

Our study of the labor market will begin by deriving the demand for labor by a firm that sells its product in a perfectly competitive market. As we saw in Chapter 7, this is the type of firm that faces a perfectly elastic demand curve for its product.

You might be surprised to learn that we have already constructed (in Chapter 4) the basic foundation of the demand for labor: the marginal physical product (MPP) of labor. Recall that the MPP of labor is the additional output obtained from adding one more unit of labor, holding other inputs constant. Remember also that after some point, the MPP of labor begins to decline. We referred to this phenomenon as the law of diminishing returns. In our discussion of labor demand we will be concerned only with the area of diminishing returns, that is, the downward sloping portion of the curve representing MPP.

In order to derive the demand for labor we need only to assign a value to MPP. Keep in mind that MPP is given in physical units of the product; we used bushels of tomatoes in the example in Chapter 4. In order to determine the value of MPP, we simply multiply the price of the product times MPP. For example, if the MPP for a certain input of labor is 7 bushels of tomatoes and the price of tomatoes is $6 per bushel, then the value of the marginal product (VMP) of this labor is $42.

The relationship between MPP and VMP is illustrated in Figure 9–1. Both curves look exactly the same, except the measure on the vertical axis is bushels for MPP and dollars for VMP. The line or curve depicting VMP is downward sloping, meaning that successive increments of the input, labor in this example, add less and less to the total value of output. The downward sloping

FIGURE 9–1
Relationship between marginal physical product and value of marginal product

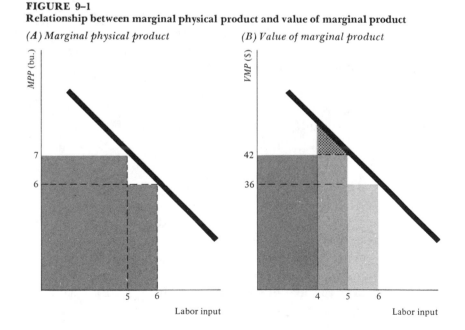

(A) Marginal physical product *(B) Value of marginal product*

characteristic of the line is due entirely to the law of diminishing returns.

Once VMP has been derived, it is possible to determine how many units of labor the firm will hire, given the price of labor. Suppose, for example, that the price of labor is $42 per day, regardless of how many units the firm hires. To choose a number from Figure 9–1(B), suppose the firm hires four units. At four units of labor, the VMP of the last or fourth unit hired is somewhat greater than $42. In other words, if the firm spends $42 for an extra unit of labor, this labor will earn somewhat more than $42 for the firm. Anytime you can spent a dollar and receive more than one dollar in return, do it. Thus the firm would definitely want to hire the fourth unit.

But would the firm want to stop hiring at four units of labor? To answer this question, assume that the firm can hire some fraction of a unit, say an hour. We can see from Figure 9–1(B) that adding an extra hour over the fourth unit also adds more to total revenue than to total cost; that is, profits are increased. Thus as long as VMP is greater than the price of the input, the firm can add to total profits by hiring more of the input. And it will continue to add more of the input until its VMP comes down to the price of the input, at five units in Figure 9–1(B). If the firm had stopped at four units it would have forgone profits equal in value to the shaded triangle in Figure 9–1(B).

At another price (or wage), say $36, the firm maximizes profits by hiring six units. Thus the VMP curve tells how many units will be hired at a given price. But this is none other than a demand curve; it is a relationship between price and quantity demanded, just as is true for a demand curve for a product. The firm's VMP curve of an input, is, therefore, the firm's demand curve for that input.

We have seen that a perfectly competitive seller maximizes profits by hiring labor to the point where labor's VMP is just equal to its price or wage. The same is true for all other inputs that the firm uses, such as machines, raw materials, power, and so forth. Economists commonly state this rule by the following algebraic expression

$$\frac{VMP_A}{P_A} = \frac{VMP_B}{P_B} = \cdots = \frac{VMP_Z}{P_Z} = 1$$

This expression says that profits will be maximized when the price of each input used is equal to its VMP, that is, when the ratio of VMP to price is one. Do not confuse this ratio with the $P/$MPP ratios of Chapter 4, which define the cost-minimizing conditions for a given level of output. The VMP$/P = 1$ ratios also satisfy the cost-minimizing rule, but in addition they define the profit-maximizing conditions from the standpoint of input use. Recall from previous chapters that the $P =$ MC or MR $=$ MC conditions also define profit maximization except in this case from the standpoint of the output level. It is somewhat more common to state the profit-maximizing conditions in terms of output rather than in terms of input, but the latter is equally correct and yields the same answer.

MARKET DEMAND

We can obtain the market demand for an input by summing all the individual firms' demand curves. The technique for summing input demand is the same as that used for summing product demand back in Figure 3–5. At each input price, all the individual quantities are summed to obtain the total quantity demanded in the market at that price.[1]

When deriving market demand for an input by summing all firms' VMP curves, we should bear in mind that this procedure implies that all other inputs used in the production process are being held constant. (Recall the definition of MPP.) Although this is a perfectly legitimate way to define market demand for an input, it is generally a bit more useful and realistic to hold the *price* of other inputs constant but allow the *quantity* of each to vary, according to its most profitable level of use. In such a situation, the firm can substitute more of a relatively cheap input for one that has risen in price. For example, when the price of labor increases relative to that of capital, producers in many cases can substitute capital for labor. (We presented the rationale underlying this phenomenon in Chapter 4.)

If we allow the quantities of related inputs to vary, then the

---

[1] We are assuming here that product price remains constant at all levels of input use. If we allowed product price to decline with increased use of the input, the market demand would be somewhat less elastic.

quantity demanded of an input will increase when its price decreases, for two reasons. First, a decline in the price of an input lowers production costs, and as a result output is increased because of the increase in product supply. (Recall the factors that shift product supply.) And as firms find it profitable to increase output, they of course increase the use of the input that has declined in price. Second, a decline in input price provides an incentive to substitute it for other inputs, as mentioned in the previous paragraph. Both factors contribute to the increased use of a relatively cheap input. Therefore the demand for an input will be more elastic when the *prices* of other inputs are held constant than when their *quantities* remain fixed.

Input demand with imperfect competition in the product market

Once the derivation of the demand for labor under perfect competition is understood, it is relatively easy to derive labor demand under imperfect competition. Because the imperfectly competitive firm faces a downward sloping demand curve for its product, the marginal revenue of an extra unit produced or sold is less than the price of this unit. Since MR is less than price, in this case we are not able to determine the value of the marginal product of an input by multiplying MPP by product price. The reason is that the price of the product must fall in order for the firm to sell any extra units produced, and this price reduction must apply to all units produced, not just the marginal unit. In this case, therefore, the value of the additional output obtained by adding an extra unit of labor is equal to MR times MPP. Economists refer to the product of MR times MPP as the marginal revenue product (MRP). Thus, where the demand curve for an input of a perfectly competitive firm is commonly denoted by VMP, the input demand of a firm in imperfect competition is known as MRP.

Since price equals marginal revenue for a perfectly competitive seller, there is really no difference in the methods of calculating input demand for the four types of firms. The abbreviations VMP and MRP are useful, however, in identifying the type of firm we are dealing with.

Since MR is less than price, it is reasonable to expect that for a given level of input use, MRP will be less than VMP. This is illustrated in Figure 9–2, where MRP declines at a faster rate than VMP. It is easier to understand this if it is realized that VMP declines only because of the law of diminishing returns. On the other hand, MRP declines for two reasons: (1) the law of diminishing returns, which is reflected in a declining MPP, and (2) the decline in marginal revenue as larger quantities of the product are sold.

FIGURE 9–2
Comparing value of marginal product and marginal revenue product

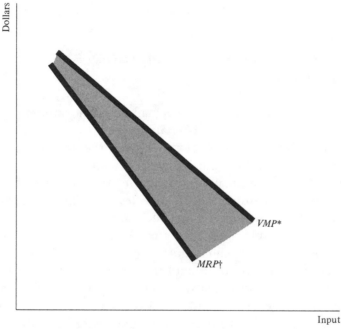

* Denotes a perfectly competitive seller.
† Denotes an imperfectly competitive seller.

The rule for using the optimum amounts of inputs by an imperfectly competitive seller on the product market is the same as the rule we presented earlier for a perfectly competitive seller. The only difference is that we now use MRP rather than VMP. Thus the algebraic expression for maximizing profits becomes

$$\frac{MRP_A}{P_A} = \frac{MRP_B}{P_B} = \cdots = \frac{MRP_Z}{P_Z} = 1$$

Although our interest in this chapter is primarily with labor, we have seen that much of the material on the demand side of the market can be applied to the use of inputs in general. Let us now turn our attention to the supply side of the labor market. Here we will see that labor possesses some unique characteristics. We begin with the labor-leisure choice.

The labor-leisure choice

From the time we are old enough to have an influence on the way we spend our time, we must decide what proportion we will spend working and what proportion we will spend on leisure. This decision has a direct effect on the supply of labor; the more time people are willing to work, the greater is the labor supply.

In our discussion of labor-leisure choice we will define labor as any activity that results in a wage or salary. This is not to say that earning good grades in school is leisure. To be sure, good students probably work as hard as, if not harder than, most "employed" people. But it will be better if we defer the discussion on schooling until Chapter 11, where we take up the economics of education.

Each person available for the labor force must decide first whether he or she will enter it. Once a person decides to do so, then the decision of how many hours to work must be made. The decisions to go to work and the type of work chosen can depend on many factors, such as the health and capabilities of the individual, self-esteem as well as the esteem of one's peers and family, and the satisfaction that results from mastering a difficult task. However, the economic factor is almost always present. Most of us have to earn a living. Moreover, the wage or salary we obtain can be expected to influence our choice of work and how much we will work.

The effect of wages and salaries on our work decisions can be made clearer if we think of leisure as a good. Like any other good, a certain amount of it brings us satisfaction. Since few of us are paid for our leisure time, the decision to spend some of our time at leisure means that we must forgo a certain amount of income. In reality then, the price of an extra hour of leisure is the income we forgo by not working this hour.

As is true for everything else we buy, price has an important bearing on the quantity we consume. Recall from the discussion of

Chapter 3 on product demand that consumers change their purchases of products with a change in prices because of the substitution and income effects. For example, if your wage increases, the price of your leisure increases. The substitution effect says that you will substitute other goods and services for leisure; you will work more. On the other hand, a higher wage also gives you a higher income, which you may use in part to "buy" more leisure.

We can illustrate the income and substitution effects between income and leisure on an indifference curve–budget line diagram similar to the one developed in Chapter 3, only now we will let the indifference curves represent the choice between money (or income) and leisure. Presumably we can visualize ourselves being equally well off with various possible combinations of money and leisure. By working a long workweek we have more money and less leisure; if we work relatively few hours per week, we have less money but more leisure or freedom to enjoy it. It is not unreasonable to suppose that two or more of such combinations could make us equally well off or satisfied. Each indifference curve drawn in Figure 9–3, therefore, denotes various possible combinations of money and leisure that could make us equally well off.

The budget line in Figure 9–3 denotes the money income earned

FIGURE 9–3
Labor-leisure choice illustrated by an indifference curve–budget line diagram

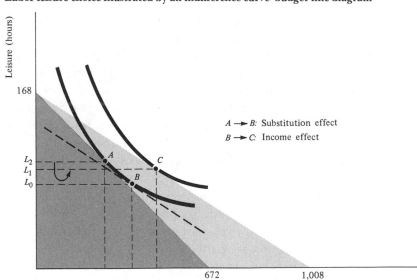

at various levels of leisure for a given wage rate. If we consider an entire week as the unit of analysis, the budget line intersects the leisure axis at 168 hours (7 days times 24 hours). In this case we would have no income but 168 hours of leisure per week. We can find the point where the budget line intersects the income axis by multiplying 168 times the hourly wage rate. For example if the wage rate is $4 an hour, the point of intersection is $672. In this case we would have no leisure but $672 income.

Of course it is not reasonable to believe that we would choose either all leisure or all money income (no leisure). At the very least we need to sleep, and most of us are willing to give up some income for the opportunity to engage in other "nonwork" activities. Assuming that we are free to choose the combination of income and leisure that provides the maximum satisfaction for a given wage rate, we can identify the combination as corresponding to the tangency point between the budget line and the highest possible indifference curve. At the $4 wage rate, this is represented by point *A* on Figure 9–3.

Now suppose the wage increases to $6 per hour. The maximum income we could earn per week at this wage increases to $1,008 ($6 × 168), so the budget line rotates in a counterclockwise fashion. As a result, the optimum money-leisure mix changes to point *C*. Notice, however, that point *C* corresponds to slightly less leisure (more hours of work) than point *A*.

The process of moving from points *A* to *C* can be separated into the income and substitution effects. The magnitude of the substitution effect is measured by drawing in a hypothetical budget line tangent to the original indifference curve and parallel to the new budget line (shown by the broken line in Figure 9–3).[2] Because of the higher wage rate, leisure has become more expensive relative to other goods. As a result people try to substitute other goods for leisure by working more. This is the substitution effect. It is shown by the movement from point *A* to *B* on Figure 9–3. Notice that the amount of leisure demanded decreases from L_2 to L_0. However, it is also true that the higher income resulting from the higher wage rate allows people to "buy" more leisure along with other goods. Therefore the income effect, shown by the movement from point

---

[2] As pointed out in Chapter 3, the substitution effect also can be shown along the new indifference curve.

B to *C* on Figure 9–3, pulls people back toward the original point. It turns out that, in this particular example, the individual ends up at L_1, which is slightly less leisure (more work) than the original amount. Of course, one could easily construct an example where the person had more leisure after a wage increase. It depends on how one draws the indifference curves. You might try to do this with a diagram of your own.

In summary, when a person's wage increases, the substitution effect pulls him or her toward less leisure, while the income effect offsets this and pulls a person back toward more leisure, or less work. Which effect prevails depends on the individual. At low levels of income, a raise in wages probably increases work and decreases leisure. At relatively high levels of income, a person can "afford" more leisure, so he or she might work less or at least not increase hours worked as the wage rate increases.

You might reasonably ask at this point whether an individual really has much choice regarding the amount of leisure that can be "purchased." After all, most jobs require the standard 40-hour workweek. However, there probably is more flexibility in this choice than one might first suppose. First, everyone has a chance to work more hours by "moonlighting" or holding two jobs. By the same token a person usually can work slightly fewer hours by increasing the rate of absenteeism or finding a job that requires a shorter workweek. If enough people wanted to work only 30 hours per week, for example, we would likely see some employers offering jobs with this option. The fact that the workweek for most occupations has averaged about 40 hours since the end of World War II is strong evidence that most people prefer to work about this many hours per week. In other words, as wages have increased, the income effect has just about offset the substitution effect during this period.

Labor supply

The supply of labor, like the supply of a product, denotes a relationship between price and quantity. As indicated by the substitution and income effects on the labor-leisure choice, we can reasonably expect the number of hours worked to increase as wages increase, at least at relatively low wage levels. At higher wage levels, however, people can afford more leisure, so we might expect a smaller degree of response to wage increases.

The changing response to wage increases is illustrated in Figure 9–4. The first three diagrams represent the supply of labor by three individuals. At $4 per hour, individual 1 is willing to supply 40 hours a week of labor. As the wage increases to $6 per hour, he increases his workweek to 45 hours. At $8 per hour he works the same amount, 45 hours, and at wages exceeding $8 he reduces

FIGURE 9–4
Wage response and market supply of labor

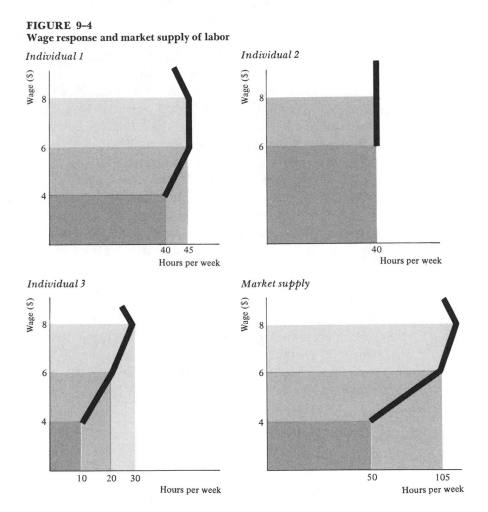

the length of his workweek. In other words, at the $8 and over wage the substitution effect does not override the income effect. Individual 2, on the other hand, does not enter the labor force until wages rise to $6 per hour. In the range of wages considered, the workweek remains at 40 hours. Individual 3 increases hours worked from 10 to 20 to 30 as wages rise from $4 to $6 to $8 per hour. These, of course, are just examples of what we might expect from different individuals. The first person might be the main "breadwinner" of a family, the second a homemaker who decides to enter the labor market at a $6 wage, and the third a college student holding a part-time job.

If we assume, to keep the example simple, that these three individuals comprise the available supply of labor, the market supply can be derived by adding together the quantity supplied at each price. At $4 per hour, individuals 1 and 3 supply 40 and 10 hours, respectively, making a total of 50 hours. At the $6-per-hour wage level, individual 2 is included in the labor force. Thus, along with the slight increase in labor offered by individuals 1 and 3, raising the wage to $6 obtains a total of 105 hours supplied.

We should take note that the market supply of labor is likely to be more elastic than the supply of individuals currently working in the market. This is because of the entrance of people into the labor market as wages rise. The result will be greater response to wage increases for the market than is true for the average individual in the market.

We should also note, of course, that in any given area there are likely to be a number of labor markets: for unskilled or semiskilled labor, for the skilled trades, and for professional and managerial personnel. In general, the more highly skilled the labor involved, the wider is the market area. For example, the market for economists is considered to be nationwide or perhaps even international in scope.

Wage determination with perfect competition in the labor market

In Chapter 6 we developed the concept that the prices of goods and services are determined by the forces of demand and supply. These same principles can be applied to the market for labor. As noted in a preceding section, the market demand for labor (of a given skill category) is a downward sloping line if employers attempt to maximize profits by hiring up to the point where the wage equals VMP or MRP. On the supply side, the total amount of labor forthcoming in any given labor market can be expected to increase with an increase in wage rates, as illustrated by the market supply curve in Figure 9–4. The wage that is determined in the market is a result of the interaction of the demand and supply of labor. The process of wage determination is illustrated in Figure 9–5(A).

FIGURE 9–5
Wage determination: Perfect competition in the labor market

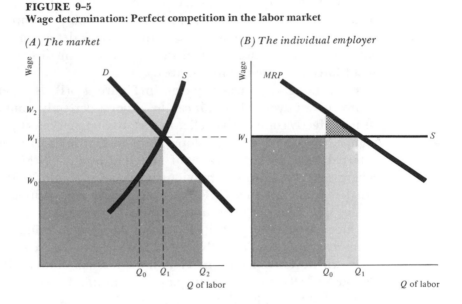

(A) The market

(B) The individual employer

If the wage happened to be above the equilibrium, say W_2, more people would be willing to work than are demanded by prospective employers. As a result there would be some unemployed people willing to work at a wage lower than W_2. Knowing this, employers will reduce wages to W_1, because they would not want to pay more than what people are willing to work for. Of course, as wages come down to W_1, the quantity of labor supplied decreases and the quantity demanded increases. At W_1 these two quantities coincide so that everyone who is willing to work at this wage is employed.

If wages are lower than the equilibrium, say at W_0, employers would like to hire more labor than people will supply. At this low wage and relatively small employment, the marginal revenue product of labor for employers in the market is greater than the wage. Thus employers can increase profits by increasing wages to induce a larger quantity of labor to be offered in the market. As wages rise, the quantity of labor offered increases and the quantity demanded decreases. The increase will continue until it reaches W_1. At this point the incentive for employers to pay higher wages to obtain more labor disappears.

If we assume that the market is in equilibrium, with wage W_1 prevailing, the perfectly competitive employer of labor faces a supply curve of labor such as that shown by S in Figure 9–5(B). Such a supply curve implies that the individual employer cannot influence the wage; the employer takes the wage as determined in the market. This situation exists if the firm hires a small share of the labor force in a community or area.

Even though the firm depicted in Figure 9–5(B) is a perfectly competitive buyer of labor, it can be either a perfectly competitive or imperfectly competitive seller in the product market. If perfectly competitive, the downward sloping line in Figure 9–5(B) could be referred to as the firm's value of marginal product (VMP) curve, whereas according to our previous notation, it would be the marginal revenue product (MRP) if imperfectly competitive on the selling side. In order to minimize confusion over notation, we refe. to the curve in Figure 9–5(B) as MRP, keeping in mind that the same reasoning would apply if we called it the VMP curve. Similarly, whenever we mention MRP in the discussion that follows or denote an MRP curve on a diagram, bear in mind that VMP could be inserted in its place.[3]

If the firm wishes to maximize profits it will hire labor up to the point where the wage W_1 is equal to the firm's MRP. If it stopped short of this point, say at Q_0, then the contribution of a marginal worker would be greater than the wage of this worker. Suppose that MRP is $6 at Q_0 and the wage is $5. By adding an extra hour of labor, the firm pays out $5 but receives $6 in return. Hence the employer gains $1 net by hiring this extra hour of labor.

---

[3] Since MR equals price for a perfectly competitive seller, it is still correct to refer to VMP as MRP, even if we are dealing with a perfectly competitive seller.

These two figures come closer and closer together as the firm continues to add labor, but total profits continue to increase. If the firm stopped hiring at Q_0, it would forgo profits equal in value to the shaded triangle shown in Figure 9–5(B).

The implication of a horizontal supply curve of labor facing a firm is that the firm has no control over the wage it pays, and if it lowers the wage slightly, the quantity of labor available to it will fall to zero. But because labor is not strictly homogeneous, like bushels of wheat or corn, the firm probably can get by with paying a slightly lower wage than the average of other employers in its vicinity. Firms that pay lower wages, however, usually attract employees who are slightly less qualified or less productive than the average. Low-wage firms also tend to have a higher turnover of personnel, which adds to the cost of training or "breaking in" employees. Thus it is not always in the interest of the employer to pay a lower than average wage. Firms that pay relatively high wages can be more selective in whom they hire and can avoid a high turnover of personnel.

At any rate, the perfectly elastic supply curve of labor facing such a firm is more accurately interpreted as a range of wages around the average. For example, if the average wage is $5.00 per hour for a given type of labor, an individual employer might pay anywhere from $4.50 to $5.50 per hour.

As individuals in the labor market, it is important to realize that we must contribute at least as much to the output of our employer as we are paid. For example, if we are paid $12,000 per year and produce only $10,000 per year of goods or services, the firm loses $2,000 per year on us. A firm that loses $2,000 per year on an employee is better off without the employee, so we could look forward to losing our job. This does not mean that employers are inhuman or heartless, but a firm that pays more out than it takes in soon goes out of business.

The situation does not change if we work for a public agency, even though the agency is not profit-oriented. Here if we produce less than our wage, taxpayers obtain less than what they pay for. Unless taxpayers wish to make a gift to us equal to the difference between our MRP and our wages, we will find our job in jeopardy. We might bemoan the fact that the world is so cruel, but it is a situation no one can change, regardless of the economic system.

It is, of course, possible for a person's wages to be somewhat greater than the individual's MRP during the period the employee is learning or getting used to a new job. In this case, the employer might anticipate that the employee's MRP would exceed the wage sometime in the future when the person is no longer a new and therefore marginal employee. It is reasonable to expect also, that in many occupations an individual's wage may not be exactly equal to the person's contribution to output. Hard-working, productive employees may be paid less than their MRP, while lazy, unproductive individuals might be paid more than what they are worth. In many instances it is not possible for employers to distinguish between employees on the basis of their MRP. The union contract may not allow it, or it may not be economically feasible for a large firm to even attempt to make such a distinction. A common method of attempting to approximate MRP differences is to pay according to a seniority scale. This presumes that older, more experienced employees are more productive than younger, less experienced ones.

Wage determination with imperfect competition in the labor market

Because most firms, even the very largest, tend to hire a relatively small proportion of the available employees in their respective labor markets, the perfectly competitive buyer of labor is the most common situation. In other words, most individual employers face a perfectly elastic supply of labor, or at least one that has a relatively high elasticity, meaning that each employer has no real power to alter the market wage. Nevertheless it is possible to conceive of situations where an employer hires a relatively large share of the labor force in a particular area. Some examples might be a "company" mining town or a large canning factory in a farming community. The latter is a better example because the factory hires labor on a relatively short-term basis. As a consequence, it may not pay for new workers to migrate into the community in response to higher wages or to leave in response to lower wages, unless the employees are migrant workers that count on the job year after year.

An employer that hires a relatively large share of the available employees in a market area faces an upward sloping supply curve of labor. Such an employer is called an imperfectly competitive buyer of labor. The upward sloping supply curve of labor implies that these employers must pay a higher wage if they wish to increase their labor force. Or, if they wish to reduce the number of people they employ, they can reduce the wage paid.

An inevitable result of an upward sloping supply curve facing a firm is that the additional or marginal cost of adding more labor exceeds the wage of the extra workers. The reason for this phenomenon is that the firm must pay a higher wage to attract additional employees, and this higher wage must then be paid to all employees.

Economists refer to the cost of adding additional labor as the marginal resource cost (MRC) of labor. At any level of labor hired, the MRC of labor is greater than the wage paid. Thus if we wish to represent this relationship on a diagram, the MRC curve would lie above the supply curve and would rise at a faster rate, as shown in Figure 9–6.

You will note that marginal resource cost on the buying side of the labor market is strictly analogous to marginal revenue (MR) on

FIGURE 9–6
Wage determination: Imperfect competition in the labor market

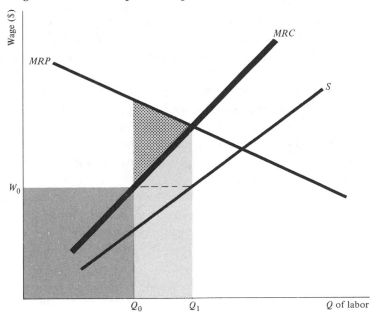

the selling side of the product market. Marginal revenue is less than price because in order to sell more, the price reduction must apply to all units sold; MRC is greater than the wage because to hire more, the higher wage must apply to all labor employed, not just the marginal workers. In other words, the MRC of an additional worker is the wage paid to this worker plus the small increase in total wages that must be paid to each of the firm's other employees.

If the firm wishes to maximize profits, it will attempt to equate the MRC of its labor with labor's MRP and hire Q_1 of labor. If it stopped short of this point, say at Q_0, the contribution of a marginal unit of labor would exceed its cost. And as we saw in the preceding section, increasing the labor hired from Q_0 to Q_1 results in an addition to total profits that is equal in value to the shaded triangle in Figure 9–6.

We should take note also in Figure 9–6 that the wage paid by the imperfectly competitive employer of labor is equal to W_0, the point on the supply curve corresponding to Q_1, the quantity of labor hired. At this quantity of labor, people are willing to work for W_0. Unlike the situation for a perfectly competitive employer, MRP is greater than the wage. This is not to say that the imperfectly competitive firm "exploits" labor. By attempting to maximize profits, this type of firm is behaving in exactly the same manner as a perfectly competitive employer. It is hiring labor up to the point where the additional cost of adding another unit of labor (MRC) is just equal to the contribution of that worker to the value of output (MRP).

We should point out also that wages paid by a perfectly competitive buyer of labor should not be any different from wages paid by an imperfectly competitive buyer of comparable labor in the same labor market. If wages were not about equal, employees would have a strong incentive to quit the low-paying employer and switch to the higher-paying one.[4]

It is important to recognize as well that it is not necessary for all employees to be mobile in order to prevent long-run wage differences between individual employers or markets. When wages paid by an employer get out of line with wages paid elsewhere, a move-

---

[4] We are assuming in this situation that the labor market consists of one or more imperfectly competitive buyers of labor and several smaller employers.

ment of a relatively small percentage of all employees from the low-to the high-wage employers usually is enough to force wages up in the low-wage markets and bring them down in the high-wage jobs. Also an inequality of wages between areas or regions usually results in some employers moving to the low-wage areas, as illustrated by the movement of northern industry to the South since the end of World War II. This has the effect of increasing labor demand in the low-wage areas and decreasing demand in the high-wage areas. As a result, wage differences tend to narrow or disappear completely.

In order to differentiate imperfect competition on the buying side of the market from the selling side, economists have labeled a market where there are few buyers as an *oligopsony*. This is comparable to an oligopoly, which characterizes a situation of few sellers in a market. If there is only one buyer of labor, the firm would be referred to as a *monopsony*, comparable to a monopoly on the selling side.

This does not mean, however, that an oligopoly on the selling side results in oligopsony on the buying side, or vice versa. The same is true of a monopsony. For example, a local light and power company might have a virtual monopoly on the sale of electricity, but in all likelihood it is a perfectly competitive buyer of labor.

Shifts in demand for labor

So far in this chapter we have studied how wages are determined in the two kinds of labor markets. Now we will attempt to explain changes in the wages and levels of employment. We noted in Chapter 6 that if a product market is in equilibrium, the only way a change in price can occur is by a change or shift in either demand or supply of the product, or both. The same is true for labor. Wages change in response to a change in market demand, supply, or both.

Let us look first at changes or shifts in the demand for labor. Most of what we will say about shifts in demand for labor can be applied to the demand for any other input as well. Recall from our discussion of the product market that an increase in demand occurs when it shifts upward and to the right, as shown by D_2 in Figure 9–7(A) or MRP_1 in Figure 9–7(B). You will notice in this case that the equilibrium or profit-maximizing wage will also in-

FIGURE 9–7
Shifts in the demand for labor

(A) Perfectly competitive market

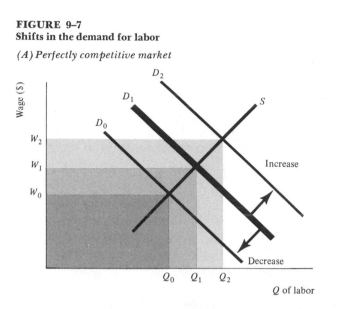

(B) Imperfectly competitive employers

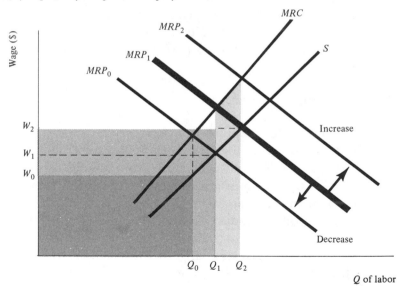

crease, and, as you might expect, a decrease in labor demand will result in a decrease in wages, as illustrated by D_0 or MRP_0 in the diagrams in Figure 9–7.

Because the value of marginal product (VMP) for a perfectly competitive buyer of labor is derived by multiplying marginal physical product (MPP) times product price, we would expect either a change in product price or a change in MPP of labor to shift the demand for labor. The same would be true for an imperfectly competitive buyer of labor because a change in price also results in a change in marginal revenue. We can conclude, therefore, that the demand for labor will shift in response to a change in product price or a change in the productivity of labor. The same would hold true for any input. The following is a summary of these changes.

1. *Change in product price.* A rise in product price, of course, results in a higher VMP or marginal revenue product for a given level of input use. The opposite is true for a decline in product price.

2. *Change in marginal physical product.* There are three major factors that can change or shift an input's MPP. These are:

   a. *Change in quantity or quality of complementary inputs.* Economists define a complementary input as one that increases the MPP of a given input when the use of the complement is increased. Consider, for example, a worker's digging a hole with a spade. When given a power shovel, the productivity or MPP will increase. Thus the power shovel would be considered a complement to labor, as would raw materials of all kinds. Without bricks, mortar, or lumber, for example, a construction worker would not be very productive.

      An increase in the quality of a complementary input has the same effect as an increase in its quantity, that is, it increases, or shifts to the right, the MPP curve of the input in question. For example, a secretary with a new electric typewriter is likely to be more productive than with a slower, manual model.

   b. *Changes in quantity or quality of substitute inputs.* Economists define a substitute input as one that decreases the

MPP of a given input when the use of the substitute is increased. For example, the use of a second worker on one spade would reduce the MPP of the first worker, because he could use it only part of the time.

It is not obvious in a given production activity whether two inputs are complements or substitutes. Furthermore, this relationship can change at different levels or mixes of input use. For example, giving the power shovel to the two workers with the spade will increase the MPP of the worker who operates the machine but decrease the MPP of the second worker if he just stands and watches.

For some labor, therefore, capital or machines serve as complements by increasing labor's productivity. For other labor, however, usually those with the lowest skills or seniority on the job, capital may be a substitute, forcing them to find other employment. It is this latter situation that we hear about most in regard to automation and unemployment. But let us defer our discussion of the effects of automation until later in the chapter.

An increase in the quality of a substitute input also has an effect similar to an increase in the quantity of such an input. In this case, quality improvement decreases, or shifts to the left, the MPP curve of the input in question. For example, an increase in the speed and capacity of a computer will decrease the MPP of a bookkeeper if it leaves the person with nothing to do.

c. *Changes in quality of the input itself.* This factor is especially important for labor. Through education and training people have become more productive, that is, they have increased their MPP, which in turn has resulted in an increased demand for their labor.

Shifts in the supply of labor

In general the supply of labor tends to be more stable than the labor demand. The overall supply of labor to the entire economy depends largely on the population. The more people there are, the more labor will be supplied at a given wage. Thus the aggregate supply of labor in the United States has increased along with its population. The proportion of the population participating in the labor force also affects the labor supply. During recent years in the United States an increasing proportion of women has joined the labor force, thus increasing the nation's overall supply of labor. And a greater proportion of college students is working part-time, which also adds to the nation's labor force.

In a sense we can also think of the increase in education and skills of the labor force as contributing to the supply of labor. If we measure labor in homogeneous "efficiency units," then a given number of highly skilled people is equivalent to more labor than an equal number of less skilled people. In the previous section, we mentioned that an increase in the skills of people tends to increase their productivity and hence their MPP and demand. An increase in the wages from increased skills requires, therefore, that the demand for skills increases more than the supply of skills.

The supply of labor facing a given industry or area would, of course, depend also on the population of the area, although in this case, the supply of labor can shift also in response to a change in wages in some other industry or area. Suppose, for example, there is a sudden increase in the demand for labor, as occurred in the recent oil discoveries in northern Alaska. The increase in wages for people to operate the oil rigs attracts more labor to this occupation. But this in turn tends to reduce (shifts to the left) the supply of labor to other nearby industries such as mining, trapping, or the service trades. It might be useful to illustrate this situation with two supply-demand diagrams of your own, one for oil drilling and the second for the other industries that employ similar types of labor. Your diagrams should predict an increase in wages in both sets of occupations.

Wages and employment changes

We know there has been a long-run upward trend in both wages and employment in the United States. We also know that because of our population growth and the increased participation of women in the labor force, the supply of labor has been increasing or shifting to the right. From this information we have to conclude that the demand for labor has been shifting to the right more rapidly than the labor supply. Otherwise, there could not have been an increase in both wages and employment.

The two main factors that shift labor demand to the right and thus raise wages have been (1) an increase in the use of complementary inputs, mainly capital, and (2) an increase in the quality of the labor force through education. Recall from the preceding section that these two factors increase the productivity or MPP of labor and thereby increase labor demand.

For individual geographic areas, industries, or firms, however, there are instances where we can observe a decrease in the demand for labor. This can occur if there is a decrease in demand for the good or service produced. As a result the firms involved reduce the quantity of inputs used that are complementary to labor, mainly capital and raw materials. There is a corresponding decline in labor's MPP and consequently a decline in labor demand, as shown in D_0 in Figure 9–7(A) above.

The logical thing to expect in this situation is a decline in wages and employment. If we were dealing with a nonhuman input, no doubt this would occur. But in the case of labor, it is rather unwise for a firm to immediately reduce the wages of its employees in response to a decrease in its marginal revenue product (MRP) of labor. An across-the-board wage cut affects all of a firm's employees and, to say the least, leaves employees unhappy. Disgruntled employees generally are not conducive to high labor productivity and profits. Moreover, if labor is represented by a union, the wage contract may forbid any decrease in wages.

Rather than reduce wages when there is a decline in demand for labor, most firms will choose to lay off some people, at least in the short run. A layoff affects only a relatively few of the firm's "marginal" employees, leaving the remainder virtually untouched. The people who are laid off may be disgruntled, but they are not around to affect the firm's productivity anyway. Of course, in the event of a severe and prolonged decline in the demand for labor in an area or by an industry, we would likely see some downward adjustment in money wages, such as occurred during the Great Depression. A more common occurrence nowadays, however, is for the wages in a depressed area or industry to remain relatively stable or to rise less than wages in the overall economy. As a result these wages tend to decline relative to wages in other areas or occupations, and some employees leave voluntarily. This kind of adjustment is a bit easier to take than an absolute reduction in money wages.

It is possible to identify occupations in which wages have increased substantially over the years but the productivity of workers appears not to have increased very much. Some examples might include teachers, barbers, and taxi drivers. One can explain the increase in wages in these cases by the upward shift in the supply curve of labor facing these occupations. If most other occupations have experienced wage increases, people will not be willing to enter occupations in which labor productivity has not increased unless they receive wages comparable to what they could earn in occupations in which labor productivity has increased. Of course, the relative prices of goods and services will tend to increase in those areas where wages increase without productivity gains. At any rate, certain occupations that do not experience gains in labor productivity still can enjoy wage increases if most other occupations in the economy experience a gain in labor productivity.

Wage differences

The large differences that exist between the wages or salaries of different people or groups sometimes seem unjustified. The movie star or professional athlete may earn $200,000 per year, working possibly six months, while the "poor but honest" laborer has to toil from dawn to dusk for a meager $6,000 per year. Why?

Wage differences can be explained largely by demand and supply. A person lucky enough to possess some scarce talent that is in relatively high demand, such as being able to throw a baseball or football exceedingly well, tends to enjoy a relatively high wage. Other talents, such as being able to push or pull a lever on a machine all day, that are in abundant supply relative to their demand are less well paid.

Some occupations require lengthy training periods, which has the effect of reducing the supply. The doctor, lawyer, or college professor who spends eight to ten years preparing for a profession must be compensated for the investment, or it would not pay to enter the profession. Of course, substantial wage differences exist within and between professions even though the educational requirement is similar. For example, the internationally known heart surgeon or Nobel Prize winner is likely to enjoy a salary (or income) several times larger than relatively unknown colleagues. In large part, these salary or income differences reflect differences in ability and productivity. One does not enjoy an international reputation without some special accomplishment.

Some professions enjoy a higher average level of income than others with similar educational requirements because of a relatively strong union. Medical doctors, for example, tend to earn substantially more than college professors with a Ph.D. The former are represented by a strong "union," the American Medical Association (AMA), while college professors are not, for the most part, "unionized." We will discuss how unions and such organizations as the AMA are able to influence the incomes of their members in a following section.

Wages or salaries also tend to reflect differences in working conditions. An occupation that requires exposure to the elements or involves some special hazard tends to pay a higher salary than those that provide comfortable, safe working conditions. Construction workers, for example, tend to earn substantially more per year than bank clerks or shoe salespersons. Similarly, steel workers who put together the superstructure of today's "skyscrapers" are well paid for the physically demanding work they do and the risks they take. In general, jobs that present special risks or other disadvantages, such as working in remote areas, have to offer higher salaries in order to attract people. We might say that the supply of people for these jobs is small relative to the demand, so their wages are high. The relatively high wages of construction workers also can be attributed at least in part to a relatively strong union, which we will discuss shortly, and to the seasonality of their work. The wages lost during days when work is not possible because of bad weather have to be made up during the days when they can work.

On the other hand, occupations that allow one to work in air-conditioned comfort tend to offer somewhat lower salaries, given the educational requirements that usually accompany such jobs. We might say that people who work in these jobs take part of their salaries in attractive working conditions. For these jobs, the supply of people is large relative to the demand, so wages tend to be lower than in less attractive jobs.

Automation

While automation, the substitution of machines for human effort in a production activity, has become popular in recent years, it is by no means new. In fact it probably began at the dawn of history when humans discovered that by using the wheel one individual could pull as much as two or three could carry. As we think of it today, automation probably began with the Industrial Revolution more than 100 years ago, although in recent years the computer has opened up more possibilities for automated production.

Is automation good or bad? Ask this question of wage earners and chances are many will say bad, especially if it is a threat to their jobs. But we must ask what life would be like if there had never been automation. Most of us would be living in caves or tents, scratching a meager living from the soil with a few crude tools. Without the aid of machines, humans are relatively unproductive creatures. Obviously we who are living in the 20th century benefit a great deal from past automation or mechanization of production.

As noted in the section on labor demand, machines or capital serve as a complement to some labor, shifting its MPP curve upward and to the right. As a person's real output increases, so do his or her wage and income. But machines or capital can at the same time be a substitute for other people, reducing their MPP and eliminating their jobs. It is this latter group of people who fear automation, and with good reason, for relatively few people like to see their jobs disappear. But the picture may not be quite so dark as might first appear. Because automation represents a more productive or cheaper method of production, the supply of the final product will be shifted to the right.

As consumers respond to the lower price of the product by purchasing more of it, the firm or industry will, of course, purchase more raw materials, which in turn will shift the MPP of the marginal workers to the right also. If the increase in output is sufficient to absorb the jobs eliminated by automation, labor can end up in the happy situation of higher pay with a greater number of jobs.

We should note also that because of population growth and the expanding economy in the United States today, most industries are increasing their output. The effect of automation in this case is for employers not to take on additional labor as they increase output, a situation that is not nearly so unpleasant to labor as losing jobs that were already in existence. A good illustration of this phenomenon exists in the growth in the service trades relative to manufacturing, where automation has been more prevalent.

A prevalent fear is that because of automation jobs will become more and more scarce. Some go as far as to say that people will have to reduce their workweek to 20 to 30 hours in order for everyone to be employed. But this fear will remain unfounded until everyone has reached a state of complete satisfaction. As long as some people desire to consume more goods or services than they now do, there is no reason why everyone who wants a job cannot be working. Knowing human nature, we should not expect to see the day soon when everyone is satiated. Contrary to popular opinion, it is not jobs that are scarce but rather people and resources to do the jobs that produce the goods and services we all desire. Of course, this is not to deny the existence of unemployment. But whatever the reason(s) for unemployment, we can be reasonably sure that it is not caused by people reaching the stage of complete contentment with the goods and services they are able to buy.

Discrimination

It is very difficult, if not impossible, to assess the full effect of discrimination in the labor market unless we ourselves have been denied a job because of our race, creed, or color. The full effect goes much deeper than the loss of income. The feeling of frustration, hopelessness, and low self-esteem can be known only by those discriminated against. Since this is a book on economics, however, we can only recognize that discrimination results in more than just economic harm.

In instances of discrimination there is a tendency to place the major blame on employers. Obviously, it is argued, employers who deny employment because of race, creed, or color are guilty of discrimination. But the problem may go deeper than this. If the hiring of people from a minority group creates bitterness, strife, and the loss of productivity among workers already employed, no employer is going to be very eager to hire these people. In this situation the blame for discrimination must be shared by employees as well as the employer.

In addition, there can well be discrimination against the output of a firm that hires from a minority group. This situation can easily prevail in the services or retail trades. For example, if consumers discriminate against stores that employ minority salespersons, employers may be reluctant to hire them. In this case the blame must fall also on the consumers.

This is not intended, of course, to furnish an excuse to the employer who discriminates against certain groups or offers only token integration. The main point is that equality of opportunity is not likely to become a reality until everyone starts accepting everyone else as individuals rather than as members of a particular race or group. The entertainment profession and the academic community must be given high marks in this regard.

Discrimination occurs also at the elementary and secondary levels of school. Since minority groups tend to live in poor neighborhoods and schools obtain a large share of their financing from local taxes, the quality of instruction tends to be much lower among minority-group children than among the children of high- or middle-income parents. The result, of course, is poor preparation for the labor market or for further training. If minority people possess only minimum skills, hence a low marginal physical productivity, they can qualify for only low-paying jobs. Thus discrimination and poverty tend to perpetuate themselves; poor schooling leads to low income, and low income results in poor schooling.

In addition to the low quality of schooling, young people from minority groups often terminate their schooling much sooner than young people from middle class neighborhoods. Since schooling is such an important prerequisite for a decent job in modern society, at first glance it appears that dropping out of high school or deciding not to attend a college or technical school is not very rational. A closer look, however, reveals that because of discrimination in the job market, it may indeed be rational not to invest in schooling. If

the jobs that can be obtained with further schooling are not open
to certain people, there is little incentive to train for them.

Women's liberation

In recent years the women's liberation movement has drawn our
attention to existing inequalities in women's salaries and opportunities in comparison with those available to men. Over a long
period of time certain occupations, such as nurse, secretarial worker,
and airline stewardess, have traditionally become associated with
women, while other occupations, such as construction worker, truck
driver, and stevedore, have been generally considered to be in the
domain of men. Many people, especially women, are now question-
ing whether these traditional roles of men and women are justified.

It might be argued, of course, that some jobs require certain characteristics that are more likely to be inherent in women than in
men, or vice versa. For example, women on the average probably
have greater manual dexterity than men, but they do not possess
as great physical strength. This may at least partly explain why
typists tend to be women and construction and dock workers tend
to be men. To the extent that physical differences between men and
women do exist and these differences are important to certain jobs,
the mix of men and women can be expected to be different. If the
occupations that require staffing by men exhibit harsh working
conditions such as exposure to the elements and hard physical labor,
additional compensation may be required in order to attract qualified people, and we can expect the average salaries of men to be
somewhat higher than those for women.

Whether the physical differences between men and women are
important enough to cause some occupations to be dominated by
one sex or the other is, of course, debatable. Those who argue they
are not can point to the Soviet Union, where women can be found
in large numbers in most occupations, ranging from street sweepers
and construction workers to medical doctors. In fact the majority of
doctors in the Soviet Union are women. Of course, it is necessary
to remember that the "liberation" of women in the Soviet Union
probably came more from necessity than design, because of the
wholesale dissipation of the male population during World War II.

It is, of course, possible to find occupations in this country in which women are doing basically the same work as men but are earning lower salaries. Mainly it is these situations that give rise to charges of discrimination. It is, however, possible to explain at least part of these wage differences without resorting to the discrimination argument. As mentioned in a previous section, employees who are new on the job tend to be somewhat less productive than experienced employees while they are "learning the ropes." If an employer can be reasonably sure that an employee will remain, there will likely be a greater willingness to pay the new employee a somewhat higher wage and to hire the employee for a management position than would be the case if the employer were less certain that the employee would stay. In the latter case, the starting salary of the new employee will likely be lower because the chance of the employer to recoup any early losses will be smaller. There are also some additional costs involved in finding, screening, and breaking in new employees that have to be met, and these costs mount when employees change jobs relatively often.

In the past, at least, the employment of women has involved somewhat more uncertainty than the employment of men. When single women marry they are more likely than men to change their place of residence and thus to change jobs. Newly married women may have babies, which at least interrupts their employment, if it doesn't halt it. When married men change jobs or are transferred, their wives usually follow. The opposite is much less likely; men usually do not change jobs because of a change in their wives' employment opportunities, although it does happen occasionally. More frequent changing of jobs also means that women on the average build up less seniority than men, which reduces their chances of moving into higher-paying management positions.

This is not to argue that women are any less reliable or stable than men. The increased uncertainty comes about because of our family and social structure. Nor do we want to suggest that discrimination against women in the labor force does not exist. The dominance of men in professions where physical characteristics are not so important, such as law and medicine, is a case in point, although there appears to be less discrimination against women in these occupations than there used to be. The main point of this section is that some wage differences between men and women can be explained on the basis of occupational differences, a greater uncertainty involved in the hiring of women, and less chance on the part of women to establish seniority.

Labor unions

The primary objectives of labor unions are to obtain higher salaries for their members and to improve working conditions. In this section we will look primarily at the methods that unions use in attempting to raise wages, together with the limitations of these methods.

The discussion of wage determination established that wages are determined by the forces of supply and demand similar to the determination of prices in the product market. It is reasonable to believe that in order for unions to modify wages, they must in some way modify or change the market for labor. There are three basic ways this can be done.

1. Increase the demand for labor. This method is probably the most desirable of all three but the most difficult. It is desirable because it results in both a higher wage and greater employment, as illustrated in Figure 9–7(A) and (B). It is difficult because in general unions do not have much influence over the demand for labor.

One means of increasing labor demand is by increasing the demand for the final product. In years past unions utilized advertising urging consumers to buy union-made products. But as more and more industries became unionized, it became more difficult to distinguish union from nonunion products.

In recent years unions have been quite active in discouraging imports of foreign-made products by lobbying for protective tariffs or quotas on imports. The success of this kind of program is difficult to gauge because limiting imports has the effect of in turn limiting our exports. If we do not buy from other nations, they understandably limit their purchases from us. As a result there is a decrease in the export demand of union-made products.

Increasing the productivity of labor (or the MPP) will also increase the demand for labor. As a result unions have attempted to improve working conditions and shorten the workweek so as to maximize each employee's potential. Unions also have encouraged education and have been active in apprenticeship programs, although, as we will see shortly, apprenticeship programs have been a more effective device for limiting the supply of labor.

Negotiating over job descriptions is another method unions have used in attempts to increase or at least maintain the demand for labor. A certain job may call for the services of employees from two or more unions, each doing a specific part of the job. In building a house, for example, the carpenters dare not infringe on any job the electricians or painters are supposed to do. Related to this is the practice of "featherbedding," which is an attempt by unions to create or maintain jobs that employers claim are not really necessary. The railroad fireman is a good example. In the days of steam locomotives, this job was, of course, necessary. With the coming of diesel and electric power, railroads argue that the fireman is now redundant, and they maintain that union insistence that this job remain constitutes featherbedding.

Any kind of make-work scheme on the part of unions cannot be very successful, however, because it invariably results in higher than necessary production costs. As consumers substitute other goods and services that are cheaper for the higher-priced union-made products, the demand for union labor will decline. Thus the union loses in the long run.

2. *Reduce the supply of labor.* By and large, unions have been more successful in raising wages by limiting the supply of labor than by increasing demand. This is particularly true among the so-called craft unions representing skilled workers. The prime vehicle for limiting entry into the profession or trade is by controlling entry into the training or apprenticeship program.

In most skilled trades or professions it is virtually impossible for an individual to find employment without a certificate or license attesting to the successful completion of the training program. Because the power to issue licenses is generally in the hands of the trade or profession itself, it is not difficult to understand why they are generally in short supply.

Shifting the supply of labor back and to the left from what it would be with free entry into the profession increases wages and reduces the number of people employed. Trade unions and professional associations such as the AMA have utilized this technique with a high degree of success because the outcome (higher wages and less employment) does not, at least in the short run, harm established members of the trade or profession. Their wages are high, and they generally do not have to fear unemployment.

The people who are harmed by this technique are both those who could obtain higher incomes if they had been allowed to enter the profession and consumers who end up paying more for services rendered. If wages and the cost of services become excessively high, however, public opinion may result in government pressure to allow more freedom of entry. Also, substitute products will begin to show up, as evidenced by "mobile homes" or factory-built housing, which results in a decrease in demand for the services of skilled tradespeople.

3. Bargain for a union wage. This technique is utilized by unions representing unskilled or semiskilled workers—the teamsters, the steel workers, and the auto workers. These are often referred to as the industrial unions, as opposed to the craft unions. Unlike the craft unions, which limit membership, the industrial union's goal is to bring all workers in the industry into union membership. The wisdom of this policy becomes clear when we remember that because the jobs represented by industrial unions require little or no training, there is always a large pool of substitute labor that can easily step in if union labor becomes more costly than nonunion labor. In addition, the success of industrial unions hinges on the condition that all firms in the industry employ union members. When unionized firms pay a higher wage and hence incur higher costs, the lower-priced products of the nonunionized firms soon take over the market.

In bargaining for a union wage, unions attempt to obtain a higher wage for their members than would be determined in a free market. As explained earlier in this chapter, this wage corresponds to the intersection of labor's demand and supply in a perfectly competitive market, as illustrated in Figure 9–8(A) by W_0. The free market wage in an imperfectly competitive labor market is also denoted in Figure 9–8(B) by W_0. The union wage is denoted by W_u in both diagrams.

In perfect competition, note that the imposition of the union wage reduces the quantity of labor employed in the market from Q_0 to Q_u^d. In order for employers to pay the higher wage they

FIGURE 9–8
Union wages in the labor market

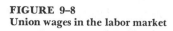

(A) Perfect competition

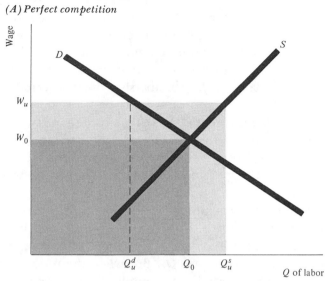

(B) Imperfect competition

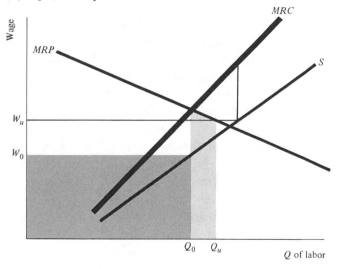

must reduce employment until labor's MRP rises to the level of the wage. If they did not cut back on personnel, the wage of the marginal workers would exceed the value of what they produce. The resulting decline in employment serves as a check on the union's bargaining power, however. Unions like to minimize unemployment, along with higher wages. Moreover, unions traditionally have not enjoyed a large, loyal membership during periods of high unemployment.

Notice also in Figure 9–8(A) that the quantity of labor seeking employment in the union wage industry increases from Q_0 to Q_u^s, resulting in an unemployed fringe equal to the distance between Q_u^d and Q_u^s. Essentially this represents the waiting list of hopeful employees.

The outcome of a union wage in an imperfectly competitive labor market, illustrated in Figure 9–8(B), is a bit surprising. You will note that in a free market the imperfectly competitive buyer of labor pays W_0 and hires Q_0. But when the union comes in and bargains for a wage, say W_u, the employer increases employment up to Q_u. This occurs because the union wage nullifies the firm's original MRC curve. The reason is that at wage W_u, the firm can hire any quantity of labor it wishes at this wage without having to pay more for additional workers. The firm's MRC curve under a union wage, therefore, consists of the solid line beginning at W_u on the vertical axis, running out to the supply curve and then extending up to join the original MRC curve of the firm.

At first glance the outcome depicted in Figure 9–8(B) appears to be highly beneficial to union members: Their wages are higher and their total employment has increased, provided the union wage is set somewhere between the original free market wage, W_0, and the point where the firm's original MRC curve intersects its MRP curve. We should point out, however, that this outcome is not likely to persist over the long run. As wages are increased, the firm's cost curves are shifted upward and to the left and profits are reduced. Those firms making only normal profits to begin with will tend to leave the business, output will decline, and the total demand facing the union for its labor also will decline. So labor still ends up with fewer jobs in the long run than would otherwise be the case. Furthermore, the prevalence of imperfectly competitive employers should not be overemphasized. The vast majority of all employers hire a relatively small proportion of the total labor force in their respective labor markets, which in turn means that they face a highly elastic supply of labor, especially in the long run.

Have unions actually increased wages? At first glance the answer may seem obvious; we continually observe negotiated wage increases in unionized trades or industries. But the question is: Would the normal forces of supply and demand result in comparable wage increases? On the basis of empirical studies, it appears that unions have been able to increase the wages of their members in the order of magnitude of 7 to 11 percent.[5] These studies also show, however, that wages of nonunion workers are about 3 to 4 percent *lower* than they would be in the absence of unionism. Since union membership accounts for about 22 percent of the U.S. labor force, with the other 78 percent nonunion, it appears that although unions have altered the structure of wages, they have not increased the overall average level of wages in the country.

It is fairly easy to see why unions have been able to raise wages by collective bargaining and by restricting entry. But why should unions cause other workers to receive lower wages? First it is necessary to recognize that an increase in wages in unionized industries results in fewer jobs in these industries or occupations than would otherwise be the case; that is, there is a movement up along the labor demand income. The people who would have worked in these jobs are forced to find employment in other nonunion occupations. This has the effect of increasing (shifting to the right) the supply of workers to these occupations. When supply increases from what it otherwise would be, price, or in this case, the wage, is lower than it would otherwise be. In other words, farm workers, retail clerks, and other nonunion workers are being forced to work for slightly less because their unionized co-workers are enjoying somewhat higher wages.

This phenomenon is illustrated in Figure 9–9. The increase in wages because of union pressure from W_e to W_u and the resulting reduction in the quantity of labor demanded from Q_1 to Q_0 are shown in Figure 9–9(A). (In this case we assume the wage increase is the result of collective bargaining by an industrial union, but the

---

[5] See H. Gregg Lewis, *Unionism and Relative Wages in the United States* (Chicago: University of Chicago Press, 1963).

FIGURE 9–9
Effect of union wage increases on union and nonunion occupations

(A) Unionized occupations

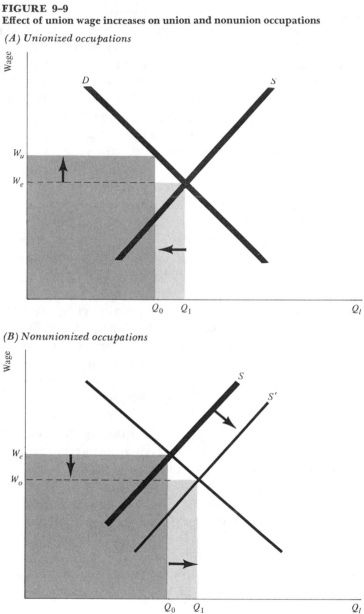

(B) Nonunionized occupations

same overall result would occur because of restricting entry into a unionized trade.) The reduction in people working in the unionized industry increases the supply of people in nonunion occupations, as illustrated in Figure 9–9(B). And, as a result, the wage level in a nonunion occupation is lower than would otherwise be the case.

Minimum wage laws

Society has attempted to protect itself against employers who pay excessively low wages by the enactment of minimum wage laws. As the name implies, a minimum wage law requires employers to pay employees covered under the law an hourly wage at least as high as the stipulated minimum. There is a federal minimum wage law that covers workers in manufacturing and industries engaged in interstate commerce. Many states, particularly northern industrial states, also have minimum wage laws of their own, especially for employees not covered under the federal law. The stipulated minimum wage, of course, has been steadily increasing in step with inflation and with the rising average level of real wages in the country. The federal law, stemming from the Fair Labor Standards Act of 1938, began with a minimum wage of 25 cents an hour in 1940 and has increased to more than $3 an hour by 1980. In recent years the minimum wage has been adjusted upward frequently to keep pace with inflation.

The people most affected by such legislation, of course, are those at the low end of the wage scale, mainly teenagers working on their first jobs and people with relatively few skills, who in large part are members of minority groups. At first glance it may appear that a minimum wage is a boon to low-wage earners. After all, if the minimum wage is $3.00 an hour, your take-home pay will be larger than if you had to work for a market-determined wage of say, $2.25 an hour. The rub comes because even though a minimum wage law can guarantee that a worker must receive at least that wage if he or she works, it cannot guarantee that a job will be available at that wage. In fact, if the minimum wage is substantially above the equilibrium wage for occupations with low hourly pay, we can expect a decline in the number of jobs available to low-wage earners.

This problem can be illustrated best with a simple market demand and supply diagram for labor (Figure 9–10). Assume here
that the minimum wage W_m, is above the market equilibrium wage,
W_e. At the minimum wage, the quantity of labor demanded, Q_d, is
less than the amount demanded at the equilibrium wage, Q_e. In
other words, by imposing a minimum wage law, people at the
lower end of the wage scale are faced with a decrease in the number of jobs available. What generally happens is that employers

FIGURE 9–10
Effect of a minimum wage law on low-income people

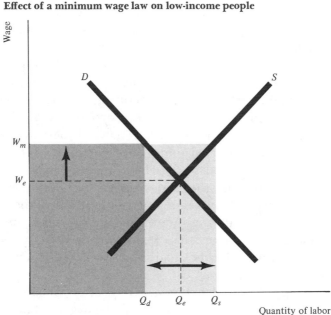

substitute capital or machines for the higher-priced labor. At the
same time, the higher minimum wage draws an increasing number of people into the market, as illustrated by the increase in the
quantity of labor supplied from Q_e to Q_s. The gap between Q_d and
Q_s, therefore, represents the number of people who would like to
work at this wage but cannot find a job (i.e., the unemployed).

The results of minimum wage laws predicted by our theoretical
framework also are substantiated by a number of recent empirical

studies.[6] It appears that the impact of minimum wage laws is felt to the largest extent by teenagers, particularly those from minority groups. In view of the relatively high unemployment rates of minorities in general, and teenagers in particular, one can seriously question whether minimum wage laws work to the benefit of those most affected. Indeed it has been argued that these laws have been mainly supported by northern industries and unions in order to protect themselves against loss of business and jobs to the South and to rural areas where wages have been lower. It is doubtful, however, that many fulltime semiskilled or even unskilled workers in manufacturing are affected by such laws. It is likely that part-time jobs, particularly those in the service trades, are affected the most.

Main points of Chapter 9

1. The labor market is primarily concerned with the demand for and supply of the services of individuals. The special attributes of labor are reflected in the market.
2. The demand for labor, or any input, by a perfectly competitive firm in the product market is equal to the input's VMP curve. Value of the marginal product (VMP) is equal to marginal physical product (MPP) times product price.
3. If market demand for an input is obtained by holding the prices of related inputs constant, then a decrease in its price will bring forth an increase in the quantity demanded for two reasons: (*a*) producers will increase output because of lower production costs and, in so doing, will increase the employment of the input in question, and (*b*) producers in many cases can substitute the now relatively cheap input for other substitute inputs.

[6] See, for example, Douglas K. Adie, "Teen-Age Unemployment and Real Federal Minimum Wages," *Journal of Political Economy* (March–April 1973), pp. 435–41; and M. Kosters and F. Welch, "The Effects of Minimum Wages on the Distribution of Changes in Aggregate Unemployment," *American Economic Review* (June 1972), pp. 323–32.

4. The demand for labor, or any input, by an imperfectly competitive firm in the product market is equal to the input's MRP curve. Marginal revenue product (MRP) is equal to MPP times marginal revenue.

5. Leisure can be thought of as a good. The more leisure we demand, the less labor we supply. The price of an extra hour of leisure is the income forgone by decreasing labor one hour.

6. The amount of leisure we take when wages are increased depends on the income and substitution effects. The income effect pulls us toward more leisure because we can afford to "buy" more, while the substitution effect pulls us toward less leisure because it is now more expensive. We will take more leisure (or work less) after a wage increase if the income effect more than offsets the substitution effect.

7. If the income effect more than offsets the substitution effect, the supply of labor will be "backward bending," meaning that less labor will be supplied at higher wages.

8. In a perfectly competitive labor market, wages are determined by the interaction of labor demand and supply. An employer will be a perfectly competitive buyer of labor if he or she hires a small percent of the labor force in a vicinity.

9. Although a perfectly competitive employer faces a perfectly elastic supply curve of labor, such an employer may have some leeway in the wage paid because labor is not homogeneous.

10. The perfectly competitive employer hires workers up to the point where the wage is equal to the MRP of an additional worker. To stop short of this point would involve an unnecessary loss of profits.

11. Imperfect competition in the labor market occurs if each employer hires a large share of the labor in a vicinity. The imperfectly competitive employer maximizes profits by hiring labor up to the point where labor's MRP is equal to the marginal resource cost (MRC) of labor.

12. The demand for labor, or any input, shifts if there is a change in the product price or the MPP of labor.

13. An increase in the use of a complementary input increases the MPP of labor, whereas an increase in the use of a substitute input decreases the MPP of labor.

14. The supply of labor shifts if there is a change in population

or in the wages paid in other labor markets. In a given labor market the supply of labor will decrease if there is an increase in the wages in alternative employment.

15. The long-run trend toward increasing wages and employment implies that the demand for labor has been increasing more rapidly than the labor supply.

16. Occupations that have not experienced gains in labor productivity exhibit wage increases because of the upward shift in the supply of labor facing these occupations.

17. In the short run, a decrease in the demand for labor by a given firm or industry tends to result in layoffs rather than a reduction in wages.

18. Wage differences between occupations occur because of differences in demand and supply conditions.

19. Automation, a new term for on old process, results in higher wages for labor. Jobs need not be eliminated if the increase in output offsets the decrease in demand for labor. In an expanding economy the substitution of machines for labor generally takes place by not replacing employees who leave.

20. Although it may appear that employers are largely responsible for discrimination in the labor market, consumers and fellow workers have a strong influence on the actions of employers.

21. Wage differences between men and women exist in part because of occupational differences, the greater uncertainty involved in the hiring of women, and less opportunity on the part of women to build up seniority.

22. Labor unions attempt to raise the wages of their members by increasing demand, decreasing supply, or bargaining for a union wage. All involve certain drawbacks, although decreasing the labor supply likely has been the most successful.

23. Empirical studies report that unions have succeeded in raising the wages of their members in the order of magnitude of 7 to 11 percent, while decreasing the wages of workers in nonunion occupations about 3 to 4 percent. The latter occurs because of the increase in the supply of workers to nonunion occupations from what it would otherwise be.

24. Although minimum wage laws place a floor on wages, they also tend to increase the amount of unemployment of people

at the low end of the wage scale, particularly teenagers looking for their first job and unskilled workers.

Questions for thought and discussion

1. If a firm wishes to maximize profits, how much of each input should
   it use?
2. Why is the VMP curve of an input also the firm's demand curve
   for that input?
3. Which is more elastic, the demand for an input when the *quantities*
   of other inputs are held constant or the demand when the *prices*
   of other inputs are held constant? Explain. Which is more realistic?
4. Suppose you apply for a job that pays $15,000 per year. What
   must be true of your VMP in order for you to obtain this job and
   keep it?
5. Suppose you are the owner of a small business and employ ten
   people. One of your main problems is absenteeism. In order to ease
   this problem, you consider raising their wages from $4.00 to $4.50
   per hour. Do you think this raise would reduce the number of days
   missed? Explain the factors that should be considered.
6. The fact that most employers tell their employees what wage they
   will receive is an indication that individual employers can set
   any wage they please. True or false? Explain.
7. Which type of employer, perfectly competitive or imperfectly
   competitive, hires labor up to the point where labor's VMP (or
   MRP) is just equal to the cost of labor? Explain.
8. The perfectly competitive employer pays a wage equal to the
   VMP of labor. The imperfectly competitive employer pays a wage
   that is less than the VMP of labor. It follows therefore that the wage
   paid by an imperfectly competitive employer is less than that of
   a perfectly competitive employer. True or false? Explain.
9. Taxicab drivers probably are not more productive now than they
   were 25 years ago but their current wages are substantially higher
   (in real terms) than they were then. Why?
10. Occasionally certain labor organizations urge consumers to boy-
    cott (not buy) the products of certain producers. If some consumers
    comply with the wishes of the labor organizations, what happens to
    demand for labor and employment in the boycotted industries or
    firms? Explain.

11. Some people argue that automation is good because it increases the productivity and the wages of labor. Others argue that it is bad because it throws people out of work. Who is right? Explain.

12. Some people do not earn much more than $100 per week, whereas others earn that much per hour. Why the large difference in earnings?

13. It is very hard to become a member of some unions, whereas it is virtually impossible not to become a member of other unions if one is working in certain industries. Why the difference?

14. Labor unions increase the wages of some people and reduce the wages of others. True or false? Explain.

15. Minimum wage laws cause unemployment. True or false? Explain.

10

The capital market

The concept of capital

In the context of business or economics, the word *capital* has taken on two slightly different meanings. Business people may think of capital as cash or money to carry on a business, as in "working capital." Economists, however, generally define *capital* as durable or long-lasting inputs such as land, buildings, machines, and tools that yield a flow of services over a period of time. The quantity of capital is generally measured in monetary terms, however. Actually the above definition of capital also could apply to consumer durables such as housing, automobiles, and appliances. They also are long-lasting and yield a flow of services over a period of time. Indeed, in view of the earlier discussion on household production (Chapter 4), consumer durables might be considered as inputs in the production of utility. Consumer durables generally are not thought of as capital, however, so the discussion in this chapter will focus on the narrower or more conventional definition of the word.

The study of capital is separated from the study of labor because there are a number of differences between these two inputs. The first and most obvious difference is that capital is an inanimate, non-living input devoid of feelings or preferences. Although the owners of capital are concerned about the wage or return it receives, they do not care about its working conditions such as the length of its workweek or whether it is employed in a prestigious occupation. Thus many of the factors that are important for labor need not be of concern in our discussion of capital.

A second difference is that capital is generally purchased for use over a relatively long period of time. For example, you may purchase an asset this year that will go on producing for you the remainder of your lifetime. Labor, or other inputs such as raw materials, are purchased for immediate or current use only. Granted there may be an understanding between employer and employee about the length of time they will be associated, but the employer of labor, unlike the employer of capital, does not usually pay the employee a lump sum for all future services. We will see shortly that this difference is quite important.

A third difference between capital and labor is that the purchase of capital may involve an expenditure well in advance of the date it begins to contribute to output. Economists refer to this time interval between the expenditure and the beginning of the flow of output as the *gestation period*. This time interval is especially important for investment in education as we will see in Chapter 11.

Annual cost of capital

What does capital cost? At first glance the answer to this question may appear obvious. Surely the cost of capital is what buyers pay the people who produce it. But the answer is not quite this simple. To return to the tomato production example, suppose you purchase a $1,000 garden tractor to increase output. It would seem a bit unreasonable to require this year's output to carry the entire $1,000 outlay. After all, the tractor will still be available for tomato production in other years. But at the same time it seems reasonable to charge at least part of the $1,000 toward current production. Thus this year's cost of the $1,000 capital item would be somewhere between $1,000 and zero. Clearly $1,000 is too much and zero is too little.

It would be reasonable to charge this year's production with at least the amount that the garden tractor depreciated in value during the year. Suppose the tractor's market value declined to $700 in that period. If you wanted, you could sell the tractor for $700 after using it the first year. Thus the depreciation cost of this capital item for the current year would be $300.

Aside from the normal operating expense, such as gasoline and oil, would the $300 be the total cost of this capital item for the current year? Not quite. Where did you obtain the $1,000 to buy the tractor? If you borrowed it from a bank, you must pay interest on the loan. If it were 10 percent per year, you would have to pay the bank $100 per year for the use of their money. Adding up the depreciation plus interest would give you $400 as the cost of this capital item for the current year.

It should not be concluded from this example, however, that the interest charge is included only when capital is purchased with borrowed funds. It would be equally necessary to include an interest charge if your own funds were used to make the purchase, because in this case you would have to forgo the interest income of the $1,000 that you could have obtained had you not purchased the garden tractor.

If the $1,000 were your own funds, however, the interest charge probably would not be quite as high as would be the case if you had borrowed the money. The reason is that individuals lend money at "wholesale" but borrow at "retail." Banks and other lending institutions that channel funds of individual lenders into a central location and then screen and loan to borrowers must be paid for their services. The difference between the interest you obtain on savings and the interest paid for a loan constitutes the payment for these services.

To summarize, the cost of capital for a given period consists of two components: depreciation and interest. The use of a capital item also involves other costs, such as fuel, repairs, and insurance, but these will depend somewhat on the kind of capital under consideration. In this section we are mainly concerned with the two components of capital cost common to most capital items.[1]

The depreciation plus interest cost of a capital item will, of course, vary from one year to the next. In the case of the garden

---

[1] Land, which in most cases does not depreciate in value, is an exception. In fact, in recent history most land has appreciated in value. We will consider land separately in a later section.

tractor, the depreciation expense for the second year probably will be somewhat lower. For example, suppose it is worth $500 at the end of the second year, resulting in a depreciation charge of $200 during that year. (We will discuss depreciation patterns in more detail in the following section.) Since you have "written off" $300 of the tractor the first year, the interest charge during the second year will be computed on the basis of $700 rather than $1,000, as it was during the first year of ownership. Thus the $200 depreciation plus a $70 interest charge ($700 × 0.10) gives a $270 annual cost of ownership for the second year on. If you had purchased the garden tractor as a one-year-old used machine for $700, the cost the first year of ownership would be $270. Although the depreciation plus interest expense will in general decline during the life of a machine, we can expect this to be offset at least in part by an increase in repairs and maintenance costs as the machine grows older.

DEPRECIATION

Because depreciation accounts for a large share of the annual cost of owning a capital item, it will be useful to examine it in more detail. There are two basic reasons a capital item depreciates: (1) the wearing out or "using up" of the item and (2) obsolescence. In regard to the first reason, it should be kept in mind that the current market value of a capital item reflects the value at the present of its expected future contribution to output. Thus, the older an item becomes, the fewer years of productive life that remain. For example, a new garden tractor may have ten years of service ahead of it, while a five-year-old machine may have only five years of life remaining. Even if the used machine could do about the same amount of work per day as the new machine, no one would pay as much for the used item because of the smaller number of work days left in it. Also there is more uncertainty involved in buying a used machine. For example, the buyer may not know whether the previous owner had taken good care of the machine. The possibility of high future repair bills will lower the price that buyers are willing to pay.

In an age of change and technological improvement, capital also becomes obsolete. If something new comes on the market that reduces production costs or increases efficiency, the demand for the old capital will decline, hence its price will fall. Thus the depreciation of capital depends not only on its own productivity but also on the productivity of the new capital being produced. Because of this it is difficult, if not impossible, to predict in advance how fast an item will become obsolete. Nor is it easy or even useful to attempt to separate how much of an item's depreciation is due to wearing out and how much is due to obsolescence; both have the same effect of reducing its market value.

Two widely used methods of estimating depreciation are (1) the straight-line method and (2) the constant-percentage method. The resulting decline in value of the item being depreciated for each of these methods is illustrated in Figure 10–1. The straight-line method amounts to decreasing the value of the capital by a constant number of dollars each year. For example, if you were depreciating your $1,000 garden tractor by the straight-line method over a period of five years, you would assess $200 per year as depreciation.

If you use the constant-percentage method, you would multiply

FIGURE 10–1
Straight-line and constant-percentage patterns of depreciation of a $1,000 garden tractor

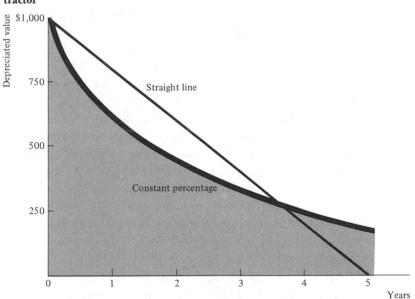

each year's market value by a constant percentage. For example, if you depreciate the garden tractor 30 percent per year, the first year's depreciation would be $300, the second year's $210 ($700 × 0.30), the third year's $147, and so on. You might notice that under the second method the annual depreciation is higher when the item is new, resulting in a lower depreciated value during its early years of use. With this method, also, the item does not depreciate to zero. After five years its depreciated value under the constant-percentage depreciation is $168. In fact, under this method the depreciated value never completely reaches zero, although it comes close.

The method of depreciation chosen and the length of time involved depend, of course, on the item to be depreciated. The constant-percentage method would seem to be a bit more realistic for most items, since depreciation usually is higher during the first few years of ownership. An automobile, for example, tends to depreciate between 20 and 25 percent per year, depending on the make, model, amount of use, and the care it has received. If you purchase a $6,000 automobile it depreciates $1,500 the first year, where the 25 percent rate applies. In calculating the total cost of ownership the first year, you should also include the interest charge, $600 if taken at 10 percent, together with gasoline, insurance, license fees, and so forth. With normal use, the total annual cost of a $6,000 automobile probably runs in the neighborhood of $3,000 the first year of ownership. Is it worth it?

The marginal product of capital

In deciding whether or not to purchase or keep a machine or other capital items it is necessary to consider both its cost and its returns. In the previous sections we looked at cost; let us now consider the returns of a capital item. In a sense capital is similar to labor or any other input in that it contributes to the output of goods and services. This contribution to output can be measured either in physical units of output by its marginal physical product (MPP), or in monetary units in terms of its value of the marginal product (VMP)—or marginal revenue product (MRP). Recall from Chapters 4 and 9 that MPP is defined as the additional output obtained from an additional unit of the input—capital in this case, and VMP or MRP, as the case may be, is the value of the additional output obtained from an additional unit of capital. (From now on, to simplify the notation, we will refer only to the MRP of capital.)

The MRP of capital can be visualized as the value of the additional output that is made possible by utilizing a machine compared with what would be produced if it were not used. Because we are interested in comparing capital's annual MRP with its annual interest plus depreciation charge, we ought to refer to the machine's annual "net" MRP. This would be the value of additional annual output less the added expense incurred by owning and operating the machine, such as fuel, repairs, additional labor, and insurance.

Once the annual net MRP of a capital item has been estimated, it is possible to compare this figure against its annual depreciation plus interest charge in deciding whether or not to purchase it. For example, in the garden tractor example, the first year's depreciation plus interest charge was estimated as $400. If the first year's net MRP of this machine were estimated to be $500, it would pay to purchase it. Anytime you can spend $400 and receive $500 in return, do so. On the other hand, if the estimated net MRP was less than $400, then, of course, the decision would be not to purchase the machine. Thus we can formulate a rule: Purchase a machine as long as its expected annual net contribution to output (MRP) is at least as great as its expected annual depreciation plus interest charge.

Of course, you might ask how it is possible to estimate the net MRP of a machine or capital item. Granted, you will probably have to make some rough calculations, but rough estimates are better than no estimates at all. The accuracy of your estimates will in part reflect your ability as a manager of capital.

The rate of return on capital

Because a capital item is generally purchased for use over a number of years, it is common to express its contribution to output during a given year as a fraction of its value at the beginning of the year. The resulting figure is commonly referred to as a rate of return. We can define the *rate of return* on capital as the amount each dollar earns each year after all expenses, including depreciation in this case, have been subtracted. It is commonly expressed as a percentage figure. For example, suppose, after subtracting depreciation and other expenses from the "gross" MRP of the $1,000 garden tractor, the first year's earnings happen to be $80. During this year its rate of return would be equal to 0.08 or 8 percent (80/1,000). In other words, each dollar earns 8 cents during the year.

You might have recognized that the rate of return on capital is essentially the same idea as the rate of return on your savings account in the bank. However, unlike a savings deposit in a bank, which goes on earning its stipulated rate of return year after year as long as the money is left in the account, the earnings of a machine or building can be expected to vary from year to year and eventually to come to an end as the item wears out.

There is one kind of capital, however, that does not tend to "wear out" or depreciate with normal care, namely land. In fact, during recent history land has generally appreciated in value. To keep the example simple, suppose you purchase a plot of land for $10,000 and expect it to remain at this price. Also suppose you can collect $1,000 per year return from the land for as long as you want to by renting it to a tomato grower. Assume also that there are no other expenses, so the $1,000 is a net return.

For an asset that can be expected to yield a stream of returns for all time to come, its annual rate of return can be computed as follows:

$$r = \frac{\text{Annual net returns}}{\text{Capital value}}$$

In the land example above, the rate of return would be:

$$r = \frac{\$1,000}{\$10,000} = 0.10 = 10 \text{ percent}$$

CAPITALIZED VALUE

By manipulating this formula slightly, we can derive another formula that is very useful for deciding the maximum price you could afford to pay for a piece of property. To make the formula more manageable, we will abbreviate, letting r represent the interest rate or rate of return, R the annual net return, and K the capital value. Now we have

$$r = \frac{R}{K} \quad \text{or} \quad K \times r = R \quad \text{or} \quad K = \frac{R}{r}$$

The resulting formula, $K = R/r$, tells us how much a piece of property is worth if we know its annual return and the interest charge. Suppose in order to purchase this plot of land you took out a $1,000 loan at 8 percent. Utilizing this formula, we find:

$$K = \frac{\$1,000}{0.08} = \$12,500$$

If you were assured of an annual $1,000 net return on this land and the money to buy it cost 8 percent per year, you could have paid as much as $12,500 for the land. Economists refer to the K in this formula, or the $12,500 in this example, as the *capitalized value* of the property. In a competitive market prospective buyers would tend to bid the price of the property up to this amount. And sellers, knowing this, will be likely to set the selling price at the capitalized value. If you are able to buy a piece of property for $10,000 that has a capitalized value of $12,500 you have made a good deal.

We should note also from this formula that for a given annual return (R), the capitalized value (K) will vary inversely with the size of the interest rate (r). If the interest rate you had to pay on your loan were 10 percent, K would have been $10,000. A lower interest rate such as 5 percent would result in a capitalized value of $20,000.

Although the relationship between the interest rate and the capitalized value is an algebraic phenomenon—the larger the denominator, the smaller is the quotient, and vice versa—it has an underlying economic rationale. At a relatively high interest rate, say 10 percent, the income that will be forthcoming many years in the future is more expensive to obtain than if the interest rate were lower. At high interest rates borrowers are required to pay more for the distant income, in terms of either an interest charge on borrowed funds or forgone interest from their own funds; hence they cannot pay as high an initial price for the capital.

In times of inflation the value of land and other real assets will tend to increase at a faster rate than the general price level, particularly in the early stages of inflation. This occurs because of expected future inflation. As inflation persists both buyers and sellers come to expect an increase in the future net returns and in the selling price when the land is disposed of. These increased values are capitalized into the current price of land.

Cash flow analysis

Most capital that might be considered for purchase, such as buildings or equipment, would not be expected to yield a stream of returns into infinity, however. As years go by, capital generally becomes less productive, and its maintenance costs rise. As a result the stream of net returns may exhibit a downward trend, eventually coming to an end when it no longer pays to keep the capital item.

As you might expect, it is somewhat more difficult to compute a rate of return to a capital item in this more common but realistic situation. To facilitate computation of capital's rate of return, economists have devised a technique called *cash flow analysis*. As the name implies, this technique involves comparing the cash outflow of a capital item, that is, its purchase price, with the inflow of cash that results from the use of the item.

We can use the garden tractor purchase also to illustrate this technique. Suppose you denote as year 0 the time you purchase the tractor. The first step is to assess, as best you can, the contribution of the tractor to your total production and sales of tomatoes during the years you expect to own it. One way to do this is to estimate your total sales during these years without the tractor and then estimate your total sales with the tractor, less the added expense such as gasoline and repairs. The difference between these two sets of figures gives the net inflow of cash that results from owning the tractor. Your figures might look something like the following:

	Year 0	Year 1	Year 2	Year 3	Year 4	Year 5
Cash outflow	−$1,000	—	—	—	—	—
Gross cash inflow	—	+$375	+$375	+$450	+$475	+$600
Less added expense ...	—	−$100	−$125	−$150	−$200	−$200
Net cash inflow ..	$1,000	+$275	+$250	+$300	+$275	+$400

It is reasonable to assume that the tractor does not begin to pay off at once. Suppose the first payoff comes about one year after you buy it—call this year 1. Also assume that you expect to use the tractor for five years. The net cash inflow figures essentially represent the tractor's net MRP for each year, except for the last year, when net cash inflow also includes the selling price of the tractor.

The added expense figures denote the expenses related to owning the tractor. They include the normal operating expense of fuel and oil, repairs, and the cost of any additional labor that is incurred by operating the tractor. This figure should also include the implicit cost of any additional hours of your own labor utilized. Notice that the added expense figures become larger as the years go by. The main reason for this is the larger amount of repairs that you can expect as the tractor grows older.

The additional expense figures, however, *do not* include the *depreciation* expense or a charge for *interest* on the $1,000. The depreciation is taken into account in the gross cash inflow figure for year 5, the year you expect to sell the tractor. The $600 gross cash inflow figure for year 5 includes both the extra value of production, say $400, and the selling price of the tractor, $200 in this example. The total depreciation over the five-year period of $800 is therefore reflected in the gross cash inflow in year 5. If there had been no depreciation, and you could have sold the tractor for the $1,000 you paid for it, the gross cash inflow would have been $1,400 in year 5.

Probably the main advantage of cash flow analysis is that we do not have to be concerned with the pattern of depreciation of a capital item. For example, if we underestimated the amount of depreciation during an early year, we would overestimate its net returns and therefore overestimate its rate of return. Also many capital items, such as machines in a factory or the factory building itself, may not have a good resale market, making it difficult to estimate their true economic depreciation during their most productive years. With the cash flow technique we need only estimate the depreciated value once, at the end of the time we expect to keep the item. Depending on how long we expect to keep it, this figure may be its scrap value. When its value is low, we are not likely to make a large error in estimating its total depreciation.

Assuming that you are fairly confident in the accuracy of your estimates of the added income and expense connected with the tractor, you still are faced with the question: Should you or should you not buy the tractor? If you add up the net cash inflows over the five-year period, you can see that the $1,000 investment in the tractor enables you to take in a total of $1,500.

Discounted present value

Before you become too optimistic about this investment, however, keep in mind that positive net cash inflows are not available to you until future years. And a dollar that you obtain, say, next year is not as valuable to you as a dollar in hand at the present, because you could always loan out or invest the present dollar at a positive rate of interest, enabling you to obtain something more than one dollar a year from now. Hence money forthcoming sometime in the future is less valuable or not worth as much as money in hand at the present because if you have the money now you could have an even greater amount in the future. For example, $100 in hand now could earn $10 interest over the course of a year and, therefore, be worth $110 one year from now if the interest rate were 10 percent. Thus $100 in hand now is worth more than $100 forthcoming one year from now.

How much is one dollar of income forthcoming a year from now worth at the present? In order to answer this question, we must specify the rate of interest that could be obtained by lending the dollar, call it r. The formula for discounting one dollar of future income to the present is given by $1/(1 + r)^n$. The n represents the number of years in the future the income is forthcoming. For example, if r is 5 percent, or 0.05, then one dollar forthcoming one year from now is worth $1/(1.05)$, or 95 cents at the present. Economists would refer to this 95 cents as the *discounted present value* of one dollar forthcoming one year in the future. Notice that if the interest rate increases, the discounted present value declines. At an interest rate of 0.10, the discounted present value of one dollar forthcoming one year from now declines to 91 cents.

By using this discounting formula you can determine the present value of the future returns of the garden tractor. Suppose that the market rate of interest is 10 percent. The present value of the returns in year 1 is $275/1.10$, or approximately $250. In year 2 it would be $250/(1.10)^2$ or $207, and so forth. The discounted present value in year 0 of the net cash inflows from years 1 through 5 is shown below:

Year 1		Year 2		Year 3		Year 4		Year 5		Total
$250	+	$207	+	$226	+	$188	+	$248	=	$1,119

It is interesting to note that the $1,500 total return from the five years' net cash inflows is worth only $1,119 at its discounted present value, assuming a 10 percent interest rate. You would of course, still consider the garden tractor to be a good investment, since the $1,000 buys $1,119 of present value. But you would not greet the prospect with quite as much enthusiasm as you might have first thought after seeing the $1,500 nondiscounted return.

This does not mean, however, that the nondiscounted $1,500 return to the $1,000 investment would always be acceptable. Suppose the interest rate you had to pay increased to 15 percent, or you have another use for your funds that would return 15 percent. Discounting the same $1,500 stream of returns back to year 0, using a 15 percent interest rate, results in a discounted present value of only $981. Here we find that the present value of the $1,500 is only worth $981. Now the tractor would not be an acceptable investment.

Benefit/cost ratio

A common way of comparing the cost of a capital item with the discounted present value of its returns is by the benefit/cost (B/C) ratio. The *benefit* of an investment is defined as the discounted present value of its net cash inflows. Dividing the value of this benefit by the cost of the investment yields the B/C ratio. In the garden tractor example, its B/C ratio is $1,119/1,000 = 1.119$ with a 10 percent interest rate. An investment is deemed acceptable if its B/C ratio is 1 or greater, preferably greater. Of course, the interest rate used to discount the returns influences the size of the B/C ratio. Recall that a 15 percent interest rate reduces the discounted present value of the garden tractor return to $981, yielding a *B/C* ratio of 0.981. In this case, the tractor investment becomes unacceptable. This example illustrates the importance of the interest rate. The higher the interest rate used to discount future returns, the lower is the discounted present value of future returns and the lower is the *B/C* ratio.

Internal rate of return

Because the interest rate that is used to discount future returns has such an important bearing on the discounted present value and *B/C* ratio, it is very important to always inquire what interest rate is used to compute these figures. An unusually low interest rate can make an otherwise unacceptable investment look good. For this reason, economists often utilize another criterion called the internal rate of return to evaluate investments. The *internal rate of return* is defined as that rate of interest which makes the discounted present value of the net cash inflows of an investment equal to its cost. The internal rate of return has a meaning that is comparable to the rate of return received on one's savings account. For example, an 8 percent internal rate of return on an investment is comparable to an 8 percent rate of return received on a savings account.

An important advantage of using the internal rate of return to evaluate an investment is that the outcome of the evaluation does not depend on the rate of interest chosen, as is the case for obtaining the discounted present value, or the *B/C* ratio. With the internal rate of return measure, the decision to invest or not to invest depends on the computed rate of return. The investment will be profitable if the internal rate of return is at least as much as the rate of interest paid on borrowed funds, or what could be earned in the next best alternative use of one's own funds.

The internal rate of return can be computed only by a trial and error process. You start out by picking a rate of interest that you think makes the discounted present value equal to the cost of the investment. If the discounted present value you obtain is greater than the cost of the investment, the internal rate of return is greater than the interest rate you have chosen. Thus you have to repeat the calculations using a higher rate of interest. If this time the discounted present value is smaller than the cost of the investment, the internal rate is smaller than the interest rate you have tried. At some point the discounted present value will be exactly equal to the cost of the investment. When this occurs you have found the internal rate of return.

In the garden tractor example, a 10 percent rate of interest discounted the $1,500 stream of returns down to a present value of $1,119. Thus the internal rate of return is slightly larger than 10 percent. On the other hand, the 15 percent rate was slightly too high; the present value of the $1,500 was reduced to $981. Thus we can conclude that the internal rate of return on the garden tractor is somewhere between 10 and 15 percent. It turns out that the discounted present value of the returns is about $1,000 ($1,006 to be exact) when the interest rate used to discount the returns is 14 percent. Thus the internal rate of return in this example is just a shade over 14 percent, but it generally does not pay to strive for greater accuracy than this. The meaning of this 14 percent internal rate of return is that the $1,000 investment pays off at the rate of 14 percent per year, or $140 per year, during the five-year payoff period. If you paid, or could have earned, 10 percent on the $1,000, you would reap a 4 percent, or $40 per year, pure profit.

Although the $140 per year net income from this investment may seem somewhat small, we must remember that $1,000 is also a relatively small investment. It does not require a very large business these days to have $100,000 or more invested. And if you obtain 14 percent on $100,000, your yearly earnings from capital are $14,000. If you borrowed the entire $100,000 for 10 percent, your pure profit per year is $4,000. Remember this is in addition to your labor income.

Most of the rich and super rich have gotten to be so by the income from capital. Moreover, most of these people, at least when they started out, utilized borrowed funds. Earning 14 percent on $1 million returns $140,000 per year. Even if you pay 10 percent for this money, you still clear $40,000 per year for letting the capital work for you. Few people except the top professional athletes, movie stars, and the highest paid executives can obtain an income over $100,000 to $150,000 per year without supplemental earnings from capital. Thus if you strive for a relatively high standard of living in the future, it is never too early to set aside part of your income for investment purposes. You must realize, though, that ownership of capital does not guarantee a high income. For example, if you borrow $100,000 at 10 percent and the capital that is purchased with the money pays off at only 5 percent, you lose $5,000 per year. When playing with stakes this high, it is important to assess rather carefully the anticipated rate of return.

To summarize, we have discussed four ways to assess the profitability of an investment: (1) comparing the annual net MRP of capital with its annual depreciation plus interest expense, (2) comparing the capitalized value or discounted present value of the stream of future returns with its purchase price, (3) comparing the B/C ratio to 1, and (4) comparing the internal rate of return with the interest rate on borrowed funds or on our own funds. Because of the variability of annual net returns of most capital items, along with the difficulty of accurately estimating the annual depreciation charge, the calculation of the discounted present value or internal rate of return by the cash flow technique tends to be the most common means of gauging the profitability of an investment.

Ranking of investment opportunities

Most business firms face an assortment of investment opportunities, some more profitable than others, and the criteria for accepting or rejecting an investment opportunity developed above are applied in these decisions. For example, in the tomato-growing endeavor you might estimate that $100 spent on garden tools (hoe, rake, etc.) would pay off at a 20 percent internal rate of return. Adding additional capital such as the $1,000 garden tractor may yield a 14 percent rate of return. Perhaps another $1,000 invested in irrigation equipment (pump, pipes, sprinklers, etc.) might be estimated to yield 10 percent. And so forth.

A convenient way to express such a ranking of investment opportunities is by a diagram. Using the figures from this example we plot the internal rate of return on the vertical axis and the cumulative amount invested on the horizontal axis. To simplify the example, assume that there is a continuous array of investment opportunities. This enables us to connect the points and draw a continuous downward sloping line, as in Figure 10–2.

Faced with these investment opportunities, you must decide

FIGURE 10–2
Cumulative ranking of investments

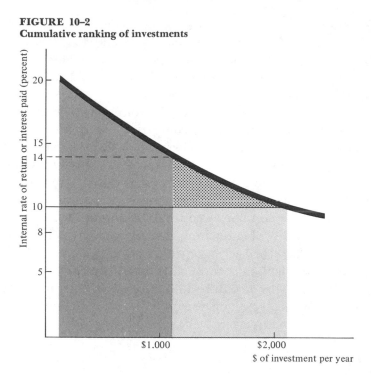

which ones to accept and which to reject for your tomato production venture. In order to make this decision, you need to know the interest rate that would have to be paid on borrowed funds or that could be obtained on your own funds. If this is 10 percent, you would want to invest in those opportunities that yield 10 percent or more. In the example depicted by Figure 10–2, the total investment for the year would be $2,100.

Stopping short of this amount, say $1,100, would reduce profits by the value of the shaded area in Figure 10–2. If you invest $1,101 instead of $1,100, you pay 10 cents per year on this extra dollar of investment and it returns 14 cents per year, so in net it adds 4 cents to your total profits (or it reduces your losses by 4 cents if you are operating in the red). Continuing to add extra dollars of investment will continue to increase profits, or reduce losses, until you reach the $2,100 point. Increasing the investment beyond $2,100, however, would reduce profits because the interest rate of return on this capital would be less than the interest charge on it.

Thus we can formulate a rule: To maximize profits a firm will continue to expand its investments until the internal rate of return on the marginal dollar invested is equal to the interest rate (explicit or implicit) that prevails. We should note, however, that changes in the interest rate change the profit-maximizing level of investment. For example, if the interest rate were 14 percent, you would invest only $1,400.

We should stress, in addition, that the cumulative ranking of investments by their rate of return is based on the *expected* profitability of each. No one knows for certain how profitable an investment will be until it has run its course. Thus a change in the degree of optimism or pessimism regarding future business conditions will likely shift the curve shown in Figure 10–2. If investors become more optimistic, for example, the curve will shift to the right, thereby increasing the total investment for a given rate of interest.

Interest rate determination

It should be apparent that the rate of interest that must be paid on borrowed funds or that could be earned on one's own funds is an important consideration in deciding whether or not to invest in a capital item. Recall that as the rate of interest increases, the discounted present value of the income stream from an investment declines. As a result, some investments that would be profitable at low rates of interest become unprofitable at high rates. In other words, as the interest rate increases, the discounted present value of fewer and fewer potential investments will remain above the cost of the investment. Or we can say that as the interest rate increases, the internal rate of return from fewer and fewer investments will remain at least as high as the interest rate. Thus we can expect that the amount of investment that will take place each year in the economy will be larger at lower rates of interest, and vice versa. Of course, as mentioned in the preceding section, the expectations of the business community regarding future sales and profits also will have an effect on the level of investment at a given rate of interest.

We might consider here how the rate of interest on loan funds is determined. A complete study of the topic would take us into the realm of macroeconomics in greater detail than is advisable at this point. However, we can say that the rate of interest on loanable funds is determined in the loan market by the demand for a supply of these funds.

Looking first at the demand for loan funds, we can identify two main sources of this demand. First, there is the demand from business firms for the purpose of financing new investment spending. Second, households demand loan funds in order to make large-scale purchases such as houses, cars, and appliances and for other purposes including education, medical bills, and travel. It is reasonable to believe that the demand curve for loan funds is a downward sloping line as shown by Figure 10–3. The fact that some

FIGURE 10–3
Interest rate determination in market for loanable funds

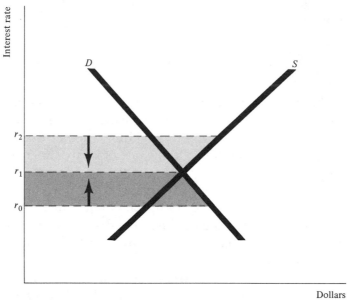

investments are less profitable than others (lower internal rate of return) means that a decrease in the interest rate will bring forth an increase in acceptable investments, which in turn means that more loan money will be demanded to finance this added investment spending. Similarly, a lower rate of interest increases the discounted present value (monetary equivalent) of the service flow from consumer durables, and in so doing increases the rate of spending and borrowing for these items.

Turning next to the supply side of the loan market, one might ask: Where do loan funds come from? In general terms, the supply of loanable funds is the amount of money people are willing to divert from current consumption to saving. Business firms also save by retaining part of their earnings and "plowing" it back into the firms for investment purposes. Of course, all business firms are owned by people so the definition still holds. There is good reason to believe that the supply curve of loanable funds is an upward sloping line as illustrated by Figure 10–3. This implies that people will supply a greater number of dollars at relatively high interest rates than at relatively low rates, other things being equal. The degree of responsiveness of savers to changes in the interest rate is still somewhat of an unsettled question in economics. However, if people buy less of an item when its price increases and more when it becomes less expensive, we should expect some increase in the rate of saving (out of a given income) when the interest rate increases. For, as pointed out in Chapter 2, an increase in the interest rate increases the price of current consumption relative to future consumption. That is, as the interest rate rises, a dollar spent on current consumption increases the amount of future consumption given up, because of the greater interest income forgone.

As in any other market, there is one equilibrium price (interest rate) and quantity that will prevail at any one time, given the demand and supply curves. This interest rate is illustrated by r_1 in Figure 10–3. At a higher rate, say r_2, a greater number of dollars will be supplied than are demanded; that is, there will be a surplus of money in the loan market. Borrowers seeing this surplus of funds will press for a rate that is more favorable to them, while lenders will have to agree to the lower rate if they wish to loan out these funds. Similarly, if the interest rate were below the equilibrium, say r_0, there would be a shortage of funds, since a greater number of dollars would be demanded than supplied at this interest rate. As a result lenders will press for a more favorable rate (to them), and borrowers will have to pay the higher rate or go without funds.

As in the product market and the labor market, the demand and supply curves of loanable funds also can be expected to shift from one position to another. The demand for loanable funds will, of course, be closely tied to investment opportunities. If prospects for future profits increase, we can expect some increase in the demand for funds to finance new investment. Or if totally new and profitable investment opportunities arise, perhaps as the result of new technology, the demand for funds also will tend to increase, or shift to the right. Given the supply of funds, the increase in demand will be expected to cause an increase in the interest rate. Of course, changes in the supply of funds also will affect the equilibrium rate of interest. For example, if people decide to increase their rate of saving, the supply of funds will increase, or shift to the right, and as a result the equilibrium rate of interest will decline. Over the long run, both the demand for and the supply of loanable funds are likely to be increasing, or shifting to the right, as the result of population growth and a rising money income in the economy.

Interest rate differences

For simplicity, we have discussed the interest rate as if there were a single rate of interest prevailing in the economy at a point in time. There are, in fact, a number of rates of interest, depending on the loan market under consideration. Banks charge a *prime rate* for their most favored customers and other, higher rates for small business, home, or auto loans. Banks and finance companies charge still higher rates for so-called personal loans, and "loan sharks" extract rates from their customers that are much higher than that.

What accounts for these differences? Basically we can say that interest rate differences reflect different demand and supply conditions in the particular loan market under consideration. If the supply of funds is large relative to the demand, then the interest rate will be low, and vice versa.

In large part, the differences in interest rates between various borrowers and types of loans are the result of differences on the supply side of the market. The major consideration here is the expected cost of making the loan. Two cost components are important. Perhaps most important is the risk of making the loan. Although lenders can never be 100 percent certain of being repaid, past experience will tell them that certain kinds of loans are much less risky than others. For example, large, reputable companies that have been in business for many years and have built up a good credit rating will likely face a supply curve of funds that lies to the right of that of small, relatively unknown borrowers. The rate of interest charged to the former is often called the *prime rate*. As the risk of default increases, lenders are forced to charge a higher rate in order to pay for the money lost through nonpayment of that type of loan. Lenders attempt to segregate potential borrowers by degree of risk in order to give lower rates to low-risk borrowers (mainly to get their business), while making high-risk borrowers pay a larger share of the cost of defaults.

In addition to risk, a second cost component that accounts for differences in the rate of interest charged is the administrative cost of making and collecting the loan. On a per dollar basis, this tends to be higher for small loans than for large ones. For example, the total cost of the paper work necessary to process a $100,000 loan probably is not much different from the total administrative cost of making a loan of $1,000. Thus the cost per dollar is higher for the smaller loan. To recoup these costs, the lender has to charge a higher rate on relatively small loans. The cost of collecting also varies. At the extreme are those lenders who employ a staff of "three-hundred-pound field men" to search out and persuade borrowers to pay up, or else! Since these lenders (i.e., the crime syndicate) must pay for these "services," they have to charge a high interest rate. If their rates are above the legal maximum, as they usually are, they also have to be compensated for the risk of getting caught and serving a prison term. One might ask: If loan sharks charge such high rates and use such violent methods of collection, why do people borrow from them? The answer, of course, is that they cannot obtain loans from reputable lenders at the legal interest rates. Ceilings on interest rates, or *usury laws* as they are called, have the effect, therefore, of forcing people who are desperate for loans and do not have adequate collateral or credit ratings into the clutches of unscrupulous lenders.

While our discussion of interest rate differences has centered on differences existing in the economy at a point in time, the entire structure of interest rates tends to fluctuate over time. During certain periods, particularly times of inflation, there are relatively high rates, while at other times interest rates are more favorable to borrowers. Again, these differences over time can be explained by changes in demand and supply conditions. For example, during times of strong demand for loans the interest rate will tend to rise to a relatively high level. The amount of inflation that borrowers and lenders expect in the future has a significant impact on the demand for and supply of loan funds and therefore affects the rate of interest in the market. To see why this occurs, we need to distinguish between the so-called money rate and the real rate of interest.

The money rate versus the real rate of interest

The interest rate we have been discussing can be called the *money rate*. The *real rate* is defined as the money rate adjusted by the rate of change of the general price level, that is, the rate of inflation. A simple example will illustrate the effect of inflation on the interest cost and returns of a loan. Suppose you lend someone $100 at 10 percent interest, to be paid back with interest one year from now, and the rate of inflation during this year happens to be 8 percent. At the end of the year you would receive $110. But the 8 percent inflation rate means that it now takes $108 to buy the same amount of goods and services that the $100 could have purchased at the beginning of the year. Thus you have gained only $2 in real purchasing power by making the loan. In other words, you received 2 percent real rate of interest on the loan. Assuming that the borrower spent the $100 on something that increased in value with the price level, say a typewriter, the $8 increase in value of the asset over what it otherwise would have been in part offsets the interest paid. In this case, the $10 interest is offset by the $8 increase in value of the typewriter, so the real rate paid by the borrower is 2 percent. The formula for finding the real rate is given below:

Real rate = Money rate − Annual percent change in price level.

Now it is possible to see why demanders of loan funds are willing to pay higher money rates of interest if they expect inflation to occur during the term of the loan. If they expect inflation to increase the value of assets purchased with the loan and thereby offset part of the interest charge, they will be willing to pay a higher money rate of interest than if they expect prices to remain stable in the future. In other words, the demand for funds will increase or shift to the right with the expectation of inflation in the future.

On the supply side, the suppliers of loan funds, that is, savers, can be expected to be less willing to save and to offer funds on the loan market if they believe that inflation will erode the purchasing power of their savings. To compensate for the loss of purchasing power of their savings, suppliers of loans will be willing to place a given amount of funds on the market only at a higher rate of interest. In other words, the supply of loan funds will tend to decrease or shift to the left with the expectation of inflation in the future. Both the increase in demand and the decrease in supply of loan funds have the effect of increasing the money rate of interest.

If there were no restriction on the level of the money rate of interest, the loan market would establish an equilibrium money rate of interest high enough to compensate for the expected inflation. In reality, upper limits on money rates of interest as set by usury laws may restrict the money rate of interest from rising to its free market equilibrium. In years of relatively high inflation, the real rate often turns out to be negative, that is, the money rate is smaller than the rate of inflation. One might ask: Why do savers offer any funds at all under such circumstances? Of course, lending even at a negative real rate is better than not lending at all and having inflation diminish one's cash even more rapidly.[2] Also, if negative real rates prevail, loans are likely to be selectively rationed to "good friends" of the lending agency or institution—usually large, low-risk borrowers.

Rationing and allocating functions of the interest rate

Market price serves as a rationing device whereby people voluntarily limit the use of goods and services that are not free, as noted in Chapter 6. Price also allocates scarce resources to the production of the goods and services that are most highly valued by society.

---

[2] Further discussion on the effect of inflation on the value of assets is contained in Chapter 3 of the companion macro book.

The interest rate, being the "price" of investment funds, also serves to ration and allocate these funds.

It goes without saying that the potential amount of investment that could conceivably be undertaken during a given year far exceeds the resources available to undertake it. As a result, the available funds have to be rationed and allocated to their most valuable uses. Since, in the private sector, investment will not be undertaken unless the expected rate of return is at least as large as the interest rate, the available investment funds are in a sense rationed or made unavailable to low-payoff, unprofitable investments.

Moreover, the interest rate has the effect of allocating the available investment funds to the areas where the expected rate of return is the highest. The greater the expected rate of return in relation to the interest rate, the more incentive investors have to allocate funds to these areas because of the expected profits. Thus the interest rate not only serves to keep funds from being invested in low-return areas, but it pulls the funds to more highly productive investments.

A great deal of investment also takes place with public funds in which profit is not a major consideration. Yet public planners also need to consider the interest rate. For a public investment to be socially profitable, its contribution to the output of society should be large enough to yield a rate of return at least equal to the before-tax marginal rate of return on alternative private investment.[3]

The stock market

The sale of stock also represents an important source of funds to finance private investment. Although the loan market and the stock market are similar in economic terms and are closely related, there is a legal difference in that the people who provide the funds in the stock market (i.e., those who save) become part owners of the business they "invest" in. Although relatively few stockholders actively participate in the management of the companies in which they invest, they nevertheless are the owners. Thus money raised

---

[3] A figure of 15 percent is frequently used as the before-tax rate of return to investment in manufacturing.

by the sale of stock is sometimes called *equity capital,* while money raised by borrowing is known as *debt capital.*

The procedure of raising money by the sale of stock can be illustrated by a simple example. Suppose you decided to form a corporation to raise $1,000 to purchase your garden tractor for your tomato production venture. After receiving a charter for your corporation, you proceed to issue 100 stock certificates, each having a face value of $10. The fact that each stock certificate carries a $10 face value does not guarantee that the 100 shares would raise $1,000, however. If prospective buyers of your stock were pessimistic about your chances for success in growing tomatoes, they might not be willing to pay the $10 price. If you were able to sell them for, say, $8 a share, the remaining $200 would have to be provided by your own funds or by borrowing. At any rate, the price of your stock would closely reflect the market's evaluation of your earning and growth potential. If you were fortunate enough to enjoy a profitable year and could pay an attractive dividend, the price of your stock would likely rise. There is no legal limit on how high (or low) it could go; the determining factor would be the market's evaluation of your profit and growth potential.

Essentially the price of existing stock is determined by the forces of demand and supply. If the demand for stocks increases relative to the supply, their prices will increase, and vice versa. Many of the short-run fluctuations in the stock market stem from changing expectations of future business conditions and/or changing expectations of the future value of the stock itself. For example, if many people who own stock believe stock prices will fall in the near future, they may attempt to sell, thereby increasing supply and lowering stock prices. Thus the "psychology" of the market can be rather important in the short run. Over the long run, however, the value of each firm's stock will tend to reflect the dividends paid and the growth in value of the firm's assets. Although people who own stock receive dividends, as opposed to interest, the meaning is virtually the same. For example, if you paid the owners of your $100 stocks an annual dividend of $5, they would in effect receive a 5 percent rate of interest on their money, assuming the stocks sold for $100.

In assessing the value of a firm's stock, a helpful guide is the firm's price/earnings (*P/E*) ratio. This ratio is obtained by dividing the current price of the firm's stock by the firm's past year's earnings on equity capital. The latter is obtained by subtracting all expenses including interest on borrowed funds and depreciation of capital from the firm's sales. If a firm has a *P/E* ratio of 5, it means that the firm's stock is selling for five times earnings. This in turn means that each $100 of stock earned $20. Another way of stating this is that the firm earned a 20 percent rate of return on equity capital. Of course, this does not mean that the firm's stockholders received a $20 dividend for each $100 of stock they own in the company. Most corporations pay out less than total earnings on equity capital, choosing instead to "plow" some earnings back into the company. Such a practice should in principle increase the value of the firm's stock because of the increase in value of assets and net worth of the firm. Because of favorable capital gains taxation, stockholders have shown a preference for growth stocks. For example, if you are in the 30 percent tax bracket and receive an extra $100 in dividends, you pay $30 of it in income taxes. But if your stock instead increases in value by $100 and you sell it for this gain, you pay a tax on this realized capital gain at only half the rate that you pay on ordinary income. In this case, the tax on the extra $100 of realized capital gains is only $15. Thus it is not difficult to see why growth stocks have become popular.[4]

Main points of Chapter 10

1. Capital, as used in the context of this chapter, refers to durable or long-lasting inputs such as machines, buildings, and land, rather than cash or money.
2. The annual cost of capital is made up of two components: depreciation and the interest charge.
3. Capital depreciates for two reasons: wearing out and obsolescence. Two common methods of estimating depreciation

---

[4] This example assumes that a person's total stock dividends exceed the $250 annual exemption from federal income taxes.

are the straight-line method and the constant-percentage method.

4. The marginal product of capital is the additional output obtained by adding one more unit of capital.

5. One method of gauging the profitability of an investment is to determine whether or not capital's annual net VMP or MRP is greater than its annual depreciation plus interest charge.

6. The rate of return on capital is the amount of income that each dollar invested earns each year after all expenses, including depreciation, have been subtracted. For example, a 6 percent rate of return means that each dollar earns 6 cents per year.

7. The capitalized value of nondepreciable capital is obtained by dividing the annual net return by the interest rate.

8. Cash flow analysis is a technique used to compare the cash outflow of a capital item, i.e., its purchase price, with the additional net cash inflows or net returns resulting from the use of the item.

9. The discounted present value of $1 to be received n years in the future is equal to $1/(1 + r)^n$, where r is the rate of interest.

10. A second method of assessing the profitability of an investment is to compare the purchase price of the capital with its capitalized value or the discounted present value of its stream of future returns.

11. The benefit/cost (B/C) ratio is obtained by dividing the discounted present value of the net cash inflow of an investment by its cost.

12. A third method of evaluating the profitability of an investment is by comparing its B/C ratio to 1. An investment is profitable if its B/C ratio is greater than 1.

13. The internal rate of return on a capital item is that rate of interest which makes the discounted present value of the stream of returns equal to the purchase price or total cost of the capital.

14. The fourth method of determining the profitability of a capital item is to compare its internal rate of return with the rate of interest that has to be paid on borrowed funds or that can be earned on equity funds.

15. To maximize profits, a firm should invest in capital until the internal rate of return on the marginal dollar invested is equal to the interest rate.

16. The rate of interest on loan funds is determined by the demand for and supply of these funds.

17. Differences in the interest paid on various types of loans are due in large part to differences in the expected cost of making the loan. These cost differences are due mainly to differences in risk and the per dollar administrative cost of making and collecting the loan.

18. The real rate of interest is equal to the money rate less the rate of inflation. During times of inflation or expected inflation, the money rate of interest tends to rise to offset the effect of inflation on the value of money and real assets.

19. The interest rate rations and allocates investment funds by making it unprofitable to invest in low-return activities, while drawing funds into high-return areas.

20. A major share of investment funds is raised by the sale of stock certificates. The value or price of each certificate also is determined by its demand and supply in the stock market.

Questions for thought and discussion

1. Labor and capital are both resources. Why are they studied separately?

2. Strictly speaking, consumer durables such as cars and appliances also are capital. True or false? Explain.

3. What is the annual cost of owning and operating a $6,000 automobile the first year of ownership if the rate of interest is 10 percent and it depreciates 25 percent? Assume it is driven 10,000 miles per year, it gets 20 miles to the gallon, and gasoline costs $1.00 per gallon. Also include insurance, license, and estimated maintenance charges. What would it cost the second year?

4. Why does capital depreciate? What are the common methods of computing depreciation?

5. *a.* What is the capitalized value of a parcel of land that yields $100 per year in net return, if the interest rate is 10 percent?

    b. In recent years farm land in the United States has been selling for three to four times its capitalized value. Why?

6. Which would you prefer, $100 in your hand now or $100 forthcoming one year from now? Why? (Assume no inflation.)

7. What is the discounted present value of $100 forthcoming five years in the future if the rate of interest is 10 percent?

8. Suppose you have the opportunity to purchase a rooming house near campus. The asking price is $100,000. It has ten rooms, each renting for $160 per month. Assume you could rent the rooms ten months out of the year. Also suppose that the annual cost of operating the house (heat, light, taxes, repairs, etc.) amounts to $8,000 per year.

    a. If you had to pay 10 percent interest on borrowed money to buy the house, would it pay to do so? Explain.

    b. Suppose because of inflation you revise your expectations and instead expect to sell the house for $140,000. Would this change in expectations have any bearing on your decision to buy the house? Explain.

    c. Compute the internal rate of return on the rooming house, first under the assumption that the house will be sold for $100,000 and then assuming that the house will be sold for $140,000.

9. Why do people have to pay a higher rate of interest when they borrow money than when they put it in a bank for savings?

10. Why are large corporations able to borrow money at a lower rate of interest than private individuals?

11. Consider a new truck that sells for $20,000. The same model of this truck that is four years old may sell for $10,000. Yet it is likely that the used truck can haul about the same amount in the first year of ownership as the new one. Why should the used model sell for about half the price of a new one?

12. *a.* Why is the money rate of interest relatively high during inflationary times?

    b. Can the real rate of interest ever be negative? Explain.

13. *a.* If different investments pay off at different rates of return, how will a decrease in the money rate of interest affect investment spending?

    b. Is it possible for investment spending and the money rate of interest to decrease at the same time? Explain.

14. How does rent control on housing affect investment in new housing?

15. Why do stock prices change?

11

The economics of education

The concept of human capital

In our discussion of the capital market in Chapter 10, we defined capital as durable or long-lasting inputs, such as buildings and equipment, that contribute to the production of goods and services. We noted that capital inputs are expensive and that the present value of their stream of returns must be greater than their purchase price for them to yield a net positive contribution to total output.

In recent years there has been a growing awareness that the acquisition of knowledge and skills by human beings also results in the creation of capital—human capital. At the same time there has been a reluctance on the part of some educators to regard education and training as a kind of capital formation. Their rationale is similar to those who have argued that labor, the services of human beings, should not be treated as an input of production subject to economic analysis. They believe it is dehumanizing to think of boys and girls learning to read and write, or of young men and women acquiring a knowledge of mathematics, history, and economics as a process that results in the formation of capital.

Surely the psychological and sociological aspects of human beings must be considered. As pointed out at the beginning of the labor market chapter, there is no reason why economists who work in the area of labor economics or human capital need to be less "human" than anyone else. Indeed, the separate study of the labor market or the economics of education allows us to take into account the uniqueness of people, as compared with nonhuman inputs such as machines, tools, and raw materials. The fact that we identify human capital as a separate field of study denotes its uniqueness. While the special characteristics of human beings are recognized, there are a number of similarities between human capital, the skills and knowledge acquired through education or training, and nonhuman capital.

First, both kinds of capital, human and nonhuman, enhance the productive capacity of society. Human beings without tools and without knowledge are very unproductive creatures. Moreover, even a cursory study of history will reveal that human capital must exist before nonhuman capital can be produced. For example, the wheel came into being when humans learned that a round object rolling along the ground encountered less friction and took less power to move than a flat object being dragged. We could point to innumerable examples of new applications of knowledge that have led to the production of new nonhuman capital.

A second similarity between the two kinds of capital is that they both pay off over a long period of time. Indeed, the stream of returns to education for most people covers 30 to 40 or more years. We will discuss shortly the kind of returns that human capital provides. For the moment it is sufficient that we become aware of the consequences of this long payoff period. First, it precipitates a great deal of uncertainty. Students are faced with the nagging question of whether the job that is being prepared for will be available when they graduate, to say nothing of 10 to 20 years in the future. At the high school and undergraduate level of training, it is virtually impossible to predict what kind of employment will be forthcoming. Since a person's job can be expected to change several times during a lifetime, it is important that training, particularly at the college level, will facilitate learning new jobs and adjusting to new environments. Another consequence to the long payoff is the need to discount future returns, as in the garden tractor example of the preceding chapter. For instance, one dollar forthcoming 40 years from now discounted back at a 6 percent interest rate is worth less than 10 cents today. With the demands of the present on a young person's resources, such as car, clothes, and travel, the decision to invest now for a payoff far into the future is difficult to say the least.

Third, human capital, like some nonhuman capital, requires a lengthy building period. With human capital, this period is generally a good deal longer. Eight years is the least amount of time that can be devoted to the process, and it may run up to 18 or 20 years for people who obtain a Ph.D. or professional degree. We will see later in the chapter that this long gestation or building period, coupled with the long payoff period, makes the discounting factor especially important in the case of human capital.

A fourth similarity between the two kinds of capital is that both tend to depreciate. The ultimate depreciation for human capital, of course, is growing old and passing from the scene. But there is a more immediate depreciation that begins the minute we learn something new—forgetting. Educators tell us that a large part of what we learn is forgotten in a relatively short time. How much do you recall of a book you read or a course you took last year, or even last quarter? Depreciation of human capital also occurs because of obsolescence. Each year new knowledge is being produced that reduces the value of existing knowledge. Skills such as the ability to repair a steam locomotive or fly a propellor-driven aircraft are no longer in demand because new knowledge and technology have come on the scene. Because of obsolescence, it is necessary for most people to continue learning throughout their lifetimes. This is particularly true for those in the professions or skilled trades. College professors who want to keep abreast of new knowledge in their field, for example, probably should spend about 20 to 25 percent of their time learning.

Human capital formation

The major part of all human capital is the result of formal schooling provided by elementary schools, high schools, trade and vocational schools, and colleges and universities. Not all schooling, of course, needs to be of this type. A good deal of learning takes place on the job, either through apprenticeship programs through learning by doing.

In addition, some learning takes place through individual study, although the truly self-made person, Abraham Lincoln, for example, always has been a rare case. In spite of the criticism levied against the traditional student-teacher arrangement in learning, it is the rare individual who can master a field or body of knowledge alone. Most of us require someone who can tell us what is important or what to study.

Personal returns to education

What does an individual obtain from education? There are two components of the personal returns to education: monetary and nonmonetary. The monetary component refers to the increased earning power that can be obtained with additional years of schooling. This increased earning power comes largely from one or both of two factors: (1) an increase in the productive capacity of the individual, and (2) the ability to conceive of and produce new goods or services that are valued more highly by society.

The contribution of education to increased productivity appears to stem, at least in part, from an increased ability to organize and use resources efficiently, including the very scarce resource, time. Surely no one appreciates the importance of time more than the student. With two or three exams coming up and a term paper to finish, the student is forced to make each minute count. The experience gained in allocating time efficiently is one of the most important advantages of a college education, at least from the standpoint of productivity of the individual. Education also enhances productivity by enabling the individual to accept new technology more readily and use it effectively. Education is particularly important with regard to technology that requires new or different skills. The more educated person seems to possess a greater capacity for self-teaching and adapting to new situations.

The effect of education on the kinds of goods and services produced is demonstrated clearly by comparing the output of a modern industrialized society that has a high proportion of educated people with that of a traditional society. The traditional society's choice of goods and services tends to be limited to a rather narrow array of low-quality items, most of which are considered necessities. The output of the more highly educated society is of a higher quality and much more diverse in nature. The world would be a dull place for the educated person if education resulted in only greater output of the traditional necessities, such as food, clothing, and shelter. Thus the monetary rewards of additional education stem at least in part from an increased ability to conceive of and produce new and different goods and services that are demanded by a more productive society.

Of course, when considering the monetary rewards of increased education, it is always possible to point out exceptions: self-made people with eighth-grade educations who have built up fortunes in the business world, or high school dropouts who made it big in show business. But if we look at large numbers of people, we find that high school graduates, on the average, earn more than people with an eighth-grade education, and people with college training earn more than high school graduates. Thus, an individual who does not achieve a high school or college education is not necessarily doomed to a life of poverty, but the chances that the person will remain poor are substantially higher than if he or she would have received the schooling.

For most people the returns to additional education exceed the monetary value of increased earnings over a lifetime. The *nonmonetary* returns to education include: (1) the immediate utility or satisfaction that a person receives during the time of schooling and (2) the long-run stream of increased satisfaction that accrues during his or her lifetime because of the educational experience.

Although few students think fondly of exams or assignments, most derive some satisfaction from being in an educational environment. The friends that are made, the dances and parties, the dates, the sporting events, the good books that are read, even the pleasure of learning all provide immediate satisfaction that is not measured in monetary terms.

But the nonmonetary rewards to schooling are not limited to the immediate time spent in school. Many friendships that begin in school endure over a lifetime. Many people meet their spouses during their school years. It would seem also that education enhances the quality of life by facilitating an awareness and greater understanding of the world around us. The lives of educated people are ruled less by superstition and fear and more by rational thought and deliberate choice. Although we do not have adequate quantitative measures of happiness, psychological studies seem to indicate that people with more education are on the average happier and find greater fulfillment in life than those with less education. Perhaps education is even more important than money in finding that elusive and nebulous good called happiness.

Social returns to education

The returns to education are not limited to those realized by the individual. Society as a whole also gains. Economists call these gains *social returns* or *externalities*, that is, the benefits that are external to the individual receiving the education.

At the family level, the education of the parents, particularly that of the mother, should have some beneficial effects on the children. For one thing it tends to broaden the children's cultural background and opportunities. Children of college-educated parents are more likely to attend college than those whose parents stopped at the grade school or high school level, although this may be less important now than it used to be because of the accessibility of community colleges. There also would seem to be a tendency for at least part of the knowledge gained by parents during their school years to be transmitted to their children. Children who gain an appreciation for the importance of knowledge have gained a great deal.

At the community level it could be argued that the education of individuals makes the community a better place to live for all. For example, one's chances of getting "mugged" appear to be somewhat greater in neighborhoods where people are poorly educated and have low incomes than those where the majority is highly educated and affluent. Granted, the income level may be the important factor in this difference, but, as we will see shortly, education has an important bearing on income. An increase in the educational level of people also seems to reduce the amount of fear and suspicion that people have of one another. Because education usually acquaints us with people of different backgrounds and ideas, it may help us become a bit more tolerant of those who happen to be different in one way or another.

It may be expected that different kinds of education would provide different degrees of social returns. It is often argued that education which imparts purely technical skills, such as programming a computer, repairing an automobile, or setting a broken bone, primarily benefits the person receiving the education because of the larger income that can be earned by selling these skills.[1] Social returns may be greatest from education that provides a better undertanding of people and society, such as the liberal arts and social sciences.

The amount of social return derived from the education of individuals is an important point because it bears on the financing of education. If social returns are important, then society ought to pay at least part of the cost of educating the individual, as is now done in public schools, colleges, and universities. The argument is that if society receives some benefit from education over and above that received by the individual, it will have to pay part of the individual's educational expense in order for the person to be willing to invest an optimum amount in education from the standpoint of society. On the other hand, if the individual receives all the benefits of the education, then it might be argued that the individual should be willing to buy the amount that provides a return equal to other investments the person could make. We will come back to the problem of financing education, but first let us look at the costs of education.

Personal costs of education

Needless to say, education is not a free good. Indeed, it is becoming more expensive each year, as every student and parent is well aware. It will be useful at this point, therefore, to itemize the major costs that students or parents bear for education. These include (1) forgone earnings, (2) tuition, and (3) books and supplies.

---

[1] Of course, the people who purchase the goods or services made possible by education also benefit.

It is a temptation to exclude forgone earnings (the money you could be earning if you were not in school) as part of the cost of an education because this cost is not paid by check or cash. It must be admitted, however, that a person who decides to go to work after high school gives up a college or technical school education. It is just as logical to argue that a person who decides to go to school gives up full-time employment earnings during the college years.

In the more developed countries of the world, forgone earnings are negligible for the elementary and junior high school student but begin to be a factor as the student finishes high school and enters college or some other kind of advanced training. In developing countries, where educational attainment is relatively low and children enter the labor force at a relatively young age, forgone earnings are relatively important even in the lower grades.

Although the average student may not feel the pinch of forgone earnings as much as the out-of-pocket costs of tuition, books, and so forth, it is necessary just the same to take this money into account when deciding how far to go in school. Considering the relatively modest salary that a high school graduate can obtain the first few years out of school, say $7,000 to $8,000 per year, it becomes clear that even a modest amount of income forgone is relatively large when viewed as a cost.

The other two cost components—tuition and books and supplies—are familiar enough that we need not go into detail here, although we should note that tuition generally does not cover the full educational costs of colleges and universities. We will consider this part of the cost in the next section.

One cost item that is conspicuous by its absence is board and room. Surely, you might argue, a student who pays $2,000 during the school year for a room and meals at the college dormitory should include this amount as a logical part of college costs. But bear in mind that everyone has to be somewhere, so if the student did not pay the $2,000 for living on or near campus, as much or more would have to be paid to live wherever the individual worked. Thus the cost items listed above include only the *extra* costs involved in attending college as opposed to doing something else. Costs are measured in this manner so they can be compared with the *extra* income that is obtained by furthering an education.

Public costs of education

From the viewpoint of the total society, all the private costs that we considered in the previous section would, of course, be a part of the total educational cost that society must bear. The operation of schools and colleges financed in part by tuition, the production of books and supplies, and the loss of earnings during school years all involve using up real resources that could have been used to produce something else had they not been used to produce education.

In the majority of our educational institutions, however, tuition does not come close to covering the cost of operating the schools. In the public elementary and high schools, tuition is zero, so the entire cost is borne by the taxpayers. In colleges and universities tuition varies a great deal; some city or community colleges set tuition at zero or close to it, while the more exclusive private schools try to cover a larger share of their operating costs by tuition. Most of the high-tuition private schools, however, must rely on endowments to make ends meet. The main point is that the total cost of education for most students is substantially greater than the cost borne by the individual student.

Financing education

The relative increase in the cost of providing educational services in recent years has prompted considerable discussion on the optimum methods of paying for these services. In the United States and most other countries of the world, a substantial share of the cost of operating educational institutions has been provided by public funds, that is, taxes. The popularity of this method of finance probably stems from a rather special characteristic of the education service. People who buy this service, namely students, have had little or no opportunity to earn and save enough to pay for it. It could be argued that many other goods and services, such as baby food and the services of pediatricians, also exhibit this characteristic, although their benefits tend to be somewhat more certain and immediate than the returns to education. By using public tax funds to finance a part of the cost of education, we are in essence spreading its current cost over several generations, as opposed to concentrating it on one or two generations, that is, parents of the students or the students themselves.

One alternative to public payment of tuition is for parents or families to pay for the education of their children. Among upper middle- and high-income people, this is frequently done. However, for a large segment of our population the cost of purchasing 12 to 16 years of quality schooling for their children would be prohibitive. It is argued that children of poor parents would continue to be doomed to a life of poverty because of an inability to buy a means of escape through education.

A second alternative to public support of education is for students to borrow to pay for it. This alternative has not enjoyed much popularity, even among students in professional and graduate schools, to say nothing of elementary and high school students. Indeed, students seem to be more willing to go into debt for an automobile than for schooling. It is not clear why, but one possible explanation is the uncertainty of the future. The automobile provides immediate and certain utility, whereas the payoff to education is both uncertain and far off. It is also true that lending agencies have not been especially eager to promote educational loans compared with auto loans, for example. No doubt, risk or uncertainty is also a prime consideration for the lender. If a person who borrows for an automobile defaults on the payments, the lender always can repossess the car. But if a person who borrows for an education defaults, it is not possible to repossess the person—or the education. Granted there are devices such as wage garnishment, but these have not been popular and they involve added legal expense and effort.

At any rate, if society desires its young people to continue to achieve 12 to 16 years of quality schooling, then it probably will have to continue to use public tax funds to finance at least a part of the cost of education. Whether such funding leads to a so-called optimum amount of education is a question that is being debated at the present time. It has been argued that such funding provides a strong incentive to overinvest in education because the full cost is not borne by the individual. That is, when the cost of something is subsidized, the individual has an incentive to buy more of it than if the person had to bear the full cost.

On the other hand, it can be argued that the uncertainty faced by the individual who must pay the entire educational cost leads to the purchase of less education than would be desirable from the standpoint of society. The argument here is that the individual faces a great deal more uncertainty regarding the payoff to education than would a large group of individuals, that is, society. Thus each individual will be inclined to invest less in education than would be the case if the person faced the same uncertainty as society as a whole. Therefore, it is argued, society will have to bear a part of the individual's education cost in order to make the individual willing to purchase as much education as he or she would if faced with the same uncertainty as society. The existence of any so-called social returns, as mentioned previously, also implies the use of public tax funds for education. However, this argument has lost some of its appeal in recent years because of our inability to quantify the magnitude of such returns or even to demonstrate their existence.

An argument for using public funds to support education also can be made on the basis of achieving a more equal distribution of income. If only the rich could "afford" to buy education for their children, the children of poor parents would likely remain poor. The use of public tax funds to finance part of the cost of education seems to have become a widely accepted means of achieving a somewhat more equal distribution of income. Education provides a means of giving people more equality of opportunity to make something out of their lives. Other income redistributive devices such as the welfare programs or a negative income tax scheme appear to be less widely accepted. In these cases many taxpayers probably feel that low-income people are not pulling their weight in society and are living off the efforts of those who are willing to work. Education provides a means of escaping poverty but it also requires considerable work on the part of those benefiting from the training. It is a way for society to help those who are willing to help themselves. It should be kept in mind, though, that students at the high school and college level will continue to bear a substantial share of the cost of schooling, regardless of how tuition is financed, because of their forgone earnings. And these forgone earnings probably loom larger in the minds of poor students than those from high-income families.

The common method of using public funds to finance education is by allocating the funds directly to the educational institutions. An alternative to this procedure would be to provide grants in the form of vouchers directly to the students or to their parents, allowing them to spend the vouchers at the school of their choice. The school would then turn in the vouchers and receive money from the government. Major advantages of this approach are that it would give people more freedom of choice and promote competition between schools. As mentioned previously, public schools now enjoy substantial freedom from competitive forces and therefore have little incentive to innovate and improve the quality of their services or to strive for greater efficiency.[2]

Returns to investment in education

Although the returns to education are reflected in more than just monetary rewards, it is helpful to obtain measures of both the costs and returns to investment in human capital or education. If education turns out to be an acceptable investment strictly from a monetary point of view, then we can be sure it is an even better investment when nonmonetary returns are considered. We will look first at the monetary returns to education.

MEASURING MONETARY RETURNS

The figures in Table 11–1 provide an indication of the monetary value of various levels of education. The figures are for 1977 and are net of federal income taxes. (State and local income taxes and social security taxes have not been subtracted, however.)

The main thing to note in Table 11–1 is the increase in the level

---

[2] For further discussion of the problems of financing education, see the report, "Investment in Education: The Equity Efficiency Quandary," workshop at the University of Chicago, June 7–10, 1971, sponsored by the Committee on Basic Research in Education of the National Research Council, in T. W. Schultz, ed., *Journal of Political Economy*, vol. 80, pt. 2 (May–June 1972).

TABLE 11-1
Mean annual income levels by education, age and sex, as of 1977*

Age	Four years high school	One to three years college	Four years college
Males			
25–34	$12,411	$13,087	$14,339
35–44	14,410	16,218	20,580
45–54	14,842	17,166	23,530
55–64	14,079	16,812	21,493
Females			
25–34	$ 8,085	$ 9,116	$ 9,786
35–44	8,253	9,240	11,017
45–54	8,538	9,068	11,171
55–64	8,421	9,998	11,420

* Current income less federal income taxes. Federal income taxes were estimated on the basis of "all returns" at the respective income levels. Income tax figures were obtained from *Statistical Abstract,* 1978, p. 271.

Source: U.S. Department of Commerce, *Current Population Reports,* "Consumer Income," Series P-60, no. 118 (March 1979), pp. 195–96.

of income as years of schooling increase. This relationship holds true for all age levels for both men and women. In order to use these figures to calculate the monetary returns to education, we must compute the *difference* in earnings between the various levels of schooling completed. For example, the monetary value of four years of college over a high school education for males in the 25–34 age group is $14,339 − $12,411, or $1,928 per year. The income differences between levels of schooling completed by age group and sex are presented in Table 11–2.

Assuming a 40-year working life, we can obtain a rough idea of the *extra* income that a person can expect to earn by completing a given level of schooling. For example, during the 25–34 age span, a man can expect to earn $19,280 additional income by completing four years of college as opposed to stopping at high school. Total lifetime earnings differences for various levels of schooling for men and women are presented in Table 11–3.

Bear in mind that the figures in Table 11–3 are *extra* income resulting from *additional* years of schooling, not total income for these groups of people. For example, the *total* lifetime earnings (after federal income taxes) are $557,730 for a man with a high school education, as obtained from Table 11–1. The total lifetime

TABLE 11–2
Annual income differences between levels of schooling completed by age and sex, as of 1977

Age	One to three years college over high school	Four years college over one to three years college	Four years college over high school
Males			
25–34	$ 676	$1,252	$1,928
35–44	1,808	4,362	6,170
45–54	2,304	6,364	8,688
55–64	2,733	4,681	7,414
Females			
25–34	$1,031	$ 670	$1,701
35–44	987	1,777	2,764
45–54	530	2,103	2,633
55–64	1,577	1,422	2,999

Source: Computed from Table 11–1.

TABLE 11–3
Total lifetime earnings differences,* by level of schooling completed and sex, as of 1977

	Males	Females
One to three years college over high school	$ 75,410	$41,250
Four years college over one to three years college	166,590	59,720
Four years college over high school	242,000	100,970

* Based on a 40-year working life.
Source: Computed from Table 11–2.

earnings of a male college graduate is estimated to be $799,420 in 1977 prices, net of federal income taxes. The contrast between male and female earnings is readily apparent in all three tables. It is not known how much of this difference is due to pure discrimination and how much is due to a greater tendency for women to be in and out of the job market over their lifetime, therefore not building up as much seniority.

Although the extra earnings over an entire lifetime add up to a substantial figure, particularly for men with four years of college, it is necessary to take into account two additional factors in order to evaluate the payoff to investment in education: (1) the cost of the schooling and (2) the fact that each additional dollar earned in the future is not worth as much as a dollar on hand at the present. Because the cost of education is incurred well in advance of the returns, the extra earnings forthcoming should be converted into present value terms using the discounting formula discussed in Chapter 10. Of course, costs are not all incurred at a given point in time either. This requires that we accumulate the costs over the years the education is taking place. We will return to this point in a moment.

MEASURING COSTS

Recall that the three major cost components of a college education are (1) forgone earnings, (2) tuition, and (3) books and supplies. In order to match the cost of college training with the returns, we estimate in this section the costs that were borne by the student who either graduated or left school in 1977. Forgone earnings are estimated as the full-time earnings of year-round workers in the 16–19 and 20–24 age categories, depending on the year in school. The earnings are adjusted down to a 40-week work year, which assumes that the student is able to obtain a comparable paying summer job. Also the earnings are net of federal income taxes, using the tax rates in the respective income categories for single persons. Tuition and fees are estimated from those of large public universities. Finally books, supplies, and miscellaneous expense are assumed to be equal to 10 percent of forgone earnings. The figures are summarized in Table 11–4.

The fact that the costs are incurred over a period of time rather than at a point in time, as in the garden tractor example, makes it necessary to "accumulate" the costs. Costs should be accumulated because the cost today of one dollar spent a number of years ago is greater than one dollar. This is because of the interest that the dollar could have earned had it not been spent on the investment in question. The formula for determining the accumulated cost of one dollar spent n years ago is $(1 + i)^n$, where i is the rate of interest. For example, the accumulated cost of \$1,000 spent four years ago is \$1,000 $(1 + 0.10)^4 = \$1,460$ using a 10 percent interest rate. In assessing the costs of education, it is common to accumulate all costs up to the end of the senior year. The procedure for accumu-

TABLE 11–4
Summary of costs for a four-year college education, 1977 graduates

	Freshman	*Sophomore*	*Junior*	*Senior*
Males				
Forgone earnings	$3,623	$3,981	$6,488	$6,902
Tuition	813	894	944	1,004
Books, supplies, and				
miscellaneous	362	398	649	690
Totals	$4,798	$5,273	$8,081	$8,596
Females				
Forgone earnings	$3,216	$3,533	$5,115	$5,442
Tuition	813	894	944	1,004
Books, supplies, and				
miscellaneous	322	353	511	544
Totals	$4,351	$4,780	$6,570	$6,990

lating the costs incurred by a male college graduate is shown below. The cost figures are from Table 11–4.

$$\$4,798(1.10)^4 + \$5,273(1.10)^3 + \$8,081(1.10)^2$$
$$+ \$8,596(1.10) = \$33,251$$

COSTS AND RETURNS

In evaluating the costs and returns to a college education it is necessary to discount the future returns back to the same point in time when costs are accumulated. In this case we use the end of the senior year as the point of reference. The procedure for discounting the future monetary returns to education is the same as that used in the garden tractor example of Chapter 10. Some of the figures for a male college graduate are presented below.

$$\frac{1,928}{1.10} + \cdots + \frac{\$6,170}{(1.10)^{11}} + \cdots + \frac{\$8,688}{(1.10)^{21}} + \cdots$$
$$+ \frac{\$7,414}{(1.10)^{31}} + \cdots + \frac{\$7,414}{(1.10)^{40}} = \$36,988$$

The results of accumulating costs and discounting returns of the four possible categories of students are presented in Table 11–5. College graduates are referred to as four-year students, while those who obtain one to three years of college are called two-year students.

TABLE 11-5
Costs and returns of a college education, as of 1977, 10 percent interest rate

	Accumulated costs	Discounted returns
Four-year males	$33,251	$36,988
Four-year females	28,366	20,443
Two-year males	13,254	11,616
Two-year females	12,017	9,791

INTERNAL RATES OF RETURN

A comparison of the attractiveness of a college education for the four groups of students is facilitated by the computation of the corresponding internal rates of return. Recall that the internal rate of return is that rate of interest which makes the discounted returns equal to the cost (accumulated in this case) of the investment. Notice in Table 11-5 that the only group in which discounted returns exceed accumulated costs is the four-year male category. Since a 10 percent rate of interest is used to obtain these figures, we can conclude that the internal rate of return is greater than 10 percent for four-year males and less than this figure for the other categories of students. The internal rate of return figures are presented in Table 11-6. Using the same procedure for obtaining costs and returns as shows for 1977, internal rate of return estimates also are presented for 1958 and 1968 (based on the last year in school).

Although there has been a slight downward trend over time in the rates of return, except for two-year females, investment in

TABLE 11-6
Internal rates of return to investment in a college education by last year in school, selected years*

	1958	1968	1977
Four-year males	14	13	11
Two-year males	16	12	9
Four-year females		8	7
Two-year females		7	8

* Income data not available for females before 1968.

a college education remained reasonably attractive in 1977. Perhaps most noticeable is the substantial decline in the rate of return to two-year males between 1958 and 1977. Bear in mind, here, that these figures apply only to college students, not to those attending technical schools. Also, one cannot escape noticing the somewhat lower rates of return to females, even assuming a 40-year working life. Recent developments against discrimination in the labor market and a stronger career orientation by many women nowadays may result in narrowing the gap in the future. Of course, in order for the rate of return to a college education to increase, earnings of women with college training must increase *relative* to the earnings of women with a high school education. If the earnings of women of all educational levels increase, the rate of return to investment in a college education need not increase. In fact, it may decrease because of higher forgone earnings and the resulting higher cost of education.

The lower rates of return to women do not mean that college is a poor investment for them. To be honest it should be acknowledged that college-educated women are more likely to meet and marry college-educated men and as a result they are able to share in the higher earnings received by their husbands. Of course, the men also benefit not only from the added earnings of women with college training should they decide on a career, but also because of the nonmonetary returns to education that women bring with them into the home. Both the husband and children benefit from the nonmonetary as well as the monetary returns.

Part-time employment

In measuring the cost of a college education, we have assumed that students receive no earnings during the school year. Yet we know that in recent years more than half of all college students work part-time during the school year. The existence of part-time earnings has the effect of reducing the total forgone earnings, which represent for most students the largest single component of the cost of a college education. Hence if we were to take account of part-time earnings, the total cost of a college education should decrease and the estimated rate of return increase.

On the other hand, one must recognize that students who participate in part-time employment during the school year must give up something. The time spent working must be taken away either from school activities (studying or extracurricular) or from whatever would be done with the time. Since these activities also have value, it would not be strictly correct to subtract part-time earnings from the cost of education without subtracting the value of the utility given up by devoting less time to other activities. Of course, the fact that many students freely decide to work part-time means that they believe they gain more from the part-time employment earnings than what they give up. It will be useful at this point to take a closer look at the effect of part-time employment on the allocation of time.

The allocation of time

In the study of the allocation of time it will be helpful to cast the student in the role of a multiproduct firm engaged in the production of three broad categories of output: (1) human capital, (2) intermediate goods via the labor market (for students who work part-time), and (3) final goods for current consumption. Because of the diversity of output we will use utility as a measure or common denominator of output. Our main interest will be the allocation of time to each of these three broad categories of activities. Hence the marginal physical product (MPP) of time is defined here as the extra utility resulting from the input of one more hour of time to any of the three activities.

In the production of human capital the student combines time with other purchased inputs such as faculty services, instructional facilities, and books. The marginal product of time in the production of human capital will, of course, depend on the inherent capability of the student as well as on the quantity and quality of complementary inputs such as the teacher and instructional materials. The marginal productivity of study time (for a given quantity) should be greater for more capable and highly motivated students than for those less well endowed with ability or motivation. Similarly the marginal product of time should be higher for students who have good teachers and effective instructional materials, or for those enrolled in high-payoff programs, than for their less fortunate counterparts.

As pointed out at the beginning of this chapter the utility (returns) derived from the production of human capital includes both monetary and nonmonetary components. It is necessary to bear in mind also that the utility that is forthcoming in the future, from either monetary or nonmonetary sources, should be discounted back to the present in order to be comparable to the utility produced through part-time employment, or household production. (We will refer to all activities other than school and part-time employment as household production.) Of course no student knows for sure how much income will be increased by education or how much education will enrich life in the future. In spite of the difficulties of assessing the utility that is forthcoming from education, each student is forced to make allocative decisions both with respect to allocating time and other inputs within the broad category of school activities, and between this category and other activities.

Students who work part-time participate in a second kind of production activity. Although work in and of itself may not result in utility, the income received yields utility through the goods and services it can buy. As pointed out in Chapter 4, these goods and services represent inputs in household production. In addition, some of the earnings may be used to purchase inputs for the production of human capital, such as in paying tuition or the purchase of books and supplies. For a given input of time to part-time employment, the higher the real wage, the greater is the MPP of this time because the extra hour of work will allow the purchase of more goods and services.

The third type of activity is household production. Here the student combines time with conventional goods, such as food, clothing, housing, transportation, and entertainment services, to produce utility. The MPP of time in household production will depend on individual tastes. For example, the student who loves to ski is likely to spend more time on the slopes than a person who receives more utility from an automobile purchased from the earnings of part-time employment. The second person is likely to spend more time working on a part-time job.

We know from the discussion in Chapter 4 that the cost of producing a given level of output (utility in this case) is minimized if inputs are used such as the P/MPP ratios are equal for all inputs. We can extend this rule and say that the cost of producing a given level of utility by the use of time is minimized if time is allocated so that the P/MPP of time is equal in all three activities. Calling to mind that the P/MPP ratio is the marginal cost (MC) of producing an extra unit of output by the input in question (time in this case), it can be said the cost of producing a given level of utility is minimized if the MC of producing utility is equal across all three categories of activities.

We noted that the MPP of time is the utility produced by an extra hour of time. But what is the price of time? In this case the price of time in any one activity is equal to its value (implicit or explicit) in the next best alternative use of this hour of time. Because the value of time is likely to differ between different people and between different days and times of the day, the price of time will vary accordingly. During the normal daytime or early evening working hours, the price of time devoted to study likely will be wages forgone (net of taxes) from a full-time job. Similarly the price of time devoted to employment during these hours would be the implicit value of time devoted to study or household activities, whichever is higher. During normal rest or sleep hours the price of time devoted to study likely would be the implicit value placed on sleep. Conversely the price of time devoted to sleep or rest will be the implicit value either of study or of employment, whichever is higher. The price of time to employment or household activities also should vary according to the proximity of examinations, rising just before examinations, when an extra hour of study may have a high payoff in terms of obtaining better grades.

One unique characteristic of time, as opposed to other purchased inputs, is that the individual by necessity must utilize 24 hours per day in total regardless of its price. The allocation of time to the various activities can and likely will vary as its price changes, but as long as a person is alive, time is being utilized in one of the three production activities. (Bear in mind that leisure and sleep are included in household production of utility.)

Because the individual always has a constant amount of time per day, week, or year, the objective should be to maximize the output of utility from this fixed value of time. As a result it is probably more useful to state the cost-minimizing rule in terms of a utility-maximizing rule. This is accomplished simply by inverting the P/MPP ratio, turning it into a ratio of the MPP of time over the price of time (MPP/P). Now we can say that the individual will maximize utility from the fixed value of time available by allocating time to the various activities such that the MPP/P ratio for time is equal across all activities. Essentially this is the same idea as the utility-maximizing rule presented in Chapter 2. If the MU per dollar of time is not equal, total utility from a given value of time can be increased by allocating more time to the activities where the MU per dollar is greater and less to those where it is smaller.

We can use this rule to predict what happens when a student engages in part-time employment. Let us begin by considering a student who is engaged only in the production of utility through school and household activities, i.e., a full-time student. Assume that the student is maximizing utility by equalizing the MPP/P ratios of time for these two activities. Now suppose an attractive job opportunity presents itself such that the MU per dollar of time becomes larger in the production of intermediate goods (purchased from the earnings) than it is in the other two activities. The opportunity of earning higher wages also increases the price of time devoted to school activities. (Recall that the price of time is its value in the next best alternative.) This has the effect of throwing the student further out of equilibrium by reducing the MPP/P of time in school activities.

The price of time devoted to household production may or may not initially increase because of the superior job opportunity. If the job is available only during normal daytime working hours on weekdays, the opportunity cost of time to household production may still be the wages that could be earned on less desirable jobs or the implicit value of study time, whichever is higher. If the job entails night or weekend work, the opportunity cost of time devoted to household production of utility will increase initially. However, as we will see in a moment, it really does not make any difference ultimately whether the job entails day, night, or weekend work; the price of time to household production will still increase once the student adjusts to the new situation.

Assuming that the job requires daytime work, say 20 hours per week, the initial consequence of the job (taking the adjustment in steps) is to reduce study time. If study time is subject to diminishing returns, as is reasonable, the reduction in study time will increase the implicit price of time to household activities (entertainment, sleep, etc.) because the MU obtained from the last hour of study time will increase. This in turn reduces the MPP/time price ratio of time devoted to household production, and as a consequence the student will begin to utilize some time that was originally allocated to household production for study. In reality the adjustment in study and household time is likely to take place simultaneously rather than in two distinct steps.

As the student approaches a new equilibrium, the amount of time devoted to study and household production must decrease a total of 20 hours per week (in this example). How much each is reduced depends on the slope of the MPP curves of time in the production of human capital and household goods. If the MPP curve of study time is steeply sloped relative to the MPP curve of household time, the largest reduction in time would come from the latter. Obviously this depends on the individual. The main point is that the decision to work part-time should result in a reduction in time allocated to study and to household activities because the MPP/time price ratios are reduced in both when a job is accepted.

We might also expect the allocation to change between different quarters or semesters. If the MPP of study time shifts to the right because of stimulating teachers or courses, for example, a greater proportion of work time would be taken away from household activities. Also the student may quit the job if the MPP of study time shifts to the right enough so that the MPP/time price ratio for study exceeds that experienced in part-time employment.

We also would expect different students to react differently to the same job opportunity. If the MPP/time price ratios for study and household activities are relatively high because the student is highly motivated, extremely capable, is attending a high–quality school, or is enrolled in a high–payoff program such as medical school, the job opportunity may well be passed up. The production of utility from part-time work may also decline after a period of work if the student has saved enough to pay for goods such as room and board for the immediate future. This can explain why students tend to be in and out of the job market.

As the real wages increase, however, the MPP/time price ratio in part-time employment also increases. As a result we may expect a greater proportion of students to find that the above ratio exceeds the corresponding ratios for study and household production. Thus an increase in real wages is likely to increase part-time employment unless the returns to education increase enough to offset this increase.

One should not conclude, however, that a reduction in study time necessarily reduces the amount of time allocated to each course. When working on a part-time job the student in many cases has the option of reducing his or her credit load while maintaining the amount of time devoted to each course. Which option the student chooses to follow depends on the value of grades (and knowledge) given up by working and maintaining a full credit load versus the cost of extending the degree program. Students who place a high value on good grades because of personal satisfaction, a belief that good grades will increase future income, or because of an intention to pursue graduate or professional school study can be expected to reduce their credit loads and extend the length of their programs if they decide to work part-time. Of course, as the hours worked per week approaches the equivalent of a full-time job, we may reasonably expect both grades and credit hours to be reduced.

Although our theory tells us that student participation in part-time employment should reduce the amount of time devoted to school *and* household activities, it does not reveal the magnitude of these reductions. Nor does it tell us whether the effect of part-time employment is to reduce grades, credit load, or both.

Preliminary evidence from a sample of students at the University of Minnesota suggests that students do some of both, that is, reduce grades and credit load, although as shown by the figures in Table 11–7, the relative effects are not the same for all students. As indicated in part (A) of Table 11–7, freshmen and sophomores who work part-time experience significant grade reductions, while juniors and seniors do not. The numbers in part (A) indicate the reduction in GPA out of a maximum 4.0 of students who work the respective hours per week in comparison with students who do not work, holding constant a number of student characteristics.[3]

---

[3] Characteristics "held constant" include hours spent on extracurricular activities, classes cut per week, high school rank, the effect on GPA of math, chemistry, and biology, and a qualitative measure of the importance of grades to the student. The latter, along with classes cut per week, was an attempt to take account of differences in motivation among students.

TABLE 11–7
Reductions in grade point averages and credits taken of students who work in comparison with students who are not employed part-time*

Hours worked per week	(A) Grade point average reductions		(B) Credit reductions per quarter	
	Freshman–sophomore	Junior–senior	Freshman–sophomore	Junior–senior
1–12	0.22	NS	NS	NS
13–25	0.31	NS	NS	1.44
More than 25	0.39	NS	1.48	2.50

NS = Not statistically significant from zero.
  * From a sample of 155 students at the University of Minnesota covering fall quarter 1973 and winter 1974. A = 4.0.
  Source: Willis Peterson "The Effect of Part-Time Employment on Student Allocation of Time and Academic Performance," University of Minnesota Staff paper P75–11, June 1975, p. 12.

On the other hand, the numbers in part (B) of Table 11–7 suggest that juniors and seniors are more likely to reduce their credit load when working part-time. These figures indicate the reduction in credits taken per quarter by students who work the respective hours in comparison with students who do not work, again holding constant the characteristics cited in the footnote. The tendency for juniors and seniors to reduce their credit loads when working probably explains why they do not suffer grade reductions. Just why juniors and seniors appears to behave differently in these respects is open to speculation. It may be that students who survive the first two years are those who receive the greatest utility from good grades and therefore do not jeopardize grades by attempting to maintain a full credit load when working.

By now it is probably evident that the management of time by college students is a very complex endeavor. Students have to assess the MPP (utility) of time not only among various activities but also within activities. For example, should a student allocate slightly more time to economics and less to some other subject, or vice versa? It is like juggling ten balls at once. In addition the optimum allocation of time is likely to change from one term to the next depending on teachers, courses, the opportunities for part-time employment, recreational and social activities, etc. How well a student is able to manage time in large part determines the individual's success in college.[4] In fact, the experience gained in managing time may be one of the most important things gained from college. This may come as a surprise to students who think that the knowledge gained from the courses taken represents the main value of a college education. Certainly this knowledge is important but learning how to manage time, a very valuable and scarce resource, is likely to be equally important.

Although the discussion in this chapter has focused on student allocation of time, the principles apply to any individual or family. For nonstudents there are only two broad categories of production: the production of intermediate goods via the labor market and the production of final goods in the context of the household activities during nonworking hours. In this case the individual should allocate time such that the MPP/time price ratios are equalized within each broad category as well as among the categories. Again the MPP of time is the utility produced by an extra hour of time, while the price of time is the value of this hour in the next best alternative activity. Whenever there is a change in MPP or in the price of time, the individual should reallocate away from the low MPP/time price ratio activities toward those that exhibit relatively high ratios.

Main points of Chapter 11

1. Economists have come to regard the skills and knowledge acquired through education as human capital.
2. A number of similarities exist between human and non-human capital: (*a*) both contribute to the real output of society, (*b*) both pay off over a long period of time, (*c*) both require a building period, and (*d*) both tend to depreciate.
3. Most human capital formation takes place as the result of

---

[4] You might have heard the story of a college student who brought home a grade report showing three F's and a D. Naturally the student's parents were concerned and inquired about the problem. After some thought the student replied, "I spent too much time on one subject."

formal schooling. A critical role of the teacher is to point out the important material to be learned.

4. The returns to education for the individual consist of two components: monetary and nonmonetary. The monetary component refers to the increased earning power that results from additional education, whereas the nonmonetary component refers to the utility that students derive from being in school and the increased satisfaction that life brings because of the educational experience.

5. Social returns to education refer to benefits derived over and above those obtained by the individual receiving the education.

6. The cost of education for the individual includes three main items: forgone earnings, tuition, and books and supplies. Forgone earnings are by far the largest cost. Board and room are not included because they must be paid regardless of what one does; they do not represent a special cost of going to school.

7. There is a temptation not to include forgone earnings as a cost of education, but giving up earnings from a full-time job to attend school is in the same category as giving up an education to go to work.

8. The public cost of education that is borne by society is, for most education, greater than the cost to the individual, because tuition generally does not cover the full cost of building and operating schools.

9. A large share of the cost of education is financed by tax funds, which tends to spread the current cost of educating society's young people over several generations. However, because the individual does not have to bear part of the educational expense, there is an incentive to overinvest in education. Offsetting this is the uncertainty faced by the individual regarding the payoff to education.

10. Income data collected by the U.S. Bureau of Census reveal that additional education results in higher incomes at every age level.

11. Monetary returns to education are measured by the differences in earnings of people with varying educational achievements.

12. In order to evaluate the payoff to investment in education

it is necessary to accumulate costs and discount future returns by an interest charge.

13. Internal rates of return to a college education for students completing or leaving school in 1977 ranged from 11 percent for four-year males to 7 percent for four-year females.

14. There was a slight downward trend in the rate of return to education between 1958 and 1977, with the greatest decline exhibited by two-year males.

15. Part-time employment reduces forgone earnings and therefore increases the rate of return to education, especially if no deduction is made for what is given up by working part-time.

16. Viewing the student as a multiproduct firm, three broad categories of production activities can be identified: (*a*) schooling, (*b*) part-time employment, and (*c*) household activities. All three result in the production of utility.

17. The MPP of time in any activity is the additional utility produced by one more hour (or unit) of time in that activity.

18. The price of time in any activity is its value (explicit or implicit) in its next best alternative.

19. The $P/$MPP ratio for time in any activity in the marginal cost of producing utility by adding one more hour of time in that activity.

20. The cost of producing a given level of utility by the use of time is minimized if time is allocated such that its $P/$MPP ratios in all activities are equal.

21. Time is a unique input in that the individual utilizes 24 hours per day regardless of its price.

22. An individual maximizes utility from a given value of time by equalizing the MPP/time price ratios across all activities.

23. The appearance of an attractive job opportunity increases the price of time to both schooling and household activities, resulting in a reduction in the MPP/time price ratio in these activities. This provides an incentive for the student to allocate some time to part-time employment and less to schooling and household activities.

24. Preliminary evidence from a sample of students and the University of Minnesota suggests that freshmen and sophomores who are employed part-time suffer a reduction in their grade

point averages, while juniors and seniors reduce their credit load.

Questions for thought and discussion

1. What similarities are shared by human and nonhuman capital?
2. Distinguish between the monetary and nonmonetary returns to education.
3. Distinguish between the personal and social returns to education.
4. Estimate the cost of your schooling this year. How much is this course costing you?
5. If the average cost of a year of schooling at the college level is $6,000, then the total cost of a four-year degree is $24,000. True or false? Explain.
6. In contrast to most other things that people buy for themselves such as food, clothing, and shelter, a substantial part of the cost of education is paid for by public tax funds. Why should education be treated differently than other goods?
7. In recent years there has been some discussion about the "voucher plan" for funding part of the educational cost of students. Under this plan, students (or their parents) would receive vouchers that they could use to pay tuition at the school of their choice.
   a. Who would likely benefit from this plan?
   b. Who would likely be against it? Why?
8. How would you go about estimating the internal rate of return to your investment in a college education?
9. The elimination of all discrimination against women and minorities in the labor market will increase the internal rate of return to their investment in a college education. True, false, or uncertain? Explain.
10. A college student can be looked upon as a small multiproduct firm. What does the student produce?
11. a. How should time be allocated so that a given amount of utility is produced at the least possible cost?
    b. How should time be allocated so that a given value of time produces the greatest possible utility?
12. College students can be observed studying hardest just before examinations. Does this behavior represent an efficient allocation of time? Explain.

13. Would the attainment of a straight A academic record represent an efficient allocation of time for most students? Explain.

14. State whether each of the following college students should allocate an "above average" or a "below average" amount of time to study and briefly explain why.

    a. A bright and highly motivated student.

    b. A student enrolled in a school where the payoff to the training is relatively high.

    c. A talented basketball player who has a chance of signing a million-dollar contract if he makes All-American.

    d. A student working as a highly paid salesperson.

    e. A student who receives relatively little utility from good grades.

15. a. When should a student engage in part-time employment?

    b. Does part-time employment reduce study time? Explain.

12

The economics of science and technology

The production of new knowledge

In Chapter 11 we developed the idea that the process of education, the transfer of knowledge from books and teachers into the minds of students, is an investment involving both a cost and a return. In this chapter we will probe a bit deeper into this process, seeking an understanding of the production of knowledge itself.

At the beginning of history the stock of knowledge that existed in the minds of people was indeed small as measured by today's standards. Hunting and fishing skills and the ability to transform nature's bounty into food, clothing, and shelter in large part constituted the body of existing knowledge. Somewhere along the way humans acquired the ability to communicate by sound. Although we now take this skill for granted, something like the instincts of animals or birds, a little reflection will suggest the tremendous advance in knowledge that the introduction of verbal skills represented. Every object, action, or thought became associated with a sound. Moreover, there had to be a common agreement, at least within an area or tribe, as to the meaning of sounds produced by human vocal cords. Anyone who has studied a foreign language can appreciate the difficulty of learning correct sounds and the advance in knowledge that this skill represents.

As the verbal skills were mastered, it became possible to pass on from one generation to the next important information that otherwise would have to be relearned anew by each individual through trial and error. Equally important, of course, was the introduction of written language, which is more efficient as a permanent means of communication and has a more far-reaching effect on the transfer and acquisition of knowledge.

A common characteristic of knowledge produced during the dawning of recorded history is that most of it came into being as a result of happy accident. In the process of sustaining themselves, people learned new things about plants, animals, and the environment. In the era of the Greek and Roman civilizations, scholars and philosophers began to pursue knowledge as a full-time occupation. And in the Middle Ages the early church emerged as a center of learning. (Mendel, one of the church's best-known monks, discovered the principle of hybridization while experimenting with peas.) Although the pursuit of knowledge by gifted individuals had important consequences, the "knowledge industry," that is, the employment of people for the sole purpose of advancing knowledge, was relatively unknown. Indeed, during the Dark Ages, the overall stock of knowledge appeared to decrease rather than grow.

Research as a production activity

In the course of history, it became apparent that if certain people could devote themselves to the full-time pursuit of knowledge, a much greater intellectual output per unit of effort was possible than when knowledge came as a by-product of daily activities. Obviously people with special talents in the development of new knowledge could accomplish more if freed from other tasks. Galileo, Newton, Edison, Franklin, and Einstein could hardly have accomplished what they did if they had been required to toil as full-time farmers or shopkeepers.

Thus the production of new knowledge through research began as a by-product of daily activities and gradually emerged as the domain of a select few. Now it has become established as a full-fledged industry. In the United States during the post–World War II years, research was one of the nation's most rapidly growing industries. In 1955 the resources devoted to all research (basic and applied) and development in the United States amounted to about $12.5 billion (1975 prices); by 1975 this figure had grown to more than $34 billion.[1]

We refer to research as an industry because it has much in common with more traditional types of production. Essentially research is a production activity. Inputs consist mainly of scientists and engineers, laboratories and testing facilities; output consists of new knowledge. The same concepts we used in our discussion of producer choice and product supply—such as marginal and average product, marginal and average costs, diminishing returns, and economics of scale—apply also to the production of new knowledge.

At the same time there are some unique characteristics of research. First, there is the difficulty of measuring output. Knowledge does not come in easy-to-measure units like bushels, pounds, or dollars. Economists have found ways of measuring knowledge indirectly, however, but we postpone until later in the chapter a discussion of this problem.

A second unique characteristic of research is that there is a possibility that in the aggregate it may not be subject to the law of diminishing returns. Recall that the law of diminshing returns refers to a situation where the addition of a variable input to one or more fixed inputs after a point results in a diminished marginal physical product to the variable input. It is conceivable to view scientists and their supporting personnel and facilities as the variable input and nature's secrets or the potential stock of knowledge as the fixed input in the production of new knowledge (that is, research). Will the addition of more scientists result in a diminishing and eventually a zero marginal product of scientific research? If nature's secrets or the potential stock of knowledge were finite, then we would reasonably expect diminishing returns at some point. But if all knowledge, both known and unknown, is infinite, then research need not be subject to the law of diminishing returns.

The question is: As we acquire more knowledge, will it become more or less difficult to add to the stock of knowledge? For those who believe that the potential stock of knowledge is finite and that we already have discovered nature's most accessible secrets, it

---

[1] *Statistical Abstract*, 1975, p. 548.

follows that the acquisition of new knowledge will be increasingly difficult. On the other hand, it can be argued that knowledge, like the universe, is boundless and that previously discovered knowledge only scratches the surface, allowing us to be even more productive in our future quest.

Unfortunately, we are not likely to be able to measure the limits of knowledge, at least within the confines of our finite lives here on earth. No one will be able to say, "We have now discovered all the knowledge there is to be known; nothing else remains to be discovered." When we consider that no two people who have lived or are living on earth are exactly the same, or that no two snowflakes have exactly the same form, we can begin to appreciate the boundlessness of nature.

We should be aware, also, that knowledge is more than having information or facts. In large part it is the ability to know what to do with information. Prehistoric people, for example, knew that fire was hot and that water moved swiftly in rivers, but they did not know that these phenomena could be transformed into sources of power. Even today the libraries filled with information do us little good unless we can apply that information.

It will be useful to probe more deeply into the activity we call "research." It encompasses a fairly wide array of endeavors, ranging from what scientists call basic research to the more applied and developmental types of activity.

BASIC RESEARCH

Basic research can be thought of as activity concerned strictly with unlocking the secrets of nature without being directed at solving a particular problem. This does not imply, though, that the output of basic research is of little use. Indeed some of the most useful research results have come from basic research.

A relatively small proportion of all research and development funds is spent on basic research. In 1975 expenditures for basic research amounted to about 12 percent of all research and development expenditures.[2] It is not difficult to understand why basic research has remained relatively small. An industrial firm invests

---

[2] Ibid., p. 548.

in research for the purpose of increasing profits. If the firm has virtually no guarantee that the research results can be applied to the firm's operation, as is true for basic research, it has little incentive to pay for it. Some large firms allow their scientists a relatively small amount of free time for basic research, but this is mainly a fringe benefit for the scientists.

As a consequence, most basic research is carried on by colleges and universities or by the federal government. But even here there has been a reluctance to "turn scientists loose." In part this might be due to a fear by the public that the funds would be squandered on scientists' pet projects, with little chance for any payoff to society. Basic research is also a very risky business. Perhaps one project out of ten really adds something significant to the fund of knowledge.

This is not to say, however, that the high degree of risk associated with basic research necessarily implies a low return to this research. The one or two successful projects out of ten can well pay for the failures. From the standpoint of risk, research is much like drilling for oil. In oil exploration, roughly one well out of ten produces a significant find, but as a rule the gushers more than pay for the dry holes.

APPLIED RESEARCH

As the name implies, applied research is concerned with solving a particular problem or finding out a specific unknown. For example, the problem might be finding a way to reduce air pollution caused by automobiles or to curb the noise of jet engines.

As a rule both industry and public institutions have been more willing to finance applied research than basic research. Understandably, the business firm is more certain that a return will be forthcoming if the research is centered on a problem of concern to the firm. Much the same holds true for publicly sponsored research. Society feels somewhat more certain that it is getting its money's worth from research if scientists work on a recognized problem.

DEVELOPMENT

The activity referred to as *development* is the almost exclusive domain of large industrial firms and the federal government. Development activities include such things as building prototypes of new products and testing them before their introduction on the market. However, it is rather difficult to separate development from applied research. In a sense, development is a kind of applied research because it is directed at finding out the unknown of a product or production technique. In fact, most industrial research is lumped together in one category and called *research and development* (R&D).

There is even some difficulty in distinguishing between the basic and applied categories of research. An applied research project can bring forth unexpected knowledge that is totally unrelated to the problem at hand. In this sense applied research has the same characteristics as basic research. It is best, therefore, to view these three categories of research as a continuum ranging from pure basic research, to applied research, to the development type of activity on the other end of the scale. Also it is important to recognize that the success of applied research and development activities depends in large part on the knowledge produced by basic research.

Research by industrial firms (R&D)

Research by industrial firms tends to be concentrated in the applied and development types of activity. The overall motivation for a firm to carry on R&D is to improve its profit position. Research and development can increase profits for the firm by (1) the development of new or improved products, which has the effect of increasing the demand for the firm's products, or (2) the development of new cost-reducing techniques of production, which reduce average and marginal costs for the firm. The production of new or improved products resulting from R&D is illustrated in Figure 12–1.

Figure 12–1(A) illustrates the situation for an imperfectly competitive firm before it undertakes the development of a new or improved product. If the R&D program is successful and a new product is developed, the demand facing the firm shifts to the right, as shown by D_1 in Figure 12–1(B). This might depict an auto manufacturer that has developed an engine that will deliver better gas mileage. Understandably, the demand for the company's prod-

FIGURE 12–1
The effect of new and improved products resulting from R&D

(A) Before R&D

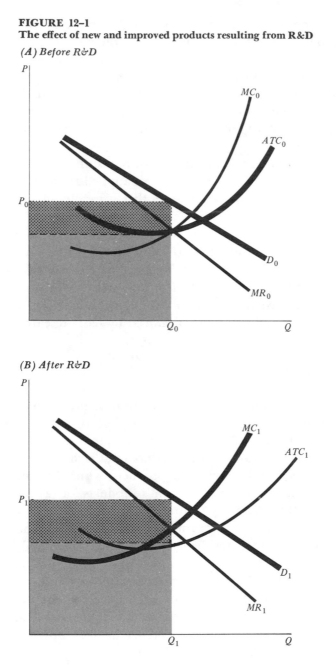

(B) After R&D

uct will shift to the right as customers switch from other companies that do not offer the improved engine.

We must keep in mind, though, that R&D is a costly activity. Hence the R&D program will have the effect of increasing the firm's average total cost (ATC) and marginal cost (MC) from what they would otherwise be. Thus ATC_1 and MC_1 in Figure 12–1(B) are drawn in slightly higher than their original position in Figure 12–1(A). In this particular example, total profits, depicted by the shaded areas, are higher after R&D than before, indicating that the additional revenue brought in by the increase in product demand more than offsets the additional cost of the R&D.

The second possibility for increasing profits through R&D is to reduce production costs through the discovery and adoption of new cost-reducing techniques. For example, a firm might develop a new, more efficient method of producing alcohol for use as a synthetic fuel. This would have the effect of shifting ATC and MC down and to the right, as illustrated in Figure 12–2. Here we assume that the product remains the same, so that the demand and marginal revenue curves are the same in both diagrams.

In this example we have assumed also that the cost saving obtained through the new technique was more than enough to offset the increase in costs brought on by the R&D. Total profits, denoted by the shaded areas in Figure 12–2, therefore increases as a result of the increased R&D expenditure.[3]

RETURNS TO INDUSTRIAL R&D

Conceptually, the decision on whether or not to carry on R&D is rather straightforward; it should be carried on as long as expected revenue increases more than expected costs. But in an actual decision-making situation, the main problem is to assess the returns to R&D. The firm has no guarantee, of course, that demand will shift to the right or costs will shift down.

The usual procedure for a firm is to begin with a rather modest R&D program, perhaps hiring an engineer to spend full time

---

[3] For further discussion on the economic aspects of research by industrial firms, see Edwin Mansfield, *The Economics of Technological Change* (New York: W. W. Norton & Co., 1968).

FIGURE 12–2
Effect on new cost-reducing techniques resulting from R&D

(A) Before R&D

(B) After R&D

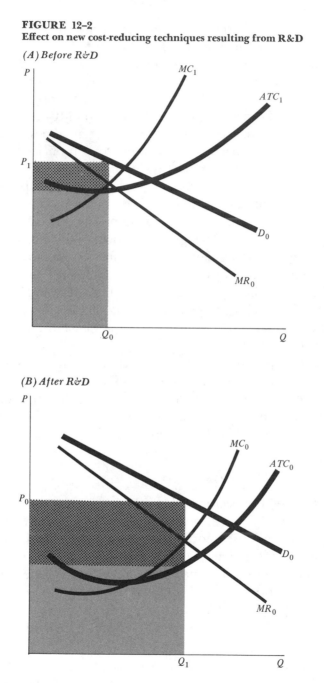

thinking up new ways of doing things. If total revenue increases more than salary and expenses, the firm may add another R&D person, and so on. In other words, decisions whether to do R&D tend to be of a marginal nature. Because of the substantial increase in R&D during recent years, we can only infer that most firms have found it profitable, hence they are doing more.

The decision by a firm to engage in R&D may be motivated as well by the desire to simply maintain a profit position. If other firms in the industry are investing in R&D to create new or improved products or to lower production costs, the firm that does not keep up soon will find itself with few customers or excessively high costs and eventually will be forced out of business. Even in this context, the effects of R&D still can be illustrated by Figures 12–1 and 12–2. Profits after R&D are higher than they would otherwise be.

In deciding whether or not to engage in R&D, the overriding consideration by the firm must be whether or not it will be possible to capture a return to its investment. If the new knowledge that is produced by R&D is readily available to competing firms, the firm that originally produced the knowledge will not be able to gain any special advantage. For example, a pharmaceutical firm that develops a new minute ingredient that might make a drug more effective will guard its secret very closely. If other firms could duplicate the ingredient, they could gain all of its advantages without paying any of the cost. No doubt this explains why some firms and governments find it profitable to employ industrial spies.

One alternative for the firm or individual who discovers or develops something new is to take out a patent with the government patent office. Patent laws forbid the duplication of the patented item or process by other firms or individuals for a period of 17 years. Without these laws or protection, it is argued, there would be little incentive to invest in R&D.

In reality, however, patent laws probably have not offered the protection that might be supposed. Although a patented item cannot be duplicated exactly, in many cases a close substitute can be developed by making a few minor changes. Patenting certain products or processes, then, may actually hasten their discovery and adoption by competing firms. For this reason it is not unusual for firms to deliberately not patent something they have developed;

rather, they try to keep it a secret. The decision whether or not to take out a patent depends mainly on the nature of the product or process. If it is something that is relatively easy to keep secret, such as an additive or minute ingredient, it might be best not to patent. But if it is something like a machine or a gadget that will be widely used, patenting provides some protection, although rarely complete protection, against copying by other firms.

Another important factor that affects whether or not a firm will invest in R&D is the absolute size of the firm. Understandably it will not pay for a small firm to engage in any sizable R&D effort. Consider, for example, your tomato-growing endeavor. Even if you were to assume that no one would copy your research results, it would not pay you to spend several thousand dollars attempting to increase tomato yields. Even if you could double the yield of each tomato plant, the return would be small compared with the probable cost of doing so.

On the other hand, a very large firm, General Motors, for example, can find it profitable to spend a great deal on something that may improve quality or decrease costs only a small amount per vehicle. Multiplying a small unit gain times a large volume can still yield a handsome return to a sizable R&D expenditure. In general, the larger the firm, the more profitable it is to invest in research and development to achieve a given percentage increase in demand or decrease in costs.

Thus far we have considered only the private returns, that is, extra profits, of industrial R&D. But keep in mind that R&D can still be a good investment from the point of view of society even if it does not provide higher profits for the firm doing the R&D. What generally happens is that the extra profits coming from a new product or a new technique of production are eventually eroded away as more and more firms copy the product or technique.

But the fact that the individual firm's extra profits from R&D eventually disappear does not mean that society's benefits from R&D disappear also. Society continues to enjoy a return from R&D long after its profits are eroded away because of the resulting new or improved products that continue to be consumed and/or the reduced costs brought about by new technology. In other words, R&D makes it possible for society to obtain a greater value of output from its limited resources. Economists refer to this benefit as a *social return.*[4]

Publicly sponsored research

An industrial firm will not choose to invest in research unless it has a reasonable assurance that it will add to profits, and the relatively small firm will not engage in research because the expense is too great to be borne by the relatively small output. However, society can benefit greatly from research that may not be profitable for an individual firm or that affects the output of industries made up of firms too small to do their own research, such as agriculture. For this reason federal and state governments either sponsor research or carry it on in their own laboratories or institutions.

Most publicly sponsored reseach is done in colleges and universities. Because of the risk involved and the small chance of capturing a profit on the knowledge produced, much of the country's so-called basic research is done in these institutions. With the exception of market research on individual products, most economic research is done in institutions of higher learning. This is true as well for the humanities and other social sciences.

The decisions on what kind of and how much public research should be done are even more difficult than for industrial research. The decision-making process is slow, cumbersome, and often based on very inadequate information. Someone, of course, must make these decisions, regardless of the information available. The basic decisions are made by society's elected representatives in the state and federal governments. They must decide how much of the taxpayers' money is to be devoted to research. Usually the amount that is allocated to research for a current year is based on what was allocated the year before, plus a little extra for increasing prices and new problems or programs.

Once the funds reach the research institutions, more decisions are required to further allocate the money. How much goes to

---

[4] For estimates of the rates of return on industrial R&D, see Edwin Mansfield, *Industrial Research and Technological Innovation* (New York: W. W. Norton & Co., 1968).

physics, how much to chemistry, economics, agriculture, and so forth? Again the current allocation is made mainly on the basis of past allocation. Marginal changes come about with changes in personnel or with the emergence or recognition of new and pressing problems such as the energy shortage.

Ideally, public research allocation should be made on the basis of the highest payoff to the research, but the main problem is to identify and measure the returns to public research.

RETURNS TO PUBLIC RESEARCH

The returns to public research, like those to education, can be classified into monetary and nonmonetary components. In the non-monetary area, society is willing to pay something to gain information about itself or about the universe, even though this knowledge may not lead to an increase in the value of real output of society. For example, society has been willing to pay a sizable amount to develop a means of getting to the moon and back. Society also considers it worthwhile to find out more about man's origin and behavior, both past and present. Even though knowledge of this sort may not add to the monetary value of real output, it presumably does add something to the utility of society.

Aside from the space program, most public research is aimed at increasing the value of output of society, that is, a dollar or monetary return. People value good health or the avoidance of the "grim reaper" before their time; hence they are willing to pay for medical research. Society places a value on a clean environment, so it supports research on ways of achieving this goal without giving up the goods and services that contribute to the pollution. Most of the basic research that is carried on, such as the work in physics, chemistry, biology, and mathematics, may not be aimed at a specific problem, but it is anticipated that the knowledge produced will somehow have a monetary value.

Measuring the monetary value of public research is indeed a difficult problem, and a great deal of work remains to be done in this area. Until some quantitative measures can be found, decisions to allocate public research will have to be made from purely subjective criteria or historical precedence, neither of which guarantees that society is getting the most for its money.

Agricultural research

We include a separate discussion of agricultural research for two reasons: (1) it is an area where some progress has been made in estimating social returns, and (2) there seems to be widespread misunderstanding about who benefits from this research.

The nation's agricultural research is carried on in about equal proportions by farm supply firms including seed, chemical, and machinery companies, and by agricultural experiment stations. The latter is funded by public tax funds. As indicated above, private firms tend to conduct research that can be incorporated into a salable product. Understandably, a firm must be able to capture a return on its investment, or else it would not pay to invest. Agricultural experiment stations tend to conduct that portion of agricultural research that private firms do not find profitable but nevertheless provides a return to society.

The overall objective of agricultural research, whether it be private or public, is to increase the productive capacity of farmers. The output of such research includes new, higher-yielding crop varieties; breeding and disease-control advances to make livestock and poultry more efficient converters of feed; completely new inputs such as herbicides and pesticides; and new and improved management practices for farmers.

As pointed out in Chapter 5 on product supply, the effect of new technology is to increase, or shift to the right, the supply curve of individual producers and the industry, as shown in Figure 12–3. For a given price, producers are willing to put more on the market or will sell a given amount for a lower price because their unit costs are lower.

The increase in productive efficiency, and hence the increase in product supply, brought about by agricultural research in effect increases the total value of agricultural output for a given amount of traditional resources such as land, labor, and capital. In other words, by producing knowledge and new, more productive inputs, society obtains more output from its scarce resources. The annual value of this additional output to society is illustrated in Figure 12–3 by the shaded area lying between S_0 and S_1, bounded on the top by the demand for agricultural products.

FIGURE 12–3
**Effect of agricultural research and resulting new
technology that shifts agricultural supply**

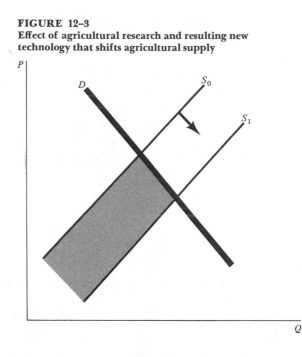

Supply curve S_0 in Figure 12–3 represents what the supply of agricultural output would be without the new technology. By measuring the increase in the productive efficiency of agriculture, economists have been able to determine the location of S_1 for a given year. The difference between these two curves, therefore, represents the annual value of output attributable to agricultural research.

By comparing the annual expenditure on research with the value of extra output attributable to research, economists have been able to obtain estimates of its social internal rate of return. The procedure used is essentially the same as we used to compute the rate of return to education. In this case the cash outflows consist of expenditures on agricultural research (both industrial and public), and the cash inflows consist of the value of additional output obtained as a result of agricultural research (value of the shaded area in Figure 12–3).

Estimates of the *marginal* internal rate of return to *additional* investment in agricultural research in the United States are in the range of 40 to 50 percent.[5] It is like the nation placing over $2 billion per year (the recent annual investment in agricultural research and extension) in a savings account and reaping a 40 to 50 percent return. This is high-payoff investment.

This brings us to our second major point. The long-run beneficiaries of agricultural research tend to be consumers of farm products rather than farmers. Of course, farmers benefit as consumers along with everyone else. Consumers benefit from agricultural research because the resulting increase in productive efficiency shifts the supply of agricultural products to the right, thereby increasing food output and reducing food prices below what they would otherwise be. It should also be pointed out that the reduction in food prices benefits low-income people relatively more than high-income individuals because the former spend a larger share of their income on food than the latter. Also the major portion of the agricultural research conducted in the public sector is paid for by taxes from middle- and high-income people.[6] Thus agricultural research has the effect of reducing the inequality of living standards between income levels. It is equivalent to achieving more equality of incomes.

Many people, particularly homemakers, would argue, though, that food prices are not cheap, judging from the prices in supermarkets these days. But one must look at the real cost of food— the proportion of a country's resources that is devoted to food production. At the present time Americans spend about 15 percent of their income on food. Contrast this to the situation in most of the world's less developed countries, where food often accounts for 70 to 80 percent of a family's budget.

Even in the United States at the turn of the century, people spent almost 40 percent of their income on food. A nation with a relatively unproductive agricultural sector must devote a relatively large share of its resources to food production. As agricultural productivity increases, more and more people leave agriculture to produce other things that make life more interesting and enjoy-

---

[5] Willis Peterson, "The Return to Investment in Agricultural Research in the United States," in Walter Fishel, ed., *Resource Allocation in Agricultural Research* (Minneapolis, University of Minnesota Press, 1971), p. 160.

[6] Luther Tweeten, "Distribution of Benefits and Costs of Agricultural Research and Education," *Oklahoma Current Farm Economics*, vol. 46, no. 3 (October 1973).

able. If 70 to 80 percent of a nation's population is required to produce food, modern conveniences such as reasonably priced automobiles, adequate medical care, and the host of laborsaving appliances that make life more enjoyable cannot also be produced. Life might have been simpler in the "good old days" when most people were farmers, but few people today would trade their standard of living for what existed in years past.

The substantial decline in the proportion of incomes devoted to food in the United States even understates the true decline in the real price of food if we call to mind the quality improvement that has occurred over the years and the increased amount of services purchased with food nowadays. There are two dimensions to the increase in quality: (1) the increase in the wholesomeness of food, meaning the reduction in disease and insect damage, and (2) the greater share of the nation's food coming from animal (as opposed to crop) sources. Both aspects of quality improvement require more resources and increase the cost of food from what it would otherwise be. Similarly the purchase of services such as those embodied in bakery bread, cake mixes, and dressed, cut, and frozen meats cost money and add to consumers' food bills. If U.S. consumers were willing to buy food of the same quality and with the same amount of services as in years past, or as now exists in the less developed countries, they would be spending considerably less than 15 percent of their income on food. Of course, there is nothing wrong with people wanting to spend some of their increased purchasing power on higher-quality food and more services.

This is not to say that agricultural research can take sole credit for economic development. Other knowledge is required as well to produce the variety of modern goods and services that raise the standard of living. But as developing nations are learning, little progress can be made without technological advance in agriculture.

Social costs of new technology

There is a growing concern in the United States and other highly developed nations that the true cost of research that produces new knowledge and technology may exceed the expenditures for research. One of the concerns is the movement of people between occupations and areas. If new technology makes a job obsolete, what is the social cost of having the person who held this job move to another occupation in another location?

It is fairly easy to measure moving costs, but there are other things to consider. People who move must leave family, friends, and familiar ways of living for the unknown. Some find moving an exciting experience; others dread it. The largest case in point is the huge rural-to-urban migration that has taken place in the United States. Most would agree that the increased concentration of population in urban areas has contributed to many present-day problems: air and water pollution and congestion of transportation systems and housing.

Without the new technology would these problems disappear? Perhaps some would. But we must remember also that problems have always plagued mankind. Consider the disease, isolation, and long hours of drudgery both in the home and on the job with which our forefathers had to contend. Even pollution existed in those days. Imagine the smell in the cities when vehicles were horse-drawn, or the smoke and soot that came forth when coal was the main source of heat and power. Indeed some of the worst pollution in the world today exists in countries that have experienced relatively little advance in technology. When dealing with present-day problems, we tend to visualize things as we would like to see them without regard to their historical background.

Main points of Chapter 12

1. The introduction of a spoken and written language early in history represented a significant advance in human knowledge.
2. At the dawning of history new knowledge came mainly as a by-product of everyday activities.
3. During the course of history humans learned that the output of knowledge could be increased if certain people devoted full time to its production. Today the production of knowledge is a large and growing industry expending billions of dollars per year in the United States alone.
4. We can think of research as a production activity in which

inputs consist of such things as scientists and engineers, laboratories, and testing facilities, and output consists of new knowledge.

5. Unlike more traditional types of production, we cannot be sure that the production of new knowledge is subject to the law of diminishing returns. If the potential stock of knowledge is infinite, diminishing returns to research may not set in, at least in the foreseeable future.

6. Knowledge is more than having information or facts; in large part it is the ability to know what to do with information.

7. Basic research is concerned with unlocking the secrets of nature without having a preconceived idea of how the knowledge might be used.

8. Applied research is concerned with solving a particular problem or finding out a specific unknown.

9. Development is an extension of applied research concerned with finding out the unknown about new products or production techniques and testing them before their introduction on the market.

10. Industrial firms are motivated to carry on R&D by the prospect of increased profits. Research and development can increase profits by the introduction of new and improved products, which shifts the demand facing the firm to the right, or the development of new cost-reducing techniques of production, which shifts the firm's cost curves down and to the right.

11. The type of research carried on by a firm is governed by the firm's ability to capture a return to the research.

12. Patent laws are intended to help firms or individuals capture a return from new products or techniques. The ability of competitors to develop close substitutes for patented items limits their protection, however.

13. In general it does not pay a small firm to engage in organized R&D because the cost cannot be spread across a large enough output.

14. Even though the private profits from R&D may decline or be nonexistent, expenditures for it can still be a good investment for society because R&D makes it possible for society to

obtain a greater value of output from its limited resources.

15. Because society can benefit greatly from research that is not profitable for individual firms, the federal and state governments sponsor or carry on research of their own. Most public research is done in colleges and universities.

16. The allocation of public research is a difficult problem because knowledge does not come in easy-to-measure units like bushels, pounds, or dollars.

17. The value to society of agricultural research has been estimated by measuring the value of the increased output brought about by the increase in the productive efficiency of farmers.

18. Consumers are the main beneficiaries of agricultural research because research increases the supply and lowers the price of food from what they would otherwise be.

19. Because low-income people spend a larger proportion of their income on food than their higher-income counterparts, the benefits of agricultural research are relatively larger for the poor than the rich.

20. There has been a growing awareness in recent years of problems associated with new technology. What is often overlooked, however, is the quality of life that existed in years past and the problems that confronted people before the advent of modern technology.

Questions for thought and discussion

1. What is research?
2. Can we be sure that the earth's resources are finite? Explain.
3. Why do business firms spend money on research?
4. Publicly funded research carried out by colleges and universities benefits all of society, whereas private R&D conducted by business firms benefits only the firms doing the research. True or false? Explain.
5. Why do we have publicly funded agricultural experiment stations but not automobile experiment stations or airplane experiment stations?

13

Micro summary

Introduction to microeconomics

Because the economic wants of every society exceed the resources available to completely satisfy these wants, it is necessary for most people to get along with less goods and services than they really would like. Hence economic decisions must be made. The decision to increase the output of any one good or service necessarily involves a cost—the amount of another good or service that must be given up. Economists call this opportunity cost. The production possibilities curve shows the various combinations of two goods that can be produced with a fixed amount of resources. Opportunity cost is shown on the production possibilities curve by the amount of one good given up to obtain more of the other as one moves along the curve.

Every society is faced with three economic questions: (1) what and how much of each good should be produced, (2) how should each good be produced, and (3) for whom? The manner in which these questions are answered differs between the private and public sectors of a market economy, and between a market economy and a communist society. In the private sector of a market economy, the decisions regarding what and how much of each good to be produced are made jointly by producers and consumers. Market prices play a key role by providing signals and incentives to both groups. A relatively high price of an item tells producers that consumers want more of the good and provides producers with an incentive to increase its output. Consumers also have an incentive to conserve on goods that are relatively high-priced.

Input prices reflect the relative scarcity of inputs and again provide producers with the incentive to conserve on those that cost the most.

The share of the output of a market economy going to each individual is determined in large part by income. Individual or family income depends on wages or salaries and the amount of capital owned. The ownership of capital depends on the amount of income saved and on inheritances.

In communist states all resources are owned by the government and everyone works for the government. The chief advantage claimed by communists is a more equal distribution of income. Among the major drawbacks of such a system are the loss of virtually all personal freedoms, lack of economic incentives, an unresponsive and inefficient allocation of resources, and the concentration of political, economic, and military power in the hands of a few people in the government.

Demand is defined as a relationship between price and quantity. The downward sloping nature of a demand curve reflects the idea that people buy more of an item when its price declines. Supply also is defined as a relationship between price and quantity. The upward sloping nature of the supply curve reflects the idea that producers place larger quantities on the market when price increases. If the market price happens to be above the equilibrium price, there will be a surplus and price will be forced down. Conversely if the price happens to be below the equilibrium, there will be a shortage and price will be forced up. The equilibrium price corresponds to the intersection of the demand and supply curves.

A change or shift in demand occurs when buyers become willing to change the quantity they will purchase at any given price. For example, an increase in demand means that buyers will take a greater quantity off the market at any given price. Similarly, a change or shift in supply occurs when sellers become willing to change the quantity they place on the market at any given price. For example, an increase in supply means that sellers will place a greater quantity on the market at a given price. The equilibrium price will increase if demand increases or supply decreases.

The five main factors that shift demand are changes in (1) prices of related goods, (2) money income of consumers, (3) expectations of consumers regarding future prices and incomes, (4) tastes and preferences, and (5) number of consumers. The five main factors that shift supply are changes in (1) resource prices, (2) prices of alternative goods that can be produced, (3) expectations of producers regarding future prices, (4) technology, and (5) number of producers (of a given size). The allocation of resources to private goods is accomplished by the forces of demand and supply, whereas the kinds and amounts of public goods produced are the result of political decisions.

Consumer choice

Producers have an incentive to cater to the wants of consumers because by doing so they enjoy higher profits. Of course, different consumers want different things because of the diversity of tastes. Utility is the amount of satisfaction received from the consumption of goods and services. The marginal unit is the extra or additional unit added to whatever we have. Hence marginal utility is the additional satisfaction received from one more unit of a good or service. Because of the law of diminishing marginal utility, the additional satisfaction received from consuming additional units of a good or service becomes less and less.

To maximize satisfaction from a given income, a consumer should arrange his or her purchases such that the marginal utility per dollar (MU/P) is the same for all goods and services. If the MU/P ratios are not equal, the total utility from a given income can be increased by reducing the money spent on the goods exhibiting low MU/P ratios and spending more on the high–MU/P goods. The utility-maximizing mix is constantly changing because of changes in MU and price.

An indifference curve is a line showing alternative combinations of two goods that yield the same utility. The shape of the indifference curve reflects the degree of substitution between the two items represented. Imperfect substitutes (the most interesting case) exhibit indifference curves that are convex to the origin, meaning that more and more of the abundant good must be obtained to compensate for the loss of the item that is becoming increasingly scarce. Indifference curves for perfect substitutes are straight, downward sloping lines, whereas those for perfect complements are rectangular.

The budget line shows alternative combinations of two items that cost a given amount. The point where the budget line intersects each axis is found by dividing the available budget by the price of the good represented on that axis. All budget lines, regardless of the degree of substitution, are straight, downward sloping lines. Utility is maximized for a given budget by consuming the mix of goods that corresponds to the tangency point between the budget line and the highest possible indifference curve that can be reached by that budget line.

Product demand

Demand is a relationship between price and quantity. It tells us the quantities of a good that will be purchased at various possible prices or the prices that people will pay for various possible quantities. A demand curve is a line showing the various combinations of price and quantity. Price is represented on the vertical axis and quantity on the horizontal axis. The downward sloping nature of the demand curve reflects the idea that people buy greater quantities of a good as its price declines.

The downward sloping nature of the demand curve is consistent with the marginal utility over price (MU/P) approach to maximizing utility; when price increases, MU/P declines, which provides an incentive for people to buy less of the good and more of other items that offer a larger marginal utility per dollar. A demand curve can be obtained from an indifference curve–budget line diagram by choosing alternative prices for one of the items represented and plotting the resulting quantities on a separate demand curve diagram. Reducing the price of the good represented on the horizontal axis causes the budget line to rotate in a counterclockwise fashion. Lower prices of the good represented on the horizontal axis give rise to larger utility-maximizing quantities of that good, resulting in a downward sloping demand curve. The income effect represents the change in quantity demanded resulting from the change in purchasing power. The substitution effect measures the change in quantity demanded because of a change in relative prices. The market demand is obtained by adding at each price the quantity demanded by each individual buyer in the market.

Elasticity of demand is a measure of the responsiveness of consumers to price changes. The elasticity coefficient is obtained by dividing the percentage change in quantity by the percentage change in price. The coefficient tells us the percentage change in quantity demanded resulting from each percent change in price. Demand is said to be elastic if E_d is greater than one, and inelastic if E_d is less than one. Goods that have good substitutes and make up a large share of consumer budgets tend to exhibit an elastic demand. Total revenue (or expenditure) will decline when price declines if E_d is inelastic.

The demand curve can and does shift (increase or decrease) because of changes in one or more of the five demand shifters. An increase in demand is represented by a shift to the right of the demand curve, meaning that people will buy more at any given price, or will be willing to pay a higher price for a given quantity. The opposite holds true for a decrease in demand. The five main demand shifters are changes in (1) prices of related goods, (2) money incomes, (3) consumer expectations regarding future prices and incomes, (4) tastes and preferences, and (5) number of consumers. Income elasticity measures the responsiveness of consumers to changes in income. The coefficient is obtained by dividing the percentage change in quantity (at a given price) by the percentage change in income. It tells us the percentage change in quantity for each percent change in income. Items that have a positive income elasticity are called superior goods, whereas those exhibiting a negative income elasticity are known as inferior goods.

Producer choice

Production is any activity that creates present and/or future utility. This includes virtually all activities. Each production activity is characterized by an output and one or more (usually more) inputs. A production function is a relationship between inputs and output. By knowing the production function, one can predict output by knowing the inputs. Marginal physical product (MPP) of an input is the additional output obtained from one additional unit of that input. MPP is measured in units of the output. The law of diminishing returns states that as more and more of a variable input is added to one or more fixed inputs, beyond some point the MPP of the variable input will begin to decline. If it were not so, the world's supply of tomatoes could be grown in a flower pot.

There are three stages of production. Stage I ends and Stage II begins at the point where the MPP curve intersects the APP curve. Stage II ends and Stage III begins at the point where the MPP intersects the horizontal axis. Diminishing returns set in during Stage I. Production should always take place in Stage II.

To minimize the cost of producing a given level of output, inputs should be utilized such that the P/MPP ratios of all inputs are equal. If they are not equal, the cost of producing a given output can be decreased by using less of the resources exhibiting the relatively high P/MPP ratios and more of these having the lowest ratios.

The degree of substitution between inputs is represented by an isoquant. An isoquant is a line that shows various possible combinations of two inputs that produce a given level of output. An isoquant representing imperfect substitutes (the most interesting case) is convex to the origin, meaning that more and more of the abundant input must be utilized to compensate for the loss of each successive unit of the scarce input. Isoquants depicting perfect substitutes are straight, downward sloping lines, whereas those representing inputs that must be used in fixed proportions are rectangular.

An isocost is a line showing various possible combinations of two inputs that cost an equal amount of money. The point where the isocost line intersects each axis is found by dividing the given cost figure by the price of the corresponding input. The least-cost method of producing a given level of output corresponds to the point where the isoquant is tangent to the lowest possible isocost line. An increase in the price of the resource represented on the horizontal axis causes the isocost line to rotate in a clockwise fashion. This increases the cost of producing a given output and changes the point of tangency, moving away from the input that has increased in price toward the one whose price has become relatively cheap.

Product supply

Costs can be classified in various ways. Explicit costs represent the money paid for purchased inputs such as hired labor, fuel, and raw materials. Implicit costs represent a charge for the resources contributed by the owner(s) of the firm. They can be measured by what the resources could earn in the next best alternative occupation. As their labels imply, fixed costs remain constant regardless of the level of output, whereas variable costs vary with changes in output.

Normal profits are defined as the amount that resources owned by the firm have to earn in order to keep them from moving elsewhere. Essentially normal profits are the same as implicit costs. Pure profits are earnings above all costs (explicit plus implicit). Pure profits provide a reward for risk taking and exist because knowledge is imperfect and the future cannot be known with certainty. During the 1949–78 period, after-tax profits (normal and pure) in the United States averaged 4.9 cents per dollar of sales and amounted to a 11.6 percent rate of return on equity capital.

Marginal cost is defined as the additional cost of producing one more unit of output; the MC curve is a mirror image of the MPP curve. Similarly the APP and AVC curves are mirror images of each other. The marginal cost curve always intersects the AVC and ATC curves at their minimum points. To maximize profits, a firm should expand output until it corresponds to the point where product price equals marginal cost. Because the MC curve indicates the output forthcoming at various possible prices, it is the firm's supply curve. If some fixed costs cannot be avoided, a firm may produce at a loss in the short run as long as it is covering its variable costs. If price falls lower than the minimum point of the AVC curve, the firm should not produce. Hence the firm's supply curve is that portion of the MC curve above the AVC curve. This also implies that production will not take place in Stage I because if the price were so low as to give rise to a level of output in this range, AVC would be greater than price. The market supply is obtained by summing the quantity supplied of all firms at the various possible prices.

Elasticity of supply measures the responsiveness of producers to price changes. It is computed by dividing the percentage change in quantity supplied by the percentage change in price. The elasticity coefficient tells us the percentage change in quantity supplied for each percent change in price. The major factor affecting elasticity of supply is time for adjustment; the longer the time allowed to adjust, the more elastic is the supply.

The supply curve can shift (increase or decrease) because of changes in the supply shifters. An increase in supply means that producers place more on the market at any given price or will take a lower price for a given quantity. The opposite is true for a decrease in supply. The five major supply shifters are changes in: (1) prices of inputs, (2) prices of other goods that can be produced, (3) producer expectations of future prices, (4) technology, and (5) number (or size) of producers. Changes in weather are an important supply shifter for food.

Demand and supply in the product market

Market prices are established by the interaction of demand and supply. Equilibrium price corresponds to the intersection of the demand and supply curves. If the price is higher than the equilibrium, quantity supplied is greater than quantity demanded, thereby causing a surplus, and as a result price declines. If the price is lower than the equilibrium, the quantity demanded is greater than quantity supplied, thereby causing a shortage, and as a result price increases. Thus if the actual market price is not at equilibrium, forces exist that will push the price toward this level.

Changes in the equilibrium price occur because of shifts in the demand and supply curves. Various combinations of price and quantity changes can occur, depending on the shifts in demand and supply. For example, an increase in the demand causes an increase in both price and quantity, whereas an increase in the supply causes price to decrease while quantity increases. Ceiling prices, if they are below their respective equilibrium levels, inevitably result in shortages, coupon rationing, and black markets. Support prices, if they are above their equilibrium values, inevitably result in surpluses.

Sales or excise taxes can be viewed as shifting the supply curve upward and to the left. In the short run, such taxes increase the prices paid by consumers and decrease the net prices received by producers. In the long run as supply becomes more elastic, consumers end up paying the major share of such taxes.

Placing a penalty on buyers of illegal goods and services has the effect of decreasing the demand for these items, thereby causing a decrease in their price and quantity. On the other hand, when suppliers bear the major penalty, supply decreases, which causes the price to increase and quantity to decrease. In most instances suppliers bear the major penalty, which explains why illegal goods and services tend to be relatively expensive.

Price serves as a rationing device by providing an incentive for consumers to limit their purchases. It is an effective rationing device because consumers impose rationing on themselves; they have no incentive to consume large amounts of scarce and expensive items. Price also serves to allocate resources by providing an incentive for producers to expand the output of goods when their demand is increasing and price is rising. Conversely producers find it to their advantage to decrease the output of items when their demand is decreasing and prices are declining.

Both demand and supply tend to be more elastic when there is a long time to adjust to price changes than when there is only a short time to adjust. As a consequence, the price change resulting from a shift in demand or supply will tend to be greatest immediately after the shift. Price then will move part of the way back to the original level as quantity adjusts more completely in the long run.

Perfect competition in the product market

A perfectly competitive firm is defined as one that has no power to alter the price it receives for its product. This situation exists when (1) each firm sells a product that is undifferentiated from that of other firms, and (2) each firm sells a small share of the market. As a result each firm is unable to sell its product at a higher price than other firms and cannot alter the market price by significantly changing the quantity supplied on the market. The demand facing the individual perfectly competitive firm is perfectly elastic, meaning that the firm can sell any reasonable quantity at the going market price.

A perfectly competitive firm will make pure profits if price is higher than ATC; zero pure profits are earned if price equals ATC; and the firm incurs a loss if price is less than ATC. A substantial number of firms earning pure profits serves as a signal for existing firms to expand or for new firms to enter. As a result, market supply increases, price declines, and pure profits are reduced or eliminated. In the event that new resources cannot enter in response to pure profits, the prices of the firms fixed inputs are bid up, thereby increasing ATC and again reducing or eliminating pure profits. The opposite adjustment occurs in the event of losses. Although there is a tendency for pure profits to be competed away, alert managers may be able to reap pure profits in the short run by adopting new cost-reducing techniques.

The long-run ATC or planning curve is an envelope of all possible short-run ATC curves. Economies of scale are said to exist in the region where LRATC is declining while diseconomies of scale occur when LRATC is increasing. If an expansion of the industry bids up resource prices for the firms within that industry or causes costs to increase because of technical diseconomies, it is known as an increasing-cost industry and its long-run supply curve will slope upward. Constant- and decreasing-cost industries exhibit perfectly elastic and decreasing long-run supply curves, respectively.

Economic efficiency requires three conditions: (1) maximum technical efficiency is obtained, (2) the P/MPP ratios of all inputs are equal, and (3) the output of each good corresponds to the point where product price equals marginal cost. The third condition maximizes the value of output to society and is met only by perfect competition.

Pollution results in a misallocation of resources because the firm perceives a lower marginal cost curve than that facing society. The control of pollution increases costs and product prices.

The perfectly competitive buyer faces a supply curve that is perfectly elastic because he or she purchases a small fraction of the total market supply. This means that the individual buyer has no control over market price but can buy any reasonable quantity at the going price. Virtually all consumers fit this description.

Imperfect competition in the product market

Firms are classified as imperfectly competitive if (1) each firm sells a sizable share of the market and/or (2) each firm sells a product somewhat different from that of competitors. If a firm sells a sizable share of the market, it can raise the market price by reducing its level of output. If a firm's product is slightly different than that of competitors, it may be able to sell its product at a slight premium. The ability to influence the price received for its product implies that an imperfectly competitive firm faces a downward sloping demand curve. Such firms can raise the price by reducing sales. Marginal revenue is the additional revenue obtained by selling one more unit of output. Marginal revenue is less than price for an imperfectly competitive firm because additional units can be sold only if price is reduced, and this price reduction must apply to all units sold.

There are three categories of imperfectly competitive firms: (1) monopolistic competition, (2) oligopoly, and (3) pure monopoly. Monopolistic competition is typical of most firms engaged in retail trade as well as small and medium-sized manufacturing establishments. The distinguishing characteristics of such firms are that each accounts for a small share of the market but sells a product slightly different from that of competitors. The profit-maximizing quantity of a monopolistically competitive firm corresponds to the point where $MC = MR$, while the profit-maximizing price corresponds to the point where a vertical line up from this quantity intersects the demand curve facing the firm.

Oligopoly exists when three or four large firms account for a major share of the sales in an industry. These firms may sell either a homogeneous or differentiated product. Pure monopoly exists when one firm accounts for the entire market. The profit-maximizing price and quantity are determined in the same manner for these firms as for those in monopolistic competition.

Imperfectly competitive firms will earn pure profits if price is greater than ATC. In the case of pure profits, more firms or re-sources are likely to flow into the industry, competing away such profits, except where entry is blocked (the case of pure monopoly). The only lasting way to block entry is by the issue of licenses by the government.

The Sherman and Clayton Antitrust Acts prohibit oligopolies from getting together to raise price. Also any success in raising price means that quantity must be reduced. This is turn means that MR is greater than MC for each firm, and as a result each firm has an incentive to increase output.

Monopoly power is measured by the P/MC ratio. For perfectly competitive firms, this ratio is one. Hence the more monopoly power, the higher is the ratio. Because of the difficulty of measuring marginal cost, the share of the market accounted for by the largest firms is often used as a proxy measure of monopoly power. During inflation imperfectly competitive firms raise prices because of an increase in their costs and/or an increase in the demand curve facing the firm. Since these shifts are out of the control of the firm, it is necessary to look for reasons other than the desire to maximize profits or monopoly power for the underlying cause of inflation.

Advertising can be classified as either informative or persuasive. The informative type provides information to consumers, enabling them to make better decisions providing it is not misleading or false. The MC curve of an imperfectly competitive firm is not its supply curve because price and quantity produced also depend on the demand curve facing the firm. However the same factors that shift supply also shift MC, and the direction of the change in price and quantity resulting from a change in MC for imperfectly competitive firms is the same as that for a change in supply in perfect competition. In general, the more differentiated its product and the larger the share of the market accounted for by the firm, the steeper is the demand curve facing the firm.

The labor market

The two primary factors of production are labor and capital. The VMP or MRP of labor is the value of additional output obtained by adding one more unit of labor. Because it pays each individual employer to add labor up to the point where the wage equals VMP or MRP, the VMP or MRP curves can be thought of as the firm's demand curve for labor. The market demand for labor can be obtained by adding at each wage the quantity of labor demanded by each firm. A somewhat more realistic way of defining the demand for labor is to allow the quantities of other inputs to vary while holding their prices constant.

When wages increase people may work more, the same, or less, depending on the income and substitution effects. The income effect pulls people toward more leisure (less work) because they can afford to buy more leisure. The substitution effect pulls them toward more work because leisure becomes more expensive when wages increase. The market supply of labor is found by adding at each wage the quantity of labor supplied.

Most wages are determined in a perfectly competitive labor market because most employers hire a relatively small share of the total labor force in their respective labor markets. Although a perfectly competitive employer may be able to pay below-average wages, it is not always in the best interest of the employer to do so. Such employers tend to attract less productive people and have a higher turnover of personnel; both add to the firm's costs. In order for an employer to retain the services of an employee, the employee must contribute at least as much to the value of output of the firm as the wages received.

An imperfectly competitive buyer of labor is defined as one who hires a substantial share of the employees in the surrounding labor market. Such a firm faces an upward sloping supply curve of labor, meaning that higher wages must be paid to attract additional employees. In this case the MRC of hiring an additional unit of labor will be greater than the wage paid because the higher wage that is necessary to attract more labor must be paid to all employees. The profit-maximizing quantity of labor hired by an imperfectly competitive employer corresponds to the intersection of the MRP and MRC curves with the wage determined by the supply curve facing the firm at this quantity.

Shifts in the demand for labor occur because of changes in the product price and in the MPP of labor. Changes in the supply of labor result from changes in labor force participation rates and in population. The latter may change because of migration of people.

Wage and employment changes result from changes in the demand for a supply of labor. Wage differences between occupations can be explained by differences in the demand for and supply of labor. Wages will be high whenever the demand for labor is large relative to the supply. People who are substitutes for machines may lose their jobs because of automation, while those that are complements will tend to receive an increase in wages. In the long run most people are able to relocate and end up earning higher wages as a result of automation. Although discrimination against minorities and women no doubt exists, some wage differences can be due to differences in skills, working conditions, and seniority.

Labor unions attempt to raise wages by (1) increasing the demand for labor, (2) decreasing its supply, or (3) bargaining under threat of strike for a wage above the market equilibrium. Unions have been most successful in the latter two strategies. Craft unions representing the skilled trades and the medical profession tend to restrict supply as their main method of raising wages. This is usually done by restricting the number of people allowed into the training program. Industrial unions representing unskilled and semiskilled workers use bargaining under threat of strike as their primary method of raising wages. Studies reveal that unions have raised the wages of their members between 7 and 11 percent. These studies also reveal that nonunion wages have been reduced 3 to 4 percent due to the reduction of workers in unionized industries and the resulting increase in supply of labor to nonunion occupations. Since unions represent about 22 percent of the U.S. labor force, it appears that unions have not had much effect on the overall average level of wages in the country. Minimum wage laws have an effect similar to union action in that they raise wages and decrease the number of jobs particularly at the low end of the wage scale, affecting teenagers and minorities.

The capital market

Capital is defined as durable inputs that yield a flow of services over a period of time. The annual cost of owning a capital item is the interest plus depreciation charge. Depreciation can be measured by the decrease in the market value of a capital item. Capital depreciates because of wearing out and obsolescence. The VMP (or MRP) of capital is the value of additional output made possible by the use of the capital item. It pays to utilize capital as long as its net annual VMP (or MRP) is at least as large as annual cost of ownership.

The rate of return on capital is its annual net return expressed as a percent of its value at the beginning of the year or period. It means the same as the rate of interest received on a savings account. Capitalized value generally refers to the present value of a capital item such as land that yields a flow of returns into perpetuity; it is found by dividing the annual net returns by the rate of interest.

In the context of cash flow analysis, cash outflow represents the purchase price of the capital item. Gross cash inflow represents the value of additional output resulting from the use of the capital, while net cash inflow is found by subtracting associated costs (excluding interest and depreciation) from the gross cash inflow figures. A dollar forthcoming some date in the future is worth less than a dollar in hand at the present because a dollar in hand now could earn interest in the meantime. The formula for finding the discounted present value of one dollar forthcoming n years in the future is $1/(1 + r)^n$, where r is the rate of interest. In addition to comparing the annual VMP (or MRP) of a capital item with its cost, there are three ways to evaluate an investment: (1) discounted present value of returns, (2) benefit/cost ratio, and (3) internal rate of return. An investment is worthwhile if the discounted present value of its return is at least as great as its cost. The benefit/cost ratio is found by dividing the discounted present value of the returns of an investment by its cost. The B/C ratio should be at least one for an investment to be profitable. The internal rate of return is the rate of interest that makes the discounted present value of the returns of an investment equal to its cost. It has the same meaning as the rate of return on money in a savings account. For an investment to be profitable, its internal rate of return should be at least as great as the interest on borrowed funds or what could be earned on one's own funds.

The interest paid on loan funds is determined in a loan market by the demand for and supply of these funds. Interest rates will tend to be lowest on large, low-risk loans because the cost of making these loans is the lowest. The real rate of interest is equal to the money rate minus the rate of inflation. During inflationary periods the money rate of interest tends to be high to compensate for the loss in purchasing power of loan funds. The interest rate rations loan funds by making it unprofitable to invest in low-return activities while allocating the funds to those investments that yield the highest rate of return.

The economics of education

Human capital refers to the acquisition of knowledge and skills by human beings. It is acquired mainly through formal schooling, although some is no doubt obtained by on-the-job training and experience. The personal returns to education include both monetary and nonmonetary components. The monetary component refers to the additional earnings made possible by education, whereas the nonmonetary returns include the present and future utility received from experiences gained as a student. It is possible that society receives a return over and above that received by the individual student through a more stable society and by the benefits received by family members, especially the children of college-educated women.

The cost of a college education is made up of three components: (1) forgone earnings, (2) tuition, and (3) books and supplies. Forgone earnings probably constitute the largest share of college costs for most students; they can be measured by the earnings of people with a high school education. Board and room are not considered a special cost of schooling because they must be paid regardless of what a person is doing. Because tuition does not cover the full cost of schooling for most students, the total cost of education for society is greater than the cost borne by the individual student. Funding part of the cost of education by public tax funds is a way for society to help young people from lower-income families to have a somewhat more equal chance to move up the income scale.

Internal rates of return in 1977 to college training in the United States ranged from 11 percent for men with a four-year degree to 7 percent for women with a four-year degree. There appears to have been a slight downward trend in the rate of return to a college education between 1958 and 1977, with the most noticeable decline exhibited by men with two years of college.

The student can be viewed as a multiproduct firm producing three broad categories of goods: (1) human capital, (2) intermediate goods via the labor market, and (3) final goods in the context of household activities. The student achieves an optimum allocation of time when the MPP/time price ratios are equalized across all activities. The MPP of time is the utility produced by an additional hour of time, while the price of time is its value (implicit or explicit) in its next best alternative activity. The theory suggests that part-time employment necessarily reduces the allocation of time to both study and household activities. Preliminary results reveal that freshmen and sophomores who are employed part-time tend to maintain their credit loads but suffer a reduction in their grades, while juniors and seniors reduce their credit loads and in so doing maintain their grades.

The economics of science and technology

Research can be viewed as a production activity with inputs consisting of scientific personnel, research laboratories, computers, etc.; output consists of new knowledge. Although the production of new knowledge through research has much in common with conventional production, it may not be subject to the law of diminishing returns if the potential stock of knowledge is infinite.

The three broad categories of research include: (1) basic research, (2) applied research, and (3) development. The last two categories are frequently combined and labeled R&D. Basic research is aimed at unlocking the secrets of nature without being directed at a particular problem. As the name implies, applied research is directed at a particular problem or product, while development activities involve the building of prototypes.

Industrial firms carry on R&D when it offers an opportunity to increase their profits. R&D can increase profits by improving the product line, and in so doing shift the demand facing the firm to the right, and/or by reducing costs. In addition to private returns (added profits), industrial R&D also yields social returns by increasing the total value of output of society. The social returns can remain even after the private returns have been competed away.

Substantial research is funded by public tax funds and carried out by firms, educational institutions, and government agencies. Much of this research is of a basic nature, which would not be profitable to private firms but nevertheless yields a social return to society. Agricultural research, about half done by private firms and the other half by agricultural experiment stations, yields a social return by increasing the supply of food. Hence it primarily benefits consumers. These returns have been measured as the area between the original and the new supply curves of agricultural products bounded on the top by the demand curve. Agricultural research also has the effect of increasing the purchasing power of low-income people compared with their middle- and high-income counterparts because the former spend a greater share of their income on food while the latter pay the major share of the public research bill.

Index

This book has been set in 11 and 10 point Baskerville, leaded 2 points. Chapter numbers are 36 point Baskerville and chapter titles are 24 point Baskerville italic. The size of the text area is 26 by 45 picas.